The Washington Lobby

CONGRESSIONAL QUARTERLY INC.
1414 22ND STREET, N.W.
WASHINGTON, D.C. 20037

Congressional Quarterly Inc.

Congressional Quarterly Inc., an editorial research service and publishing company, serves clients in the fields of news, education, business and government. It combines specific coverage of Congress, government and politics by Congressional Quarterly with the more general subject range of an affiliated service, Editorial Research Reports.

Congressional Quarterly was founded in 1945 by Henrietta and Nelson Poynter. Its basic periodical publication was and still is the CQ *Weekly Report,* mailed to clients every Saturday. A cumulative index is published quarterly.

CQ also publishes a variety of books. The CQ *Almanac,* a compendium of legislation for one session of Congress, is published every spring. *Congress and the Nation* is published every four years as a record of government for one presidential term. Other books include paperbacks on public affairs and textbooks for college political science classes.

The public affairs books are designed as timely reports to keep journalists, scholars and the public abreast of developing issues, events and trends.

They include recent titles such as *Dollar Politics, Third Edition, The Soviet Union* and *Budgeting for America.* College textbooks, prepared by outside scholars and published under the CQ Press imprint, include recent titles such as *American Politics and Public Policy: Seven Case Studies, Origins of Congress, Second Edition,* and *Congress and Its Members.*

In addition, CQ publishes *The Congressional Monitor,* a daily report on present and future activities of congressional committees. This service is supplemented by *The Congressional Record Scanner,* an abstract of each day's *Congressional Record,* and *Congress in Print,* a weekly listing of committee publications.

CQ Direct Research is a consulting service that performs contract research and maintains a reference library and query desk for clients.

Editorial Research Reports covers subjects beyond the specialized scope of Congressional Quarterly. It publishes reference material on foreign affairs, business, education, cultural affairs, national security, science and other topics of news interest. Service to clients includes a 6,000-word report four times a month, bound and indexed semi-annually. Editorial Research Reports publishes paperback books in its field of coverage. Founded in 1923, the service merged with Congressional Quarterly in 1956.

Printed in the United States of America

Library of Congress Cataloging in Publication Data

Main entry under title:

The Washington lobby

Bibliography: p.
Includes index.
1. Lobbying — Law and legislation — United States. 2. Lobbying.
I. Congressional Quarterly, inc.
KF4948.Z9W37   1982   328.73'078   82-12525
ISBN 0-87187-240-4

Editor: Nancy Lammers
Assistant Editor: Robert S. Mudge
Supervisory Editor: John L. Moore
Major Contributor: Bill Keller
Contributors: Judy Aldock, Irwin B. Arieff, Sharon Clayton, Harrison Donnelly, Edna Frazier-Cromwell, Ann Pelham, Andy Plattner, Judy Sarasohn, Elizabeth Wehr
Indexer: Nancy A. Blanpied
Design: Mary McNeil
Cover: Richard Pottern
Graphics: Ray Driver, George Rebh, Bob Redding, Cheryl Rowe

Book Department

David R. Tarr *Director*
Joanne D. Daniels *Director, CQ Press*
John L. Moore *Associate Editor*
Michael D. Wormser *Associate Editor*
Martha V. Gottron *Senior Editor*
Barbara R. de Boinville *Senior Editor, CQ Press*
Susan Sullivan *Developmental Editor, CQ Press*
Margaret C. Thompson *Senior Writer*
Diane C. Hill *Editor/Writer*
Sari Horwitz *Editor/Writer*
Nancy Lammers *Editor/Writer*
Mary McNeil *Editor/Writer*
Robert S. Mudge *Editor/Writer*
Janet Hoffman *Indexer*
Carolyn Goldinger *Researcher/Editorial Assistant*
Patricia M. Russotto *Researcher*
Esther D. Wyss *Researcher*
Patricia Ann O'Connor *Contributing Editor*
Elder Witt *Contributing Editor*

Congressional Quarterly Inc.

Eugene Patterson *Editor and President*
Wayne P. Kelley *Publisher*
Peter A. Harkness *Executive Editor*
Robert E. Cuthriell *Director, Research and Development*
Robert C. Hur *General Manager*
I.D. Fuller *Production Manager*
Maceo Mayo *Assistant Production Manager*
Sydney E. Garriss *Computer Services*

Contents

Editor's Note. *The Washington Lobby, Fourth Edition,* traces the history of lobbying from its colonial beginnings through the remarkable growth of special interest groups in Washington in the 1970s and 1980s. The book discusses lobbying in the context of the actual issues, participants, methods and legal restrictions that define this vital, constitutionally protected activity. One chapter outlines the development of the methods used by lobbyists over the years, with special attention given to the new, sophisticated techniques of the contemporary lobbyist. Another is devoted to the increasingly important role of executive branch lobbying. Here the book highlights the new dimension that President Ronald Reagan gave to presidential lobbying through his efforts to enact his economic and New Federalism plans. A sampling of federal programs traditionally supported by loyal lobbies also is included in the new edition. Other chapters recount the history of lobby regulation and give an explanation of the rise of political action committees, which followed federal restrictions on campaign contributions in the 1970s. The last two chapters describe the part many lobbyists play in today's campaign fund raising and the methods by which interest groups rate members of Congress.

A substantial part of the book is devoted to case studies of specific lobby interests, such as the new Christian right, small businesses, and foreign agents. The book also includes a selected bibliography and an extensive index. *The Washington Lobby, Fourth Edition,* is one of CQ's public affairs books designed as timely reports to keep journalists, scholars and the public abreast of issues, events and trends.

The Washington Lobby

The Washington Lobby

From Alaska lands to zero population growth, every conceivable issue has attracted the attention of competing interest groups, and across the country they and their lobbyists have become a potent force in the political process. Their ranks include the traditional rich and powerful Capitol Hill lobbies, as well as the many grass-roots coalitions that derive power from their numbers and determination.

"America is no longer a nation. It is a committee of lobbies," wrote Charles Peters, editor-in-chief of *The Washington Monthly*. The goals these groups espouse are diverse and, from their point of view, their causes just.

Although their objectives may differ, the various groups pressuring Congress in the 1980s increasingly were using similar, often highly developed, strategies to get what they wanted. At one time lobbying may have meant a persuasive soloist pleading his case to a senator or representative; but as often as not the contemporary lobbyist depended far less than his predecessors on individualistic methods and more on coordinated, indirect techniques made possible by modern means of communication.

As it grew in size and sophistication, the lobbying profession lost much of the stigma attached to it from past scandals and the activities of unscrupulous influence peddlers. But concern lingered that some individuals and groups, despite their polish and adherence to laws and proprieties, might be having too much sway in Congress, to the detriment of the public interest.

Peters continued in his article to say that "Politicians no longer ask what is in the public interest, because they know no one else is asking. Instead they're giving each group what it wants...." In his farewell address to the nation delivered Jan. 14, 1981, President Jimmy Carter also expressed concern about the proliferation of single-interest groups, which he said was "a disturbing factor" that "tends to distort our purposes, because the national interest is not always the sum of all our single or special interests."

But comments like these have produced little in the way of restrictions on lobbies or the way they operate. The dilemma for would-be reformers was that lobbying derives from basic American rights, and any efforts to control it must avoid any entanglement with those rights.

Constitutional Protection

Lobbying has been recognized as a legitimate, protected activity from the earliest years of the United States.

The First Amendment to the Constitution provided that "Congress shall make no law ... abridging the freedom of speech or of the press; or the right of the people peaceably to assemble and to petition the Government for redress of grievances."

But there is a potential for corruption and conflict of interest inherent in protecting the rights of groups to petition, and James Madison was credited with foreseeing it. His classic statement in *The Federalist* (No. 10) defended the need for a strong federal government to act as an effective counterbalance: "Among the numerous advantages promised by a well-constructed union," he wrote, "none deserves to be more accurately developed than its tendency to break and control the violence of faction.... By a faction, I understand a number of citizens, whether amounting to a majority or minority of the whole, who are united and actuated by some common impulse of passion, or of interest, adverse to the rights of other citizens, or to the permanent and aggregate interests of the community."

By the early 19th century, corruption and conflicts of interest were commonplace and, although they discomforted many, were taken as a matter of course. Abundant evidence accumulated that venal and selfish methods often were used to get legislative results. Chief among the indiscretions was bribery, where legislators traded influence for money.

The term "lobbyist" came into usage about this time, and the unsavory reputations of the early practitioners gave the word a pejorative sense that lobbyists have been trying to shake ever since. By 1829 the phrase "lobby-agents" was being applied to special favor-seekers hovering in the New York Capitol lobby at Albany. By 1832 the term had been shortened to lobbyist and was in wide use at the U. S. Capitol. Newspaper reporters and political cartoonists compounded the lobbyists' stereotypical image by portraying them as sinister, portly, cigar-smoking individuals who held legislatures completely in their control.

An often-cited example of a conflict-of-interest problem arose in the 1830s when Congress became embroiled in President Andrew Jackson's battle with the Bank of the United States. It was disclosed that Daniel Webster, then a senator from Massachusetts, enjoyed a retainer from the bank. On Dec. 21, 1833, Webster complained to bank President Nicholas Biddle: "My retainer has not been renewed or refreshed as usual. If it is wished that my relation to the Bank should be continued, it may be well to send me the usual retainers."

Lobbyists Seek More Public Respect

Many lobbyists saw the 1980s as a pivotal time for their profession. Of chief concern to many was promoting a positive image that reflected more accurately the Washington lobbyist's part in the legislative process. In 1979 a professional group, the American League of Lobbyists, was formed with this goal in mind. Its prime concerns were "professionalism, rules of conduct and image improvement."

Roland A. Ouellete, the group's 1982 president and the assistant director of General Motors' Washington office, offered a definition that the group was trying to promote: "Lobbyists are first and foremost experts in government — its structure, its programs, its policies and its legislative process. Lobbyists provide information, advocate and implement policy positions and defend economic, political, technical and social 'philosophies.' And, in addition to being the principal contact with the political policy-makers, they are integrally involved in planning and executing the related strategies to accomplish political objectives."

Among other things, the League members were formulating in 1982 a code of conduct as well as an accreditation process and career growth program for lobbyists.

Over the years, often in response to lobby scandals, Congress tried to control influence buying, passing lobby registration and disclosure laws. But the effectiveness of those laws continued to be disputed into the 1980s.

Nevertheless, lobbyists gradually gained a more positive image. The public began to recognize that pressure groups and their agents perform some important and indispensable jobs. Such services today include helping to inform both Congress and the public about problems and issues, stimulating public debate, opening a path to Congress for the wronged and needy, and making known to members the practical aspects of proposed legislation — whom it would help, whom it would hurt, who is for it and who against it. The result of this process has been considerable technical information produced by research on legislative proposals.

Growth of Lobbying

Despite the deep and pervading sense of ambivalence that surrounded their profession, lobbyists continued to be attracted to Washington in the 20th century. Their legions grew steadily after the New Deal of the 1930s, paralleling the growth in federal spending and the expansion of authority into new areas. Over the next four decades the federal government became a tremendous force in the nation's life, thus expanding the areas where changes in federal policy could spell success or failure for special interest groups.

Then in the 1970s a series of congressional reforms opened up meetings, diminished the seniority system, forced more publicly recorded votes and increased the power of subcommittees. Power once concentrated in the leadership and held by committee chairmen was diluted among many members, as well as in the ranks of professional staffers that had swelled throughout the 1960s. Lobbyists found they had to influence more people, members and staffers alike, to get something accomplished.

Because of the unspecific — and some would say unenforceable — lobby registration laws, it was impossible to come up with an exact number of lobbyists in Washington. But whether they referred to themselves as political consultants, lawyers, foreign representatives, legislative specialists, consumer advocates, trade association representatives or government affairs specialists, there were an estimated 10,000 to 20,000 people lobbying in Washington in 1982 — either periodically or throughout the year. Even the lower end of this estimate showed a dramatic increase from the figure of 4,000 estimated for 1977.

Lobby Techniques

A Washington lobby group wants results. It pursues them wherever they are likely to be found in the governmental process. Many organizations, directed by professionals in the art of government, focus major efforts at key points where decisions are made and policy interpreted into action. They use the methods they deem appropriate for the circumstances within the limits of their resources, group policies and ethical outlook.

If a group loses a round in Congress, it can continue the fight in the agency charged with execution or in the courts. A year or two later, it can resume the struggle in Congress. The process sometimes continues indefinitely. On a long-range basis, groups strive to build up what they consider a sympathetic or at least neutral attitude in places of power where their particular interests are affected.

Coalition Organizing

The concerted exercise of influence is as old as government itself, but most lobbyists agree that during the 1970s and into the 1980s coalition lobbying became a commonplace ritual in Washington. The ad hoc coalition, the working group, the alliance, the committee — these became the routine format of all but the most obscure lobbying campaigns.

While the movement toward coalitions had accelerated after World War II, it was far from new even then. As early as 1950 the House Select Committee on Lobbying Activities said in a report: "The lone-wolf pressure group, wanting nothing more from other groups than to be left unmolested, is largely a thing of the past."

Cooperative Efforts

The explosion of the lobbying business, aimed at comprehending and staunching the flow of government activism, meant many voices competing for the ear of Congress. One advantage for lobbyists and members alike was that collective lobbying allowed a sorting out of competing aims before going to Congress, almost like lawyers settling a case out of court.

And so although at one time a lobbyist may have individually pleaded his case, by the 1980s a person with a cause found his first task was to persuade members of his own organization or group to support him, then to line up help from natural allies in other interest groups. These ad hoc lobby coalitions often are composed of a mix of corporate, association and business federation lobbyists, as well as unions and any other interests that can be enticed into a marriage of convenience. Allies on one issue sometimes become opponents on the next one.

These temporary alliances do their initial work off Capitol Hill, in a community possessing its own committees, leadership, staff, communications network, service organizations and culture. Participants contribute time, legal help, printing and mailing costs according to their resources and their stake in the battle.

Ideally, before the lobbyist approaches a member, compromises within the coalition have been made, congressional sponsors for the bill have been identified, legislation has been drafted to satisfy a wide range of allies, priorities have been assigned, and a strategy has been mapped out. When the lobbyist finally does go to Congress, he is likely to be in a team of two or three — perhaps with one individual representing the member's district — selected to dramatize the breadth of support for, or opposition to, the legislation.

Although labor, consumer groups, environmentalists, arts and education advocates, charities and many other groups merge into short-term alliances, business groups clearly demonstrate superior mastery of the technique, helped along by money and a naturally cohesive political outlook. A historic example of the broad coalition was the protectionist bloc, which was effective in raising protective U. S. tariffs to their highest point ever in 1930. More recently, coalitions during the 97th Congress labored to protect favored programs from Reagan budget cuts, to extend the Voting Rights Act and to protect the Clean Air Act.

Enacting Legislation

Traditionally, the best-known coalitions have been directed primarily at stopping new government initiatives — a federal consumer protection agency, a common situs picketing bill or labor law reform legislation. Successfully ushering legislation through Congress always has been a much more ambitious task than preventing passage, which can be accomplished by a single subcommittee blockade or a crippling amendment.

This developed by design. The bicameral structure of the legislative branch and the constitutional separation of

For Hire: A Dozen Reagan Insiders

Following are some of the Washington lobbyists, political consultants, lawyers and publicists with ties to Ronald Reagan's campaign or administration, along with a sampling of their clients based on federal lobby registrations as of March 5, 1982.

Robert Keith Gray. Public relations man Gray was a communications adviser in the Reagan campaign and co-chairman of the Reagan inaugural. Gray headed the Washington office of the Hill and Knowlton Inc. public relations firm for 20 years, breaking away in March 1981 to organize Gray and Co. The firm is the registered lobbyist for 15 clients, including the American Iron and Steel Institute, American Trucking Associations, El Paso Natural Gas, General Telephone and Electric, the Health Insurance Association of America, Motorola Inc. and Republic Airlines. Gray is a registered foreign agent for a Guatemalan businessman named Domingo Moreira, the German shipbuilder Thyssen Nordsweekwerke, Italian Aerospace Industries Inc., Kuwait Petroleum Corp. and the Embassy of Venezuela.

William E. Timmons. Timmons, a White House aide in the Nixon and Ford administrations, took a leave from his lobbying firm to organize state campaign operations and help congressional relations in the Reagan campaign. His firm is the registered lobbyist for 15 clients, including the American Petroleum Institute, the Association of Trial Lawyers of America, Chrysler Corp., G. D. Searle and Co., H. J. Heinz and Co., Major League Baseball, the National Rifle Association and Northrop Corp.

Peter D. Hannaford. A former Reagan speech-writer and consultant, Hannaford heads the sister firms of Hannaford and Co. and Hannaford International. The firms offer public relations, lobbying and international business consulting. Hannaford bought out former partner Michael K. Deaver, who became Reagan's deputy chief of staff; he also bought an international consulting firm from Richard V. Allen, Reagan's national security adviser until his forced resignation Jan. 4, 1982.

The firm is a registered lobbyist for 12 clients, including General Motors Corp., Northwest Alaska Pipeline Co., and Trans World Airlines Inc. It is a registered foreign agent for the China External Trade Development Council and the Taiwan government.

Black, Manafort & Stone. Charles Black, Paul Manafort and Roger Stone are campaign, advertising and lobbying partners who were campaign operatives for Reagan and several Republican congressional candidates. The firm of Black, Manafort & Stone is registered to lobby for the Air Transport Association of America, American Newspaper Publishers Association, and Tosco Corp.

Charls E. Walker. Tax lawyer and lobbyist, Walker chaired Reagan's campaign tax policy task force and was a top economic adviser in the transition. Charls E. Walker Associates is a registered lobbyist for 46 clients, including Amax, American Telephone & Telegraph Co. (AT&T), Bechtel Corp., Bethlehem Steel, the Chicago Mercantile Exchange, Dresser Industries, Eastern Air Lines, Ford Motor Corp., General Electric, International Paper Co., Procter & Gamble Co., and Union Carbide.

Dean Burch. Former chairman of the Republican National Committee and Federal Communications Commission (FCC) chief in the Nixon administration, Burch is a specialist in communications law for the firm of Pierson, Ball & Dowd. He was Vice President George Bush's staff chief in the 1980 campaign, and helped pick FCC members as part of Reagan's transition team. Pierson, Ball & Dowd is registered to lobby for 11 clients, including companies aiming to keep AT&T out of new computer markets.

Stanton D. Anderson. Anderson was a lawyer for the Reagan campaign and transition. The law firm of Anderson, Hibey, Nauheim and Blair, started in February 1981, is a registered lobbyist for seven clients. Among them are the Atlanta and San Francisco rapid transit districts, Morgan Guarantee Trust Co., Burlington Industries and Texas Air.

The firm is a registered foreign agent for several Japanese companies and for the government of Haiti.

Lyn Nofziger. Franklyn C. (Lyn) Nofziger, a longtime Reagan political adviser, left a White House job as assistant for political affairs to open Nofziger and Bragg Communications in February 1982. According to an aide, Nancy Guiden, the firm did not plan to lobby Congress, but would give political advice to candidates and corporations, including where political action committees should spend money.

John P. Sears. Lawyer Sears, a former Nixon deputy counsel, was Reagan's campaign manager until a messy falling out with other top Reagan aides in February 1980. Now a partner in Baskin & Sears, he said his work is mainly to "interpret current events and give advice," with "very little" lobbying.

Baskin & Sears is registered to represent foreign clients, but not to lobby Congress. The firm's principal client is the government of South Africa, which pays $500,0000 a year for representation. Other foreign clients include Japan Airlines, the Japanese Automobile Manufacturers Association, and Poongsan Metal Corp. (a Korean small-arms maker).

William E. Tucker. Tucker is a Denver lawyer who acted as a regional political director in the Reagan campaign, a consultant to Reagan's counsel in the transition and early administration. Tucker opened a Washington office of his firm, Tucker & Brown, in October 1981. The firm is a registered lobbyist for Johns-Manville Corp. (asbestos mining) and Petro-Lewis Corp. (oil and gas).

powers gave a considerable natural advantage to defensive lobbying efforts. Political scientist David B. Truman wrote that these structures "operate as they were designed, to delay or obstruct action rather than to facilitate it." He added: "Requirement of extensive majorities for particular kinds of measures and the absence of limits on the duration of debate have a like effect as do numerous technical details of the parliamentary rules. Finally, the diffuseness of leadership, and the power and independence of committees and their chairmen, not only provide a multiplicity of points of access...but also furnish abundant activities for obstruction and delay, opportunities that buttress the position of defensive groups." By combining their knowledge and resources, members of coalitions improve their chances of overcoming the natural obstacles to new legislation, and they have a better chance of killing bills they oppose. In the early 1980s lobby coalitions increasingly were on the offensive to move legislation and to roll back existing laws.

"Up until now, you didn't have a chance to get things passed. All you were trying to do was put out the fires your opponents started," said R. Hilton Davis, vice president of legislative and political affairs for the U. S. Chamber of Comerce. Davis said he believes the arrival of a Republican administration and Senate majority in 1980, along with several years of practice at team-building, are responsible for that chance.

A notably successful collective effort was one mounted by the Alaska Coalition, which in 1980 won passage of the lands bill that preserved much of the state from development. More recently, the political environment created by Reagan's leadership contributed to the success of a formidable business coalition, the Carlton Group, that worked to gain passage of the so-called 10-5-3 capital depreciation tax write-off. The 10-5-3 proposal became law as part of the Economic Recovery Tax Act of 1981.

Direct Lobbying

The changes in Congress that occurred in the 1970s worked to enlarge the job of Washington lobbyists. They not only had to become more active — to communicate their messages to a much broader range of members and staff — but they also had to adopt more effective techniques. As access to members became more available, more groups formed to protect or enlarge their turf and competition between lobbyists increased.

Lobbyists using the direct approach continue to meet with members of Congress and their staffs, provide in-depth information and give testimony at congressional hearings. But their methods are more sophisticated, relying more on information than on personal connections.

One legislative aide observed: "I think there's a new breed of lobbyist around. There's less of the slap-on-the-back, 'I've been dealing with you for 15 years, let's go duck hunting' kind of approach. Now it's 'Here's a 20-page paper full of technical slides, charts showing the budget impact, a table on how it meets the threat situation and some language in case you'd like to introduce an amendment.' "

Access Prerequisite

A lobbyist's strategy focuses on the interaction between his group and those on Capitol Hill and in the executive branch. To communicate with the power brokers, the advocate first needs access. So whether he is a partner in a Washington law firm or an in-house employee of a union, trade association or business, more often than not the lobbyist already has close ties with Congress. Many lobbyists have spent time as staff aides on Capitol Hill, and some were members of Congress. *(Former members as lobbyists, case study, p. 93)*

A consensus never has existed on whether it is contacts that ultimately count, but many people believe that insider credentials are a good investment. Charles Black, a one-time campaigner for presidential candidate Ronald Reagan and a member of a political consulting firm, put it this way: "No. 1 is the access — to get them in the door and get a hearing for the case. The second thing is the development of the case and how to present it. Knowing the individuals personally, knowing their staffs and how they operate and the kind of information they want...that kind of personal knowledge can help you maximize the client's hearing." *(Tosco Corp., case study, box, p. 6; Reagan insiders, box, p. 4)*

It also is possible to gain access by taking part in the Washington social circuit. Some lobbyists become well known, even notorious, for giving lavish dinner and cocktail parties. Until his downfall in the 1977-78 "Koreagate" scandal on Capitol Hill, South Korean lobbyist Tongsun Park was a noted Washington host. "His flamboyant social style earned him enormous good will and access in the Washington political community," noted a Washington commentator. "That could often be cashed in for reciprocal good will and generosity toward the country he represented."

Another help in opening doors is the sheer size of the interest group represented, such as the senior citizens' lobby. According to Norman Ornstein and Shirley Elder in

Do Connections Really Help?...

The 1980 presidential election was cause for dejection at the Los Angeles headquarters of Tosco Corp.

The company had worked hard to win President Carter's imprimatur on a federal loan guarantee for a proposed shale oil venture in western Colorado, but time was running out. Now it seemed likely the idea would have to be sold to a whole new cast of politicians — including a new president who had campaigned as a free-market enthusiast, specifically criticizing the Carter administration for supporting synfuels subsidies.

To make matters worse, the company lacked good Republican connections. Tosco executives had been betting on the Democratic Party. Just six weeks before the election, Tosco chief executive Morton M. Winston had donated $10,000 to the Democratic National Committee and company Chairman Isadore M. Scott another $5,000. The company's political action committee and much of the executive hierarchy had pitched in to help Carter.

But any gloom over government financial help at Tosco was dispelled nine months later, when President Reagan announced the government would stand behind Tosco's borrowing of $1.1 billion. And in November of 1981, the government went further and agreed to be not just the guarantor of the loan, but the actual lender.

Nevertheless, the project, one of the nation's first large attempts to squeeze synthetic oil from shale rock, collapsed May 2, 1982. Exxon Corp., 60 percent owner of the Colony Project, said rising costs and plentiful oil supplies were driving it out of the project. Exxon planned to write off its investment and buy out Tosco, its junior partner. Tosco was expected to repay the government the approximately $80 million it already had received, while making a profit of about $100 million on the deal.

Despite the ultimate outcome, the selling of Tosco represents a distinctive type of lobbying campaign, where the issue involves high stakes for a few participants, where much of the activity takes place off of the public stage and where the lobbyists cannot take the time or do not see the potential to arouse a great outpouring of popular pressure.

In that type of lobbying, political or personal connections are premiums. Connections may not command favors or guarantee a successful outcome, but they bring quick access, credibility and rapport, first-hand understanding of how the key government players think and conduits to the information upon which strategies are built.

Cabinet Clash

Reagan's administration inherited three synthetic fuels proposals that already had acquired momentum under the Carter administration. They were so-called "fast-track" projects financed through a 1980 amendment to the Defense Production Act of 1950 rather than through the conventional machinery of the Synthetic Fuels Corporation (SFC), which then still was being organized. Fuel from the fast-track plants was to be available for military use.

One project was designed to produce 48,000 barrels per day of liquid petroleum from shale rock on Colorado's western slope. Exxon was to handle construction and operation, while Tosco contributed technology and shale-bearing land. Exxon's 60 percent share of the project was not government-backed, and the company was not visibly involved in the loan guarantee lobbying effort.

An Energy Department assessment in 1981 rated Tosco's as the most promising of several synfuels ventures then proposed for government aid, but noted that Tosco could not afford to participate without government backup.

The new administration split sharply over how to handle this legacy. Energy Secretary James B. Edwards emerged as the leading proponent of the guarantees, backed by Transportation Secretary Drew Lewis, a fellow member of the Cabinet-level Council of Energy and Natural Resources. Office of Management and Budget (OMB) Director David A. Stockman became the leading critic. Edwards pointed to the national interest in energy independence, Stockman to the virtue of letting private enterprise pay its own way.

Considering the split within the administration, all the projects moved to approval smoothly, escaping Stockman's budget knife in February 1981, percolating through Cabinet-council meetings in June and July and winning Reagan's blessing by early August. In November 1981 the Tosco contract was signed.

Tosco's Guns

In the lobbying that was organized to keep this process moving, Tosco's fellow pleaders, Union Oil and American Natural Resources, were not without their inside moves. But Tosco, by comparison with the other companies' ordinary efforts, hired so many lobbyists that one participant would later joke about discovering a new American minority: people *not* on Tosco's payroll. For Tosco, the 1981 effort was just the climax of a methodical lobbying drive that, among other achievements, had helped create the 1980 Defense Production Act amendment authorizing synfuels loan guarantees.

"The most recent events have been very dramatic, but they've been just sort of the last push in a very, very long effort to get this thing done," said Camilla S. Auger, Tosco executive vice president, who recruited and directed her company's lobbying

...Tosco Corp. Did Not Gamble

team. While some companies entrust their legislative affairs to a few in-house lobbyists, Tosco prefers to "use people in a very selective, rifle-shot manner," she explained. "We like to have people who are very highly specialized, who do one or two things for us, who have special knowledge of a particular area or a particular constituency, and we're very selective who we get."

Newspapers singled out one of Tosco's rifles: former Reagan publicist and speech writer Peter D. Hannaford, retained promptly after the 1980 presidential election. In November of 1981, columnists Rowland Evans and Robert Novak reported "suspicions of impropriety bordering on conflict-of-interest," because Hannaford had been touting Tosco's project at the same time he was buying out his former public relations partner, Michael K. Deaver, Reagan's deputy chief of staff.

Hannaford told Congressional Quarterly he never discussed Tosco with Deaver, but that he did talk to other White House officials, including presidential counselor Edwin Meese III; he said he did not recall the timing or details of any discussions.

August said Hannaford's primary value was in helping cast the company's arguments in language that would appeal to conservatives. "It's not his contacts so much as his years of experience in conservative politics," she said. "The sort of work we do with him is mainly conceptual rather than a discussion of this personality or that personality."

But Hannaford was just one circuit in a lobbying campaign with more connections than a telephone switchboard. Besides Hannaford and the company's in-house advocates, chiefly Auger and Washington office director William J. Robinson, the team included at least a dozen other hired consultants:

● Marcus W. Sisk Jr., a Washington Lawyer retained by Tosco for more than 10 years, and partner John P. Foley Jr. "Mark Sisk was the chief negotiator and probably the key person on the deal," said a Tosco spokesman.

● David Mixner, a liberal California activist whose consulting firm counts Tosco among its clients. Mixner had warm relations with the Carter White House. "After the election, our influence on the loan guarantee diminished," said Mixner. A Tosco official called him seeking advice, and Mixner recommended Hannaford. "You had a Republican administration," he explained. "I think [hiring a Republican lobbyist] is the normal procedure."

● Anne Wexler, President Carter's former assistant for public liaison, and Robert Shule, a former Senate lobbyist for the Carter administration. Wexler had been an advocate of synfuels while in the White House. After the change in government, she and Shule became partners in a new lobbying firm,

and Tosco signed up as a client a few months later.

● Charles Black and Paul Manafort, political consultants who worked on the campaigns of Reagan, Kansas Sen. Robert Dole and other Republicans. They expanded their business to include lobbying after the 1980 elections, and Tosco was among their first clients. Their main function was to keep in touch with congressional Republicans.

● Walt Klein. A former administrative assistant and campaign manager for Sen. William L. Armstrong, R-Colo., Klein left his Senate post to become a consultant to Tosco during the synfuels fight.

● William S. Moorhead, a former Democratic representative from Pennsylvania (1959-81), who, as chairman of a House Banking subcommittee, was the author of the amendment creating subsidies for such "fast-track" projects as Tosco. Although he did not publicly register to lobby, Moorhead worked actively with former colleagues to line up House support for the Tosco project and to head off trouble. He also provided analysis of the legislation he helped write.

● Robert C. Farber, a consultant based in Arlington, Va. Auger said he was hired for his "knowledge of specific constituencies" — presumably meaning organized labor, because Farber has written for union publications. Farber also was close to Rep. Eugene V. Atkinson, R-Pa., an influential member of the subcommittee investigating synfuels subsidies.

● Harry K. Schwartz, a former Carter domestic policy adviser, retained by Tosco as a specialist in environmental issues.

● Harold Miller, a former Hughes Aircraft Co. lobbyist retained by Tosco several years earlier because, Auger said, he "knows the Congress backwards and forwards."

How much any of these advocates may have influenced the final outcome is impossible to tell. Even without the lobbying blitz, the administration would have faced intense pressure on Tosco's behalf from Congress. In February 1981, as Stockman was pruning the budget, Rep. Jim Wright, Texas, and other House Democratic leaders wrote to the administration urging that synfuels be left alone. Later in July, as the issue went to the Cabinet, a barrage of well-aimed letters went out from Congress, including one from Senate Armed Services Chairman John Tower, R-Texas, to Defense Secretary Caspar W. Weinberger; one from Sen. Robert Dole, R-Kan., to the president; and one from House and Senate leaders.

A lot of what the lobbyists did, in fact, was to channel and reinforce congressional support by supplying executive branch reconnaissance, information networks, fact sheets memo-drafting, and cues on the best timing and wording of congressional letters to the White House.

their book entitled *Interest Groups, Lobbying and Policymaking*: "Beyond the direct political translation of size into votes, a large group representing many citizens has a built-in legitimacy; it 'speaks' for a sizable part of America, not just for a handful of individuals." When a large group speaks out loudly and vehemently, as the National Rifle Association does, its cause must be taken seriously by lawmakers.

Prestige alone also provides a strong incentive for members and staff people to listen. The Business Roundtable, a group composed of the chief executive officers of major corporations such as General Motors, IBM and AT&T, can feel confident that its leaders will be heard when they present their opinions and requests on Capitol Hill.

Information and Expertise

Access is crucial, but knowledge and technique are just as critical because lobbyists traditionally have provided information as well as expertise to hard-pressed members and committees. According to Ornstein and Elder, political expertise and reputation are essential to the successful lobbyist: "Knowledge of the ins and outs of the legislative process — including the important stages of the process, the relevant committees and subcommittees, the key actors, the best moments to act or withdraw, the personal characteristics, strengths, and weaknesses of members and staff — is vital to a group's legislative success...."

Direct lobbying most often begins at the committee or subcommittee level, as approval of a measure by a congressional panel usually ensures final passage. Except on highly controversial issues, committee decisions are almost always upheld by the full chamber. A thorough lobbyist provides to the committee and its professional staffers extensive background and technical information on the issue of interest, precise legislative language for a proposed bill or amendment, lists of witnesses for the hearings and the name of a possible sponsor for the bill.

The decentralization of power in Congress, resulting in the expansion in the number and importance of subcommittees, directly affected the lobbyist's job. As the number of people having power increased, so did the number of pressure points. It became advantageous for an interest group to have a supporter in power. Thus in the Congresses of the 1980s it was not unusual for a lobbyist to back a particular member for a slot on a favored committee, or for a leadership position on a panel.

Also, as "sunshine" laws and rules opened markup sessions, hearings and conferences to the public, the lobbyist no longer was left hovering outside the closed door excluded from the action; rather he could be right there watching every move — in many cases suggesting legislative language and compromise positions. This kind of help is especially useful during consideration of highly technical legislation. Also, recorded votes on amendments, and open knowledge of who introduced them, makes it easier for the lobbyist to monitor the action and apply pressure where most needed.

Political scientist Lester W. Milbrath in his book *The Washington Lobbyists* noted that "failure to locate such key persons (members and staff) may result in the sending of many superfluous messages, and if the key persons cannot be persuaded, there is a high likelihood that the decision will go adversely."

It also behooves the successful lobbyist to be accurate and complete, alerting the member to any negative aspects of the legislation he seeks to advance. Former White House aide Douglass Cater said in *Power in Washington*: "The smart lobbyist...knows he can be most effective by being helpful, by being timely, and, not least, by being accurate. According to the testimony of lobbyists themselves, the cardinal sin is to supply faulty information which puts a trusting policy-maker in an exposed position."

Ornstein and Elder expressed a similar opinion: "A group's or lobbyist's political reputation — as an honest political broker and honest information source, as well as the general reputation for political influence — is a crucial element in political success."

Most contemporary lobbyists carefully avoid approaches that the member could interpret as threatening or as constituting excessive pressure. An adverse reaction by a member could lead to unfavorable publicity or even a damaging congressional investigation.

Political scientist Donald R. Matthews described the lobbyist as a "sitting duck — their public reputation is so low that public attack is bound to be damaging.... To invite public attack, or even worse a congressional investigation, is, from the lobbyist's point of view, clearly undesirable." Matthews added: "It is the threat of and use of these countermeasures which help explain why so little lobbying is aimed at conversion. A lobbyist minimizes the risks of his job, the cause which he serves, and his ego by staying away from those senators clearly against him and his program. For, of all types of lobbying, attempts at conversion are most likely to boomerang."

Grass-Roots Techniques

In conjunction with direct lobbying, many organizations seek to mobilize constituents into pressuring senators and representatives. High election turnovers gradually have created a Congress less wedded to old loyalties and more skittish about constituent pressures. This trend contributed to the current prominence of indirect, "grass-roots" lobbying — inducing constituents back home to bring pressure on Congress.

Constituent Power

Confirming what has come to be conventional wisdom in the lobbying trade, the public relations firm of Burson-Marsteller interviewed 123 congressional staffers and found that constituent letters, telegrams and calls counted more than anything else in influencing their bosses.

Nearly every trade association or public interest group of any stature has developed its own grass-roots network to ensure that what its Washington lobbyists says is reinforced by an outpouring from back home. For those interests that do not have such a network, a thriving intermediate industry has grown up that promises clients it can take a whisper of public interest and amplify it into a roar of public pressure.

Traditional grass-roots pressure methods include maintaining a steady stream of correspondence with the lawmaker, even when not demanding a specific favor; arranging recess visits to local establishments; and dealing frequently and skillfully with local newspapers and television. These tools are not new to established groups; what is new is the magnitude and sophistication of them.

Modern Techniques

A fact of modern lobbying is that home-district pressure frequently does not spring spontaneously from the public. The genuine grass-roots support often is enhanced by the highly technical orchestration of a special-interest group, the more subliminal stimulation of a professional public relations campaign, and occasionally the persuasion of an employer or union.

Still the oldest and favorite instrument of the organized grass-roots lobbying campaign remains the postage meter. Computer technology and high-speed, low-cost telegram services enabled interest groups in the 1970s and 1980s to target mailings where they would do the most good.

Some lobby experts maintain that grass-roots pressures might not change a lawmaker's mind, but concede that they do attract attention to issues. According to political scientists Roger H. Davidson and Walter Oleszek in their book *Congress and Its Members*, "Legislators understand that lobby groups orchestrate 'spontaneous' outpourings of letters and postcards. Pressure mail is easily recognized, because each piece is nearly identical to all the others. Members may discount the content of such mail, but its volume is sure to attract their attention as they think about the next election."

Richard A. Viguerie, a conservative widely recognized as the pre-eminent expert on mass mail, said that — contrary to his image as primarily a fund-raiser — most of his work was grass-roots lobbying. Viguerie said 90 percent of the 60 million-70 million pieces of mail his computers would disgorge in 1982 for groups such as the National Right to Work Committee and the Conservative Caucus would urge the recipient to do something other than contribute — sign a petition, write a letter to Congress, send a post card or boycott a product.

In a departure from the general belief that personalized letter-writing campaigns are more effective, Viguerie used the technique of bombarding Congress with thousands of preprinted post cards or clip-out coupons. He admitted that members of Congress would recognize his campaigns as orchestrated and that they did not value the opinions expressed in a standardized post card as much as a thoughtful, individual letter. But neither could they ignore them, he argued.

His view was supported by the Burson-Marsteller study, which found that "orchestrated mail," while not so effective as spontaneous constituent letters, ranked "surprisingly high" as an influence on lawmakers.

Another grass-roots lobbying technique involves gaining attention through mass media campaigns — on the radio, television, or in newspapers and magazines. Thoughtful editorials in well-known or more obscure newspapers in members' districts often stimulate readers to write their congressman. John Shattuck, executive director of the American Civil Liberties Union (ACLU), said that many lobbyists underestimated the importance of developing close relationships with newspaper editors and editorial writers, whose influence upon constituents, and thereby upon members, could be pivotal on controversial issues.

Attention also is purchased through paid advertising. According to Ornstein and Elder, "Nearly every day, *The Washington Post* — a popular outlet for lobbying appeals, because of its universal circulation among Washington politicians — has full or half-page ads placed by groups, either urging public and congressional support for or opposition to a particular legislative proposal, or promoting a general viewpoint on a broad public policy issue."

The technological age also offers the contemporary lobbyist a back door into the public print through "media distribution services." North American Precis Service, the largest of its kind, claimed it could "generate tons of letters to legislators" by getting clients' views placed in smaller newspapers, and on radio and television stations. North American would package a company or trade group pitch as an editorial or light feature, with a title such as "Washington Wants to Know" or "Capitol Ideas." The firm's brochure promised the articles would be run verbatim in hundreds of outlets without being labeled as paid public relations. One North American brochure promised: "Our IBM 5120 computer will address your material to the editors who are most likely to print it."

Some newspapers, including *The Washington Post*, viewed such products as propaganda masquerading as news and barred them from their news or editorial columns. They refused to use editorial pieces written by public relations or media distribution firms. The president of North American defended his company's releases as always fair and accurate, aimed at "increasing public awareness of the truth so that you generate massive public support."

Campaign Support

Campaign contributions to members of Congress serve two important functions for lobbying organizations. Political support not only can induce a congressman to back the group's legislative interests, but also can help to assure that members friendly to the group's goals remain in office.

While corporations have been barred since 1907, and labor unions since 1943, from making direct contributions to campaigns for federal office, contributors have found numerous ways to get around the restrictions. Labor pioneered in setting up separate political arms, such as the AFL-CIO's Committee on Political Education (COPE), that collect voluntary contributions from union members and their families and use the money to help elect senators and representatives favorable to their cause. It also is legal for unions to endorse candidates.

Similarly, corporations can organize political action committees (PACs) to seek contributions from stockholders and executive and administrative personnel and their families. Corporate PACs have proliferated, especially after the Federal Election Commission SunPAC decision in 1975, and their influences have come to rival, if not surpass, those of labor. The SunPAC decision allowed business PACs to solicit employees and not just stockholders, vastly expanding their potential to raise money. *(Chapter on political action committees, p. 41)*

Twice a year union and corporate political action committees are allowed to seek anonymous contributions by mail from all employees, not just those to which they were initially restricted.

The same general resources for political support and opposition are available to members of citizens' groups and, indeed, to a wide range of organizations seeking to exert political pressure on members of Congress.

In approaching the typical member, a pressure group has no need to tell him outright that future political support or opposition depends on how the member votes on a particular bill or whether, over a long period, the member acts favorably toward the group. The member understands this without being told. The member knows that when the vital interests of some group are at stake, a vote supporting those interests normally would win the group's friendship and future support, and a vote against them would mean the group's enmity and future opposition.

Lobbyists themselves frequently deny this is the intention of their campaign support. But lobbyists do admit that political support gives them access to the legislator that they otherwise might not have.

3

The Presidential Lobby

The president is the strongest source of pressure on Congress. No one else can subject the legislative branch of government to as much influence as the president and his helpers in the executive branch. No one else can organize the pressure as thoroughly or sustain it as long as the president.

How does he do it? The Constitution is tight-lipped. Presidents have had to find their own ways. Strong presidents have done so. Strong presidents have learned to lobby Congress directly, in person or through staff. They've influenced Congress indirectly, by focusing public opinion. They have used government jobs, contracts and other forms of patronage. They have threatened to veto bills, and — when all else failed — they have gone ahead and vetoed them. These are the main ways presidents pressure Congress.

The Constitution vests Congress with "all legislative powers" and vests the president with "the executive power." Despite this apparent separation, the president has become, over the years, a *maker* of laws in his own right. Bertram M. Gross, in his book *The Legislative Struggle: A Study in Social Combat*, goes as far as to call the president "the most important legislative leader in the government," adding that "except in wartime, Presidents are now judged more by the quality of the legislation they propose or succeed in getting enacted than by their records as executives."

The president's role as lawmaker begins with his constitutional duty to "from time to time give to the Congress Information of the State of the Union, and recommend to their Consideration such Measures as he shall judge necessary and expedient." To these bare bones Congress has attached other requirements. The president is required, for example, to send Congress an annual budget message, setting forth his plans for taxes and spending, and an economic report, giving his program for achieving "maximum employment, production and purchasing power," as outlined in the Employment Act of 1946.

The Constitution only hints at how a president is supposed to go about persuading Congress to pass his economic program, his tax and spending plan and the other measures he deems necessary and expedient. "He may, on extraordinary Occasions, convene both Houses, or either of them." And "he shall nominate, and by and with the Advice and Consent of the Senate, shall appoint Ambassadors, other public Ministers and Consuls, Judges of the

Supreme Court, and all other Officers of the United States, whose Appointments are not otherwise provided for, and which shall be established by Law: but the Congress may by Law vest the appointment of such inferior Officers, as they think proper, in the President alone, in the Courts of Law, or in the Heads of Departments."

Finally, the Constitution gives the president the power to "return . . . with his Objections" any bill Congress has passed but that he disapproves of. This is the veto power.

Over the decades, a sort of gentleman's understanding has evolved concerning what is proper and what is improper presidential salesmanship. The understanding is that direct pressure generally is acceptable, but spending money to solicit outside pressure on Congress is not.

A criminal statute adopted in 1919 appears to prohibit the executive branch from spending money to influence votes in Congress. Violation is punishable by a $500 fine, a year in jail and removal from office. But the statute is so ambiguous that it never has resulted in an indictment or prosecution. Alleged violations have been tried in the press, in congressional hearings and General Accounting Office reports, but never in a courtroom.

Weak presidents have discovered in the law's near silence an excuse for inactivity. Strong presidents have taken silence to mean they may do anything not expressly forbidden. But a strong president's success at pressuring Congress depends on many things, among which are: Congress' own strength, the popularity of the president and his program, whether the issue is foreign or domestic, and whether the White House and Congress are in the hands of different political parties.

It was House Speaker Henry Clay, not the president, who set the domestic agenda during the administrations of Madison and Monroe. Clay conceived and promoted his American Plan — a program of improvements at home and tariff protection against imports from abroad.

Woodrow Wilson was master of virtually all the arts of pressure — direct lobbying, public opinion and patronage. But when Wilson failed to persuade the public of the need to join the League of Nations, the Senate rejected the League.

Between World War II and Vietnam, Congress kept presidents on a short leash at home but let them run far abroad. "The postwar Presidents, though Eisenhower and Kennedy markedly less than Truman, Johnson and Nixon, almost came to see the sharing of power with Congress in foreign policy as a derogation of the presidency. Congress in increasing self-abasement, almost came to love its impotence," wrote Arthur M. Schlesinger Jr. in his book *The Imperial Presidency*.

No president has ever come to office more schooled in the ways of Congress than Lyndon B. Johnson. He had worked at the Capitol 32 years — as a secretary, member of the House, senator, Senate minority leader, majority leader and vice president. With President Johnson cracking the whip in 1965, Congress passed the most sweeping domestic program since Franklin Roosevelt: aid to schools, voting rights, health care for the aged, rent supplements for the poor and freer immigration.

According to a Congressional Quarterly study, Congress in 1965 approved 68.9 percent of Johnson's requests, the highest since CQ began keeping score in 1953. Two years earlier, President John F. Kennedy had scored only 27.2 percent.

Yet Johnson understood that success was fleeting. "I have watched the Congress from either the inside or the outside, man and boy, for more than 40 years," he remarked early in 1965, "and I've never seen a Congress that didn't eventually take the measure of the president it was dealing with."

Unhappy with the war in Vietnam and its attendant inflation, the voters elected 47 more Republicans to the House in 1966. Johnson proposed open housing legislation in 1966 and 1967. But it languished until 1968, when Martin Luther King Jr. was killed and many U.S. cities erupted in racial violence. Johnson declined to seek re-election.

Like Presidents Kennedy and Johnson, Richard Nixon had served in Congress before the White House. Unlike his predecessors, however, Nixon had a Congress controlled by the opposition party. Within 15 months of his inauguration, the Democratic Congress had rejected two Nixon nominees for the Supreme Court, both of them Southerners.

In 1971 Nixon set "Six Great Goals" for his administration: welfare reform, revenue sharing with the states and localities, comprehensive health insurance, clean air and water, government reorganization, and full employment. By the end of Nixon's first term, Congress had approved only revenue sharing.

In Nixon's second term, the Democratic Congress imposed the first congressional limits on a president's power to act in international emergencies. It passed the Budget Act to limit the president's power to impound money appropriated by Congress. The uproar over the Watergate scandal finally forced Nixon to resign the presidency, the first president ever to do so.

Having a Congress of the president's own party is no guarantee of success, however. Although Jimmy Carter had a Democratic House and Senate, he was inept at pressuring Congress, either directly or through public opinion. Congress rejected, or drastically changed, many of Carter's big legislative proposals. Among Carter's most notable failures were proposals for a 10-cent-per-gallon gasoline tax as an energy conservation measure, controls on ballooning hospital costs, labor law changes and tax revision. Nevertheless, Carter managed to score some significant legislative and foreign policy victories.

Nor does opposition control of Congress necessarily spell a president's defeat. In 1981 Ronald Reagan put together a coalition of Republicans and Southern Democrats to force his tax and spending plans through a House "controlled" by Democrats.

PRESIDENTIAL LOBBY: MORE OPEN, ELABORATE

Since the birth of the Republic, presidents have lobbied Congress, in person or through helpers. Careful of the form if not the substance of separate powers, early presidents kept their congressional lobbying discreet and their helpers few. In recent years, presidential lobbying has become more open and more elaborate.

George Washington visited the Senate to try to win its advice and consent to an Indian treaty. Washington expected to force quick action. He failed. After that, the first president stayed away from the Capitol, except to deliver annual messages. Instead, he sent Secretary of State Thomas Jefferson and Treasury Secretary Alexander Hamilton for private talks on foreign and fiscal matters. Hamilton became so influential that the House established its committee on Ways and Means to defend against him.

When Jefferson became president, he used a series of Virginia representatives, beginning with William B. Giles, as his eyes, ears and hands in Congress.

In this century, Woodrow Wilson made his lobbying as discreet as possible. His chief congressional lobbyist was Postmaster General Albert Burleson, a Texas Democrat who had quit the House to take the Cabinet job. With postmasterships and post offices at his disposal, Burleson had considerable influence over members of Congress.

At Burleson's suggestion, Wilson enlisted another Texas Democrat, John Nance Garner, to act as his confidential lobbyist *inside* the House. Garner was a member of the Ways and Means Committee and later was to become Speaker and vice president. The Wilson-Garner relationship was hidden from the House Democratic hierarchy. Supposedly on private business, Garner left Capitol Hill twice a week by streetcar, got off near the White House, entered through a side door and was ushered into Wilson's private study where he reported to the president.

But Wilson knew how to apply pressure in person, too. In pursuit of tariff revision, he dropped by congressional committee meetings. In the Senate, every Democrat voted for the tariff bill.

Franklin D. Roosevelt used White House aides James Rowe, Thomas G. Corcoran and Benjamin Cohen to exert pressure on Congress. As their official duties included drafting legislation, they were natural choices to lobby to get bills enacted. Postmaster General James A. Farley was also the Democratic national chairman. Farley used both the postal and the political power to influence votes in Congress. Like Roosevelt, Harry S Truman used White House assistants Clark Clifford and Charles Murphy in part-time legislative liaison.

By not publicly naming their congressional lobbyists, wrote Neil MacNeil in his book *Forge of Democracy*, "Wilson, Roosevelt and Truman ... kept up a pretense of staying within the traditional strictures of the assumed independence of the President and the Congress. They felt the need for such intimate contact with the members of Congress, but they hesitated to offend the sensibilities of the House and Senate as institutions."

Beginning with Dwight D. Eisenhower, presidents have appointed full-time legislative liaison officers to their White House staff. In addition, all federal departments now have their own congressional liaison forces. The practice began in 1945, when the War Department created the office of assistant secretary for congressional liaison, centralizing congressional relations that had been handled separately by the military services.

Eisenhower named Bryce N. Harlow, long an employee of the House Armed Services Committee, as his top special assistant for congressional affairs, a post he held under various titles for eight years. The position no longer was anonymous, nor did Harlow have other White House assignments.

According to MacNeil, Harlow "normally operated from his White House office, answering and making telephone calls, perhaps as many as 125 a day." MacNeil's account of Harlow's liaison methods continues: "Only rarely did he slip up to the House of Representatives and usually then only to have a private lunch with Charles Halleck of Indiana, one of the Republican leaders.... Harlow kept the Republican party's congressional leaders informed of forthcoming Eisenhower legislative proposals and kept in touch with Democratic leaders. Frequently he escorted Speaker Sam Rayburn and Senate Majority Leader Lyndon Johnson into the White House late in the day for a highball and chat with the President.... Harlow tried to satisfy the requests of members and tried to persuade them to support the President's programs. 'In this game,' he said, 'it's what you've done lately that counts.'"

Kennedy-O'Brien Liaison Team

President Kennedy sought to beef up the liaison function, appointing his long-time associate Lawrence F. O'Brien as chief lobbyist and giving O'Brien full authority to speak for him on legislative matters. O'Brien was given co-equal rank with other top White House aides and was assigned assistants for both House and Senate. MacNeil reports that "to even the most influential senators who telephoned Kennedy in the first weeks of his presidency, the President had a stock reply: 'Have you discussed this with Larry O'Brien?'"

At the outset of the Kennedy administration, O'Brien organized a series of cocktail parties, all held in House committee rooms, where he sought to meet House members on a purely social basis. Later, O'Brien invited House members in groups of 50 for coffee at the White House. For committee chairmen, he set up private discussions with the president. At a dinner with the Democratic Study Group, a bloc of about 100 House liberals, O'Brien promised that the president would support them for re-election if they backed his legislative program. "The White House certainly remembers who its friends are," MacNeil reported of O'Brien, "and can be counted on to apply significant assistance in the campaign."

Clearing their activities with O'Brien, Cabinet officials sought to cultivate congressional leaders. Defense Secretary Robert S. McNamara courted House Armed Services Committee Chairman Carl Vinson, D-Ga. (1914-65), Vinson's Senate counterpart Richard B. Russell (1933-71) (also a Georgia Democrat) and other key members of the House and Senate military committees. Treasury Secretary Douglas Dillon kept in close touch with House Ways and Means Committee Chairman Wilbur D. Mills, D-Ark. (1939-77). Agriculture Secretary Orville L. Freeman consulted frequently with congressional leaders on the president's farm program. Other Cabinet officers and their liaison staffs made similar contacts.

Kennedy and O'Brien made extensive use of the congressional liaison offices of the Cabinet departments and executive agencies. When an administration bill was introduced in Congress, the department involved was given prime responsibility for getting the measure through subcommittee and committee. When the bill neared the House or Senate floor, O'Brien and his corps of White House lobbyists joined forces with the agency liaison teams. There were about 35 agency lobbyists working during the Kennedy-Johnson era although not all of them devoted full time to legislation.

The Kennedy tactics often were successful in removing major legislative obstacles, but the obstacles appeared so frequently that the president's program foundered in Congress. Some members, primarily the older, more conservative ones, resented the pressure treatment. As Meg Greenfield, a newspaper and magazine writer, reported in 1962: "The most widely shared and loudly voiced grievance that Congress has against administration practices concerns the unremitting attention it receives from those it describes simply and without affection as the 'young men.' They badger, to hear the members tell it. They hector. They even chase.... Legislators who still cherish the notion that they themselves will decide how to vote appear to have been at various times amused, confused and infuriated by the discombobulation of incoming messages.... 'Why are you calling me, son?' an august legislator asked an all but anonymous administration phoner not long ago.... To the White House counterclaim that pushing and prodding sometimes helps and never hurts, one congressman replies by citing the case of a young liaison man, the very sight of whom at the cloakroom door, he claims, is enough to cost the administration 25 votes. Under questioning, he lowered the figure to three, but this time he seemed serious."

Liaison Under Johnson

The liaison system Kennedy nurtured paid dividends during the Johnson administration. Loyal Democrats had picked up a working margin of seats in the 1964 election, and with O'Brien still supervising the liaison job, almost all of the old Kennedy measures sailed through Congress. Even when Johnson appointed O'Brien postmaster general, he continued as chief White House lobbyist, after Johnson himself.

O'Brien abided by one self-imposed rule. He would not enter the public congressional galleries, either to listen to debate or watch the members vote. "He could read the debate and count the vote in the *Congressional Record* the next day," wrote MacNeil. "To appear in the gallery, however, might smack of an impropriety; it might seem that he was asserting an undue pressure on the members of Congress. O'Brien's sensitivity here was a trace, a faint trace, of the old constitutional separatism between the executive and legislative branches of the government. There were scarcely any others left. The rest had been eroded by the imperious demands of modern America."

Nixon and Ford

Although President Nixon sought to slow down the furious pace of legislation that had marked the Johnson years, he still relied on a large liaison staff to push key administration bills. As chief lobbyist, he named Bryce Harlow, who came back to the White House after eight years of lobbying for the Procter & Gamble Co. In Nixon's first two years, his lobby force lost critical battles over two Supreme Court nominations and over restrictions on the administration's Southeast Asia policy but won a notable victory on funds for deployment of a controversial antiballistic missile system.

Harlow served Nixon until April 1974, four months before Nixon's resignation. In addition to Harlow, during the Nixon years, much of the day-to-day congressional liaison was handled by William E. Timmons, who had served in both Senate and House offices.

When Timmons resigned as chief liaison officer, President Gerald R. Ford promoted Max L. Friedersdorf to the position. A former newspaper reporter, Friedersdorf had been an administrative assistant to a House member and a congressional relations officer with the Office of Economic Opportunity.

Problems for Carter

A newcomer to Washington, President Carter got off to a bad start by appointing another Georgian and an equally inexperienced hand, Frank B. Moore, as his chief congressional lobbyist. Moore quickly offended congressional sensibilities by failing to return phone calls, missing meetings and neglecting to consult adequately about presidential appointments and programs. He broke with precedent by organizing his 20-man staff around issues rather than geographical areas. This hampered vote-trading. As a former Carter aide explained, a White House liaison officer "is no longer in a position to discuss a sewage treatment plant in the context of a foreign aid vote, because the liaison aide who handles foreign aid does not also handle environmental issues."

Six months after taking office, Carter reorganized his liaison team by geography and added several Washington veterans, including William H. Cable, a respected House staffer who was put in charge of lobbying the House. Moore also adopted some of Lawrence O'Brien's techniques for pushing major bills through Congress, including close coordination of White House and department lobbyists and personal intervention by the president before key votes. The White House also began using computers to analyze past votes and target supporters for the future.

These "task force" techniques were used to help persuade Congress to stop development of the B-1 bomber, ratify the Panama Canal treaty and revise the civil service system.

After its shaky start, the Carter liaison team also learned to work through the Democratic leadership in the House and Senate. Carter himself met with the leaders every Tuesday. But according to most observers, Carter's team never recovered totally from its beginnings.

Attention to detail is one of the factors that set President Reagan's legislative liaison team, headed initially by Max Friedersdorf, apart from the Carter team that preceded it. Friedersdorf had worked on congressional relations under Nixon and Ford. His chief assistants, Powell E. Moore in the Senate and Kenneth M. Duberstein in the House, had substantial experience on Capitol Hill.

Reagan built a reputation for a winning way with Congress during his first years, thanks mainly to a few major showdowns on the budget, taxes and the sale of the AWACS radar planes to Saudi Arabia. One news magazine summed up that particular week in October with a cover photograph of a gleeful president and the headline, "He Does It Again!"

During 1981 Duberstein was Friedersdorf's principal deputy in the House, where he became known as an effective, discreet and partisan go-between. These qualities would hold him in good stead, as Friedersdorf stepped down from his post at the end of the year and Reagan

turned the job over to Duberstein. *(Duberstein profile, box, p. 19)*

MOVING CONGRESS BY GOING TO THE PEOPLE

When even the most skillful direct pressure fails, presidents often turn to the public for help in moving Congress. Going over congressional heads to the people has always required cultivation of reporters and others responsible for gathering and transmitting the news. Today, radio and television permit a president to go over reporters' heads, too, in marshaling public opinion.

Among the early presidents, Andrew Jackson was the most skillful at public relations. Jackson arranged to have official documents leaked to his favorite newspapers. According to James E. Pollard in his book *The Presidents and the Press*, Jackson "knew what he wanted, he meant to have his way, and he was fortunate in finding journalists devoted to him and capable of carrying out his desires."

Lincoln found himself on the defensive with Congress in regard to his war policies. But he overcame congressional opposition with public support, generated by the stories he passed out to reporters and editors and by letters he wrote that found their way into print. The press also published Lincoln's eloquent speeches. While Lincoln "paid some heed to the sanctity of military secrets, he declined to worship at that shrine," wrote George Fort Milton in his book *The Use of Presidential Power*. "He knew that the people had ears, whether the walls had them or not, and took advantage of every appropriate occasion to tell his innermost thoughts."

Andrew Johnson was the first president to grant a formal interview to the press. He gave 12 exclusive interviews, most of them on his troubles with Congress over Reconstruction. But press coverage failed to generate enough public sympathy to save Johnson from impeachment by the House. He escaped conviction in the Senate by a single vote.

Theodore Roosevelt made himself easily available to reporters. Credited with having invented the "background" press conference, Roosevelt launched "trial balloons" to test public opinion before deciding on a course of action. Under Roosevelt, the White House began issuing regular news releases.

Roosevelt saw the White House as a "bully pulpit," to be used to mobilize public support. Eager to show the American flag abroad, Roosevelt sent the U.S. battleship fleet around the world, even though the Navy lacked funds to pay for the cruise. The public was so impressed with this display of American naval power that Congress lost no time in appropriating the necessary funds.

Woodrow Wilson began the practice of holding regular and formal press conferences. Until the war in Europe took most of his time, Wilson met the press an average of twice a week. But Wilson was most effective with his appeals directly to the public. Several weeks after Wilson's inauguration, the new president issued a statement attacking the "extraordinary exertions" of special interest groups to change his tariff bill, according to *The Presidents and the Press.* "The newspapers are filled with paid advertisements," he said, "calculated to mislead the judgment of public men not only, but also the public opinion of the country itself."

While Wilson succeeded in having his way with the tariff, the technique failed him in 1919, when he conducted a whistle-stop tour of the country to drum up support for the League of Nations. He was followed by a "truth squad" of senators opposed to the league. In the end, the Senate rejected the Treaty of Versailles, which contained the Covenant of the League.

Like his distant relative Theodore, Franklin D. Roosevelt viewed the president as more than a chief executive. "The presidency is not merely an administrative office. That is the least of it," he said during the 1932 campaign. "It is pre-eminently a place of moral leadership."

FDR: Master of the Art

Probably no other president has used the news media so skillfully as FDR. He showered attention on White House reporters, holding 998 press conferences during his 147 months in office. According to Pollard, Roosevelt "was on an unprecedented footing with the working press. He knew its ways, he understood many of its problems and he more than held his own in his twice-weekly parry and thrust with the correspondents."

But it was in the radio that Roosevelt found a powerful new tool for shaping public opinion and pressuring Congress. At the end of his first week in office, Roosevelt went on the radio to urge support for his banking reforms. He addressed a joint session of Congress, too. His reforms were passed that very day.

Similar radio messages followed, and they became known as "fireside chats." As Arthur Schlesinger Jr. put it, these radio talks were effective because they "conveyed Roosevelt's conception of himself as a man at ease in his own house talking frankly and intimately to neighbors as they sat in their living rooms."

According to Wilfred Binkley in the book *President and Congress*, Roosevelt "had only to glance toward a microphone or suggest that he might go on the air again and a whole congressional delegation would surrender. They had no relish for the flood of mail and telegrams they knew would swamp them after another fireside chat to the nation."

So Congress went on, in the spring of 1933, to approve a spate of Roosevelt proposals, pausing to change scarcely so much as a comma. At the time, the president's program was known as the "Roosevelt Revolution," but he said he preferred "New Deal." In Roosevelt's first 100 days, Congress approved the bank bill, a 25 percent cut in government spending, farm relief, public works, relief for the states, the Civilian Conservation Corps and other important measures. Although the going got much tougher later on, Roosevelt still won passage of the Trade Agreements Act, Social Security and the Public Utilities Holding Company Act.

Television Becomes Important

President Eisenhower permitted his news conferences to be filmed and then televised, after editing by the White House. President Kennedy permitted live telecasts of his news conferences. For the first time, the public saw the actual questions and answers as they occurred, unedited. While these TV encounters with the press helped make Kennedy popular, they were not sufficient to pressure Congress into passing his program.

President Johnson succeeded in getting both public and Congress to accept his Great Society program at home. Johnson was a master at moving members of Congress in person. But his televised address to Congress on voting

White House legislative liaison, Kenneth M. Duberstein, third from left, and aide Powell A. Moore, far left, accompany GOP congressional leaders at a strategy session at the White House.

rights proved that he could move the people, too. Finally, the war in Vietnam soured both his public and his congressional relations.

In 1966 Congress showed that TV can be as powerful a weapon against a president as for him. When the administration asked for more money to conduct the war, the Senate Foreign Relations Committee turned the televised hearing into a full-scale debate on the war itself.

President Nixon tried to go over the heads of the Washington press corps, which he regarded as hostile, by holding press conferences outside of the capital. He also tried to generate public support through TV, with mixed results. His televised veto of a Labor-HEW money bill in 1970 brought 55,000 telegrams down on the Democratic House, which upheld the veto.

But Nixon's TV appearances failed to erase Watergate from the public mind. On Nov. 17, 1973, Nixon told a startled nation: "I am not a crook." Meanwhile, the Senate Watergate Committee's televised hearings and the House Judiciary Committee's televised impeachment proceedings undermined public support for Nixon. He resigned the presidency Aug. 9, 1974.

President Ford took office promising an "open administration." Indeed, at the end of 1975, the National Press Club praised him for conducting 24 news conferences in 19 months in office, compared with Nixon's 37 in 5-1/2 years. But the club criticized Press Secretary Ron Nessen for being unprepared and devious in his briefings.

President Carter campaigned as a Washington outsider and continued to cultivate that populist image after he took office. Carter's inaugural walk with his wife Rosalynn up Pennsylvania Avenue, "town meetings," fireside chats and bluejeans — all conveyed to the people through television — failed, however, to generate enough support in the country to move his program through Congress. "We used to be frightened to death that he would go over the top of Congress and appeal directly to the people," said Rep. Timothy E. Wirth, D-Colo., "but there's not enough cohesion in his program to do that. There's no reason to feel threatened."

An exception was the televised signing, in March 1979, of the peace treaty between Israel and Egypt, following the Camp David summit meeting, which Carter called in 1978. That ceremony played a part in persuading an otherwise stingy Congress to give foreign aid to Israel and Egypt.

President Reagan, a former actor, enjoyed early success with TV. In May 1981, Reagan made a televised address to a joint session of Congress to appeal for passage of his budget package, one that cut social spending and increased spending for defense. It was Reagan's first public appearance since the attempt on his life, March 30. A few days after his address, the Reagan budget easily passed the Democratic House.

Reagan also dispatched top administration officials to congressional districts to drum up public support for his program. Reagan named Elizabeth Hanford Dole to be his official liaison with the public.

Her stock in trade included invitations to White House briefings by the president, Cabinet members and staff for business and community leaders, farm groups and others. Dole herself gave numerous speeches. And it became her office's job to arrange for presidential greetings, on film or tape, for a fledgling Hispanic radio service or a Teamsters' convention.

Her operation was but a piece of a broader effort to win public support for the president's program. For many,

the president himself emerged as his own best lobbyist. After the Reagan budget passed the House in May 1981, Speaker Thomas P. O'Neill Jr., D-Mass., called the Reagan effort "the greatest selling job I've ever seen."

PATRONAGE: FAVORS FOR VOTES

Another means of exerting pressure on Congress is patronage — the president's power to fill government jobs, award government contracts or do other political favors. Patronage can create a debt that is repaid by voting the president's way on legislation. At least it creates an atmosphere of friendly familiarity between the president and members of Congress. "Broadly conceived, patronage involves not only federal and judicial positions, but also federal construction projects, location of government installations, offers of campaign support, access to strategic information, plane rides on Air Force One, White House meetings for important constituents of members, and countless other favors both large and small," wrote Roger H. Davidson and Walter J. Oleszek in their book *Congress and Its Members*. "Their factual or potential award enables presidents to amass political IOUs they can 'cash in' later for needed support in Congress."

In this century, civil service and postal reform has reduced the number of jobs the president has to fill. But award of government contracts and other favors remains a powerful lever in the hands of presidents.

How effective patronage is as a pressure tool is a matter of debate. Neil MacNeil reported that Sen. Everett M. Dirksen of Illinois (1951-69), a Republican leader in the 1960s, called patronage a "tremendous weapon," adding that "it develops a certain fidelity on the part of the recipient." But Rep. Paul J. Kilday, D-Texas (1939-61), said in 1961 that a congressman usually has 100 applications for every job. According to MacNeil, Kilday said: "You make 99 fellows mad at you and get one ingrate."

George Washington thought that government jobs should be filled by "those that seem to have the greatest fitness for public office." The framers of the Constitution, meanwhile, sought to protect members of Congress from the president's patronage power. The Constitution says: "No Senator or Representative shall, during the Time for which he was elected, be appointed to any civil Office under the Authority of the United States, which shall have been created, or the Emoluments thereof shall have been increased during such time; and no Person holding any Office under the United States, shall be a member of either House during his Continuance in Office."

"In other words," wrote Rep. DeAlva Stanwood Alexander, R-N.Y. (1897-1911), in 1916 in *History and Procedure of the House of Representatives*, "a legislator was not to be induced to create an office, or to increase the emoluments of one, in the hope of an appointment; nor was the Executive able to appoint him while he continued in Congress. But in practice these constitutional limitations neither preserved the legislator's independence nor restrained executive influence. In fact, the President's possession of an ever-increasing patronage has enabled him at times to absorb the legislative branch of Government."

Agency Lobbyists: 'President's Shock Troops'

Almost every sizable subdivision of the executive branch has someone in charge of dealing with Congress. The Cabinet-level departments and agencies have congressional relations staffs headed by officials who usually rank one notch below the secretary.

In addition, several independent agencies, such as the Environmental Protection Agency and the National Aeronautics and Space Administration, and some Cabinet subdivisions, such as Transportation's Federal Aviation Administration, have significant congressional relations offices of their own.

In the Reagan White House, Kenneth M. Duberstein's office of legislative affairs kept a roster of 26 separate agency lobby offices, employing a total of nearly 600 people. Even that number understated the resources devoted to influencing Congress.

For example, it did not count the 215 who worked for "legislative liaison" offices run by the military services. Many of these staffers had cubbyhole offices in the Rayburn House and Russell Senate office buildings, and performed services ranging from setting up a military escort for a committee chairman traveling abroad to telling a taxpayer how to apply for a Pentagon contract.

Congressional relations officers do not make the administration's policies, but they help shape them by interpreting administration views to Congress and bringing back impressions about what will pass and what will not.

William J. Gribben, a Duberstein deputy who kept tabs on the departments' congressional relations staffers, described them as "the president's shock troops." But their jobs often were less visible and more complicated than that, involving reconnaissance and logistics as much as hand-to-hand combat.

A sample: On Nov. 12, 1981, Defense Secretary Caspar W. Weinberger and his top deputies met with members of the House Appropriations Defense Subcommittee to press the administration's case for funding of the B-1 bomber and MX missile. Russell A. Rourke, Weinberger's assistant secretary for legislative affairs, set up the meeting. He polled the congressmen to see what points Weinberger should address, briefed the secretary and his aides on congressional concerns, and then watched the whole performance to see if any follow-up was required.

Later, Rourke prepared a list of senators and representatives for Weinberger or President Reagan to phone on the legislation, with notes on "talking points" of importance to each lawmaker. "We're kind of orchestrators," Rourke said of his job.

Scratching Itches

Sometimes congressional relations people do the face-to-face selling of administration policy — although, because of vague legal limits on executive branch persuasion, they are reluctant to use the word "lobbying." Sometimes they hover behind the technical specialists.

The less glamorous side of congressional relations work is scratching the many little itches of lawmakers and their constituents.

At the Agriculture Department (USDA), it may mean fetching an explanation for the constituent whose federal loan application was denied. At the State Department it may be answering a query from a voter whose father died on vacation in Europe. Justice officials will get the letter from the woman who wrote to her congressman about the awful conditions in the prison where her son is serving time.

At the Interior Department, Assistant to the Secretary Stanley W. Hulett said, fully 75 percent of the congressional relations staff time was spent processing complaints to Congress from "people who have run afoul of the bureaucracy" — over such matters as grazing leases or land condemnations.

Most departments have a steady flow of federal grants and contracts to announce, and members of Congress want to do the announcing so they can bask in the glory. In time-honored fashion, the party in power is notified first.

These activities may seem menial, but how they are handled has a lot to do with a department's reservoir of good will on Capitol Hill. By the midpoint of the 97th Congress (1981-83), Capitol Hill had acquired some sense of who the departmental lobbyists were in the Reagan administration, how they worked and how well.

There had been complaints of foul-ups, of some initial slowness in filling key lobbying positions and of instances of inexperience or insensitivity to the Congress. But the slip-ups had not undermined the administration's reputation for effectiveness — especially compared with the legendary (and possibly exaggerated) blunders of the Carter administration.

"I think there's clearly greater sensitivity to Congress in this administration than in the last one," said Rep. Dick Cheney, R-Wyo., chairman of the House Republican Policy Committee and a White House aide in the Ford administration.

To keep track of its far-flung lobbying operations, the Reagan White House received written weekly reports from each of the major congressional liaison offices. White House officials also insisted that departmental messages to Congress be cleared by the Office of Management and Budget (OMB), a longstanding procedure, but one that sometimes had been loosely observed.

"One of the first things Max Friedersdorf [Duberstein's predecessor] said to me is, 'There is no such thing as a departmental position. There is an administration position,'" said one departmental liaison aide.

While the Constitution forbids members of Congress to hold other federal jobs, it does not forbid appointment of his friends, family and supporters. With the emergence of political parties in the first decade of government under the Constitution, party loyalists started demanding federal jobs.

Spoils System: Created, Perfected

The inauguration of Thomas Jefferson in 1801 marked the first change in political parties at the White House. The new president found himself surrounded by Federalist party officeholders appointed by Washington and John Adams. Jefferson replaced enough of the Federalists with Democratic-Republicans to assure, he said, a more even distribution of power between the parties.

Jefferson initiated the "spoils system, which allows victors to appoint their own people to public office. But it was Andrew Jackson, 20 years later, who perfected and justified spoils. According to Martin and Susan Tolchin in their book *To the Victor: Political Patronage From the Clubhouse to the White House,* Jackson was "the first to articulate, legitimize, and translate the spoils system into the American experience." The spoils system engendered power struggles. Jackson had a House controlled by his own Democratic Party and a Senate in the hands of the opposition Whigs. The president and Congress spent much of their time fighting over patronage.

In the Senate, Jackson was challenged by John Tyler and John C. Calhoun, who led the battle against confirming some of the president's appointees and conducted a formal inquiry into the extent of federal patronage. According to the Tolchins, Calhoun said that "patronage made government too big: if this practice continued, he warned, states' rights would be crushed under the force of an ever-expanding federal bureaucracy. His investigation revealed the shocking fact that the 60,294 employees of the federal government, together with their dependents and other pensioners, made up a payroll of more than 100,000 people dependent on the federal treasury."

President Abraham Lincoln used patronage to promote a constitutional amendment abolishing slavery. Unsure whether enough states would ratify the amendment, Lincoln sought to hasten the admission of a new state, Nevada. The Nevada bill was bogged down in the House, when Lincoln learned that the votes of three members might be up for bargaining. When Assistant Secretary of War Charles A. Dana asked Lincoln what the members expected in return for their votes, Lincoln reportedly replied: "I don't know. It makes no difference. We must carry this vote. . . . Whatever promises you make, I will perform." Dana made a deal with the three representatives, and Nevada entered the Union. The new state then voted for the 13th Amendment.

President William McKinley appointed members of Congress to commissions, thus breaching the constitutional prohibition against members holding other federal offices. McKinley appointed them to make peace with Spain, settle the Bering Sea controversy, set the boundary between Alaska and Canada, arrange a commerce treaty with Great Britain and gather information on Hawaii. McKinley asked the Senate to confirm senators named to the Hawaiian commission, but it declined to do so.

Perhaps the most successful dispenser of patronage ever to hold the presidency was Woodrow Wilson, who made patronage an important instrument of his party leadership. Although patronage jobs had been cut back severely under President Grover Cleveland, as part of his civil service reform, Wilson used what patronage was left him with maximum effect. According to the *New York Sun,* Wilson's use of patronage "was never better illustrated than last Saturday, when at four o'clock, it became apparent that the senators from the cotton-growing states of the South had effected a coalition with the Republican side to kill the war-revenue bill or suspend it until legislation was put into the measure for the relief of the cotton planters. Immediately a strong arm was extended from the White House which promptly throttled the movement within thirty minutes after the fact of the revolt became known to Postmaster General Burleson, with the immense post-office patronage of the country at his disposal. . . . When the test came, four hours later, three of the eight revolters faltered and the scheme collapsed."

FDR, Eisenhower, Kennedy and Johnson

The next Democrat in the White House, Franklin Roosevelt, also made effective use of his patronage power. His patronage chief, Postmaster General Farley, asked patronage seekers such questions as "What was your pre-convention position on the Roosevelt candidacy?" and "How did you vote on the economy bill?" If a member was asked to vote for a presidential measure against local pressures, the matter was put "on the frank basis of quid pro quo."

The Eisenhower administration used patronage more as a stick than a carrot. The president's patronage dispenser, Postmaster General Arthur Summerfield, frequently set up shop in the office of House Minority Leader Charles A. Halleck, R-Ind. (1935-69), and berated Republican representatives who broke party ranks. Insurgents were warned that key jobs such as postmasterships might be cut back unless they got behind the president's program. The president himself sought to broaden the spoils, however, by removing 134,000 classified jobs from the Civil Service.

Presidents Kennedy and Johnson both assigned the task of dispensing patronage to John Bailey, chairman of the Democratic National Committee. Although clever use of patronage swayed votes on several key bills, Kennedy preferred the pressure of direct lobbying. Johnson was a master at dispensing jobs and other favors. He invited members of Congress to the White House for tete-à-tetes, danced with the wives, telephoned them on their birthdays and invited them to his Texas ranch.

Richard Nixon presided over the dissolution of a large piece of the president's patronage empire when he signed a bill that converted the 141-year-old Post Office Department into the politically independent U.S. Postal Service. While the main reason Congress passed the bill in 1970 was to solve the postal system's money problems, the measure ended the power of politicians to appoint or promote postmasters and other postal workers.

While the president's power over government jobs has declined, his power over the award of federal contracts and the location of federal installations has remained strong. According to Nelson W. Polsby in his book *Congress and the Presidency,* a president can use this power "to reward and punish congressional friends and foes quite vigorously. . . . Small Business Administration and Area Redevelopment Administration loans to certain areas may get more and more difficult to obtain, as applications fail to qualify. Pilot programs and demonstration projects may be funneled here rather than there. Defense contracts and public works may be accelerated in some areas, retarded in others."

Duberstein: Reagan's Chief Lobbyist

As Republicans basked in President Reagan's tax cut victory of August 1980, his chief ambassador to Congress, Max L. Friedersdorf, foresaw problems. By winter, Friedersdorf remarked with a faint smile, Reagan would "be blamed if anything goes wrong . . . snow, bubonic plague. . . ."

After the tax cut victory, the road did indeed get rougher for Reagan. As political fallout mounted in Congress, the task of coping with it fell to Kenneth M. Duberstein. Duberstein became chief of White House legislative affairs Jan. 2, 1982, when Friedersdorf's resignation took effect.

House Republican leader Robert H. Michel, R-Ill., expressed pleasure with Duberstein's appointment: "I gave him my highest recommendation," Michel said. Friedersdorf, Michel conceded, had much more experience than the then 37-year-old Duberstein, and "there's no substitute for experience in dealing with 535 doggone prima donnas up here."

However, Duberstein's assets included a quick grasp of legislative procedure and its importance, his candor and his loyalty, the GOP leader said. "He really keeps me informed, and I can tell him anything and know he'll hold a confidence," Michel said.

House Majority Whip Thomas S. Foley, D-Wash., said Democratic leaders were less familiar with Duberstein because the administration largely had ignored them after an initial display of attention in the spring of Reagan's first year in office.

Friedersdorf's Departure

Friedersdorf's departure did not reflect dissatisfaction with his part of the administration, according to White House Communications Director David R. Gergen. The lobbyist was named consul general in Bermuda. An asthma attack had sent Friedersdorf to the hospital during the final campaign for the tax bill in mid-1981, but his health was not a factor in the resignation, Gergen said.

Members of Congress praised Friedersdorf's skill in guiding Reagan's far-reaching economic program through a skeptical Congress in 1981. They also suggested that Duberstein would have his hands full continuing to convince Congress in 1982 and later.

Duberstein acquired Capitol Hill experience as an aide to former Sen. Jacob K. Javits, R-N.Y. (1957-81), and became an executive branch lobbyist during the Nixon and Ford administrations. He directed congressional relations at the General Services Administration (1972-75) and then at the Department of Labor (1976-77). During the Carter administration he was director of business and government relations for a New York-based foundation, the Committee for Economic Development.

Whereas Friedersdorf generally was perceived as

Kenneth M. Duberstein

"mellow, a smoothie," in Michel's phrase, Duberstein struck some who had dealt with him as more partisan. "He is a conservative who had an instinct to be a strong voice," said Rep. Tom Loeffler, R-Texas. Loeffler, who held Duberstein's House liaison job in the Ford White House, and Rep. Charles W. Stenholm, D-Texas, credited him with cementing the House alliance in 1981 between Republicans and conservative Southern Democrats.

Grasp of Procedure

A Republican tactician in the House said Duberstein's strong suit was his quick grasp of procedural intricacies. When House Democrats designed a complex rule to govern debate on the budget cut package known as Gramm-Latta II, "it was inside baseball stuff, but he was able to boil it down so that his staff could go around and explain it to members we needed," the tactician said. The result was the Reagan coalition's critical procedural victory of June 25, 1981.

Duberstein's mastery of House procedures also was valued by Hill operatives who counted on him to head off unrealistic White House schemes. While Friedersdorf worked during the prolonged honeymoon between Congress and the president, Duberstein was expected to operate in a more strained atmosphere.

Election year pressures likely would make Duberstein's job especially difficult, as would the touchy issues facing Congress including additional budget-cutting and the renewal of clean air legislation. Duberstein appeared to relish his plateful of political indigestibles. To survive in his job, he said, "You have to be able to say this is fun *and* that this is important for the country."

Distribution of contracts and installations became increasingly important as the federal budget grew after World War II. The greatest beneficiaries were members of the House and Senate Armed Services committees and Defense Appropriations subcommittees. In return for their support of military requests, they received defense plants and installations in their states and districts.

Meanwhile, presidents have shown varying degrees of skill at handling the small change of patronage. President Carter did not enjoy socializing with congressmen. *Congress and Its Members* recounted this story of a House Democrat: "When I came here, President Kennedy would have six or seven of us down to the White House every evening for drinks and conversation. Johnson did the same thing, and they created highly personal, highly involved relationships. With Carter, he has 140 people in for breakfast and a lecture." The Carter White House refused a request from House Speaker Thomas P. O'Neill Jr., D-Mass., for extra tickets to the Carter inaugural.

President Reagan enjoyed swapping small talk and stories with members of Congress of both parties. Reagan had Speaker O'Neill to dinner, and the White House staff invited O'Neill to a surprise birthday party for the president.

VETO THREAT: ULTIMATE WEAPON

When surprise parties and tickets, Army bases and jobs, lobbying on the Hill and at the grass roots all fail to move Congress, a president may resort to his most powerful defensive weapon, the veto.

A president uses the veto not only to try to kill unpalatable bills but also to dramatize his policies and put Congress on notice that he is to be taken seriously. Short of a veto itself, a presidential threat to veto legislation is a powerful form of lobbying.

The Constitution says that any bill Congress passes must go to the president. The president must either sign it or send it back to Congress with his objections. If he does neither while Congress is in session, it becomes law without his signature. A pocket veto occurs if Congress adjourns and the president does not sign a bill within 10 days after receiving it.

A two-thirds vote of each house is required to override a veto. The Supreme Court ruled in 1919 that two-thirds of a quorum, rather than two-thirds of the total membership, is enough for an override.

The veto is powerful because a president usually can muster the support of at least one-third plus one member of a House or Senate quorum. Woodrow Wilson said the veto power makes the president "a third branch of the legislature." From 1789 through 1981, presidents vetoed 2,393 bills, and Congress overrode only 92.

The concept of veto (literally, I forbid) originated in ancient Rome as a means of protecting the plebeians from injustice at the hands of the patricians. Roman tribunes, representing the people, were authorized to veto acts of the Senate, dominated by the patricians. English rulers were given absolute veto power, and in 1597, Queen Elizabeth I rejected more parliamentary bills than she accepted. The

English veto, which cannot be overridden, is still nominally in effect but has not been used since 1707.

Early American presidents conceived of the veto as a device to be used rarely and then only against legislative encroachment on the prerogatives of another branch of government. Washington vetoed only two bills; Adams and Jefferson, none. Although Madison and Monroe vetoed seven bills between them, they cited constitutional grounds for doing so in all except one case. John Quincy Adams did not veto a bill.

Jackson's View of Veto

The concept of the veto underwent a marked change under Andrew Jackson, who vetoed 12 bills, mostly because he took issue with their content or purpose. Jackson's most noteworthy veto was of a bill to recharter the Bank of the United States, which Jackson considered a creature of special interests. Binkley described Jackson's veto message as "a landmark in the evolution of the presidency." Binkley says: "For the first time in American history, a veto message was used as an instrument of party warfare. Through it, the Democratic Party, as the Jacksonians were now denominated, dealt a telling blow to their opponents, the National Republicans. Though addressed to Congress, the veto message was an appeal to the nation. Not a single opportunity to discredit the old ruling class was dismissed."

President John Tyler's veto of a tariff bill in 1843 brought on the first attempt by Congress to impeach a president. An impeachment resolution, introduced in the House by Whig members, charged the president "with the high crime and misdemeanor of withholding his assent to laws indispensable to the just operation of the government." When the impeachment move failed, Henry Clay proposed a constitutional amendment to enable Congress to override the president's veto by a simple majority instead of the required two-thirds. The president's right of veto gave him power equal to that of almost two-thirds of Congress, Clay said, adding that such power would ultimately make the president "ruler of the nation."

Use of Veto After the Civil War

When, after the Civil War, President Andrew Johnson vetoed a bill to protect the rights of freedmen, Congress passed the measure over his head — the first time Congress had overridden the president's veto on a major issue. The civil rights bill was only the first of a number of measures to be passed over Johnson's veto. Among others was the Tenure of Office Act, which led indirectly to Johnson's impeachment. When Johnson refused to abide by the provisions of the act, which prohibited the president from removing appointed officials from office until their successors had been confirmed, the House initiated impeachment.

During the rest of the 19th century, presidents used the veto mainly to prevent corruption through the passage of private bills. Grover Cleveland vetoed 584 bills (346 directly and 238 by pocket veto), including 301 private pension bills, which previous presidents had signed routinely. While meant to discourage fraudulent claims, Cleveland's veto incurred the wrath of veterans' groups.

Cleveland's veto record stood until Franklin Roosevelt, who disapproved 635 bills, 372 directly and 263 by pocket vetoes. Nine Roosevelt vetoes were overridden.

Under Roosevelt, vetoes increased both in absolute

Dole: White House Link to Public

In the frescoed "hall of states" at the U.S. Chamber of Commerce headquarters in Washington, Elizabeth Hanford Dole, President Reagan's public liaison chief, was preaching to the converted.

Scores of Washington representatives for trade associations savored a champagne toast to the victory of the first fiscal 1982 budget resolution, which was to be voted on in the House the next day.

The May 6 audience listened appreciatively as Dole invited them to bring their ideas and problems to her White House Public Liaison Office. Part cheerleader, part listening post, Dole was charged with building support for Reagan and his policies, and defusing criticism.

She thanked her audience for the effort they already had put into lobbying for the budget resolution. Their support included lavish newspaper and television advertisements, messages mailed to stockholders and visits paid to members of Congress by corporate executives.

"We're in the same business," Dole assured the assembled lobbyists, "communication, coalition-building, outreach."

Elizabeth Hanford Dole

Indirect Pressure

Like the White House's legislative liaison operation, Dole's office brought pressure to bear on Congress to pass the president's programs. But she did it in an indirect fashion, going to members' constituent groups, never to the lawmakers themselves. "Public opinion and attitude play an enormous part in what Congress does," said House Majority Whip Thomas S. Foley, D-Wash.

Essential to Dole's credibility with outside groups was her ability to appear as a White House insider. Only then would groups turn to her office in their quests for presidential access. If such groups liked their welcome, they could offer a president either sophisiticated Washington lobbying for his programs or the funds and networks essential to spur grass-roots support — or both.

Dole's impact was inseparable from factors such as Reagan's personal popularity and the work done by other White House officials including chief lobbyist Kenneth M. Duberstein and the hundreds of people who made up the White House office of legislative affairs. But clearly the whole team was doing something right. For example, the U.S. Chamber of Commerce, with a $70-million-a-year annual budget, concentrated its lobbying in 1981 on promoting Reagan's economic program.

Like Duberstein and other White House officials, Dole had to be careful not to step outside the bounds of a federal law prohibiting federal employees from seeking to influence Congress. She, too, maintained she was in the information business. "The more information we provide, the more people will understand President Reagan's program." However, some observers, such as Rep. Tony Coelho, Calif., chairman of the Democratic Congressional Campaign Committee, perceived Dole's operation as "wholly political."

Impeccable Credentials

Dole's assets included impeccable professional and political credentials and her own contagious enthusiasm. As a commissioner of the Federal Trade Commission (FTC) from 1973 to 1979, she gained an insider's knowledge of business and government. Colleagues at the FTC lapsed into superlatives when asked to recall her tenure. Hard work, keen intelligence and North Carolina charm made Dole "very, very easy to work with and very good," said David Clanton, acting FTC chairman.

Dole brought a strong consumer orientation to the FTC from assignments as executive director of a presidential commission on consumer interests (1968-71) and as deputy director of the White House office of consumer affairs (1971-73).

In 1979 Dole resigned her FTC position to assist her husband, Sen. Robert Dole, R-Kan., in his brief, unsuccessful presidential campaign. As chairman of the Senate Finance Committee, her husband was one of the best-placed members of Congress, a factor that worked to her advantage.

numbers and in relation to the number of bills passed. This, according to Professors Binkley and Malcolm C. Moos in their book *A Grammar of American Politics: The National Government*, reflected the growing complexity of America, which in turn was reflected in legislation. While Cleveland focused his vetoes on private pensions, Roosevelt took on the full range of issues. Until Roosevelt, no president had vetoed a revenue bill, and it was assumed that precedent exempted tax bills from the veto. Roosevelt first vetoed a revenue bill during World War II.

Presidents Truman and Eisenhower continued to make extensive use of the veto. Truman used it to safeguard organized labor against industry and agriculture. When, during the coal and rail strikes of 1946, Congress passed a bill restricting strikes, Truman vetoed it, and Congress sustained the veto. The votes to sustain came mainly from members representing big cities. In 1947, Truman vetoed the Taft-Hartley Labor Act, claiming it was unfair to labor. By then, however, Republicans were in control of Congress and the veto was overridden.

Eisenhower used the veto and the veto threat to defeat or limit social programs favored by the Democrats, who controlled Congress during six of his eight years in office. To fight liberal measures, Eisenhower put together a coalition of the Republican minority and conservative Southern Democrats. In 1959, for example, he vetoed two housing bills and another to promote rural electricity. Congress was unable to override either veto. That same year, Eisenhower used the threat of veto to defeat Democratic proposals for school aid, area redevelopment, a higher minimum wage and health care for the aged.

Presidents Kennedy and Johnson seldom had to use the veto or threaten it. They were activist presidents whose main interest lay in getting their programs through a Congress controlled by their own party. But in 1965 Johnson vetoed a military construction authorization bill that required advance congressional review of presidential decisions to close military bases.

Like Eisenhower, Presidents Nixon and Ford used the veto and its threat to prevent enactment of Democratic programs. Nixon often justified his vetoes on grounds that the bills were inflationary. When Congress passed a Labor-HEW appropriations bill that exceeded his request by $1.1 billion, Nixon vetoed it on national radio and TV. The Democratic House sustained the veto. Congress also sustained him on his vetoes of bills authorizing funds for the war on poverty and for manpower training and public service jobs.

But in 1973 Congress approved legislation to limit the president's power to commit armed forces abroad without congressional approval. Nixon vetoed the bill but Congress overrode him.

Ford vetoed 17 major bills in 1975 alone and was sustained in all but four of those. Seven of the 17 bills concerned energy and the economy. Not one of these vetoes was overridden. In 1975 both houses passed a consumer protection bill. The measure never went to conference, because Ford threatened to veto it.

Jimmy Carter was the first president since Truman to have a veto overridden by a Congress in the hands of his own party. In 1980 he disapproved a debt limit bill that included a section killing an import fee he had imposed on foreign oil. Only a handful of senators and representatives, all Democrats, voted to sustain the veto. Later that year, Congress voted overwhelmingly to override Carter's veto of a bill to increase salaries of doctors at veterans hospitals.

Carter enjoyed a couple of notable triumphs. In 1977 he threatened to veto the public works appropriations bill because it contained money for dams and other water projects that Carter said were wasteful. Congress passed the bill anyway, and Carter made good on his threat. Defying its own leadership, both Democratic and Republican, the House voted to sustain the president. The vote was 223-190, which was 53 short of the two-thirds needed to override. The House in 1978 also sustained Carter's veto of a weapons procurement bill that authorized funding for a nuclear-powered aircraft carrier that he opposed.

During his first year, President Reagan vetoed two bills. In November 1981 he disapproved a continuing appropriations bill on grounds that it was "budget busting." Instead of trying to override the veto, Congress regrouped and sent Reagan a bill he could sign. Reagan's other 1981 disapproval was a pocket veto of a bill that would have reduced bankruptcy fees. According to Reagan, the bill would have helped but one company.

Wielding his veto power twice in two days, President Reagan vetoed two versions of the same supplemental appropriations bill in mid-1982 and threatened to veto it a third time unless Congress rewrote it to his satisfaction. Earlier in the year he rejected a standby oil allocation bill.

4

Sacred Cows

Some federal programs seem to lead charmed lives. Year after year, they survive the budget drill of successive administrations, the barbs of critics, the popular pressure for smaller federal deficits, the competition of newer priorities. Their legendary life expectancy on Capitol Hill prompted David A. Stockman, director of the Office of Management and Budget, to describe them as "the thundering herd of sacred cows."

Something more than merit shields these programs. In some cases it is a broadly based, politically sensitive or especially vocal constituency. Sometimes it is the paternal pride of a few highly placed protectors in Congress. Some programs are left alone due to longstanding mutual protection pacts with sponsors of other programs. Bureaucrats within an agency can undercut administration austerity efforts aimed in their direction.

But in 1981 Capitol Hill became treacherous terrain, populated by self-styled fiscal conservatives and watched over by a determined president. Novel budget rules — called reconciliation — were designed to force compliance with overall spending targets.

How did the untouchables of past years stand up to these new hazards? Congressional Quarterly culled a few examples from the "thundering herd" and followed their steps across this newly hazardous budget course. The programs chosen were impact aid, the Clinch River breeder reactor, the Export-Import Bank, the A-7K attack airplane, Public Health Service hospitals, Amtrak passenger trains, the Head Start program and the peanut allotment program.

The sample programs were not selected for their size or importance, nor for their merits or lack of them. Programs were picked for their proven resistance to attack. Though they represented dramatically varied federal activities, each had something going for it beyond its value to the public — benefactors or assets that immunized it to past economizing moves.

The stories of these programs provide vignettes rather than a full picture; they offer clues rather than conclusions. But they help to illustrate the transformation of budget politics during President Reagan's maiden legislative voyage.

The first and easiest observation is that even sacred cows no longer can rest easy. Some of the once-inviolate programs examined here suffered budget cuts far greater than past critics ever were able to inflict. That was thanks in large part to the machinery of reconciliation. The packaging of encyclopedic program changes under the general rubric of "spending cuts" circumvented the committees that traditionally have authorized programs and appropriated money for them. Lobbyists no longer could count on being rescued by the familiar and friendly committees they customarily had dealt with.

In addition, the cast changes brought about in Congress and in the White House through the elections meant the absence of longtime defenders of particular projects and the arrival of newcomers with no allegiances to the work of the past. The near-elimination of the Clinch River breeder reactor showed that some of these new members were willing to carry budget-cutting a good deal farther than Reagan wanted. The tensions in the farm bloc, discussed in the saga of the peanut program, provided further evidence of this change.

But the tales related below also indicated that the dynamics that had kept programs viable remained in operation. All but two of the programs discussed made it through 1981 alive — barely alive in a few cases, but alive — and were in training for future rounds.

A few additional observations about the care and feeding of sacred cows in 1981:

Constituency. Strong, broad constituent support is still the sturdiest shield a program can have.

Reagan and reconciliation forced Congress to do things it had been unwilling to do in the past. But the notion that they forced Congress to do politically risky things probably was an exaggeration. Where threatened programs had vocal support from a broad, voting constituency, Congress showed a willingness to resist Reagan's vaunted "mandate," and Reagan himself showed a willingness to compromise.

Impact aid and Amtrak were two cases where popular pressure from beneficiaries traditionally had overcome economy-minded critics. In 1981 Reagan failed to cut the two programs as deeply as he wanted — a failing he did not experience in other areas with smaller or quieter constituencies. Further evidence of the potency of constituency could be found in the administration's wary approach to Social Security cuts or in Congress' resistance to proposed cuts in the Farm Belt's rural electric loan program.

Jobs. The word "jobs" traditionally has been more powerful than "abracadabra" at warding off the Office of Management and Budget. Clinch River and the Export-

Import Bank were helped by their promise of putting Americans to work.

In 1980 Stockman, then a member of the House, in challenging continued funding of the massive Tennessee-Tombigbee waterway project, jested that if employment was the main criterion, Congress might as well "go whole-hog and build a pyramid in every state, because that would generate a lot of jobs." On this issue, Stockman stood as a minority voice within the Reagan administration, which supported continued work on Tennessee-Tombigbee and many other pyramid-sized water projects.

Rich Pastures. In general, sacred cows stand a better chance if they graze in richer pastures. Where the fiscal pressures are less intense, sacred cows continue to dine on federal money. Although for a while it looked as though the A-7K aircraft would benefit from this larger truth, in the end it lost its funding as the pressure intensified to make some cuts in the healthy defense budget.

Still, this theme could be enlarged to include tax cut legislation. While Reagan was taking away on the spending side of the ledger, he was giving rather generously on the tax side. As a result many lobbyists were finding the tax-writing committees a good deal less inhibited than their budget-writing counterparts.

Friends. Powerful friends still count; some of the power, however, had changed hands. The 1980 election defeats of Sen. Warren G. Magnuson, D-Wash. (1944-81), and Rep. John M. Murphy, D-N.Y. (1963-81), doomed the long-protected public health service hospitals. But the Clinch River reactor survived the conservative tide in part because of an early appeal from the Senate majority leader, Howard H. Baker Jr., R-Tenn., whose state was home for the project.

Human Needs. Compassion is not a strong selling point for social programs. Nutrition, housing, job training, welfare, health, legal aid for the indigent and other "human needs" programs fared rather poorly. A few "do-gooder" programs survived, however. As the Head Start story illustrates, programs for the poor stand the best chance if they

are sold on the basis of "proven" success, have a well-organized constituency and are politically non-threatening.

Budget Tricks. Creative accounting can spare a program that might otherwise suffer. A traditional technique for keeping dams, highways and other public works projects from the ax is to stretch out construction time so that each project gets built in smaller installments, keeping down the annual total.

Budget Process. The reconciliation process, which forced Congress to vote for or against spending totals, proved a formidable weapon for curbing spending. It was intended to be such a restraint. But where a president was willing and a Congress pliable, it also could be a device for protecting programs.

The last-minute rescue of Clinch River from the hands of spending critics was accomplished using reconciliation for shelter. In the House, the Republican reconciliation alternative helped ensure that the Export-Import Bank would be financed more generously than the president recommended.

Clinch River Reactor

Powerful friends, heavy lobbying and 1981's confused congressional budget process combined to keep alive the nuclear industry's favorite project, the Clinch River (Tenn.) breeder reactor. The episode showed how the arrival in Congress of conservative, uncommitted newcomers shook the old loyalties that held some programs inviolate — in this case, nearly carrying budget-cutting much farther than Reagan wanted.

Before Jimmy Carter became president, Clinch River was the nation's premier energy project. It was to be a demonstration plant that would produce more nuclear fuel than it consumed while making electricity for the Tennessee Valley Authority. The project became the symbolic centerpiece of the national fight over nuclear power.

Throughout his term, Carter tried to kill the project, arguing that the plutonium it created could result in the spread of atomic weapons. Carter was aided by strong opposition from environmental and taxpayer groups. But he never was able to overcome the alliance of nuclear believers, Tennessee lawmakers and utility lobbyists; each year Congress appropriated funds for Clinch River.

Between 1970 — the year Congress first authorized the program — and 1981, more than $1 billion had been spent, and actual construction had not even begun. The estimated cost of the project had grown from $700 million to $3.2 billion. The nation's utilities and the nuclear industry expected the Reagan administration to move quickly ahead on programs dear to them, including Clinch River, in which both groups had a large financial stake.

But Reagan's choice of Stockman to be director of the Office of Management and Budget sent shivers through Clinch River supporters. As a first-term congressman from Michigan in 1977, Stockman had written a study concluding that the federal government should abandon the project on economic grounds.

Stockman's initial draft of the fiscal 1982 budget did not include Clinch River funding. However, when Reagan presented the budget in March 1981, $254 million for the project was included. The president had inserted the funding, over Stockman's objections, at the request of Senate Majority Leader Baker, a vigorous supporter of the project for his home state of Tennessee.

An artist's conception of the proposed $3.2 billion Clinch River (Tenn.) breeder reactor, at right, which withstood 1982 budget pressures.

Stockman, who lost few other battles in preparing the budget, told reporters that "I am not running this government single-handedly."

Committee Opposition

Clinch River opponents were led by lobbyists Renee Parsons of Friends of the Earth and Jill Greenbaum of the National Taxpayers Union. To the administration's dismay, it was apparent that Stockman's 1977 argument helped convince several of the new members to oppose the project.

The House Science Committee had voted 22-18 May 7 to terminate the $3 billion project. The vote came on an amendment to the fiscal 1982 DOE authorization bill, which later was included in the reconciliation package. However, with House adoption of the Republican backed Gramm-Latta substitute, the committee action was overturned.

Ironically, it was the administration's own insistence on a free market in energy that opponents of the project used as their argument for killing the project. That argument apparently appealed to new members of the panel; 10 of the 13 new members voted to terminate the reactor. The vote was viewed as primarily an economic rather than an anti-nuclear vote.

Reconciliation Results

The committee vote turned out to be only a short-lived blow to Clinch River supporters. Opponents of the project never got a chance to find out if the new fiscal conservatism of the Science panel was shared in the rest of Congress. Ironically, it was the new budget process designed to force sacrifices in the name of austerity, that saved the high-priced Clinch River project from facing that test. The Senate reconciliation bill did not address the issue, but the Senate Energy Committee assumed the project would continue to be funded. And in preparing the substitute reconciliation bill that the House eventually adopted, the White House added Clinch River as a sweetener to attract the votes of Southern Democrats.

In the end, despite extremely close calls in both chambers, an ample $195 million was appropriated for Clinch River in the fiscal 1982 energy and water appropriations bill. Stockman explained to William Greider in the re-

nowned series of interviews for *The Atlantic* that the issue "just wasn't worth fighting.... This [economic] package will go nowhere without Baker, and Clinch River is just life or death to Baker."

Peanut Allocations

Passing farm legislation always has been a logrolling tournament. Farmers of wheat or peanuts or dairy cows cannot command a majority in Congress, but they traditionally have found strength by huddling together — with food stamp funding included in the same legislation as an inducement to urban representatives.

In 1981, as Congress wrote its quadrennial farm bill, the Reagan administration inched a wedge into the farm bloc and pounded on it. "My strategy," Stockman explained to Greider for *The Atlantic*, "is to come in with a farm bill that's unacceptable to the farm guys so that the whole thing begins to splinter."

For peanut farmers, the administration proposed an end to the longstanding allotment system that gave a limited number of established permit holders the exclusive right to grow peanuts. Commercial peanut purchasers and consumer advocates said this system was archaic and inflationary, and the administration agreed. The ultimate outcome was a compromise that pleased no one entirely.

Peanuts Debated

"If I went out and planted 500 acres of peanuts, would I go to jail?"

In one blunt question to the Senate Agriculture Committee, Sen. Roger W. Jepsen, R-Iowa, summed up the case against the federal peanut program. For years the program, one of the last remnants of restrictive, Depression-era farm policies, quietly guaranteed a select few farmers the right to grow peanuts. Others who might have tried to crash that exclusive club and grow the lucrative crop for market would not have been jailed. But they would have faced severe fines if they ever got past the regional grower associations that control U.S. peanut sales.

President Reagan wanted to begin opening up the program to any farmer who wished to grow peanuts. Sen. Richard G. Lugar, R-Ind., wanted even more drastic action.

A timely mix of weather, budget politics, unsettled relations among farm groups and new farm leadership in Congress meant that Reagan and Lugar had an extra edge in loosening up the program.

The budget process became central to the peanut issue. The program's relatively modest cost of $17 million to $30 million a year was not the issue, but the process itself disturbed the vote-trading that succeeded in shielding the controversial structure of the program up until 1981.

Peanut program defenders, such as Sen. Howell Heflin, D-Ala., argued that peanuts were a uniquely risky crop, uniquely deserving of special federal protection. The peanut grower associations spoke with a single voice in praise of it and it was that view, voiced by representatives such as former Rep. Dawson Mathis, D-Ga. (1971-81), that was most often heard in Congress. Mathis counseled Georgia Peanut Growers.

Not all peanut growers liked the program, although the dissatisfied were not often heard in Congress. In 1981, however, Gene Miller of Lumpkin, Ga., told congressional agriculture committees he wanted to see the whole program scrapped. Miller and like-minded farmers did not think they should pay someone else for permission to grow peanuts, as they traditionally had to do.

Unless a farmer inherited a farm with a peanut allotment — in effect a license to grow — or bought a farm with one, he had to rent an allotment from an owner at a cost as high as $200 per acre for the most fertile acreage in Georgia and Alabama. The allotments were handed out by the federal government shortly after World War II — to farmers already in the peanut business. They could be transferred only by their owners and could not be sold separately from the land to which they were assigned.

Heflin and his allies insisted that widows and children and the rural elderly who own allotments would suffer cruelly if the system were ended. "Is it *evil* for the widow at 80 years of age to lease her property?" Heflin demanded of the Agriculture Committee. Program advocates also argued that the allotments had become part of the owners' net worth, and that the Congress should not abruptly devalue the peanut acres.

But Lugar said the whole system was "out of kilter. It's feudal." Although the Agriculture Department could not confirm the figure, Lugar maintained that 70 percent of U.S. peanuts were not grown by those who held the allotments. Lugar indicated that the program had survived his attack in committee in 1981 because it was "special interest agricultural policy at its least defensible."

Congressional Agriculture committees reflect the regional nature of farming, with individual members most often representing one or two specific commodities such as dairy, soybeans, grains, livestock, or the Southern crops of tobacco and peanuts, rice and sugar. Members habitually vote for each other's programs to ensure support for their own. In the past, with skilled vote-trading and the ever-expanding federal budgets, the regional tensions among different farm interests generally were subordinated to crafting farm bills that all could support.

But in 1981 commodity interests found themselves in direct competition for federal funds. Some Midwestern grain or soybean producers who lived for years with high-risk, low-support federal programs were becoming resentful of the special status accorded peanut producers. Lugar touched on that feeling when he remarked that "nothing I could propose for [Indiana] corn producers would come close to what peanut growers want."

With the budget having fixed the size of the federal pie through the reconciliation process, "there's only so many cherries, and everybody is a little more parochial," said Mathis. "It's not the same old game of 'you do something for me, and I'll do something for you,'" said John Baize, Washington director of the American Soybean Association.

Of the three million U.S. farms, only 54,000 grow peanuts, according to Agriculture Department figures. The highest-yielding peanut farms are those in the Southeast, represented for years by such high-yield politicians as former Senate Agriculture Committee Chairman Herman E. Talmadge, D-Ga. (1957-81).

Talmadge and before him Sen. Allen J. Ellender, D-La. (1937-72), crafted "gentlemen's agreements" that guaranteed the survival of the closed peanut and tobacco programs that are so important to the rural South, according

Before 1981 it was illegal to grow peanuts as a cash crop without an allotment from the federal government. Most peanut farmers rented allotments from non-farmers.

Impact aid has traditionally received support from conservatives. Yet the program was threatened in 1981 by Reagan administration budget cuts.

to Robert Mullins of the National Farmers Union.

Congress wrote new peanut marketing limits into the 1977 farm bill. Although these cut program costs dramatically, they did not open up the program.

Nature set up the procedures for the 1981 struggle when the previous year's drought cut peanut production in half, causing supermarket prices for peanuts and peanut butter to soar.

Besides setting commodity groups against each other, the 1981 budget process undermined the clout of committee chairmen, such as Talmadge's successor at the Agriculture panel, Sen. Jesse Helms, R-N.C. By relocating overall spending decisions outside of the authorizing committee, the process left Helms far less room for negotiations.

Another sensitive factor that neither farm leaders nor members would discuss openly was Helms' adamant personal style, which many found far less conciliatory than that of Talmadge. Lobbyists said they could not remember a time when an attack such as Lugar's on a farm program could have come out of "their" Agriculture Committee, much less with the support of three other committee members.

Final Outcome

Offered in a House-Senate conference by a peanut friend, Rep. Charlie Rose, D-N.C., the compromise for the first time opened the exclusive peanut-growing club to any farmer who wanted in. However, current participants received lucrative special advantages — higher price supports, and preferential access to the domestic market. Both sides grumbled about the outcome, with consumer groups ending up more aggrieved than producers. With consumer advocates and some commodities groups urging disapproval, the final farm bill limped through the House by a two-vote margin, and the administration proclaimed victory.

The year's events may not have marked the end of the farm block, but some saw them as the beginning of the end. "Concern over government spending, and the conviction that the government is the problem, have broken up the

New Deal coalition responsible for passing farm bills in the past," said Rep. Bill Alexander, D-Ark.

Impact Aid

Impact aid is the perennially popular program that compensates schools for educating children whose parents live or work on untaxed federal property. The moral of its story may be that you *can* teach an old cow new tricks. Every president since Dwight D. Eisenhower tried to trim the program, complaining that it passed out money indiscriminately to rich and poor schools alike.

Every president since Eisenhower failed because, for one thing, a program that gives money to 3,900 school systems sprinkled among nearly every congressional district is bound to have a following in Congress. Impact aid has had such a following that each year, before the House Appropriations Subcommittee on Education approves the impact aid budget, the most die-hard conservatives show up to testify in support.

For fiscal 1982 Reagan proposed cutting the program sharply, to $401 million from about $725 million disbursed in 1981. From the outset, it was evident to impact aid supporters that things would be more difficult than in past years. When school districts began their annual round of phone calls and visits to their representatives, they found that many longtime supporters — especially conservative Republicans and Southern Democratic "Boll Weevils" — felt bound to support the president's budget cuts.

"It's not that they don't like impact aid," lamented James Maza, director of the National Association of Federally Impacted Schools, which orchestrates lobbying by about 1,000 school districts. "It's that they like fiscal austerity more." Just as important, the budget device of reconciliation meant that "we didn't get a lot of clean shots," Maza said. Proponents never got a yes-or-no vote in the House on their program, because it was packaged in a larger parcel, loosely labeled "less spending."

Tuition Threat

So supporters of impact aid tried a different approach. School districts in a few states warned that if impact aid underwent drastic cuts, they would begin billing military families for tuition. Fanned by the impacted schools association, the idea spread. Virginia passed a law allowing schools to charge tuition if impact aid was cut; then North Carolina followed suit; then Texas. By June, tuition charges were under serious discussion in at least seven states with large military installations.

The strategy was partly successful. While the administration publicly refused to back down, the military was alarmed about the potential impact of tuition charges on morale and enlistment. Base commanders and military families began telling their congressmen of their fear, and Defense Department aides began lobbying within the administration for a higher impact aid budget.

On June 24 there was a Senate hearing on the tuition flap — not in the Labor and Human Resources Committee, which governs impact aid, but in the Armed Services Committees, where Chairman John Tower, R-Texas, had heard the alarm bells. The next day, Tower and a group of cosponsors, mostly conservatives, offered an amendment to the reconciliation bill increasing impact aid to $500 million. Pentagon officials had told Tower that would be just enough to stave off the tuition attempts.

Sen. Pete V. Domenici, R-N.M., floor manager of the reconciliation bill, pointed out that Tower's amendment would exceed the budget ceiling assigned to the Labor Committee, of which Tower was not a member. But Domenici said he had looked at the list of cosponsors and decided it was useless to protest. He let the amendment go by on a voice vote.

Close Call

In the House, impact aid had one perilous moment when the Education and Labor Committee, under enormous budget pressure, voted to wipe out the program altogether. Though the committee did not say so, there was speculation that committee leaders believed threatening to kill such a popular program might force the House to come to the rescue of social programs in the panel's jurisdiction.

When it became clear the House probably would never get a clear vote on the issue, the Education Committee put back the money. It turned out not to matter, because the Republican version of reconciliation, which ultimately passed in the House, contained the president's funding level of $401 million.

Thanks in part to the anxiety over the military tuition issue, the fiscal 1982 funding level for impact aid ended up higher than Reagan's recommendation — but not by a lot. Congress authorized $475 million in the reconciliation bill in July 1981. Considering the mood of Congress, aid defenders said they were probably lucky to have that.

Export-Import Bank

How can Congress cut programs for the poor but refuse to demand the same sacrifices of Boeing, Westinghouse, General Electric and other major corporations? That is how the debate over the Export-Import Bank — which finances exports by U.S. firms — was framed by the bank's antagonists in the administration and Congress.

One answer was jobs. The exporting firms and their subcontractors employed legions of people throughout the country, and they claimed thousands of those jobs depended on exports financed by the Export-Import Bank. Another answer was that the administration's heart was not fully in its proposals to cut the program. At several points along the way, bank supporters found only soft resistance when they tried to restore the money. As a result, the program Reagan picked to prove that business must suffer alongside social programs ended up showing just the opposite.

Ambivalence

The Export-Import Bank makes low-interest loans to foreign firms and countries that buy goods and services from American companies selling overseas. Two-thirds of the loans traditionally benefit seven large corporations exporting nuclear plants, aircraft and similar high-technology products.

It probably would be an exaggeration to call the Export-Import Bank sacrosanct, for the bank never has received the level of lending authority exporters would have liked. But the program is well defended by its large corporate borrowers, exercising their first-name connections and their constituent relations with prominent members of Congress.

President Reagan singled the program out in his televised economic speech in February 1981, pointing to the bank as proof that his budget cuts would not spare "profitable corporations." He proposed cutting the bank's direct lending authority to $5.1 billion in fiscal 1981, and $4.4 billion in 1982, both well below President Carter's requests. From the beginning, according to congressional and industry sources, the administration was ambivalent about these cuts. Industry lobbyists, members of Congress and officials of Ex-Im all told reporters they were getting mixed signals about administration policy on the bank's future.

One view, emanating primarily from budget director Stockman, was that the Ex-Im Bank violated the spirit of a free marketplace. On the other side, U.S. Trade Representative William E. Brock III and Commerce Secretary Malcolm Baldrige were more sympathetic. Baldrige was acquainted with the bank from his days as a corporate executive; before joining the Cabinet he sat on the board of at least one company, AMF Inc., that used Ex-Im to finance a variety of overseas sales.

Baldrige and Brock told corporate executives they believed the bank was an important equalizer for American companies doing business overseas, but it would be bad public relations to excuse business from the general budget-cutting. Business leaders generally were marching with the president on his economic plan, and most were at first reluctant to break step over one favored program. Only a handful of big companies, in league with the International Association of Machinists, took Ex-Im's case to Congress, and the initial lobbying was low key.

In the first round, that was enough. Bank users, explained a Senate aide, "are very large companies, and they are very large employers. I don't think there's a senator here who doesn't know if one of those plants is in his state, and doesn't know what the bank means to those companies."

Sen. Nancy Landon Kassebaum, R-Kan., whose state was home to several aircraft makers, won an amendment in the Senate Budget Committee that restored about a third of the loan authority Reagan had cut. Senate supporters found little administration resistance, and word began to

spread that the White House did not care that much. "Some administration officials even encourage lawmakers privately to soften the proposed cutbacks," *The Wall Street Journal* reported.

Industry Lobbying

By May 1981, when the issue heated up in the House, much of industry's restraint had dissolved, and the major bank users had begun putting pressure on Congress. Boeing, Westinghouse, the machinists and others had joined together and begun sending industry-labor lobbying teams to Capitol Hill. Boeing had hired a former Senate aide to remind lawmakers that the company had 3,500 subcontractors in 44 states.

"I would say the companies most affected have overcome their inhibitions," said an official at one major company in early May. He added that the administration had not pressed bank borrowers to toe the line. "It could be that the whole budget issue has gotten past the stage where they need a symbolic cut in the industrial sector."

The uninhibited lobbying proved necessary as a 1981 supplemental appropriation bill made its way to the House floor. In a May 12 amendment promoted not by Republicans but by Democrat David R. Obey of Wisconsin, the House voted to give the bank exactly what the president had asked. Obey said he had nothing against Ex-Im, but that it should suffer along with everyone else. He won an odd majority made up of conservatives who were not fond of the bank and liberals angry about other budget cuts.

Overnight, backers of the bank rallied. Bank supporters met in the office of Democrat Norman D. Dicks, from Boeing's home state of Washington, then fanned out. Machinists focused on liberal friends. Members of a House export task force cornered colleagues on the floor. Subcontractors called their congressmen. The following day, with one of Reagan's best House friends, Rep. Thomas B. Evans Jr., R-Del., leading the charge, the House reversed itself and broke the president's Ex-Im budget by $400 million. The overnight lobbying, focusing on the jobs issue, changed about 70 votes.

"I am for jobs, and I am going to vote for this motion," said one of the converts, John F. Seiberling, D-Ohio, "but I am getting sick and tired of being told that we have to cut spending, we have to quit subsidizing the poor and the disadvantaged, and at the same time we are going to have more subsidies for big business."

Ex-Im Bank supporters won successive victories in the fiscal 1981 supplemental appropriation bill, the fiscal 1982 reconciliation measure and in the 1982 foreign aid appropriation. The final 1982 appropriation bill gave the bank $4.4 billion in direct loan authority (compared with a $3.9 billion Reagan request) and $9.2 billion for loan guarantees (Reagan wanted $8.2 billion).

On the House floor Dec. 11, 1981, Rep. Harold L. Volkmer, D-Mo., offered an amendment to cut $500 million from the loan figure, but conceded that "undoubtedly the individual industries that are affected by this Export-Import Bank have sufficient clout on this floor in order to make sure that they win the day whatever the amount." His amendment failed without a roll call.

Amtrak Train System

The "Perils of Amtrak" constitute one of the great continuing cliffhangers of Congress.

Since the national railroad's creation by Congress in 1970, White House economizers regularly have attempted to truncate the heavily subsidized passenger railroad network. But friends of the railroad just as regularly have ridden to the rescue, aided by popular and nostalgic support for passenger trains and the loyalty of individual lawmakers for their home-state routes.

In 1981 the melodrama of the passenger railroad followed the familiar script, with the added tension of brinkmanship. Administration officials did succeed in cutting the budget for Amtrak but not enough to shut down its major, politically sensitive routes. "I understood the political problems of Amtrak. [But] we got most of what we wanted," Transportation Secretary Drew Lewis said.

A National System

Reagan proposed a $613 million budget for Amtrak in fiscal 1982, $380 million less than President Carter's request. Taxpayers, Reagan said, should not subsidize the travel of a few. Amtrak officials soon translated the dollars into miles of railroad: Reagan's proposal, they said, would require a shutdown of all service outside the Northeast Corridor, which links Washington, New York and Boston.

The full system includes 22,000 miles of routes running through most states and many congressional districts.

Amtrak said $735 million was the minimum needed, along with some legislated cost-saving measures, to maintain what it calls "a national system." Reagan officials protested that Amtrak was playing an old trick, exaggerating the breadth of the cuts in hopes of scaring Congress into boosting the budget. At first, the Republican-run Senate Commerce Committee agreed to go along with the cuts out of loyalty to the president's economic goals. The committee approved a $613 million subsidy for fiscal 1982.

But as hometown newspapers churned out editorials protesting the threat to local service and hundreds of letters from constituents supporting Amtrak started pouring into members' offices, lawmakers began to get uneasy. Senators contacted their colleagues on the Commerce panel, with much of the alarm coming from the new Republican majority. David Durenberger, R-Minn., spearheaded the drive among non-committee members. Conservative Strom Thurmond, R-S.C., wrote the committee to support Amtrak. Staffers and Amtrak backers said there was tacit or public support from Republicans Dan Quayle, Ind., Arlen Specter, Pa., Mark O. Hatfield, Ore., and others. Missouri Gov. Christopher S. "Kit" Bond lobbied Surface Transportation Subcommittee Chairman John C. Danforth, R-Mo. California Gov. Edmund G. Brown Jr. contacted Sen. S. I. "Sam" Hayakawa, R-Calif. Committee member Kassebaum lent her support.

Howard W. Cannon of Nevada, the committee's ranking Democrat, was an early and formidable dissenter on Amtrak cuts. As the previous chairman, he had operated by consensus with GOP members, never asking for much for himself. When he pressed for more funds for Amtrak, other members could not easily dismiss him. Also, any train service that helped Cannon's state would also please Reagan's close friend, Sen. Paul Laxalt, R-Nev. J. James Exon, D-Neb., turned over to the panel a petition signed by 7,000 of his constituents asking for increased funding to spare the train that runs through Nebraska.

Panel Votes $735 Million

Meanwhile, the House Energy and Commerce Committee voted the $735 million Amtrak wanted. Norman F. Lent, N.Y., the Transportation Subcommittee's senior Republican, took the public lead. Also vital were subcommittee Chairman James J. Florio, D-N.J., and committee Chairman John D. Dingell, D-Mich., whose state would have lost its Detroit-to-Chicago service under the Reagan proposal.

Supporters framed the issue as one of national energy and transportation policy, but no one lost sight of the local consequences. "They're certainly not going to take the chairman's train away," a Dingell staffer said. "That's a fairly constant political standard."

On June 10, Senate Commerce Chairman Bob Packwood, R-Ore., called OMB Director Stockman. According to Packwood's aides, the senator told Stockman he did not want to ask his colleagues to support the Reagan budget request — cutting their own trains and incurring the political consequences — if the administration intended to give in during an eventual House-Senate conference. Just how serious was the administration about these cuts, Packwood asked.

The answer was that the administration was not firm about the cuts, so long as the panel met its total budget targets. The committee then approved a $735 million

Amtrak budget. Packwood said the vote was based on a belief in the importance of a "national system," not in parochial concerns. But he conceded the senators found it easier to vote for Amtrak knowing their own trains would be retained. In his case, that meant two trains that traverse Oregon, the Seattle-to-Salt Lake City *Pioneer* and the Seattle-to-San Diego *Coast Starlight*.

Amtrak did some route restructuring to save money, but its one controversial change proved to be short-lived. On Sept. 30, 1981, Amtrak stopped service on the little-used *Cardinal*, from Washington, D.C., to Chicago by way of West Virginia. The train was a pet of Senate Minority Leader Robert C. Byrd, D-W.Va. At his urging, the conference report on the Department of Transportation appropriations bill inserted language ordering Amtrak to keep operating the train.

One footnote to the story shed a little extra light on Amtrak's survival record: Though the House version of the transportation appropriations bill did not contain language dealing with the *Cardinal*, House Transportation Appropriations Chairman Adam Benjamin Jr., D-Ind., later sent Indiana reporters a press release announcing that he had "directed the service resumed." As the release noted, the train stopped in Gary, Richmond, Muncie, Marion and Peru, Ind.

Head Start

In a year when many programs for poor people underwent sharp spending cuts, the Head Start preschool education program stood out as a major exception. The program was spared a budget reduction and even managed to win a sizable increase. A combination of good statistics, political clout and a non-controversial objective saved Head Start from the budget-cutting tide that overwhelmed other education and anti-poverty programs.

The Head Start program provides education, health and social services to low-income and handicapped children aged 3-5. In 1981 it enrolled some 375,000 children in 1,262 local programs. The program got off to a good start during the budget battle when President Reagan included it in his "social safety net" and his budget asked for $950 million, which was $130 million more than the preceding year.

Lobbyists for the program pointed to the political advantages for the administration in preserving the program. Unlike most of the other safety net programs, Head Start was focused solely on the poor, thus emphasizing the administration's commitment to the "truly needy." Unlike the main programs for the poor, Head Start spending was not large, so any increase would have cost relatively little.

"They were looking for a real poor people's program. The Republicans wanted to show they were not anti-poor or anti-black," said Joseph Williams of the Children's Defense Fund, a non-profit children's advocacy group funded by foundations.

Stressing Results

Williams and other program backers preferred to stress Head Start's successful results with children as the chief reason for its budget survival. They could point to a substantial body of data showing that Head Start was effective and could even save money in the long run.

Most importantly, the studies showed that spending for Head Start led to reduced future spending for other programs. In the area of education, for example, Head Start children had been shown to need less special help when they entered public school, and to be more likely to continue in school. According to one estimate, the benefits of Head Start, in terms of reduced special education and increased projected lifetime earnings of participants, outweighed its costs by more than 2-1.

Head Start also provided health screening, treatment and immunizations that helped to reduce subsequent health care costs. There also was evidence that the preventive health aspects of Head Start "pay off in the prevention of long-term and debilitating health problems," according to Sen. Alan Cranston, D-Calif.

A unique feature of Head Start — and a major reason for its political success — was the program's emphasis on parental participation. Unlike other education programs for the disadvantaged, in which parents had at most an advisory role, Head Start gave parents real power over their local programs. Parents' councils participated in hiring and firing decisions, for example. The parents' sense of social involvement and confidence — so often absent in poor people — carried over into politics.

"We trained the parents to become advocates for their children. The parents would be involved and continued their involvement with the children's development," recalled Dennis Murphy, a former local Head Start program administrator who left to research the reasons for Head Start's relative budget success at Long Island University.

The training in advocacy gave the program a much more active base of mass support than most other programs for the poor. "The Head Start parents are incredibly vocal. Whenever there is a threat to the program, they are very well heard on the Hill," said one congressional aide with extensive experience with the program.

Other programs for the poor, notably legal services and community action programs, also stressed participation by recipients. Yet those programs were targeted for sharp budget attacks.

The difference was that Head Start attacked no one and did not make anyone angry. While the other programs pushed "empowerment" of the poor, through activities such as class action suits and tenant strikes, Head Start concentrated solely on helping the poor improve themselves. Its internal focus did not threaten established interests that might lobby against it. Head Start programs sometimes ran into conflict with local education authorities over personnel and other issues. However, the education lobby in Washington generally supported the program.

Finally, cuteness counts. Three- to five-year-olds were among the most appealing members of the low-income population, and it was a rare member of Congress who was unaffected by a visit to a local Head Start center.

Final Outcome

Congress obliged Reagan's initial request by authorizing $950 million for Head Start in its 1981 reconciliation bill. Later the safety net proved not quite so inviolate — Reagan asked for a 12 percent cut in all program appropriations, and Congress gave him 4 percent nearly across the board. Nonetheless, Head Start ended up with appropriations of $912 million, a significant increase from $820 million in fiscal 1981.

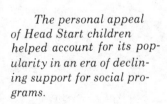

The personal appeal of Head Start children helped account for its popularity in an era of declining support for social programs.

The A-7 Jet Fighter

The A-7 tactical fighter aircraft was designed for the jungles of Southeast Asia, but it showed great prowess in the jungles of Capitol Hill as well. The acquisition of A-7 attack planes for the Air National Guard was opposed by most secretaries of defense, including Caspar W. Weinberger, as less important than the hardware needs of the active services. But — until 1981 — the plan had always survived, thanks to active lobbying by an "iron triangle" composed of the manufacturer, Texas lawmakers and National Guardsmen and reservists who liked training in the plane.

The Air Force had bought A-7s in various versions, but the one at issue was the A-7K, a two-seat model used by the Air National Guard to train reserve pilots in the basics of A-7 warfare. The A-7K was one of the few military items deliberately omitted from the Reagan administration's expansive military budget request to Congress. Moreover, Air Force Chief of Staff Gen. Lew Allen Jr. in May urged the House Armed Services Committee not to add the plane to the budget.

In this the Reagan administration was following the lead of its predecessors, which had argued, first, that the A-7 was an outmoded, Vietnam-era aircraft, and second, that buying planes for the National Guard was a lower priority than keeping the combat-ready Air Force well equipped.

Each year, however, Congress ordered the Pentagon to buy more A-7Ks. In 1981, 30 were deployed at various National Guard units, and the guard wanted 12 more to round out its force, at a cost of about $155 million. Defenders of the A-7K maintained it was a quality aircraft, its two-seat configuration indispensable for "over the shoulder" instruction. They chastised the Pentagon for neglecting the guard in favor of the active services.

Samuel S. Stratton, D-N.Y., chairman of the House Armed Services procurement subcommittee, chided the Air Force at a May hearing that "it would be somewhat inappropriate if, when we called up the reserves, they didn't have any equipment to go along with them."

Critics of the A-7K had less charitable explanations for its popularity in the Air National Guard. "Some people have been so cynical as to suggest that every state Air National Guard has a general, and generals are usually too old to fly high performance jets by themselves," said Robert M. Sherman, defense adviser to anti-A-7 Reps. Dennis M. Hertel, D-Mich., and Thomas J. Downey, D-N.Y. "A two-seater gives them the chance to keep flying."

'Iron Triangle'

Whatever its merits, the A-7K had some heavy political armor. The legs of the triangle were the Dallas-based Vought Corp., which made the plane, and the Texas congressional delegation, which considered the company a cherished constituent. The lobbying of the former and the influence of the latter help waft the plane through the yearly budget cycle.

More important was the base of the triangle, the National Guard itself, and its proxy lobbying arm, the National Guard Association of the United States, made up of guardsmen and alumni. The association was a practiced and professional lobby. Guard commanders were sent an annual "Red Book," outlining the service's legislative wish list and giving tips for visiting congressmen ("Wear civilian clothes. . . . Be honest and informative") and writing letters to Congress ("Write on your civilian business letterhead. . . . Avoid pattern phrases and sentences that give the appearance of 'form' letters").

At strategic moments in the law-making process, the association sent "Action Grams" to its members, urging them to consult their Red Books and then write to members of Congress.

"The guard is grass-roots America," explained Merle F. Allen Jr., executive assistant of the association. He gestured at a desk piled high with folders, each containing onion-skin copies of letters guard officers had written to their representatives in the 1981 campaign to save the A-7K.

The association considered its letters especially influential because the guard tended to attract more educated and influential people than the active services — businessmen rather than blue-collar workers. "We've got some master letter-writers in the guard," Allen said. "And of course, a lot of them know their congressman on a first-name basis. You don't get that in the other services."

In 1981 the A-7K had something else going for it. While other committees were being ordered to make spending cuts, the House and Senate Armed Services committees were given roughly a one-third increase in their budgets for military hardware. They felt little of the financial pressure

When key support in Congress dissolved and pressure by the manufacturer was eased, the Air National Guard's A-7 jet fighter was struck from the budget.

Staten Island's PHS hospital, which was among the island's largest employers, was desperately needed, said Rep. Guy V. Molinari, R-N.Y. He argued that the tight supply of hospital beds on the island made it a "life and death matter."

that crushed programs in other committees.

By the time Gen. Allen appeared before the full committee May 5, Stratton's subcommittee already had decided to add the planes. "We looked in vain through all of your [budget] appeals to find a single aircraft or vehicle that was specifically requested for the reserves," Stratton said. "And so we had to turn to the National Guard Association and the Reserve Officer Association, these quasi-official organizations that support the reserves...."

The full committee agreed two weeks later. By then the Senate already had routinely tucked the money into its bill.

Trade-off Attempt

But if critics could not cut the plane, perhaps they could outsmart it. With the defense authorization bill on the House floor July 16, Rep. Toby Moffett, D-Conn., offered an amendment to strike the A-7s and replace them with F-16s, a newer fighter plane.

It was a clever offer. The guard would have gotten a more modern, faster plane. Because the Air Force already was buying 160 F-16s, it could have gotten the extras at a discount price — 13 for the price of 12 A-7s. Moreover, the F-16 was being built in Texas, by General Dynamics.

The Air Force supported the move, and A-7 critics circulated a letter from an Air National Guard colonel saying the guard did too. But the Texas delegation — noting that the A-7 meant more to Vought than a few extra F-16s to the other company — opposed the move. So did the guard association, arguing that the A-7 units would be completed before the newer plane.

Moffett's amendment failed, 148-268.

Final Outcome

Indeed, the Pentagon in 1981 seemed an especially cozy refuge for the A-7K. Both the House and Senate Armed Services committees voted to authorize about $150 million to purchase a dozen more planes. But in September, two legs of the protective iron triangle gave way when President Reagan, confronted by soaring deficit estimates, opened the Pentagon budget to limited cutting. Faced with

a Reagan request for $2 billion in defense trims, House and Senate conferees on the fiscal 1982 defense authorization bill agreed to drop A-7Ks from the budget.

According to *The Fort Worth Star-Telegram*, the deciding factor was Senate Armed Services Chairman Tower, who decided he no longer could support the home-grown A-7K over higher Pentagon priorities. Without his support, House defenders Martin Frost and Charles Wilson, both Texas Democrats, could not save the plane. Another factor, the paper said, was that Vought Corp., revived by the prospect of new A-7 sales overseas and by larger contracts on such weapons as the B-1 bomber, decided not to press the issue as hard as in the past.

Bruce Jacobs, deputy executive vice president of the National Guard Association, insisted the guard was not distressed by the decision: "As far as we're concerned it's a dead issue. Congress has made a decision. We accept it. Period."

Public Health Service Hospitals

If Guy V. Molinari chaired an Appropriations Committee, he might have pulled it off — as Sen. Magnuson had done for years. As it was, Molinari did as well as a freshman House Republican could expect. He helped delay, but could not prevent, the Reagan administration's plan to cut off funding for the Public Health Service (PHS) hospital in his Staten Island (New York) district. It and seven other PHS hospitals were scheduled to be shut down unless local groups would take them over. "If I were chairman of a committee, there wasn't a chance in hell they'd close that hospital," said Molinari. "I wouldn't allow it."

Every administration since Eisenhower's had targeted PHS hospitals, trying to reduce federal spending. Until 1981 Congress successfully resisted, thus continuing a tradition begun in 1798. In that year legislators set up the hospitals to treat merchant seamen, free of charge, because of fears they might bring back exotic diseases from overseas. Though there once were 28 hospitals, all but eight had been closed by 1981.

Magnuson and Murphy

For years, these hospitals, as well as 27 clinics, were shielded successfully from executive branch budget-cutters by powerful friends such as Magnuson, the Washington Democrat who chaired the Senate Appropriations Committee, and John Murphy, who headed the House Merchant Marine Committee. Magnuson was especially protective of the hospital in Seattle, and Murphy's favorite PHS hospital was located in the Staten Island district he represented.

Both were defeated in 1980 and, according to those involved in the long tug-of-war over the hospitals, that change made all the difference. "There were two key things in the past — one was named Magnuson and the other was named Murphy," said Dr. John Marshall, who headed a special PHS hospital task force as acting associate administrator of the Health Services Administration.

Harley Dirks, who for several years directed the staff of Magnuson's Labor and Health Appropriations Subcommittee, also credited Magnuson. "If you're chairman of a committee and president pro tem of the Senate, you've got some clout," he said. "If you're a congressman, then you're kind of flapping your arms." Dirks joined a consulting firm, Washington Counsel — Medicine and Health.

Magnuson used all the tricks of a well-placed senator to protect the hospitals. For example, when President Nixon tried in 1973 to shut down all the hospitals at once, Magnuson responded by putting into law a prohibition against the closures unless Congress specifically agreed. He craftily attached the provision to a veto-proof weapons procurement bill. Magnuson also used the annual appropriations bills to encourage use of the hospitals and clinics by federally funded programs such as drug and alcoholism treatment or childhood immunization.

In the 1950s and 1960s, public health professionals and the then-strong maritime unions rallied to save the PHS system from threatened budget cuts, although some individual hospitals were closed. When Nixon went after the entire system in the early 1970s, and Congress took up the cause, the other supporters became less active — and they could afford to be.

Talmadge Simpkins, who headed an AFL-CIO umbrella group for several maritime unions, said his group again tried in 1981 to save the free care for seamen. However, they found that supporters in Congress "got hit with so much at one time" with the budget cuts that "I guess they saw stuff more important to them," Simpkins said.

Reagan Success

Although Molinari and friends gained a little more time for the hospital system, Reagan succeeded in stopping the flow of federal dollars. The administration originally wanted the hospitals to stop admitting patients July 1, 1981, and to shut their doors by Oct. 1 of that year. However, the House, in its reconciliation bill for fiscal 1982, agreed to pay the costs of shutting down the hospitals — or for transition costs, should state or local governments agree to take over operation. A Senate floor amendment authorized similar funding through March 1982. Sponsor of the amendment, Sen. Alfonse D'Amato, R-N.Y., happened to be Molinari's Washington housemate.

Repealed was the 200-year-old "entitlement," or legal right, that seamen had to free medical care. Also eligible for free care had been fishermen, oil rig workers, the Coast Guard, marine engineers, waterway operators and others, for a total of about 400,000 beneficiaries. This group had constituted about a third of the patients treated by the PHS facilities.

Military personnel, and particularly their families, also had been major users of the PHS hospitals through an arrangement between the PHS and the Defense Department. Local residents, through a variety of programs, had made up a major share of patients at three hospitals — Staten Island (28 percent), Seattle (24 percent) and Baltimore (30 percent). Other PHS hospitals were located in New Orleans, San Francisco, Boston and Nassau Bay, Texas. In addition to treating seamen and the military, the hospitals in the past had been used to care for Cuban and Indochinese refugees and victims of hurricanes and other natural disasters.

Advocates of the system, such as former Director Edward Hinman, contended that closing the hospitals would not save the federal government money. Instead, it would be more costly to provide private care for those treated by PHS personnel, he said. Hinman became executive director of Group Health Inc., a health maintenance organization in Washington, D.C.

The most determined advocate for the hospitals was Molinari, who focused on little else after his November 1980 election. Staten Island's PHS hospital, which was among the island's largest employers, was desperately needed, said Molinari. He argued that the tight supply of hospital beds on the island made it a "life-and-death matter." Though hampered by his lack of power in Congress, Molinari did manage a meeting on the question with President Reagan and Vice President George Bush. He also met with Stockman, director of the Office of Management and Budget.

Molinari also was prepared to vote against Reagan's budget in the House, despite his firm support for the administration. The Republican reconciliation bill originally provided no funds to upgrade the hospitals to meet minimum standards or to otherwise help close them or turn them over to other agencies. But Molinari convinced House Republican leaders and Stockman to add hospital funding — in return for his vote. (The deal was made moot when Republicans decided not to try to delete the Democratic version of Energy and Commerce Committee provisions, which included transition funding for the hospitals.)

Though Molinari urged Stockman to close just those PHS hospitals that were not cost-effective, leaving open the others, he said that Stockman refused. "He [Stockman] said as long as the system exists, you have the potential for a powerful member of Congress to use leverage, say, if he has a local hospital in distress, to try to bring it into the PHS system," Molinari said. "And that would be too risky for the budget."

5

Lobbying and the Law

Although lobbying is protected by the First Amendment guarantees of freedom of speech, and the right of citizens to petition the government for a redress of grievances, abuses led to periodic efforts by Congress to regulate lobbying.

In 1876 the House adopted a resolution requiring lobbyists to register during the 44th Congress with the clerk of the House, but the bill never became law. Beginning with the 62nd Congress in 1911, federal lobbying legislation continued to be considered in practically every session. Yet by 1982 only one comprehensive lobbying regulation law and a handful of more specialized measures had been enacted. In many cases, congressional investigations of lobby corruption, in response to the public outcry over corruption, took the place of tightening the rules.

Lobby Regulations

The principal method of regulation was disclosure rather than actual control. In four laws, lobbyists were required to identify themselves, who they represented and their legislative interests. In one law, lobbyists also were required to report how much they and their employers spent on lobbying. But definitions were unclear, enforcement minimal. As a result, the few existing disclosure laws produced only limited information, and their effects were questionable.

One reason for the relative lack of limitations on lobbies was the difficulty of imposing effective restrictions without infringing on the constitutional rights of free speech, press, assembly and petition. Other reasons included a fear that restrictions would hamper legitimate lobbies without reaching more serious lobby abuses, the consolidated and highly effective opposition of lobbies, and the desire of some members to keep open avenues to a future lobbying career. Congress succeeded in enacting two major lobbying laws, the Foreign Agents Registration Act of 1938 and the Federal Regulation of Lobbying Act of 1946.

The Foreign Agents Registration Act was enacted in 1938 amid reports of Fascist and Nazi propaganda circulating in the United States before World War II. It was amended frequently after that, and its history was as much a part of this country's struggle with internal security as it was a part of efforts to regulate lobbying.

The one existing omnibus lobbying law, the Federal Regulation of Lobbying Act, was enacted as part of the 1946 Legislative Reorganization Act. Its vague language and subsequent court interpretations combined to reduce seriously the effectiveness of the law's spending and lobbying disclosure provisions.

The political spending of pressure groups also was the object of numerous campaign finance bills enacted over the years by Congress. The ability to promise electoral support or opposition gave pressure groups one of the most effective devices in their attempts to influence Congress on legislation.

Precisely for this reason, Congress attempted on several occasions to limit campaign contributions made by corporations, organizations and individuals in connection with federal elections. The limitations were intended to prevent those with great financial resources from using them to dominate the selection of members of Congress and thereby its legislative decisions. *(Political action committees, chapter, p. 41)*

Following are brief discussions of the lobby laws arranged in chronological order.

Utilities Holding Company Act

Section 12 (i) of the Public Utilities Holding Company Act of 1935 required anyone employed or retained by a registered holding company or a subsidiary to file certain information with the Securities and Exchange Commission (SEC) before attempting to influence Congress, the Federal Power Commission or the SEC itself, on any legislative or administrative matter affecting any registered companies. Information required to be filed included a statement of the subject matter in which the individual was interested, the nature of the individual's employment and the nature of the individual's compensation.

Merchant Marine Act

Section 807 of the Merchant Marine Act of 1936 required any persons employed by or representing firms affected by various federal shipping laws to file certain information with the secretary of commerce before attempting to influence Congress, the Commerce Department and certain federal shipping agencies on shipping legislation or administrative decisions. The information included a statement of the subject matter in which the person was interested, the nature of the person's employment and the amount of the person's compensation.

Foreign Agents Registration Act

The Foreign Agents Registration Act of 1938, as amended, required registration with the Justice Department of anyone in the United States representing a foreign government or principal. Exceptions were allowed for purely commercial groups and certain other categories. The act brought to public view many groups, individuals and associations that, while not necessarily engaged in lobbying Congress directly, carried on propaganda activities that might ultimately affect congressional legislation and national policy.

The Foreign Agents Registration Act was amended frequently following its passage in 1938 — for example, in 1939, 1942, 1946, 1950, 1956, 1961 and 1966 — without changing its broad purposes. From 1950 on, the Justice Department followed the practice of reporting annually to Congress, in the form of a booklet listing registrants under the act and their receipts and the names of the foreign principals of registrants.

The 1966 amendments sought to clarify and strengthen the act by imposing stricter disclosure requirements for foreign lobbyists, by adding to the scope of activities for which individuals must register, by requiring them to disclose their status as agents when contacting members of Congress and other government officials, and by prohibiting contingent fees for contracts (where the fee was based upon the success of political activities) and campaign contributions on behalf of foreign interests.

In 1974 the Justice Department toughened its enforcement policy toward the activities of foreign agents. The department adopted a General Accounting Office suggestion and began to make use of the Section 5 inspection clause of the act, which encouraged more detailed and accurate reports. Increased litigation resulted. Between the adoption of the new policy and 1982, 14 civil actions had been initiated by the registration unit, most of which were resolved by consent decrees.

Federal Regulation of Lobbying Act

The Federal Regulation of Lobbying Act was passed as part of the Legislative Reorganization Act of 1946. The lobbying provisions prompted little debate at the time and, despite frequent attempts to change the law since, as of 1982 it had not been subsequently amended.

The 1946 act did not in any way directly restrict the lobbyists' activities. It simply required any person who was hired by someone else for the principal purpose of lobbying Congress to register with the secretary of the Senate and clerk of the House and to file certain quarterly financial reports so that the lobbyists' activities would be known to Congress and the public. Organizations that solicited or received money for the principal purpose of lobbying Congress did not necessarily have to register, but they did have to file quarterly spending reports with the clerk detailing how much they spent to influence legislation.

In 1954 the Supreme Court in *United States v. Harriss* upheld the constitutionality of the 1946 lobbying law but narrowly interpreted its key aspects. Opportunities for evading the loosely written law increased after that, and some critics described the statute as "more loophole than law."

One loophole opened by the decision involved collection or receipt of money. As interpreted by the court, the law did not cover groups or individuals that spent money to influence legislation, unless they also solicited, collected or received money for that purpose.

Another loophole involved the term "principal purpose." A number of organizations — including the National Association of Manufacturers for nearly 30 years — argued that because influencing Congress was not the principal purpose for which they collected or received money, they were not covered by the law regardless of what kind of activities they carried on.

The court held, in addition, that an organization or individual was not covered unless the method used to influence Congress contemplated some direct contact with members. The significance of this interpretation was that individuals or groups whose activities were confined to influencing the public on legislation or issues (the so-called grass-roots lobbying) were not subject to the 1946 law.

The decision left vague precisely what kind of contacts with Congress constituted lobbying subject to the law's reporting and registration requirements. The law specifically exempted testimony before a congressional committee, and in 1950, in *United States v. Slaughter*, a lower federal court held that this exemption applied also to those helping to prepare the testimony. Other direct contacts presumably were covered, but a gray area soon emerged, with some groups contending that their contacts with members of Congress were informational and could not be

---

IRS Tax Ruling

On March 20, 1978, the Internal Revenue Service issued rulings clarifying the kind of business activities the agency regarded as non-tax-deductible "grass-roots" lobbying.

Section 162 of the Internal Revenue Code distinguished between "direct" lobbying, the costs of which were deductible by business organizations, and "indirect" or grass-roots lobbying expenses that were not deductible.

The IRS said in the rulings, "No deduction is allowable for expenses incurred by a corporation in preparing and placing advertisements in major state newspapers and regional magazines setting forth objections to proposed legislation of direct interest to the corporation." The gist was that costs of direct communication with a legislative body were deductible, but not the costs of informing others of a corporation's views.

The IRS also said a trade association could deduct the costs of urging its members to contact their congressmen on legislation of direct interest to the group, but it could not deduct the cost of informing prospective members or of asking its members to urge their employees or customers to communicate with Congress.

considered subject to the law.

Another weakness was that the law applied only to attempts to influence Congress, not administrative agencies or the executive branch, which originated much legislation enacted by Congress and which put into effect many regulations similar to legislation.

The law also left it up to each group or lobbyists to determine what portion of total expenditures were to be reported as spending for lobbying. As a result, some organizations whose Washington office budgets ran into the hundreds of thousands of dollars reported only very small amounts spent on lobbying, contending that the remainder was spent for general public information purposes, research and other matters. Other organizations, interpreting the law quite differently, reported a much larger percentage of their total budgets as being for lobbying. The result was that some groups gained reputations as "big lobby spenders" when, in fact, they simply were reporting more fully than other groups spending just as much.

Finally, reinforcing all the other weaknesses was the lack of enforcement. The 1946 law did not designate anyone to investigate the truthfulness of lobbying registrations and reports or to seek enforcement. The House clerk and Senate secretary were not directed or empowered to investigate reports they received or to compel anyone to register. Since violations were made a crime, the Justice Department had power to prosecute offenders but no mandate was given the department to investigate reports. In fact, the Justice Department eventually adopted a policy of investigating only when it received complaints, and its prosecutions were rare.

Efforts to enact a lobby disclosure statute that covered all significant lobbying of Congress — something no one claimed the existing 1946 act did — were pursued throughout the 94th, 95th and 96th Congresses. Both the House and Senate passed a new bill in 1976 but conferees were unable to resolve differences between the two versions before Congress adjourned. Although similar bills were introduced almost each year after that, including one the House passed in 1978, no new lobbying disclosure law had been enacted as of 1982.

Opposition from lobbyists for many different interests doomed the legislation. Disclosure of organized grass-roots campaigns turned out to be the hardest-fought obstacle to new lobbying legislation.

Lobbying Investigations

Over the years investigations of lobbying practices stemmed from a wide range of motives and these studies sought to achieve nearly as broad a range of objectives. Lobby investigations were used to respond to intense public concern about lobbying, to gather information on the workings of existing regulatory legislation and to help prepare the way for, and to shape, proposed new regulatory legislation.

Since 1913 most sessions of Congress have been marked by investigations of lobbying activities in general or of specific alleged abuses. Following are summary accounts of selected major lobbying investigations.

Business Lobbying, 1913

The first thorough investigation of lobbying was undertaken by the Senate in 1913 in reaction to President Woodrow Wilson's charges of a massive grass-roots lobbying effort against his tariff program. Wilson was enraged by alleged lobbying activity of the National Association of Manufacturers and other protectionist groups on the Underwood tariff bill. He denounced what he called an "insidious" lobby that sought to bring on a new tide of protectionism.

"I think the public ought to know," Wilson said, "that extraordinary exertions are being made by the lobby in Washington to gain recognition for certain alterations in the tariff bill. . . . Washington has seldom seen so numerous, so industrious, or so insidious a lobby. . . . There is every evidence that money without limit is being spent to sustain this lobby. . . . The government ought to be relieved from this intolerable burden and the constant interruption to the calm progress of debate."

The Senate hearings disclosed that large amounts had been spent for entertainment and for other lobbying purposes both by the interests seeking high tariff duties and by those interested in low duties, such as the sugar refiners. Following the hearings, a lobby registration bill was introduced, but farm, labor and other special interests warded off a vote on it.

Also in 1913, Col. Martin M. Mulhall, lobbyist for NAM, published a sensational account of his activities in a front-page article in the *New York World*. Among other disclosures, Mulhall said he had paid "between $1,500 and $2,000" to help Rep. James T. McDermott, D-Ill. (1907-14, 1915-17), for legislative favors.

A four-month inquiry by a select House committee found that many of Mulhall's allegations were exaggerated. The panel established that Mulhall had set up his own office in the Capitol, had paid the chief House page $50 a month for inside information, had received advance information on pending legislation from McDermott and House Republican leader John W. Dwight, N.Y. (1902-13), and had influenced the appointment of members to House committees and subcommittees. Six of seven House members implicated by Mulhall were exonerated, but the panel recommended that McDermott be "strongly censured." The House adopted the panel's recommendations. Although McDermott was not expelled from the House, he resigned in 1914 and was re-elected to another two-year term.

Tax and Utilities Lobbying, 1927

Interest in lobbying activities was rekindled in the 1920s after the American Legion and other veterans' groups obtained passage of a bonus bill over the veto of President Calvin Coolidge.

In 1927 an investigating committee under Sen. Thaddeus H. Caraway, D-Ark. (1921-31), conducted extensive public hearings on lobbying efforts. One of the immediate reasons was the pressure being applied to the Ways and Means Committee for repeal of the federal estate tax.

The American Taxpayers League brought more than 200 witnesses, including one governor and many state legislators, to Washington to testify. All travel expenses were paid and some of the witnesses received additional compensation.

The second activity to which Congress objected at the time was the establishment of Washington headquarters by the Joint Committee of National Utility Associations to block a proposed Senate investigation of utility financing. The joint committee succeeded in having the investigation transferred to the Federal Trade Commission, but that agency took its assignment seriously and gave the utility situation a thorough going-over.

At the end of the investigation, the Caraway committee recommended a sweeping registration bill. It defined lobbying as "... any effort in influencing Congress upon any matter coming before it, whether it be by distributing literature, appearing before committees of Congress, or seeking to interview members of either the House or Senate." A lobbyist was defined as "... one who shall engage, for pay, to attempt to influence legislation, or to prevent legislation by the national Congress." The Senate passed the bill unanimously but a House committee pigeon-holed it.

Despite failure of the Caraway bill, the Senate Judiciary Committee's report on the measure contributed greatly to the public's knowledge of lobbying. The panel asserted that about 90 percent of the 300 to 400 lobbying associations listed in the Washington telephone directory were "fakes" whose aim was to bilk unwary clients.

These organizations, according to the committee report, included groups that purported to represent scientific, agricultural, religious, temperance and anti-prohibition interests. "In fact," the panel said, "every activity of the human mind has been capitalized by some grafter." The committee estimated that $99 of every $100 paid to these groups "go into the pockets of the promoters." Caraway himself disclosed that one of the lobbyists had collected $60,000 in one year from business interests by simply writing them every time a bill favorable to business was passed and claiming sole credit for its passage.

Naval Armaments, 1929

The next congressional probe of lobbying came in 1929, when a Senate Naval Affairs Subcommittee looked into the activities of William B. Shearer, who represented shipping, electrical, metals, machinery and similar concerns interested in blocking limitation of naval armaments and in obtaining larger appropriations for Navy ships. The path to Shearer's exposure had been paved when he filed a suit in the New York courts to recover $257,655, which he said was owed to him by the New York Shipbuilding Co. Shearer claimed the money was due for lobbying services he had performed in Washington and at the Geneva naval limitation conference of 1927.

Testimony showed that shipbuilding interests sent Shearer to Geneva, where he did everything he could to torpedo an agreement. Following the conference, at which no agreement was reached, Shearer had led industry lobbying efforts for bigger naval appropriations and for merchant marine subsidies. His other activities included preparing pro-Navy articles for the Hearst newspaper chain, writing articles for the 1928 Republican presidential campaign, in which he characterized peace advocates as traitors, and writing speeches for the American Legion and like-minded lobby groups.

Utilities Lobbies, 1935

A decade of congressional concern over the influence exerted by private utilities led to a stormy probe of that industry's lobbying activities in 1935. Although Congress nine years earlier had instructed the Federal Trade Commission to investigate utility lobbying, a two-year FTC probe had been largely inconclusive.

Intensive lobbying that threatened to emasculate an administration bill to regulate utility holding companies prompted President Roosevelt to send Congress a special message describing the holding companies as "private empires within the nation" and denouncing their lobbying techniques. The bill's congressional supporters demanded an investigation to determine how far the power interests' lobbying had gone.

A special Senate investigative panel was set up under the chairmanship of Hugo L. Black, D-Ala. (1927-37), an administration stalwart who later became an associate justice of the Supreme Court. Following a sometimes raucous hearing, Black concluded that the utilities had spent about $4 million to defeat the bill and had engaged in massive propagandizing to convince the public that it was an iniquitous invasion of private rights and a sharp turn toward socialism. Among other findings, Black's panel stated that the utilities had financed thousands of phony telegrams to Congress, using names picked at random from telephone books.

Amid a furor over the telegrams, Congress passed the Public Utilities Holding Company Act, which required reports to federal agencies on some utility lobbying activities. The Senate and House also passed lobbyist registration bills. A compromise was agreed upon but the House rejected the agreement and final adjournment came before a new agreement could be reached. The measure's defeat was attributed to the combined efforts of hundreds of lobbyists.

Munitions Lobby, 1935

Another Senate investigation during 1935 looked into activities of the munitions lobby. The Special Committee Investigating the Munitions Industry, headed by Gerald P. Nye, R-N.C. (1925-45), disclosed bribery and arms deals in Latin America and Great Britain, prompting sharp responses from leaders there.

Further Studies, 1938 and 1945

The Temporary National Economic Committee, which Congress set up at President Roosevelt's request under the chairmanship of Sen. C. Joseph O'Mahoney, D-Wyo.(1934-53, 1954-61), included lobbying among its subjects of study in 1938.

The Joint Committee on the Organization of Congress, established in 1945, studied lobbying activities along with other matters pertaining to Congress. On the basis of the committee's recommendations, Congress in 1946 passed the Legislative Reorganization Act, including the Federal Regulation of Lobbying Act.

Omnibus Lobbying Probe, 1950

A House Select Committee on Lobbying Activities headed by Frank M. Buchanan, D-Pa. (1946-51), investigated the lobbying activities of a wide range of organizations in 1950. The probe had been prompted largely by President Truman's assertion that the 80th Congress was "the most thoroughly surrounded ... with lobbies in the whole history of this great country of ours." Truman said: "There were more lobbyists in Washington, there was more money spent by lobbyists in Washington, than ever before in the history of the Congress of the United States. It's disgraceful...." Most of the publicity centered on the Committee for Constitutional Government's efforts to distribute low-cost or free "right-wing" books and pamphlets designed to influence the public.

To determine more accurately the amount of money spent to influence legislation, the House investigating com-

Public Charities, Lobbying and Tax Status

Congress changed the rules of the lobbying game as played by 273,000 tax-exempt public charities when it cleared a sweeping revision of the nation's tax laws Sept. 16, 1976. By 1982 the number of affected organizations had swelled to 325,000.

The revision, said House Ways and Means Committee Chairman Al Ullman, D-Ore. (1957-81), was meant to provide "a new elective set of standards for determining whether a tax-exempt charity has engaged in so much lobbying that it loses its exempt status and can no longer receive deductible contributions."

The changes concerned Section 501 (c) 3 of the Internal Revenue Code, which grants tax-exempt status to non-profit charitable, religious, scientific, cultural or educational groups and to groups engaged in "testing for public safety" or in preventing cruelty to children or animals.

These "public charities" can lose their eligibility to receive tax-deductible contributions if the Internal Revenue Service judges them to be engaging in "substantial" lobbying. Charities fear this loss because it removes a prime inducement for people to give them money.

Some public charities complained that the "substantial" test under Section 501 (c) 3 was so vague that even the IRS did not understand it. It prohibited the organizations from engaging in partisan political activity or devoting substantial efforts to "carrying on propaganda, or otherwise attempting, to influence legislation." This applied to activities at all levels of government.

New Tests Provided

The 1976 revision allowed charities to decide whether they wished to be judged on a vague standard of assessing their lobbying activities, as under existing law, or on their specific lobbying expenditures, as stipulated in the revision.

Excluded from coverage were churches, church groups and private foundations. Many church groups had expressed alarm that the new terms, if applied to them, would infringe upon their constitutional rights by violating the First Amendment separation of church and state. Church spokesmen contended that the IRS had no authority to monitor church activities. Charities electing to comply with the law would forfeit their tax-exempt status if they exceeded their spending limits by more than 50 percent over four years.

Specifically, Section 2503 of the tax revision:

● Set the basic level of allowable lobbying expenditures at 20 percent of the first $500,000 of the organization's exempt-purpose expenditures for a given year, plus 15 percent of the second $500,000, plus 10 percent of the third $500,000, plus 5 percent of any additional expenditures.

● Set a maximum annual expenditures limit of $1 million.

● Restricted "grass-roots" lobbying (attempts to influence general public opinion on legislation) to not more than one-fourth of the total lobbying expenditure.

● Allowed eligible charities to choose for themselves whether to be subject to its terms, or to remain under the existing law.

● Set an excise tax of 25 percent of a charity's excess lobbying expenditures as the penalty for exceeding either the general spending limit or the grass-roots spending limit.

● Provided that a charity exceeding the spending limits by more than 50 percent over four years would lose its exempt status.

● Provided that sanctions and penalties would operate automatically rather than at the discretion of the IRS.

● Defined "influencing legislation" broadly, and defined "legislation" as action by national, state or local legislative bodies, or by the public in initiatives, referenda or similar procedures.

● Excluded from its definition of lobbying: communications between an organization and its members; provision of information to legislative bodies at their request; provision of research or non-partisan studies; and instances of "self-defense" lobbying, when a pending legislative decision might directly affect an organization's existence, powers or tax status.

● Required charities electing to be governed by the bill's limits to disclose total lobbying expenditures.

● Excluded churches, church-related organizations and private foundations from the terms of the bill.

Court Ruling

In a related development, a federal appeals court ruled March 26, 1982, that the special tax status Congress gave veterans' groups was unconstitutional unless it also was extended to other 501 (c) 3 organizations that lobbied. Writing for the full U.S. Court of Appeals for the District of Columbia, Judge Abner Mikva said the right to receive tax-deductible donations must either be taken away from veterans' groups that lobby or be granted to other non-profit charitable and educational groups. The "substantial" lobbying test had not previously applied to veterans' organizations.

The appeals court's ruling came on a legal challenge brought by a tax-reform group, Taxation With Representation, that in 1974 was denied the right to receive tax-deductible donations because it lobbied Congress and the executive branch on tax laws.

mittee requested detailed information from 200 corporations, labor unions and farm groups. Replies from 152 corporations showed a total of $32 million spent for this purpose from Jan. 1, 1947, through May 31, 1950. More than 100 of these corporations had not filed reports under the 1946 Federal Regulation of Lobbying Act. Reports of the 37 that did showed expenditures of $776,000, which was less than 3 percent of the amount reported by respondents to the committee questionnaire. In releasing the survey results, Chairman Buchanan noted that it covered activities of only 152 of the country's 500,000 corporations. "I firmly believe," he said, "that the business of influencing legislation is a billion-dollar industry."

The House committee recommended strengthening the 1946 lobbying law but no action was taken.

Omnibus Lobbying Probe, 1956

In 1956 a major lobbying inquiry was conducted by the Senate Special Committee to Investigate Political Activities, Lobbying and Campaign Contributions. The inquiry was initiated against a background of an alleged campaign contribution to Francis H. Case, R-S.D. (1951-62), in connection with voting on a natural gas bill. The panel was chaired by John L. McClellan, D-Ark. (1943-77).

Following a long investigation, McClellan on May 31, 1957, introduced a new lobbying registration bill designed to replace the 1946 act. The bill proposed to tighten the existing law by making the comptroller general responsible for enforcing it (there was no administrator under the 1946 act); by eliminating a loophole that required registration of only those lobbyists whose "principal purpose" was lobbying; by extending the coverage to anyone who spent $50,000 or more a year on grass-roots lobbying; and by eliminating an exemption that made the law inapplicable to persons who merely testified on proposed legislation.

The bill was opposed vigorously by the Chamber of Commerce of the United States and was criticized on certain points by the National Association of Manufacturers, the Association of American Railroads and the American Medical Association, although the latter endorsed the measure as a whole. The bill did not reach the floor and died with the close of the 85th Congress.

Retired Military Lobbyists, 1959

In 1959 the House Armed Services Subcommittee on Special Investigations held three months of hearings on the employment of former Army, Navy and Air Force officers by defense contractors, and the influence of the retired officers in obtaining government contracts for their new employers. The subcommittee found that more than 1,400 retired officers with the rank of major or higher — including 261 of general or flag rank — were employed by the top 100 defense contractors.

In its report in 1960, the subcommittee said that "The coincidence of contracts and personal contacts with firms represented by retired officers and retired civilian officials sometimes raises serious doubts as to the objectivity of these [contract] decisions." Congress largely accepted subcommittee recommendations for tighter restrictions on sales to the government by former or retired personnel.

Foreign Lobbyists, 1962

Lobbying in connection with the Sugar Act of 1962 led the Senate Foreign Relations Committee to launch an investigation of foreign lobbies and the extent to which they attempted to influence U. S. policies. At the request of Foreign Relations Committee Chairman J. William Fulbright, D-Ark. (1945-74), and Sen. Paul H. Douglas, D-Ill. (1949-67), the Finance Committee, which had jurisdiction over the sugar bill, had queried sugar lobbyists on their arrangements with their employers, mostly foreign countries. A compendium of the answers, made public June 26, 1962, showed that some payments to sugar lobbyists were made on the basis of the size of the sugar quotas granted by Congress.

Hearings conducted some months later by the Foreign Relations Committee produced evidence that some lobbyists also lobbied their own clients. Fulbright disclosed, for example, that Michael B. Deane, a Washington public relations man hired by the Dominican Sugar Commission, apparently had given the commission exaggerated, sometimes inaccurate reports.

Deane admitted that he had reported falsely that the president had invited him to the White House and that he had talked with the secretary of agriculture. Deane said he occasionally gave himself "too much credit," but "one tends to do that a little bit when they have a client who is outside of Washington." Similar testimony was elicited from other sugar lobbyists.

The Fulbright probe continued well into 1963 and, at its conclusion, Fulbright introduced a bill to tighten registration requirements under the 1938 Foreign Agents Registration Act. The bill passed the Senate in 1964 but died in the House. It was revived in the 89th Congress and enacted in 1966.

'Koreagate,' 1978

On Oct. 24, 1976, *The Washington Post* disclosed that the Justice Department was probing reports that South Korean agents dispensed between $500,000 and $1 million a year in cash and gifts to members of Congress to help maintain "a favorable legislative climate" for South Korea.

Tongsun Park, a Washington-based Korean businessman and socialite, was named as the central operative. Park fled to London shortly after the story appeared. He stayed there until August 1977, then went to Korea. He later returned to the United States to testify at House and Senate hearings on Korean influence-peddling.

By 1978 the House and Senate ethics committees had ended their probes without recommending any severe disciplinary action against colleagues linked to the scandal. The House investigation, which began in early 1977 with reports that as many as 115 members of Congress had taken illegal gifts from South Korean agents, ended in October 1978 with the House voting its mildest form of punishment, a "reprimand," for three California Democrats: John J. McFall (1957-78), Edward R. Roybal and Charles H. Wilson (1963-81).

Two former representatives were prosecuted for taking large sums of money from Tongsun Park: Richard T. Hanna, D-Calif. (1963-74), pleaded guilty to a reduced charge and went to prison, and Otto E. Passman, D-La. (1947-77), was acquitted in 1979.

While the Senate Ethics Committee recommended no disciplinary action against any incumbent or former senator, a third committee investigating U.S.-Korean relations echoed the conclusion that South Koreans had bribed government officials to win support for what was called the "authoritarian" government of Park Chung Hee. Also, the House Subcommittee on International Organizations said that illegal Korean activities had gone beyond lobbying.

6

Political Action Committees

To some, political action committees (PACs) represent a healthy new way for individuals and groups to participate financially in the political process. To others, they are an insidious outgrowth of Watergate-inspired legislation. But all sides agree that PACs are an increasingly important force in the financing of congressional races.

In 1972 only 14 percent of all contributions to House and Senate general election candidates came from PACs. By 1980 the PAC share had swelled to 25 percent. And the total number of PACs, barely 600 at the end of 1974, exceeded 2,900 by the end of 1981.

Altogether, PACs raised nearly $140 million in the 1980 campaign and contributed $55 million to House and Senate candidates. That figure was more than PACs raised and contributed in the 1976 and 1978 elections combined.

More than two-thirds of the contributions in 1980 went to House candidates, where the campaign budgets were smaller and the opportunities greater for PAC contributions to make an impact. But with a flock of endangered liberal Democrats providing a target, PAC spending in Senate races also reached a record high. *(PAC role in congressional elections, 1972-80, graph, p. 45)*

Traditionally, PACs have steered most of their money to incumbents. Because Democrats held a majority of seats in both houses of Congress until January 1981, their candidates routinely received most of the PAC money.

But with the Republican resurgence, the increased willingness of many non-labor PACs to support GOP challengers, and the growing fund raising for so-called negative campaigns aimed at incumbents, it was possible the Democratic advantage could evaporate by the 1982 elections. *(Non-connected PAC 1981 receipts and expenditures chart, p. 53)*

Vehicles for Political Involvement

The term "PAC" is not precisely defined in the Federal Election Campaign Act (FECA), the law that provides the basic ground rules for the financial conduct of federal campaigns. FECA does define a non-party political committee as any committee, club, association or other group of members that has either receipts or expenditures in a calendar year of at least $1,000, or operates a separate, segregated fund to raise or disburse money in federal campaigns. Committees that fit this definition have come to be known as PACs.

Because corporations and labor unions are prohibited by federal law from using corporate and union treasury funds for political contributions, PACs have become a tightly regulated vehicle for political involvement by business and unions. Campaign contributions by political action committees must come from voluntary gifts to the PACs. But corporate and union funds may be used to administer PACs and solicit money for them.

Most PACs are affiliated with corporations or labor unions. But there are a large number of political committees affiliated with trade, membership and health organizations and a growing number of independent, non-connected PACs set up by groups interested in a particular cause, such as abortion or the environment.

Impetus for PACs

Labor unions began forming political action committees nearly a half century ago to maximize their influence in the political process. But the real impetus for PAC formation did not come until the 1970s when the federal campaign finance laws were overhauled. Crucial were the 1974 amendments to the FECA, which clamped a $1,000 limit on the amount an individual could contribute to a House or Senate candidate in a primary or general election. PACs were permitted to give $5,000 per election, with no limit on how much a candidate could receive in combined PAC donations.

Overnight the political landscape was changed. Before 1974 little need existed for PACs outside the labor movement. Individuals — whether business executives or wealthy political philanthropists — could give unlimited amounts to the candidates of their choice. But the 1974 legislation ended this era of unbridled giving and forced wealthy individuals, corporations and other organizations to seek new outlets to remain financially involved in the political process.

The PAC Debate

For many, PACs were the answer. In the wake of the Watergate scandal and the exposure of illegal corporate contributions, they offered a centralized and well-organized way to participate politically.

Foes of PACs, however, view them quite differently. They contend that the committees are a corrupting influence on the political process, filling a vacuum created by the strict federal limitation on contributions and the decline of political parties as basic campaign organizations.

"PACs tilt the system dramatically toward incumbents," complains Common Cause President Fred Wertheimer. "PAC giving is a form of political investment in government decisions."

Critics claim that PAC contributions buy influence. They cite examples such as a June 1979 House amendment to weaken the windfall profits tax, which drew the support of 95 percent of the House members who received more than $2,500 from oil company PACs the previous election.

But PAC defenders contend that any favorable vote in Congress reflects a shared philosophy, not influence-buying. In 1979 Republican William F. Clinger Jr. told a newspaper in his central Pennsylvania district that PACs obtained access to him as a result of their contribution, but that was all. "I've encountered no vote that I've made," Clinger said, "where I've thought, 'Gee, I better vote this way because they gave me $2,000.'"

PAC supporters maintain that the political committees are a practical exercise of their constitutional rights. Explained former Republican Rep. Clark MacGregor of Minnesota, the chairman of the United Technologies Corp. PAC in 1979: "We're talking about voluntary contributions, not windfall profits by some insensitive corporation."

Legislative Background

The legislative groundwork for the PAC boom of the 1970s was laid by the FECA of 1971. When the decade began, the political activities of corporations and unions were tightly restricted.

Corporate gifts of money to federal candidates had been prohibited since 1907 by the Tillman Act. In 1925 the ban was extended by the Federal Corrupt Practices Act to cover corporate contributions of "anything of value." Labor unions were prohibited by the Smith-Connally Act of 1943 and the Taft-Hartley Act of 1947 from making contributions to federal candidates from their members' dues.

The 1971 act modified these bans by allowing the use of corporate funds and union treasury money for "the establishment, administration and solicitation of contributions to a separate, segregated fund to be utilized for a political purpose." Administrative units of those funds became known commonly as PACs.

But the 1971 act did not modify the ban on political contributions by government contractors. This resulted in many corporations holding back from forming PACs. Labor unions, many of which had government manpower contracts, also became concerned that they would be affected and led a move to have the law changed to permit government contractors to establish and administer PACs. That change was incorporated into the 1974 amendments to the FECA.

SunPAC Decision

But labor's efforts had unexpected consequences. While the easing of the prohibition against government manpower contractors forming PACs removed a headache for organized labor, it also opened the door for the formation of corporate PACs.

Yet in the wake of Watergate many corporations remained skittish about what they were permitted to do. Not until November 1975, when the Federal Election Commis-

sion (FEC) released its landmark ruling in the case involving the Sun Oil Company's political committee, SunPAC, did many businesses feel comfortable in establishing PACs.

The FEC decision was in response to a request from Sun Oil for permission to use its general treasury funds to create, administer and solicit voluntary contributions to its political action committee, SunPAC. The company also sought permission to solicit its stockholders and all employees for PAC contributions and to establish a separate "political giving program" among corporate employees that could be financed through a payroll deduction plan. Sun Oil indicated that employees would be allowed to designate the recipients of their contributions.

By a 4-2 vote, the bipartisan commission issued an advisory opinion approving the requests, although the FEC emphasized that SunPAC must abide by guidelines ensuring that the solicitation of employees was totally voluntary.

The two dissenting commissioners — both Democrats — objected to the scope of SunPAC solicitations. They argued that because federal law permitted unions to solicit only their members, SunPAC should be restricted to soliciting only its stockholders.

Labor was incensed by the ruling, since it greatly enlarged the potential source of funds available to corporate PACs. The unions pressed hard to have the commission's decision overturned, and they succeeded in the 1976 FECA amendments in having the range of corporate solicitation restricted from all employees to a company's management personnel and its stockholders. Corporations and unions were given the right to solicit the other's group twice a year by mail.

The 1976 amendments also permitted union PACs to use the same method of soliciting campaign contributions as the company PAC used, such as a payroll deduction plan. And the law sought to restrict the proliferation of PACs by maintaining that all political action committees established by one company or international union would be treated as a single committee for contribution purposes. The PAC contributions of a company or an international union would be limited to no more than $5,000 overall to the same candidate in any election no matter how many PACs the company or union formed.

In the short run, the 1976 amendments were a victory for labor, because they curbed some of the benefits for corporate PACs authorized by the FEC's SunPAC decision. But the legislation did nothing to undercut the primary effect of the SunPAC ruling: abetting the formation of PACs within the business community. Moreover, the law explicitly permitted trade associations, membership organizations, cooperatives and corporations without stock to establish PACs.

Corporate PAC Boom

Prior to the SunPAC ruling, there were more labor than corporate PACs; but that situation changed quickly after the FEC's controversial decision. Within six months of the November 1975 SunPAC opinion, the number of corporate PACs had more than doubled — from 139 to 294 — while only 20 new labor PACs had formed.

After that, the disparity between the number of business and union PACs grew even wider, with corporate PACs numbering 1,251 in July 1981, more than four times the number of labor units (303). These totals did not include the myriad corporate PACs that are active only in state and local races and do not have to register with the FEC. *(PAC growth graph, p. 45)*

Viewed another way, corporate PACs, which represented less than 20 percent of the total number of federally registered political committees in November 1975, comprised nearly half of the total number in mid-1981.

In spite of their fewer numbers, labor PACs were able to run ahead of their corporate counterparts in contributions to federal candidates throughout the 1970s.

Several heavyweight unions provided the edge. In 1978, for example, five labor PACs — affiliated with the United Auto Workers (UAW), the AFL-CIO, the Steelworkers, the United Transportation Union and the Machinists — each contributed between $500,000 and $1 million to congressional candidates. In contrast, no single corporate PAC that year gave House and Senate candidates even $200,000.

The situation was similar two years later. The PAC of the Winn-Dixie stores led the corporate category with contributions of barely a quarter million dollars to federal candidates in the 1980 election. *(Leading PACs in 1980, box, pp. 50-51)*

But the financial activity of individual corporations can be understated. While some businesses and labor unions have more than one PAC, most of the state and local labor committees report their financial activity on a single report filed by their international committee. Many of the subsidiary corporate PACs, however, file separately and their reports must be aggregated to obtain the complete campaign finance picture of some corporations.

A prime example is the American Telephone & Telegraph Co. (AT&T). In 1980 it had a PAC for each of its Bell System subsidiaries. While a *Washington Post* study found that none of the 23 subsidiary PACs came close to rivaling the contribution total of Winn-Dixie, the aggregate contributions of the AT&T subsidiaries to federal candidates surpassed $650,000.

AT&T, however, is clearly in a class by itself. Dow Chemical, with eight PACs and $300,000 in donations to federal candidates in 1980, was a distant second in aggregate corporate contributions.

Many of the multiple PACs are subsidiaries concerned only with a region or state — such as the PACs for Pacific Bell Telephone or New York Telephone. They do not provide a national corporation any financial advantage, since a single contribution ceiling applies for each corporation or union regardless of how many PACs it has.

Labor Competes

Altogether in 1978, labor PACs provided congressional candidates $10.3 million, a half million dollars more than the amount provided by corporate PACs. But labor lost its advantage two years later. At the same time that union PACs were increasing their contributions to House and Senate candidates by about 25 percent (to $13.1 million), corporate PACs were nearly doubling their contributions (to $19.2 million). *(1979-80 PAC contributions to House and Senate candidates, p. 47)*

Political experience was one factor in the turnabout. While some corporations were establishing federal PACs for the first time in the late 1970s, many had gained experience by running PACs for years at the state and local level. Other corporations new at the PAC game used 1978 as a trial run and demonstrated far more sophistication in 1980.

But the sheer volume of corporate PACs was probably the deciding factor that enabled the business community to outstrip labor in direct contributions. While the average

corporate PAC contribution is not that large — under $1000 —the category is expanding rapidly. More than 400 corporate PACs were created between December 1978 and December 1980, producing a whole new pool of dollars for political campaigns that even the experienced labor heavyweights could not match. During the same time, only 80 new labor PACs were established, many of them at the local level.

And labor could be at an even greater disadvantage in the future. While there is a finite number of labor unions, most of them already organized, the universe of possible business PACs is huge and relatively undeveloped. The 1,251 corporate units in existence in July 1981 represented only 26 percent of the 4,788 U.S. companies with reported assets of $100 million or more and a paltry 4 percent of the 29,383 companies with reported assets of $10 million or more. Both figures are based on 1977 data published in January 1981 by the Treasury Department.

What is bad news for labor is also bad news for their traditional allies, the Democrats. Throughout the 1970s, the Democrats capitalized on strong labor backing and incumbency to garner the lion's share of PAC dollars.

But the Democrats' fund-raising equation began to break down in 1980 as the party's majorities in Congress dwindled. Incumbency traditionally was the sole reason many business PACs donated to Democratic candidates. As the prospect of a Republican Congress brightened, this lure lost much of its appeal.

Labor support for the Democrats remained solid in 1980, as 93 percent of all direct union contributions went to Democratic House and Senate candidates. But the surge in corporate PAC giving, most of which went to Republican candidates, reduced the overall Democratic advantage. In

1978 Democratic House and Senate candidates received 56 percent of all PAC contributions. Two years later, the Democratic share had fallen to 52.5 percent. *(1980 PAC contributions by category, box, p. 47)*

PAC MONEY: GETTING IT, GIVING IT

Although the law permits corporate PACs to solicit stockholders, very few do. A survey of 275 corporate PACs, coordinated by the Business-Industry Political Action Committee (BIPAC) in 1981, found that only 18 percent of the corporate PACs asked stockholders for contributions.

"Stockholders are a broad and very diverse group," explained Frank S. Farrell, chairman of the Burlington Northern PAC in 1978. "Many of them have differing political complexions and points of view. It's a question of whether it's worth the time and effort."

Corporate Solicitations

Management personnel are the main target for the corporate PACs, but corporations vary widely in how low into the management ranks they reach to solicit. In the late 1970s, General Electric was soliciting its 540 top executives. About two-thirds participated. On the other hand, Lockheed was soliciting its full management group, and approximately 600 — about 5 percent of the number solicited — were contributing.

By the early 1980s, more corporations were following the Lockheed example, soliciting throughout their management ranks. The corporate PACs in the BIPAC survey had an average of 388 donors, giving about $160 apiece.

The frequency of solicitation also differs greatly among corporations. Some solicit annually, others more or less frequently. The primary methods of solicitation are mail, personal contacts, small group presentations and combinations of all three.

Most of the corporations surveyed use payroll withholding plans for their employees to make contributions, although some major companies have held back. They have been concerned that the confidentiality of the contributors might be breached if that information were part of the company's payroll system.

Some corporations permit a PAC contributor to designate which party is to receive the money or to allow the PAC to use it at its discretion. Decisions about which candidates will receive PAC contributions are almost always made by special committees of the corporate PAC. But in some instances a PAC may not use a formal committee, instead following the recommendations of the PAC manager, a specialist within the company on politics and government affairs, or the firm's Washington lobbyist.

On the average, the 275 corporate PACs surveyed by BIPAC contributed $471 to House candidates and $824 to Senate candidates in 1980.

Labor Solicitations

Among labor unions less variation exists in solicitation practices. Generally a union business agent or steward will solicit union members in person or in a group on an annual basis, although, according to an AFL-CIO spokesman, more and more unions are using payroll withholding for voluntary political contributions.

If a company uses payroll withholding to collect contributions from its executives, federal law requires that payroll withholding automatically be made available for a union to collect the political contributions of its members who work for the company. If a company does not use payroll withholding, then a union may negotiate for it.

"We're a big unwieldy national organization," observed Bernard Albert, public relations director of the AFL-CIO COPE (Committee on Political Education). Payroll withholding "is just beginning to pick up steam. The big payoff is down the road."

The Steelworkers is one major union that has adopted the plan. It employs a checkoff system that lets union members give either 2 cents a workday or $5 a year to the PAC.

The national boards of union PACs usually contribute to candidates on the recommendations of their local officials. For the AFL-CIO COPE in each state to make a contribution, however, a candidate traditionally has had to receive a two-thirds vote at a state labor convention or from a body designated by the convention.

Machinists' Suit

In October 1979, the International Association of Machinists mounted an assault on the solicitation methods of major corporations. It filed a complaint with the FEC, maintaining that 10 leading corporations — including Dart Industries, General Electric, General Motors, Grumman and Winn-Dixie — were engaging in "inherently coercive" practices to collect PAC contributions from their employees.

The Machinists charged that the companies' solicitation practices were "pregnant with coercion" because the job security of mid-management employees was not protected either by union membership or contracts; employees frequently lacked anonymity — they were sometimes solicited in person and by their supervisors; employees had no control over the distribution of their contributions, which often went out of state; and employees rarely declined to contribute. Many employees made contributions in exactly the same amount, which the union contended indicated orchestration by the corporation. The Machinists added that the average amount of contributions to corporate PACs was far greater than the average contribution made by members of the general public with comparable incomes.

In summary, the Machinists noted that there was "no possible room for a conclusion that the corporate PACs are operating with employee contributions that are genuinely free and voluntary political donations."

Corporations saw the union complaint as a thinly disguised effort to drive their PACs out of business, and saw no merit in the charges. Many business officials shared the view of Robert Hibbard, president of the Pennsylvania Chamber of Commerce, who denied in 1979 that corporations were pressuring employees for PAC contributions. "It would hit the paper right away if an employee's arm was twisted," maintained Hibbard. "It would be the dumbest thing for a business to do."

The FEC tended to agree. The commission's general counsel concluded that all of the allegedly coercive prac-

Growth of Political Action Committees, 1974-81

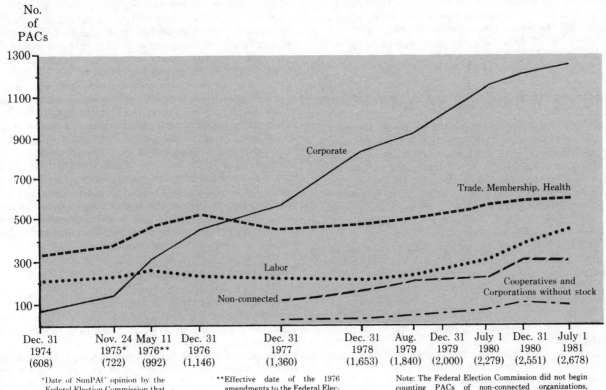

No.
of
PACs

Date										
Dec. 31 1974 (608) | Nov. 24 1975* (722) | May 11 1976** (992) | Dec. 31 1976 (1,146) | Dec. 31 1977 (1,360) | Dec. 31 1978 (1,653) | Aug. 1979 (1,840) | Dec. 31 1979 (2,000) | July 1 1980 (2,279) | Dec. 31 1980 (2,551) | July 1 1981 (2,678)

*Date of SunPAC opinion by the Federal Election Commission that prompted the subsequent rapid growth in corporate PAC's.

**Effective date of the 1976 amendments to the Federal Election Campaign Act.

Note: The Federal Election Commission did not begin counting PACs of non-connected organizations, cooperatives and corporations without stock in separate categories until 1977.

Source: Federal Election Commission

PAC Role in Congressional Elections, 1972-80

Percent of total candidate receipts

Political action committee contributions as a share of the total campaign receipts of House and Senate candidates in general elections.

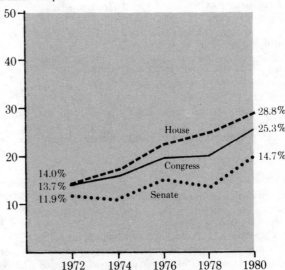

Note: Prior to the 1976 election, campaign spending data were compiled by Common Cause. The Common Cause studies in 1972 and 1974 covered shorter time periods than the FEC surveys. The FEC studies covered the 24 months through the end of the year in which the election was held.

28.8%
25.3%
14.7%
14.0%
13.7%
11.9%

Source: Federal Election Commission 1976-80; Library of Congress publication by Joseph E. Cantor, 1972-74

tices cited by the union were permissible under the law. By a 4-0 vote the FEC decided in December 1979 to dismiss the complaint.

Machinists challenged the dismissal and on April 6, 1982, the District of Columbia federal circuit court of appeals held that the FECA amendments did not violate the Constitution. As of July 1982 the case was pending on appeal before the U.S. Supreme Court.

Deciding Where to Spend

For PACs, the decision on whether to spend money in a particular campaign involves more than simply winning and losing. Winning is the most important thing, but it is not, as it was for the old Green Bay Packers, the only thing. A lot depends on the candidate's ideology, his standing in Congress and even internal PAC politics. An unsuccessful but attention-drawing challenge to a strong and famous senator may have as much claim on PAC resources as a close House campaign somewhere else.

Most PACs still say, of course, that their primary job is rewarding friends and punishing enemies. "You have good guys and you have bad guys, and we're for the good guys," said William Holayter, political director of the Machinists union. Not surprisingly, Holayter's idea of a good guy is a Democrat who supports organized labor. Of the 248 candidates he and the Machinists supported in 1980, only six were Republicans.

But most PACs are trying simultaneously to make the "bad guys" a little friendlier by teaching them some respect. "When we were just a lobby and didn't have a PAC, some members didn't pay attention," said Charles Orasin, executive vice president of Handgun Control Inc., which wants stricter government firearms regulation. "Now that we can hurt the members, they listen."

PACs with a particular regional interest often will invest in most of the campaigns in their region, even when victory is certain or defeat a foregone conclusion. The UAW has a hard time staying out of any district in Michigan, its headquarters state. In 1980, the UAW contributed to Democrats in all but one of the state's 19 House elections. The only contest they avoided involved the re-election of Republican Guy Vander Jagt, who had no major party opposition and won with 97 percent of the vote.

For the American Medical Association (AMA), special considerations are professional, not regional. The AMA faces a problem when a doctor runs for Congress, and the group's staff prefers his opponent. "We can be under a lot of pressure from our membership to give to the physician," said an AMA official.

The Human Factor

Deciding on which candidates to help and with how much money is a subjective process. As with other things human, perceptions can be flawed.

Most PACs manage to know who their friends are. But many of them make bad calls on how much support the friends need. The Communications Workers of America (CWA) still regret that they gave California Democrat Lionel Van Deerlin only $2,000 for his House re-election campaign in 1980. Republican Duncan L. Hunter, lightly regarded early in the year, outspent Van Deerlin and defeated him. "There was a bit of feeling that Van Deerlin wasn't in as much trouble as he was," said Loretta Bowen,

the union's political director. "That snuck up on us. We made a mistake."

In the early days of the 1982 campaign, PACs were struggling to make sure that they had the proper intelligence about congressional districts newly drawn all over the country. Often they had to target and then un-target as more information on the new districts became available.

Sometimes, the quality of the candidate or the shape of his district becomes less important to a PAC than the adequacy of his campaign organization. That was the case in Washington's 5th District in the 1980 elections. In light of his narrow 1978 victory, Democratic Rep. Thomas S. Foley seemed highly vulnerable against a well-regarded Republican, John Sonneland.

Many conservative PACs gave heavily to Sonneland. But one "New Right" strategist who thought him a waste of money was Paul Weyrich, executive director of the Committee for the Survival of a Free Congress. "We only gave Sonneland $500 because he had a very poorly run campaign," said Weyrich. "He had no precinct-level organization. We could have put in $1 million, and he couldn't have won." In a close race, Sonneland lost.

The Local Connection

Many PACs face the problem of disagreements between their Washington staffs and their local affiliates. Sometimes they are drawn into a race to appease local opinion and are forced to spend far more than they would have liked.

Local considerations also can hinder a PAC's national political objectives. Consider the case of John Glenn, Bob Carr and the CWA, which favors liberal Democrats.

Ohio Democrat Glenn easily won a second Senate term in 1980, outspending his little-known opponent by a margin of 3-1. Although Glenn obviously did not need the money very much, the CWA sent him the full $10,000 allowed by law. Meanwhile, Michigan Democrat Bob Carr, swamped financially and narrowly defeated for a fourth House term, received a mere $400 from the union.

Why did Carr, a solid liberal and friend of the CWA, fare so badly? "We simply ran out of money," said the CWA's Bowen. "We were broke three or four weeks before election day."

But why did they have to give Glenn money they needed elsewhere? "Glenn is close to Marty Hughes, our vice president for Michigan and Ohio, who insisted Glenn get the full 10," said Bowen. "There was not a heck of a lot we could do."

If that sounds unreasonable, it is not uncommon. Ignoring the wishes of the local membership makes for headaches. From the Washington perspective, however, it is important to have local members in a targeted state or district because it helps offset the charge that "outside money" is being used to influence an election.

The Loyalty Issue

Some PACs concentrate almost exclusively on rewarding friends and influencing the powerful. Others are more vengeful, willing to spend a great deal of money and effort to make life difficult for members they find personally or ideologically offensive.

PAC managers like to say that they have long memories. "We did nothing for Barry Goldwater [in 1980]," said George Meade, vice president of government relations for the American Trucking Associations, "because we had

PAC Congressional Contributions:
Corporate Groups Double Their Giving

(In millions of dollars)

Jan. 1, 1977 - Dec. 31, 1978*

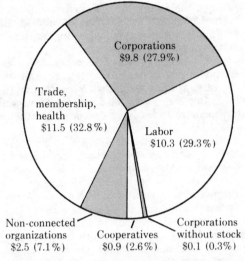

Total PAC contributions: $35.1 million

Jan. 1, 1979 - Dec. 31, 1980*

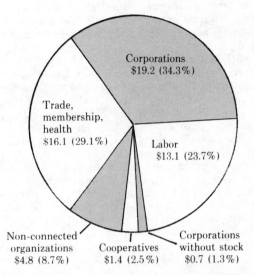

Total PAC contributions: $55.3 million

*Each category's percentage of total PAC contributions to House and Senate candidates during the 1978 and 1980 election cycles is listed in parentheses.

PAC Contributions to House and Senate Candidates in 1980

Type PAC	Total Contributions 1979-80	Increase from 1977-78 cycle	Party Affiliations		Candidate Status		
			Democrat	Republican	Incumbent	Challenger	Open
Corporations	$19.2	+$ 9.4 (+96%)	36%	64%	57%	31%	12%
Trade, Membership, Health	16.1	+ 4.6 +40	44	56	64	23	13
Labor	13.1	2.8 +27	93	7	71	17	12
Non-connected	4.8	2.3 +92	32	68	32	49	19
Cooperative	1.4	0.5 +56	65	35	81	6	13
Corporations without stock	0.7	0.6 +600	56	44	73	17	10
Totals	$55.3	+$20.2 +58	53	47	61	26	13

Source: Federal Election Commission

problems with him in committee. Lowell Weicker's asked us to fund raise, and we've given him an emphatic 'no.' "

Helping a group on a particular issue may not be enough to please its PAC, no matter how important the issue is. Republican Rep. Lyle Williams of Ohio joined with the Steelworkers in 1979 in a suit designed to block U.S. Steel's plans to close two mills in the Youngstown area. But the union PAC still gave to Williams' unsuccessful 1980 challenger, a labor-supporting Democrat. PAC leaders cited a vote by Williams to weaken the windfall tax on oil and chose to ignore his 68 percent favorable rating from the AFL-CIO in 1980.

Nearly all PACs, however, use the word "loyalty" in describing their standards for financial help. Labor spent most of its money in 1980 in an effort to protect friendly Democratic incumbents, many of them moderate and liberal Democrats in Northeastern and Midwestern states. The few Republican beneficiaries of union largesse, such as Sens. Jacob K. Javits of New York and Charles McC. Mathias Jr. of Maryland, had pro-labor records.

But in spite of union assistance, many labor favorites went down to defeat in 1980. Fearful of more congressional losses in 1982, PACs for the major unions began to raise money earlier and to distribute it sooner than ever before. The re-election committees for Democratic Sens. Edward M. Kennedy of Massachusetts and Howard M. Metzenbaum of Ohio, for instance, each raised nearly $100,000 in the first half of 1981 — about two-thirds from labor PACs.

Although labor committees have a tradition of supporting candidates in the early stages of a campaign, spending activity increased dramatically in the first six months of 1981 in comparison with the corresponding period before the 1980 election. An informal survey by Congressional Quarterly's *Campaign Practices Reports* found that the PACs for the Machinists, Steelworkers, United Mine Workers and the National Education Association (NEA) all contributed more than twice as much to federal candidates in the first six months of 1981 than they did in the first half of 1979.

The loyalty standard can create some awkwardness when two of a PAC's best friends run against each other. In 1980 the National Abortion Rights Action League (NARAL) was faced with a dilemma when two of its allies, Javits and Democratic Rep. Elizabeth Holtzman, fought for Javits' New York Senate seat. The PAC solved the problem by giving $5,000 to Javits in the primary and $5,000 to Holtzman in the general election. Javits, beaten for renomination by Alfonse D'Amato, ran on the liberal line in the fall but got nothing from NARAL at that time. D'Amato edged Holtzman by less than 80,000 votes in a bitter contest; Javits finished a distant third.

Access and Influence

In deciding where to invest, PACs spend a lot of time weighing who the future congressional powers will be. The approach for years has been to invest in access and influence and often to ignore real constituent needs.

Democrats have enjoyed an overall financial edge in the past because of incumbency. Republicans are catching up in PAC receipts, due to heavier giving to GOP challengers by corporate and trade association groups.

To be sure, business committees make certain not to neglect powerful Democrats. As the majority party in both houses during the 96th Congress, Democrats — particu-

larly senior ones — benefited from business giving. According to a Common Cause study released in April 1981, 28 Democratic House leaders received an average of $35,000 from corporate and business-related trade association PACs in 1980.

House Majority Leader Jim Wright of Texas reportedly drew $155,680 from business-related groups; Rep. Dan Rostenkowski of Illinois, the House Ways and Means Committee chairman, $106,450; and Rep. James R. Jones of Oklahoma, the House budget chairman, $104,851.

The Common Cause figures dovetailed with the conclusions of a study by the liberal Democratic Study Group (DSG) in the fall of 1980.

"Business PACs," the DSG concluded, "(give) support to Republican challengers running against Democrats whose seats are not secure, while continuing to buy access to those Democrats who have safe seats and who are generally responsive to business concerns. In other words, help the healthy and shoot the sick."

Other PACs have tried to discipline themselves to forego the "access and influence" method and spend their money on candidates who need it. More and more PACs in the business world have been willing to break new ground and support non-incumbents with a free enterprise outlook.

Their willingness to set aside some of their money as "risk capital" was evident in 1980. Although as in earlier years the bulk of corporate contributions went to congressional incumbents, the share given challengers increased from 20 percent of all corporate PAC contributions in 1978 to 30 percent in 1980.

The increased volume of corporate giving in 1980 and the larger share for challengers represented good news for the GOP. Corporate PACs have been less partisan than labor's, but still decidedly Republican in preference. Nearly two-thirds of all corporate PAC contributions in 1980 went to GOP candidates.

Both the National Republican Congressional Committee (NRCC) and the National Republican Senatorial Committee (NRSC) have provided GOP candidates assistance in meeting PAC representatives. For a time in the 1970s, the Republican National Committee (RNC) even had a PAC division to encourage the formation of business PACs.

As in 1978, much of the corporate PAC money poured into the coffers of GOP congressional candidates late in the campaign. In 1978 many business PACs — some participating in their first campaigns — apparently set aside at least one-third of their budgets for contributions to many Republicans and some moderate Democrats in the final weeks before the election.

In 1980 the late giving spree was even more pronounced. From the beginning of 1979 to Labor Day 1980, corporate PACs contributed nearly $12 million to House and Senate candidates, with slightly more than half the money going to GOP candidates. In the final weeks of the campaign, the business community poured more than $8 million into congressional races, with more than three-quarters earmarked for Republican candidates.

The PACs were guided in their last minute giving by the national party committees and major business organizations such as the Chamber of Commerce. They made available lists of pro-business candidates in close races who needed funds.

While not the only factor in the Republican successes at the polls in 1980, the surge of business PAC money undoubtedly had an effect.

Labor's Consolation

Although labor has taken a back seat to corporations in direct contributions, it still retains several advantages. One is partisan internal communications, a technique used frequently by labor but sparingly by corporations.

Unions, like corporations, which can direct their appeals only to stockholders, executive and administrative personnel, can communicate only with their members. The unions helped candidates by means of "apolitical" communications, such as newsletters exempt from FEC regulations, as well as by direct advocacy.

Partisan Communications

According to an FEC study, most of the partisan communication money in the 1976 election — 87 percent — went for direct mailings. Other expenses included brochures, phone banks, posters, car stickers and peanuts.

In 1976, labor groups reported spending $2 million on communication with members compared to just $31,045 spent by corporations. The disparity was even greater in 1980. While 57 labor organizations spent close to $3 million, just one corporation made internal communications and their expenditures totaled less than $4,000.

Part of the reason for labor's advantage is that union memberships generally are more cohesive and more easily mobilized through phone banks and targeting techniques than a company's executives and its stockholders, who are scattered throughout the country.

Internal communications have become a traditional way labor can lend additional help to its candidates. Corporations, on the other hand, are more comfortable channeling money through direct contributions.

"I question whether it is our business to educate people (stockholders and executives) on behalf of one candidate with stockholder money," commented Stephen K. Galpin, secretary of the General Electric PAC in 1978. "There is a credibility problem. Would it do any good?"

Among the 10 groups that reported spending the most money on internal communications in 1980, eight were labor groups — including the American Federation of State, County and Municipal Employees ($532,538), the AFL-CIO ($441,064) and the UAW ($402,280). But the front-runner was a membership organization, the National Rifle Association (NRA). After spending about $100,000 to communicate with its members in 1976, the NRA spent more than $800,000 in 1980.

In both 1976 and 1980, most of the expenditures for partisan communications were made in the presidential races rather than in congressional contests. In both years, the major beneficiary was Jimmy Carter. Nearly $1.2 million was spent advocating his election in 1976, and more than $1.5 million promoting his re-election bid in 1980.

In contrast, less than $75,000 was spent each election by groups favoring the Republican presidential candidate. In 1980, much more was actually spent by groups urging the defeat of Republican Ronald Reagan ($254,130) through internal communications than by organizations favoring his election ($64,784).

Unreported Expenditures

While labor's reported expenditures for internal communications have reached seven figures, that amount is just a small portion of the extra help that unions regularly provide the Democratic Party.

Campaign finance expert Herbert E. Alexander wrote in *Financing the 1976 Election* that "only messages sent directly to [union] members and that focused on specific candidates were reported to the FEC. Admonitions to vote Democratic, for example, did not have to be reported, and direct advocacy of a specific candidate did not have to be reported if the basic purpose of the communication was not political or if the total cost did not exceed $2,000. Almost every labor newsletter mailed to members in September and October praised Carter or criticized Ford, and a picture of Carter usually was on the cover. Little of this communication was reported to the FEC, presumably because the material appeared in regular publications that report on union business."

Millions of dollars more were spent in union treasury money for ostensibly "non-partisan" activities such as voter registration and get-out-the-vote drives. Labor unions have become very skilled in these non-partisan techniques, which often are designed to be of particular help to one candidate: An example of this would be a get-out-the-vote drive in an area where pro-labor voters predominate.

Although non-partisan political expenditures do not have to be reported to the FEC, campaign finance expert Michael Malbin estimated in a 1977 *National Journal* article that organized labor the previous year had spent about $11 million on reported and unreported partisan communications, voter registration and get-out-the-vote activities. A significant factor in Carter's victory, the labor expenditures represented about half the amount the Democratic presidential campaign received in public funds for its general election drive that year.

POWER GROWS FOR OTHER PACS

Corporate and labor units together were responsible for nearly 60 percent of all direct PAC contributions to congressional candidates in 1980. The rest of the money was provided by four other categories of PACs: cooperatives, corporations without stock, trade, membership and health as well as non-connected.

Although the lucrative PACs of the Associated Milk Producers and the Mid-America Dairymen are numbered among the cooperatives, most political committees within the cooperative and corporation-without-stock categories are relatively insignificant. In mid-1981, the two categories combined had barely 100 PACs, and together they provided only 4 percent of all contributions to House and Senate candidates in 1980.

Trade, Membership and Health PACs

The large group of trade, membership and health PACs, however, is a different story. In the 1980 election they contributed $16.1 million to House and Senate candidates, nearly 30 percent of all PAC gifts. About two-thirds of the contributions from trade, membership and health PACs went to incumbents, and slightly more than half the donations went to Republican candidates.

Leading PACs in 1980 Election...

...In Gross Receipts and Expenditures

Committee and Affiliation	Category	Receipts	Expenditures
1 Congressional Club	N	$7,873,974	$7,212,754
2 National Conservative Political Action Committee	N	7,600,637	7,464,533
3 Fund for a Conservative Majority, The	N	3,163,528	3,150,496
4 Realtors Political Action Committee (National Association of Realtors)	T	2,753,139	2,576,077
5 Citizens for the Republic	N	2,356,751	2,384,210
6 Americans for an Effective Presidency	N	1,920,377	1,874,312
7 UAW Voluntary Community Action Program (United Auto Workers)	L	1,792,406	2,027,737
8 American Medical Political Action Committee (American Medical Association)	T	1,728,392	1,812,021
9 Committee for the Survival of a Free Congress	N	1,647,556	1,623,750
10 National Committee for an Effective Congress	N	1,570,788	1,420,238
11 Gun Owners of America Campaign Committee	T	1,414,951	1,398,670
12 Committee for Thorough Agricultural Political Education (Associated Milk Producers Inc.)	Co	1,323,567	1,274,931
13 Texas Medical Association Political Action Committee-TEXPAC (Texas Medical Association)	T	1,286,003	1,237,893
14 Automobile and Truck Dealers Election Action Committee (National Association of Automobile Dealers)	T	1,271,857	1,392,745
15 ILGWU Campaign Committee (International Ladies' Garment Workers' Union)	L	1,256,116	925,065
16 Transportation Political Education League (United Transportation Union)	L	1,162,113	1,196,241
17 AFL-CIO COPE Political Contributions Committee (AFL-CIO COPE)	L	1,129,378	1,196,938
18 Americans for Change	N	1,072,549	1,061,123
19 NRA Political Victory Fund (National Rifle Association)	T	1,044,879	1,125,123
20 California Medical Political Action Committee (California Medical Association)	T	1,039,172	895,350

Categories: Co - Cooperative; L - Labor; N - Non-connected; T - Trade, membership, health

*Statistics are based on interim reports for the 1979-80 election cycle filed with the Federal Election Commission.

...In Contributions to Federal Candidates

Committee and Affiliation	Category	Expenditures
1 Realtors Political Action Committee (National Association of Realtors)	T	$1,546,573
2 UAW Voluntary Community Action Program (United Auto Workers)	L	1,422,931
3 American Medical Political Action Committee (American Medical Association)	T	1,360,685
4 Automobile and Truck Dealers Election Action Committee (National Association of Automobile Dealers)	T	1,035,276
5 Machinists Non-Partisan Political League (International Association of Machinists and Aerospace Workers)	L	847,608
6 Committee for Thorough Agricultural Political Education (Associated Milk Producers Inc.)	Co	740,289
7 AFL-CIO COPE Political Contributions Committee (AFL-CIO)	L	715,327
8 Seafarers Political Activity Donation (Seafarers International Union of North America)	L	686,748
9 United Steelworkers Political Action Fund (United Steelworkers of America)	L	681,370
10 National Association of Life Underwriters PAC (National Association of Life Underwriters)	T	652,112
11 American Dental Political Action Committee (American Dental Association)	T	648,875
12 MEBA Political Action Fund (Marine Engineers Beneficial Association)	L	615,295
13 American Bankers Association BANKPAC (American Bankers Association)	T	593,910
14 Transportation Political Education League (United Transportation Union)	L	583,969
15 Active Ballot Club (Food & Commercial Workers International Union)	L	569,775
16 Carpenters Legislative Improvement Committee (United Brotherhood of Carpenters & Joiners of America)	L	554,175
17 ILGWU Campaign Committee (International Ladies' Garment Workers' Union)	L	493,810
18 CWA-COPE Political Contributions Committee (Communications Workers of America)	L	449,520
19 NRA Political Victory Fund (National Rifle Association)	T	434,303
20 National Committee for an Effective Congress	N	427,387

The trade, membership and health category is diverse. Many of the committees within the category — such as the PACs for the National Association of Realtors and the National Automobile Dealers Association — have ties to the business community. The health-related PACs — such as the committees affiliated with the American Medical Association (AMA) and the American Dental Association — also fall into this group. And finally, there are the membership organizations — such as the NRA and the Gun Owners of America — that are rooted in a political ideology or issue.

Like organized labor, the category is anchored by a few heavyweights. In 1978 the AMA PAC ($1.6 million), the Realtors PAC ($1.1 million) and the Automobile Dealers PAC (nearly $1 million) topped all political committees in contributions to House and Senate candidates. These figures represented donations just from the national committees; the totals would have been even higher if the contributions of state affiliates to federal candidates had been included. In 1980 the three were among the top four PACs in all categories in total contributions. The Realtors led all PACs with $1.5 million in donations to federal candidates.

The 1975 SunPAC decision — which spurred a rapid increase in the number of corporate PACs — also prompted growth in the number of trade, membership and health PACs. Within six months, nearly 100 new committees were formed. But the creation of trade, membership and health PACs tapered off after that; only 125 new units were established between May 1976 and November 1981.

Strict regulations on the solicitation of contributions have been a major factor in discouraging faster growth. Trade associations raise funds from employees in member corporations. But they must obtain permission from the corporation each year before they may solicit their executive and administrative personnel. The associations maintain this is very costly and want the one-year limitation removed so they can solicit until a corporation withdraws its approval.

Ideological PACs' Influence

About 500 political committees fall into a unique, catch-all category called non-connected PACs. They are independent organizations without a parent body. But the leading non-connected PACs have thousands of contributors who are regularly tapped by direct-mail, fund-raising appeals.

Unlike most other PACs, which are motivated by economic concerns, the principal interests of the leading non-connected PACs are ideological. The most successful ones have been stridently conservative.

According to a *New York Times* analysis published in May 1981, the three PACs that raised the most money in the 1980 campaign were well to the right on the political spectrum: the three were the Congressional Club, formed by backers of Republican Sen. Jesse Helms of North Carolina, which raised nearly $7.9 million; the National Conservative Political Action Committee (NCPAC), which had receipts totaling $7.6 million; and the Fund for a Conservative Majority, an outgrowth of the Young Americans for Freedom, which raised $3.1 million.

Aided by conservative direct-mail, fund-raising expert Richard Viguerie, the Congressional Club and NCPAC have emerged as financial successes by developing mailing lists of more than 300,000 contributors each. In contrast, the leading non-connected PAC with a liberal identification, the National Committee for an Effective Congress (NCEC), has a much smaller mailing list and in 1980 raised less than one-fifth as much as either of the conservative giants.

Altogether, the non-connected PACs collected $40 million in 1980, more than either the corporate ($34.1 million), labor ($25.7 million) or trade, membership and health PACs ($33.7 million). But while the corporate and labor PACs contributed more than half of what they raised to congressional candidates, the non-connected PACs pumped less than $5 million directly into the coffers of congressional candidates, barely 10 cents out of each dollar they collected.

Much of the money raised by the ideological PACs was plowed back into costly direct-mail programs, an expense not incurred by corporate or union PACs. Their administrative costs were covered by the corporation or union, and they were able to raise money from members, employees or stockholders without expensive mass appeals.

With the rest of their funds, the leading non-connected PACs found several ways to become involved in congressional campaigns. In addition to making direct contributions or independent expenditures, some hired national experts on polling, media and other facets of modern-day campaigning which they made available to their candidates. Other PACs sponsored candidate training schools and provided research information from their Washington offices.

Since the ideological PACs were not restrained by affiliation with a parent organization that depended on access to members of Congress, they took greater risks than other PACs in supporting non-incumbents. In 1980 more than two-thirds of all direct contributions from non-connected PACs to House and Senate candidates went to challengers or candidates for open seats. All the other PAC categories channeled a majority of their donations to incumbents.

Most of the recipients of these direct contributions from non-connected PACs were Republicans. Over two-thirds of their donations in 1980 went to GOP candidates; corporate PACs gave 64 percent of their donations to Republicans. *(1980 PAC contributions by category, p. 47)*

But the ideological committees made their greatest mark on the 1980 campaign through independent expenditures that benefited Republicans in particular. The independent spending route was especially enticing to the well-heeled conservative PACs since it was not subject to the legal ceilings on direct contributions. PACs can independently spend an unlimited amount in a federal race as long as they do not make contact with the candidate that they favor.

Particularly controversial was NCPAC's nationwide media campaign to defeat six Democratic senators in 1980, including George McGovern of South Dakota, Frank Church of Idaho, John C. Culver of Iowa, Birch Bayh of Indiana, Alan Cranston of California and Thomas F. Eagleton of Missouri. Known as "Target '80," the independent spending drive, which cost $1.2 million, was largely successful: all but Cranston and Eagleton were defeated.

Liberal PACs Compete

Within several months of the 1980 election, five major new liberal PACs had been formed. While they differed

Non-connected PACs Fund Raising and Spending in 1981

Conservative Groups	1981 Receipts	1981 Expenditures	1980 Receipts	1979 Receipts
Congressional Club	$5,323,566	$5,809,007	$7,094,707	$1,185,007
National Conservative Political Action Committee	4,143,132	4,224,109	5,316,693	2,242,608
Fund for a Conservative Majority	1,060,727	1,063,878	2,874,421	289,216
Citizens for the Republic	1,049,680	927,839	1,117,456	1,239,307
Committee for the Survival of a Free Congress	889,207	912,827	1,065,109	582,456
Americans for Change	336,863	330,106	1,072,551	*

Liberal Groups

	1981 Receipts	1981 Expenditures	1980 Receipts	1979 Receipts
National Committee for an Effective Congress	$972,863	$1,029,430	1,216,157	$354,741
Fund for a Democratic Majority	861,091	636,196	*	*
Independent Action	684,282	673,100	*	*
Committee for the Future of America	678,469	399,219	*	*
Democrats for the 80's	600,108	287,249	*	*
Progressive Political Action Committee	205,033	165,765	*	*

*Committee did not exist.

Source: Federal Election Commission

from the conservative PACs in their goals and their leadership — political consultants started two of them, the leading Democratic presidential hopefuls for 1984 were behind two more and a party elder statesman began the other — their rhetoric was similar.

Through all their fund-raising appeals sounded the refrain that liberal causes were imperiled by the Republican capture of the Senate and the White House in 1980 — and by the chance that the GOP could win the House in 1982.

NCPAC figured as the arch-villain in virtually all the liberal money pitches. Unfailingly, their financial pleas cited the superior financial power of NCPAC and other "New Right" groups, whose treasuries were much fatter.

The new PACs with the most ambitious fund-raising objectives, the Progressive Political Action Committee (PROPAC) and Independent Action, were founded by political consultants who specialized in direct mail. Victor Kamber's PROPAC expressed hopes of raising $1.5 million for the 1982 campaign, while Roger Craver's Independent

Action set a budget goal of $2 million. Kamber previously had done most of his work for labor PACs, while Craver's clients had included the Democratic National Committee (DNC) and independent presidential candidate John B. Anderson.

Democrats for the '80s, created by former New York Gov. Averell Harriman and his wife, Pamela, was expected to raise most of its money at social events that drew wealthy, longtime Democratic contributors. This was the traditional fund-raising method for establishment Democrats such as the Harrimans.

Sen. Kennedy's Fund for a Democratic Majority and former Vice President Walter F. Mondale's Committee for the Future of America were widely perceived as vehicles for their sponsors' presidential ambitions. Kennedy's PAC planned to raise funds by tapping the mailing list of 1980 contributors to the senator's White House campaign, while Mondale's relied more heavily on fund-raising events.

Two other organizations were established to combat the "New Right" — former Democratic Sen. George Mc-

Govern's Americans for Common Sense and television producer Norman Lear's People for the American Way. These two, though, were not PACs and planned to fight conservatives through media ads about specific issues, such as abortion and television programming.

All the liberal groups had as their main goal economic support of liberal candidates. But only one of the five planned to concentrate on independent expenditures aimed at vilifying conservatives it deemed vulnerable in 1982. That one was Kamber's PROPAC.

Due to its association with NCPAC and the controversial "Target '80" campaign, the independent expenditure concept had a particularly bad name among many liberals PROPAC hoped to tap for funds.

Sensitive to this, the group defended negative independent spending as a necessary evil. "Nobody likes it, but the right wing has developed it extensively," said a PROPAC representative. "So where it needs to be done, we will have to do it." *(Profiles of NCPAC, PROPAC, pp. 57-59)*

Fund Raising for 1982

By the end of 1981, the new liberal groups, struggling against the financial and technical advantages of the right, still had a long way to go to catch up with the conservatives. As the 1982 congressional elections approached, the conservative groups were raising record funds and outspending their liberal counterparts by a ratio of more than four to one. *(Non-connected PAC 1981 receipts and expenditures, p. 53)*

The FEC disclosure reports showed the six largest conservative PACs had raised a combined war chest of $12.8 million in 1981 — an amount well over the $5.5 million raised by the five among them that existed in 1979, a comparable off-election year.

The Congressional Club topped the list in 1981 in both fund raising and spending, raising more than the top six liberal groups combined. The North Carolina-based group raised over $5.3 million in 1981 and spent just over $5.8 million, the difference being money carried over from 1980. The amount raised was only $1.7 million less than the group's total for 1980, an election year in which it broke all previous fund-raising records.

During 1981, Congressional Club activity included $1,000 contributions to the re-election campaigns of North Carolina GOP Reps. Bill Hendon and Eugene Johnston, a $5,000 in-kind contribution to the Connecticut Republican senatorial primary campaign of author Robin Moore, and a $1,000 loan to the 1982 House campaign of former Rep. Robert E. Bauman, R-Md. (1973-81).

The Congressional Club was followed closely by NCPAC, which raised over $4.1 million. The figure was just shy of twice what NCPAC raised in 1979 and about $1 million less than it raised in 1980. The group spent $4.2 million in 1981, less than $1 million short of its 1980 expenditures.

Although NCPAC is best known for its negative independent campaign tactics, the group also digs into its coffers to help conservative candidates directly. 1982 NCPAC loans included $5,000 to Rep. Robert K. Dornan's, R-Calif., Senate race, $3,000 to Rep. Stan Parris, R-Va., and $2,000 to Bauman's campaign.

Bauman also received a $500 contribution from the Fund for a Conservative Majority, a group that raised, as well as spent, about $1 million in 1981.

Citizens for the Republic was the only one of the top six conservative groups to raise less in 1981 than in 1979 — just over $1 million as compared with $1.2 milllion. In 1980, the group was a fund-raising vehicle for Ronald Reagan and like-minded candidates.

Conservative activist Paul Weyrich's Committee for the Survival of a Free Congress raised $889,207, just $175,000 less than its 1980 total. The committee's 1981 expenditures were $912,827.

Americans for Change, the newest of the conservative groups, raised $366,863 and spent $330,106. The PAC did not exist in 1979, but raised and spent over $1 million — mainly supporting Reagan — in 1980.

If all these figures were sobering for liberals, some consolation could be taken from their good year in 1981, at least compared to 1979 when only one of the top six liberal groups in 1981 fund raising existed. Although the liberal PACs raised a comparably modest $4 million in 1981, in 1979 the one liberal group that existed raised the slim sum of $350,000.

The group was the NCEC, the oldest liberal PAC and still the most active. In 1981 NCEC raised just under $1 million, only $240,000 less than the group raised in 1980. The group spent $1,029,430 in 1981, including contributions to Sens. Kennedy and Quentin N. Burdick, D-N.D., and Reps. Michael D. Barnes, D-Md., Paul Simon, D-Ill., and Patricia Schroeder, D-Colo.

Kennedy's PAC, the Fund for a Democratic Majority, raised $861,091 in 1981, its first year, and spent $636,196. That gave it a second ranking among liberal PACs. Mondale's PAC, Committee for the Future of America, raised just over $675,000 and spent just under $400,000. The committee raised 68 percent of its funds in the second half of the year.

Independent Action spent $673,100 in 1981 and raised $684,282. The group contributed to five Democrats, including Rep. Morris K. Udall of Arizona. Democrats for the '80s raised $600,108. Of that, $200,000 came from an Averell Harriman birthday fund-raising party. The group gave $10,000 each to the Democratic Congressional Campaign Committee and the Democratic Leadership Circle.

PROPAC came at the bottom of the liberal list. Kamber's group raised $205,033 and spent $165,765 — some of it on independent expenditure attacks on GOP Sens. Orrin G. Hatch of Utah, Helms, and Harrison "Jack" Schmitt, of New Mexico.

These 1981 figures confirmed what political analysts had been saying since the 1980 election. "The New Right is light years ahead," observed Herb Alexander. "They've been at it for years, and it's unrealistic to think the liberals can get near them soon."

While the liberals still had to go through the long task of assembling contributor lists, the conservatives had theirs in hand. "If you want to get money from the ones on the street during Vietnam," explained Viguerie, "you have to realize that they're 28, 30, 32 now and spend their money buying shoes for the kids every four months. By the time the kids are gone, those people have turned conservative."

But liberal PACs argued that a conservative White House and Senate had sufficiently energized fellow believers to make their financial plans successful. They maintained that many liberals were eager to give, pointing to the $8.3 million that Anderson raised for his independent presidential quest in 1980.

But the New Right clearly had momentum. Conservatives, long regarded as bloody but unbowed losers, had their political appetites whetted by the victory of Reagan and many of his Republican allies in 1980. "Everyone's mailings have gone through the roof since November," Viguerie told *The Washington Post* in March 1981. "Conservatives, in our lifetime, have never had any victories before, and they are excited and enthusiastic."

ATTEMPTS TO CURB SPECIAL INTERESTS

Even before the 1980 election, leading Democrats were concerned about the financial success of corporate and conservative PACs. In 1979 they moved to pass legislation that would curb contributions by PACs to House candidates.

While the proposal drew bipartisan support — Democrat David R. Obey of Wisconsin and Republican Tom Railsback of Illinois were the principal co-sponsors — it received most of its backing from the Democratic Party and its traditional allies, such as the AFL-CIO and the public affairs lobby, Common Cause. Republican leaders as well as business groups and conservative organizations strongly opposed the measure.

Legislative Attempts

The Obey-Railsback bill was unveiled on the heels of the release of a Harvard University study of federal election laws. The study, commissioned by the House Administration Committee, concluded that the post-Watergate revisions designed to clean up campaign finance had a number of unintended consequences, including a decline in grass-roots fund raising and a burgeoning role for PACs.

"PACs have increasingly supplanted other sources of money in politics and candidates for Congress have become increasingly dependent (on them)," the study explained. "If one of the original intentions of campaign finance reforms was to limit the appearance of special interests in the political process, the law has, in practice, had the opposite effect."

Armed with the conclusions of the Harvard study, the Obey-Railsback bill was introduced in the House in July 1979. Supporters of Obey-Railsback claimed that the growth in PAC contributions was undermining the effectiveness and integrity of Congress. "PAC giving is giving with a purpose," declared Obey. "It is money given by groups who then follow up their contribution with lobbying activities in behalf of their particular interests."

PACs were a "centrifugal force," Obey argued, that pulled members of Congress away from broad consensus-building and toward narrowly defined goals. He warned that action must be taken quickly before PACs became too powerful to curb. Proponents of Obey-Railsback maintained that PACs were fueling a political arms race, with the cost of congressional campaigns escalating out of control.

But opponents of the measure countered that more money was needed in politics, not less. "More dollars were spent on fireworks last year than all congressional elections combined," claimed Rep. Guy Vander Jagt, a Republican from Michigan.

Rather than be restricted, opponents contended that PACs should be encouraged. Although most PAC money went to incumbents, they claimed that Obey-Railsback was an "incumbent protection measure." Critics of the bill contended that PAC contributions were vital to challengers, particularly in the important early stages of a campaign when most of them had little name recognition and fund raising was difficult.

Opponents also doubted that Obey-Railsback would bring the new emphasis on small contributors that proponents anticipated. Instead, they saw a rise in wealthy candidates who would finance their own campaigns, a movement by many PACs into independent expenditures to avoid the limits on contributions and more burdensome paperwork and bureaucracy.

Finally, Republicans maintained that while Obey-Railsback effectively curbed direct contributions — the staple of corporate PACs — it did nothing to restrict the huge labor expenditures for internal communications and "non-partisan" activities.

Although opponents succeeded in delaying floor action for a time, the House passed the compromise measure on Oct. 17, 1979, by a vote of 217-198. A large majority of Northern Democrats supported the bill; most Republicans and Southern Democrats opposed it. House passage proved to be the high-water mark for the drive to curb PAC spending. The bill quickly bogged down in the Senate, and never was passed.

One drawback for Obey-Railsback was that most of its supporters also backed public financing of congressional races. Although the House Administration Committee had rejected legislation in May 1979 that would have established public financing for House general election campaigns, opponents were afraid that passage of the PAC limitation bill could renew interest in public financing.

Also many senators feared that passage of Obey-Railsback would set a precedent that could lead to PAC spending ceilings in Senate races. Supporters of the bill felt compelled to emphasize that they had no plan to put a cap on PAC spending in Senate elections because they considered it to be a less severe problem than in House campaigns.

The conservative Republican gains in 1980 interrupted, at least temporarily, attempts to curb PAC spending. Senate Minority Leader Robert C. Byrd, D-W. Va., introduced a version of Obey-Railsback at the beginning of the 1981 session and several moderate House members introduced a PAC limit bill later in July. But neither measure sparked much enthusiasm, and no action was taken.

Parties Seek Control

The growing clout of the conservative PACs understandably concerned Democratic Party officials, who viewed NCPAC and its allies as a disrupting influence in congressional races. In early 1981 Democratic National Committee (DNC) Chairman Charles T. Manatt named New York lawyer and former Kennedy adviser Theodore C. Sorensen to head a party panel that would explore ways to curb independent spending.

Manatt invited the RNC to participate in a joint study of the independent spending question, but the committee's Chairman Richard Richards declined. Instead, the RNC set up its own committee in June 1981 with the broader mandate of reviewing and recommending changes in the federal election law and the presidential nominating process. Republican National Committeeman Ernest Angelo of Texas was named the committee chairman.

But Richards did voice concern that the conservative PACs were loose cannons in Republican campaigns. While their negative advertising might soften up Democratic incumbents, Richards warned, the conservatives were prone to overdo their attacks and ultimately might prove an albatross to GOP candidates.

At the urging of then Reagan political adviser Lyn Nofziger, Richards met privately in May 1981 with conservative PAC leaders, including Viguerie, NCPAC Chairman John T. "Terry" Dolan and Tom Ellis, the director of the Congressional Club.

Richards asked the conservative PACs not to make independent expenditures in campaigns where GOP candidates or Republican state chairmen objected to their involvement.

But the conservative groups expressed little interest in an agreement. "Our conclusion," said Dolan the following month, "is that we cannot have any kind of formal agreement from a legal point of view, nor would we want to from a political point of view."

With hopes of an agreement dashed, Richards began issuing public warnings. In July 1981 he urged NCPAC to stay out of the 1982 Massachusetts Senate race, indicating that attacks on Kennedy would backfire against his Republican challengers.

PRESIDENTIAL PACs: REAGAN LEADS THE WAY

In establishing PACs, Kennedy and Mondale were merely following the lead of Ronald Reagan, who launched the Citizens for the Republic after his unsuccessful presidential bid in 1976.

From the beginning, the Reagan PAC operated with a scope that dwarfed any imitators. Possessing a $1 million surplus from 1976 and a mailing list of more than 100,000 names, Reagan created his PAC in early 1977. By the time it was operating in full swing, it employed a staff of nearly 30, a crew of consultants and a cartoonist. With a multimillion-dollar budget, the Santa Monica, Calif.-based organization emerged as an off-year refuge for many longtime Reagan advisers, including Lyn Nofziger, who headed the PAC in 1978.

Citizens for the Republic relied heavily for money on its carefully developed mailing list, but augmented it with fund-raising events and campaign management workshops around the country. By the end of 1978 the Reagan PAC had spent $4.5 million and still had more than $200,000 left in its treasury.

Presidential Hopefuls Compete

An FEC study found that in 1978 the Citizens for the Republic exceeded all other non-party PACs in gross receipts and expenditures. But because of its high overhead, its level of contributions to federal candidates trailed PACs established earlier by large business and labor organizations.

Yet the size and scope of the Reagan effort was un-

precedented for a presidential hopeful in a midterm election. Citizens for the Republic listed contributions to 400 Republican candidates across the country: 25 running for the Senate, 234 for the House, 19 for governor and 122 for other offices, which ranged from lieutenant governor of California to clerk of Clinton County, Mo. Reagan's wide-ranging activities also extended into intra-party affairs, with contributions to candidates for several state chairmanships.

Citizens for the Republic clearly overshadowed the other PACs formed by presidential hopefuls in 1978 — the John Connally Citizens Forum, George Bush's Fund for Limited Government and Robert Dole's Campaign America. The Connally PAC listed contributions to only 80 candidates, the Bush PAC to 51 and the Dole PAC to 17.

The Bush and Dole groups had limited objectives, serving primarily as speaking bureaus for their sponsors. Connally's PAC had more ambitious ideas, but fell short of its projected $1 million budget when it encountered difficulty in developing a reliable base of direct-mail contributors.

Unlike Reagan, the other GOP hopefuls had to form their PACs from scratch. Both Bush and Dole, former RNC chairmen, relied extensively on personal contacts with business leaders around the country to raise money. A Bush PAC spokesman claimed funds were raised by the "rifle shot technique," which consisted of Bush's brother or some other aide on the telephone.

Altogether the four PACs spent more than $5.6 million during the 1978 campaign, most of it eaten up by heavy start-up and operating costs and unitemized travel expenses. Of the $809,330 the PACs listed on their campaign spending forms as contributions, more than two-thirds went to House and Senate candidates. The remainder went to candidates at the state and local level and various party organizations.

A substantial minority of the contributions were made by providing in-kind services rather than direct donations. Forty percent of the contributions listed by the Citizens for the Republic, for example, were in the form of in-kind services, such as television and radio tapes by Reagan, travel expenses for a Reagan appearance and polling data commissioned by the PAC.

New Route to White House

While PAC spokesmen stressed that the basic purpose of their organizations was to help Republican candidates in 1978, there was little doubt that they also had 1980 on their minds. "The PACs are a new way a presidential candidate can pick up chits," observed Steve Stockmeyer, the executive director of the National Republican Congressional Committee in 1978.

The PACs were a logical extension of the traditional non-presidential election year appearances by White House hopefuls at fund-raising dinners along the "rubber chicken" circuit. When Richard M. Nixon, for example, was laying the groundwork for his 1968 presidential campaign, he traveled 30,000 miles on behalf of GOP congressional candidates in 1966. His travels, plus the salary and expenses of one assistant, cost $90,000.

While all of the 1980 Republican hopefuls made their greatest efforts in their home states — Texas for Bush and Connally, Kansas for Dole and California for Reagan — they showed particular interest in contests in the early presidential primary states.

New Hampshire, traditionally the first primary state, got special attention from the presidential PACs that belied its small size. Led by a $5,000 contribution from the Citizens for the Republic, all four PACs gave to Gordon Humphrey, the upset Senate winner over Democratic incumbent Thomas J. McIntyre. The Bush PACs contribution of $500 was sent two weeks after the election, the PAC's only post-election contribution.

The GOP PACs also funneled most of their donations to conservative non-incumbents. None of the PACs listed a contribution to prominent moderate Republicans such as Sens. Mark O. Hatfield of Oregon or Charles H. Percy of Illinois, who were seeking re-election in 1978. The small number of contributions to moderate Republican candidates came from the Bush and Dole groups.

Bush lent campaign assistance to Reps. William S. Cohen of Maine (in his successful Senate race), William A. Steiger of Wisconsin, who died after winning re-election, and Illinois' John Anderson, later Bush's rival for the GOP presidential nomination. Dole campaigned for two Republican House members endorsed by the UAW, Elwood Hillis of Indiana and Matthew J. Rinaldo of New Jersey.

Like the other Republican PACs, the Citizens for the Republic made its greatest effort on behalf of challengers and candidates for open seats. In House races, GOP opponents of Democratic members elected in 1974 and 1976 were major recipients. But the Reagan group provided a lot of other help to long-shot candidates.

The other three Republican PACs worked more closely with the RNC and its congressional, senatorial and gubernatorial affiliates in determining which candidates to support.

The presidential PACs represented a significant new Republican fund-raising source in 1978. Not only did the White House hopefuls make contributions, but their appearances raised millions more for GOP candidates and the party. Spokesmen for the Bush and Connally PACs both claimed that fund-raising appearances by their sponsors helped raise upwards of $2.5 million for Republican candidates in 1978. While the possibility existed that presidential PACs could pose a threat to the financial base of traditional party organizations, friction appeared to be minimal in 1978. "We're not in competition with them to raise money," explained Stockmeyer, "but we're gleefully joining with them to give it. They've opened a new area of candidate money."

Of the Republican PACs active in 1978, only the Citizens for the Republic remained in operation afterward, and it on a somewhat scaled-down basis. With Reagan mounting his own presidential campaign, the PAC raised "only" $2.4 million in 1979-80. In the first six months of 1981, it had collected about $600,000 more.

Although some of the presidential PACs were short-lived, there was agreement among their directors that a PAC is a necessity for a presidential hopeful under the existing campaign finance law. No longer are candidates permitted to tap sympathetic individuals or groups for large donations, nor can they count on a single aide or their congressional staff to handle scheduling requests throughout the increasingly long presidential campaigns. "The law forces top national candidates into PACs," observed Paul Russo, the executive director of Dole's Campaign America. "How else would you pay for travel?"

Another PAC spokesman agreed with Russo, but put it more bluntly: "Any potential candidate has to ally himself with this type of structure," he said. "They have to move around the country and meet party leaders. The law forces us to set up dodges called PACs."

PAC PROFILES

Most political action committees are created for the same reason — to help elect those candidates who reflect their own political views. But individual PACs may go about achieving their goals in different ways.

Some, such as the National Conservative Political Action Committee (NCPAC) and the Progressive Political Action Committee (PROPAC), specialize in so-called negative campaigns. Rather than actively promote a specific candidate, these groups run campaigns against incumbents who disagree with their views on the issues. Another kind of PAC, represented by the Women's Campaign Fund, spends as much of its money and effort on finding and training candidates as financing them.

Yet another group, the Council for a Livable World, makes its impact by suggesting to its supporters those candidates it favors. Supporters then contribute to specific candidates by sending checks to the Council, which passes them on to the candidates who thus know why they are getting the money.

Profiled below are several political action committees and the ways they raise and spend campaign funds.

NCPAC's Campaigns: A New Twist in Politicking

One of the most controversial PACs is NCPAC, which uses a number of campaign techniques including negative advertising to defeat liberal incumbents. "Our goal is a conservative Senate, and this is the best way to get it," says NCPAC's chairman, John T. "Terry" Dolan, of his organization's decision to advocate defeat of an incumbent without openly promoting any opponent.

NCPAC's tactics have been hailed by some as an effective use of legal campaign practices, but castigated by others as Machiavellian and dishonest. Regardless of whose perception is right, the group's tactics have caught the attention of the political world. In 1980 NCPAC targeted six liberal Democratic senators; four of them were defeated.

NCPAC continued to target candidates in the 1982 elections. In the Senate, Lowell P. Weicker Jr., Conn., was among the group of eight targeted incumbents. The group also campaigned against liberal House members.

But the 1982 NCPAC campaigns could be blunted by a backlash of sorts. Targeted incumbents took steps to minimize the damage that NCPAC ad campaigns might inflict, several television stations refused to carry NCPAC ads and some Democratic organizations challenged NCPAC on the grounds that it was violating federal campaign spending laws.

NCPAC was one of the first political action committees to take advantage in a major way of the loophole created by the Supreme Court's decision in *Buckley* v. *Valeo*. That allowed political action committees to spend unlimited amounts of money in federal elections providing they had no contact with the candidates involved. In the 1979-80 elections cycle, NCPAC's independent expenditure efforts were the most visible — and the second most expensive. NCPAC spent $3.3 million in its independent effort, of which $1.2 million was spent opposing the candidacies of the six targeted Senate incumbents. Most of the remainder was spent promoting candidates, primarily Ronald Reagan. By the end of 1981, NCPAC had raised a total of $4.1 million, nearly twice as much as it raised in 1979, a comparable non-election year.

Targeting

The six senators marked for defeat in 1980 were Birch Bayh, D-Ind., Frank Church, D-Idaho, John C. Culver, D-Iowa, George McGovern, D-S.D., Alan Cranston, D-Calif., and Thomas F. Eagleton, D-Mo. Only Cranston and Eagleton won re-election.

In each of the six states, the conservative PAC ran television and newspaper ad campaigns that pointed out what NCPAC considered to be the incumbent's weak points. Bayh, Church and Culver, for example, were derided through an advertising "baloney" blitz. These ads featured slices of baloney with multimillion-dollar price tags equaling the amount of deficit spending the target senator purportedly voted for. "One very big piece of baloney is Birch Bayh telling us he's fighting inflation," the announcer said.

In Idaho NCPAC tried to portray Senate Foreign Relations Committee Chairman Church as opposed to a strong national defense by airing television advertisements showing empty Titan I missile silos in the state. Church claimed the ads were misleading because the Titan I missiles had been replaced by another generation of missiles.

Charges persist that NCPAC deliberately distorts the political positions of incumbents it opposes. In at least one instance, misrepresentation may have actually helped the incumbent. NCPAC in 1981 mounted a campaign against John Melcher, D-Mont., sending a letter to Montanans in which it misstated Melcher's position on three of the six issues discussed. When Melcher complained, NCPAC wrote a letter of apology. Dolan denies that the misrepresentations it has circulated are intentional. However, he has acknowledged that he once said: "A group like ours could lie through its teeth and the candidate it helps stays clean." Dolan claims that comment, which initially appeared in *The Washington Post*, was taken out of context.

A Real Difference?

Some political observers question whether NCPAC's negative campaigning actually works. They note that the four defeated liberal senators targeted by NCPAC in 1980

represented very conservative states, were vulnerable before NCPAC began its campaigns and may have lost even if the negative advertising had not been run.

Others warn that NCPAC's power should not be underestimated. They point to the case of Paul S. Sarbanes, Maryland's liberal Democratic senator up for re-election in 1982. NCPAC made Sarbanes one of its early targets in 1981, running a similar tough negative advertising campaign portraying Sarbanes as "too liberal for Maryland." At first it looked as though the ad campaign might have backfired.

Sarbanes got his own campaign organized sooner than he might otherwise have, and his major conservative opponent subsequently determined that she could not defeat Sarbanes and so dropped out of the race. For a few months it appeared that the NCPAC campaign had benefited its target.

But a February 1982 poll taken by *The Baltimore Sun* found that while Sarbanes' approval rating had held steady compared with a similar poll conducted in the fall of 1981, the number of voters who disapproved of his performance had increased from 22 percent to 29 percent. How much of that increase, if any, could be attributed to the continuing NCPAC ads was unclear, but the poll likely encouraged the controversial committee to continue its campaign.

Opposition

NCPAC has been criticized by Republican opponents of targeted incumbents and by some state Republican organizations who fear a voter backlash to what many consider NCPAC's unsavory tactics. But NCPAC is getting most of its opposition from the people it is trying to defeat — liberal Democrats. A series of complaints have been filed with the Federal Election Commission, the Internal Revenue Service and the Justice Department, but they have failed to stop the organization.

The most recent attack comes from the Democratic National Committee (DNC) and the Democratic congressional campaign committees charging that NCPAC has violated federal election law by consulting with some Republican candidates.

Meanwhile, some liberals have decided to give conservatives a taste of their own medicine. One group — the Progressive Political Action Committee (PROPAC) — was established in 1981 to use negative campaigns to help defeat conservative incumbents.

Liberal Independent PAC Copies Conservatives' Strategy

For a group that did not exist during the 1980 elections, PROPAC has some very big plans. Starting in December 1981, the new liberal committee began an advertising campaign designed to unseat four conservative Republican senators, including a leader of the New Right, Sen. Jesse Helms, R-N.C.

What PROPAC had in mind, according to founder Victor Kamber, was a liberal version of what NCPAC did in 1980 — attack specific legislators with negative campaigns. *(NCPAC profile, p. 57)*

"We plan to use [NCPAC Director] Terry Dolan's exact logic that we're only exposing their [the legislators'] records," Kamber said.

PROPAC's early campaign cost $30,000 to $50,000. In addition to Helms, the political action committee initially targeted Sens. Orrin G. Hatch, R-Utah, S. I. "Sam" Hayakawa, R-Calif., and Harrison "Jack" Schmitt, R-N.M. Hayakawa dropped out of the race in January 1982, and PROPAC later decided not to take an active part in the Hatch campaign.

The ads, run in the three states concerned, were pointed. In Utah an oil well gushed money next to the words: "When Orrin Hatch says he likes the Houston Oilers, he's not talking about football." In New Mexico Schmitt was pictured looking at a mirror while the caption read: "Jack Schmitt may not get much done in the Senate, but he sure looks good doing it." In North Carolina "Policeman" Helms shined a flashlight on a couple in bed next to the words: "If you think Jesse Helms is against big government, think again!"

Kamber, a former AFL-CIO official who ran a firm of public and governmental affairs specialists, said the ads would focus on the perceived weaknesses of the candidates — Schmitt's lack of legislative activity, Helms' anti-abortion stance, and Hatch's relationship with big business.

Helms was not up for re-election until 1984 and Kamber admitted the North Carolinian was picked to help PROPAC raise funds. But Kamber also believed Helms was vulnerable and said targeting him then would begin the process of weakening him in the voters' minds.

PROPAC is not wealthy, raising approximately $200,000 in 1981. But the group mailed 800,000 solicitations early in 1982 that Kamber hoped would help raise between $750,000 and $800,000. The PAC planned to spend as much as $400,000 on negative campaigns in 1982.

Kamber is aware many fellow liberals have criticized groups such as NCPAC for negative campaigning. Some Democrats had sought to disassociate themselves from PROPAC and the head of the Democratic Party in Utah had asked PROPAC to stay out of the state, warning that negative campaigning could backfire and ruin the party's chances to defeat Hatch.

But Kamber believes liberals ought to take advantage of the election law that permits unlimited negative campaign spending. "Someone's got to do this kind of stuff," he concluded, "and we're prepared to do it."

Women's PAC Focuses On Developing Candidates

While most political action committees limit their activity to contributing funds to candidates, the Women's Campaign Fund spends as much time and money finding and training candidates as it does making financial contributions to them.

The bipartisan fund has existed since 1974 "exclusively to help women get into the political process and get into public office," according to Executive Director Ranny Cooper. Although the fund only aids women candidates, not all women office seekers qualify. Recipients must take "progessive" stands on women's issues, specifically the

Equal Rights Amendment (ERA) and abortion rights; have a chance of winning; and need the fund's technical assistance.

The fund helped the campaigns of most women serving in Congress in 1982, including Reps. Shirley Chisholm, D-N.Y., Millicent Fenwick, R-N.J., Patricia Schroeder, D-Colo., and Sen. Nancy Landon Kassebaum, R-Kan. The only other woman in the Senate, Paula Hawkins, R-Fla., did not receive fund support because of her conservative views on women's issues, Cooper said.

Races between progressive women and progressive men pose tough decisions for the fund, Cooper said. The fund stayed out of two 1980 races involving women they otherwise would have supported — Republican Mary Buchanan, who challenged Sen. Gary Hart, D-Colo., and Rep. Marge Roukema, R-N.J., who defeated Rep. Andrew Maguire, D-N.J. Hart and Maguire are strong supporters of women's issues. The fund decided it was better to spend its limited resources on women candidates elsewhere.

When women candidates run against each other the fund looks beyond stands on issues in deciding whom to support. In 1980, two women with progressive records, Bess Myerson and Rep. Elizabeth Holtzman, D-N.Y., were candidates in New York's Democratic senatorial primary. The fund chose to support Holtzman, an early supporter of the fund, because her campaign was better organized than Myerson's, Cooper said. Holtzman won the primary but lost in the general election.

Approximately 70 percent of the fund's contributions go to candidates in primary elections. The fund concentrates on providing support for candidates early in their campaigns because a lack of "seed money" often keeps women out of races or causes them to lose.

The fund's most recent priority has been aiding state and local candidates by developing a network of politically active women. About a third of the approximately $200,000 the fund spent in 1980 went to non-federal races, particularly in states that had not ratified the ERA. It planned to use half of the $400,000 it hoped to raise for 1982 races on state and local candidates.

In addition to giving money to candidates the fund also acts as a "brokering agent" for women candidates. It sets up meetings with other political action committees for candidates, helps the candidates plan strategies and hosts seminars on campaigning and fund raising for women candidates.

Business PAC Has Difficult Act to Follow

The Business-Industry Political Action Committee (BIPAC) had an enviable problem: it was so successful supporting pro-business candidates in 1980 that a repeat performance in 1982 likely would be quite a task.

BIPAC supported almost twice as many winners as losers in 1980. The unaffiliated group — supporting mainly non-incumbent candidates — participated in 126 races, including primaries, and enjoyed an 81-to-45 win-loss record.

By all accounts 1980 was a banner year for pro-business candidates and a number of well-known legislators opposed by BIPAC are no longer in Congress. "We've done a good job in defeating those people," said Bernadette A. Budde, BIPAC's director of political education. The result, she said, was that many of BIPAC's 1982 races would be "obscure."

Candidates qualifying for BIPAC support are first identified by local business leaders, then must be approved unanimously by a six-member panel of BIPAC directors. The panel consists of three Republicans and three Democrats. For a candidate to receive support, various criteria must be met. The race must be clearly business-related, the contest must be close and there must be a need for money.

With this in mind, Budde described the 1982 Maine senatorial race as "the best-shaped race in the country." BIPAC supported Rep. David F. Emery, R, in his challenge to incumbent Sen. George J. Mitchell, D, who had a BIPAC legislative rating of five (out of a possible 100). Emery's House record earned him a rating of 77.

Another Senate race attracting BIPAC's early attention was Rep. Robin L. Beard's, R-Tenn., challenge to Sen. Jim Sasser, D-Tenn. Beard had a 100 rating compared with Sasser's 44. BIPAC has aided Rep. Cleve Benedict, R-W.Va., in a race against Senate Minority Leader Robert C. Byrd, D-W.Va. BIPAC gave Benedict, a House freshman who had not yet received a rating, $2,093 in direct and in-kind contributions during his 1980 House race. Byrd's rating was seven.

BIPAC helped Republican businessman William J. Moshofsky in his bid for the House seat held by Rep. Les AuCoin, D-Ore. (rating 25). Moshofsky, vice president for government affairs of the Georgia-Pacific Corporation, was a member of BIPAC's board of directors.

BIPAC shuns independent expenditures in favor of in-kind contributions — primarily mailings to other political action committees soliciting support and contributions. Most mailings are carried out in consultation with candidates. Other solicitations go out to individuals from political or business figures such as Sen. James Abdnor, R-S.D., or Amway executive Richard DeVos, BIPAC regional vice chairman for the Midwestern states.

Abdnor was himself a BIPAC recipient in the 1980 elections, receiving $1,132 in in-kind contributions for his primary race and $2,500 in direct general election contributions. In total, BIPAC gave out $11,139 in in-kind contributions and $135,500 in direct contributions.

Arms Control Committee Funnels Campaign Funds

How does an arms control political action committee tap opposition fallout from the Reagan administration's big defense spending program? The Council for a Livable World does it by making sure candidates it supports know exactly from where their campaign money is coming.

The 20-year-old council, which only endorses Senate candidates because senators have a direct role in shaping U.S. arms policy, uses an unusual technique for fund raising and contributing.

The council mails profiles of candidates it has endorsed to over 13,000 supporters. Supporters choose the candidate or candidates they wish to help and write their check to the candidate's election committee. But instead of mailing the check directly to the candidate's committee, they funnel it through the council.

The council acts as a conduit for funds to let candidates know donations reflect their support for arms control. In addition, the group avoids the $5,000 primary and general election contribution limits for PACs because the money does not actually come from the council itself.

The council's candidate assistance program garnered a 50 percent success ratio in 1980, a year when defense policy was a central election issue.

In addition to $14,000 in direct council contributions, the group channeled $216,267 from its supporters to 14 candidates including: Sens. Christopher J. Dodd, D-Conn.; Gary Hart, D-Colo.; Dale Bumpers, D-Ark.; Alan Cranston, D-Calif.; Thomas F. Eagleton, D-Mo.; and Charles McC. Mathias Jr., R-Md.

To be endorsed by the council, a candidate must strongly support arms control and have an opponent with clearly opposing views. The council usually stays out of campaigns waged between two major arms control supporters.

Candidates must also have a "solid chance to win," without being considered a lopsided favorite. The council prefers to concentrate on races in smaller states and on primary elections where the money can make a greater difference.

According to John Isaacs, the council's Washington-based legislative director, the organization hoped to double its 1980 financial assistance to candidates in 1982. As of December 1981, the council had raised approximately $60,000 to support five candidates: Rep. Toby Moffett, D-Conn., who was running for the Connecticut Senate seat held by Republican Lowell P. Weicker Jr.; and Sens. John H. Chafee, R-R.I.; Howard M. Metzenbaum, D-Ohio; Paul S. Sarbanes, D-Md.; and Jim Sasser, D-Tenn.

Isaacs anticipated the council would also endorse incumbent Sens. George J. Mitchell, D-Maine, Donald W. Riegle Jr., D-Mich., and Robert T. Stafford, R-Vt.

Anti-handgun PAC Aims To Trigger New Members

What could be tougher than waging legislative battles in Congress with such politically powerful giants as the National Rifle Association (NRA) and the Gun Owners of America? Ask Handgun Control Inc. (HCI), a group founded for just that purpose, and the answer might be raising money for its political action committee.

Like a number of other PACs affiliated with what the government designates "corporations without capital stock," HCI's PAC has been hindered by a Federal Election Commission (FEC) fund-raising rule. The commission's regulations restrict organizations such as HCI to soliciting PAC contributions only from members — people who, in this case, have contributed to the parent organization. This has meant the PAC has had a limited universe from which to solicit funds.

PAC Director Charles Orasin hopes that a Sept. 4, 1981, federal appeals court decision may change that. The court ruled that the National Right to Work Committee —

a group with a similar corporate structure to the anti-gun group — could solicit PAC contributions from outside its membership if the solicitations were directed at people who had shown support for the committee's goals.

The appeals court refused a rehearing and the FEC has asked the Supreme Court to review the decision. In the meantime HCI's PAC is gearing up for a supporter identification drive it calls "One Million Strong."

According to Orasin, the idea is to identify the names of gun control supporters around the country — names that later will be used for PAC solicitations. The campaign coincides with the publication of HCI Chairman Pete Shields' book *Guns Don't Die — People Do* and a new bumper sticker and poster campaign. The PAC's spending power could be greatly enhanced if the new identification campaign gets off the ground.

In 1980 the PAC spent approximately $150,000, raised from 65,000 donor/members of its parent organization. Orasin hoped to raise as much as $600,000 for use in the 1982 election. The money would come from an estimated 470,000 supporters identified through the new campaign, as well as from donor/members who contributed to HCI.

Orasin said the number of HCI donor/members had increased in 1981 to 150,000, a 131 percent rise. He cited the handgun shootings of President Reagan and former Beatle John Lennon as major reasons for the increase.

"Lennon's death changed a lot," Orasin said, adding that college students are now much more aware of the issue when HCI tries to galvanize their support on campuses.

But HCI's PAC is still fighting an uphill battle. The NRA has approximately 2.1 million members, many organized in easily approachable gun clubs. In 1980 the NRA's Political Victory Fund spent approximately $1 million on campaign contributions and independent expenditures. In addition the NRA outdid even labor unions in communicating with members concerning which candidates to vote for and which ones to vote against. According to FEC figures, the NRA spent $808,839 on such communications.

7

Washington Fund-Raisers

When Mark Green headed up Ralph Nader's Congress Watch in Washington, he used to say that no one knew more than he did about the influence of campaign money on Congress. And as a co-author of the book *Who Runs Congress?*, Green helped popularize the idea that special-interest political action committees (PACs) "own" Congress.

But when Green decided to run in 1980 for Congress himself, from New York's 18th District, he scheduled a modest $100-a-head fund-raising dinner, and guess who was invited: mentor Ralph Nader, economist John Kenneth Galbraith, a lot of liberals ... and a passel of PACs.

Green explained in an interview, "I have to raise money now.... Otherwise, it would be like playing tennis and refusing to hit the ball." Ironic as this may sound, Green's fund-raising efforts simply provided evidence that he had learned the elementary lesson of modern campaign finance: Get the Washington money.

The most popular way to do that is to throw a party and offer potential donors the opportunity, for a price ranging from $100 to $1,000 a head, to sip cocktails, munch canapés, and mingle with members of Congress and their staffs. The donors usually are lobbyists who buy their tickets with money from PACs organized by businesses, labor unions or trade associations.

As political campaign costs have escalated and PACs have proliferated, Washington fund-raisers have kept pace, becoming a commonplace institution in the capital. Almost every available source agrees that there are more Washington fund-raisers — perhaps double the number in 1976 — that ticket prices have soared, and that they are scheduled earlier in each campaign cycle. Because fund-raisers are not just attended by representatives of special interests, but also frequently are organized by them, they are more than just another campaign endeavor. Directly or indirectly, they are lobbying events as well.

While many in Washington see that as harmless, or even a beneficial stimulant to the political process, an outspoken minority thinks this trend has brought fund raising and law making too close for comfort. Lobbyists, these critics say, use their fund-raising prowess to win extraordinary access to members of Congress. At the same time, legislators may be tempted to abuse their lawmaking power to extract campaign contributions from the people who petition them for help.

"It's not a question of buying [votes]," said Fred Wertheimer, president of Common Cause. "It's a question of relationships that get built, obligations and dependencies that get established.... It puts PACs at the head of the line, as opposed to the great bulk of a congressman's constituents."

The Washington fund-raiser is a "phenomenon that is getting bigger and bigger and bigger," remarked Joseph S. Jenckes, a lobbyist for Abbott Laboratories. "If I don't get 400 invitations in a year, I'd flip. No, maybe more."

"They are awfully numerous," agreed Rep. Thomas S. Foley, D-Wash., who, as chairman of the House Democratic Caucus during the 96th Congress and majority whip during the 97th, attended a fair number of fund-raisers himself. "For the people who are going to these things, it must get very tiring."

There are good reasons for the proliferation of fund-raisers. Most obviously, candidates for federal office are finding they need more and more money to wage a campaign these days, more than they can easily raise from contributors in their own states.

House candidates in 1978 spent $88 million, up 44 percent from 1976. Republican and Democratic House candidates on the average spent $107,795 on their races. But close races cost a lot more. In the 74 districts where the winner received 55 percent or less of the vote, the average combined campaign cost for the candidates was $448,000.

Running for the Senate was even more expensive. A total of $65.5 million was spent on 35 Senate contests in 1978, up from $38.1 million for 33 seats in 1976. Moreover, 21 Senate candidates spent more than a million dollars compared to 10 in 1976.

"As long as there's a source of money somewhere else, why take it all out of your district?" commented Jay Stone, an aide to Rep. Henson Moore, R-La. In Moore's district, he noted, funding sources in 1980 were milked dry by a high-priced gubernatorial campaign and a spate of local races — as well as by the 1982 Senate and House races.

Impact of Campaign 'Reforms'

Ironically, the passage in 1971 and 1974 of a series of comprehensive reforms in the federal election process may have been the single most significant reason for the increasing popularity of Washington fund-raisers. The laws allowed corporations and unions to become campaign contributors through the vehicle of political action committees and at the same time restricted the amounts individual donor could give. *(PACs, chapter 6, p. 41)*

PACs flourished — increasing from none in 1972 to 608 by the end of 1974, and to more than 2,600 by mid-1981. Cash-hungry candidates eagerly reached out to them. Because the highest concentration of PACs is in Washington, the Washington fund-raiser became a logical way to get money from them. The candidate needed simply to schedule a party, charge for the tickets, and convince as many PACs as possible to attend.

"PAC money," explained Common Cause's Wertheimer, "is the cheapest and the easiest money to get if you're an incumbent." *(Incumbents and challengers, box, pp. 72-73)*

"Washington is not full of big Republican givers," commented independent political consultant Robert J. Perkins, who organizes fund-raisers for Republican politicians. "But the concentration of PACs is greater here than anywhere else. So Washington fund-raising events concentrate on PACs."

Early Bird Fund-raisers

As the competition for PAC dollars has become more intense, candidates have begun to schedule their fund-raising events earlier and earlier in the election cycle. Cocktail parties and receptions for the 1982 election began to occur almost immediately after the debts were paid off for the 1980 election.

Once a member decides to hold a Washington fund-raiser, he or she has plenty of places to turn for logistical help. A member's congressional staff can lend a hand, though federal law forbids a staffer from helping out during office hours or even while physically in the office. The House and Senate party campaign committees also can be of some assistance. They can provide candidates with advice, mailing lists, and help with planning and organizing an event and making follow-up telephone calls to the targets of the candidate's invitations — all at no cost to the candidate.

So great has the demand for fund-raising dates become that the Democratic and Republican congressional campaign committees even play traffic cop. To avoid scheduling conflicts, every three to four weeks they mail out complete listings of upcoming Washington fund-raising events.

A lot of candidates, though, want more specialized help. Some will seek out professional fund-raisers who — for a fee — will do all the work of organizing and putting on the event. *(Fund-raisers, box, pp. 66-67)*

Help from Lobbyists

More often, though, incumbents find that they can get the same kind of help — at no cost — from lobbyists. Lobbyists can help in a number of ways. They can donate mailing lists for the invitations, and then make the follow-up telephone calls to push for the ticket sale. Or, a lobbyist actually can throw the fund-raiser, hosting it as well as donating the organizing time, the food and drinks, the mailing list and even the location. Inevitably, the lobbyists who help out also turn out to have a professional interest in the member's legislative activities.

Rep. Joseph P. Addabbo, D-N.Y., chairman of the House Appropriations Subcommittee on Defense, raised $23,375 in 1979 at a fund-raiser heavily attended by defense contractors. The assistant treasurer of the effort was James McDonald, a lobbyist for Northrop Corp., the huge aircraft and weaponry company. McDonald said he has been helping the chairman organize fund-raisers since 1972, because "Joe Addabbo and I have been friends for 15 years." He said he only handles "a small part" of Northrop's Washington interests.

McDonald also helped raise money for Rep. Leo C. Zeferetti, D-N.Y., and half a dozen others, he said, and for many years was a principal fund-raiser for former Rep. Thomas Morgan, D-Pa. (1945-77), chairman of the House Foreign Affairs Committee. Other examples:

● Abbott Laboratories' Joseph Jenckes helped organize a $150-a-head breakfast prior to the 1980 elections for Rep. James R. Jones, D-Okla., a key member of the Ways and Means Committee, which handles much of the health legislation of concern to Abbott. Jenckes also helped out Rep. Tom Loeffler, R-Texas, and Sen. John Glenn, D-Ohio. Glenn and Loeffler both come from states where Abbott has plants.

● William R. Edgar, vice president for government relations of the General Aviation Manufacturers Association, called colleagues to solicit support for Rep. Robert Duncan, D-Ore., chairman of the House Appropriations Subcommittee on Transportation. Duncan's campaign was unsuccessful.

● Robert Barrie, lobbyist for General Electric, and Thomas H. Boggs, whose clients include several energy giants, were co-hosts for a $1,000-a-head dinner in March 1980 for Sen. Mike Gravel, D-Alaska, chairman of subcommittees on energy taxation and water resources. Gravel also lost his bid for re-election.

● Lucinda Williams, a lobbyist for the Federation of American Hospitals and active on many members' fund-raising steering committees, frequently assists members who work on committees handling health legislation. In 1979 her beneficiaries included Ways and Means member Ken Holland, D-S.C., and the Commerce Committee's James D. Santini, D-Nev.

● Jack H. McDonald, a former congressman (R-Mich., 1967-73) turned lobbyist — his clients include American Express Co., Burroughs Corp. and the Sugar Association — helped promote a successful event for Rep. Guy Vander Jagt, R-Mich., of the tax-writing Ways and Means Committee. He said he also had aided at least five other members of Congress. "I just work for my friends," McDonald said. "In a lot of cases, I've never lobbied them."

"Beyond the $100 or $200 you can give to a candidate, the more important thing is helping him arrange his fund-raiser," said Linda Jenckes, lobbyist for the Health Insurance Association of America. "It's a double way to say, 'Thank you, and I hope you get elected.'" She added: "Those that don't get this kind of support get the message: 'Hey, maybe I'm not doing a good job.'"

Hits, Flops and Power

Though there may be many reasons why a particular fund-raiser turns out to be a hit or a flop, some factors clearly are more important than others. Perhaps the key consideration is the power of the candidate for whom the fund-raiser is being thrown, and the candidate's willingness to use that position of influence to promote ticket sales.

For this reason, junior members and challengers often do better staying away from the Washington fund-raiser altogether. They usually are better off raising their money in some other way. For the more senior members, on the other hand, the longer they have been around and the more powerful their committee assignments, the better are the odds of turning an evening of handshakes and cocktails into a tidy list of contributors.

"The number of people who think you are wonderful tends to increase as you climb the ladder," explained veteran fund-raiser Leslie Israel, who was labor coordinator of the Kennedy for President campaign. One way incumbents try to take maximum advantage of their seniority is by targeting their invitations to the lobbyists and PAC officials they feel are least able to turn them down.

"The most important thing is your list," Response Marketing's Bradley Sean O'Leary explained. "You've got to reach everyone who would have the faintest reason for wanting to have your candidate elected." Lists, often in the form of computer tape, can be borrowed from lobbyists or bought from professionals. Perhaps the most popular is a PAC list available, free, to almost any member of Congress from the political arm of the American Trucking Associations.

While some lists are accorded a certain mystique or financial value (the truckers report donations of their list as an in-kind contribution worth $20, while the Americans for Constitutional Action value theirs at $1,200), most experts agree all are the same basic roster of PACs with a history of attending fund-raisers. Usually the list is supplemented with names of the congressman's friends and official contacts, and targeted to PACs interested in issues in which the lawmaker has made a name for himself.

Just as important are the follow-up telephone calls that are made after the invitations have gone out, preferably by close friends or influential associates of the invited guests. If the checks still do not seem to be pouring in, a candidate can up the ante by scheduling a second, more intimate gathering with a few lobbyists who might be willing to pay for his company.

In February 1980, for example, officials of energy PACs got a letter from General Electric lobbyist Robert Barrie reminding them of an upcoming fund-raiser for Gravel. Noting that at a price of "only $200" this was likely to be a large, impersonal affair, Barrie invited his friends to "make the night better for Mike" by attending a more exclusive dinner later in the evening, at $1,000 per guest.

Tailored to Transportation

An example of a fund-raising effort carefully tailored to exploit a member's legislative position was a pair of Washington events prior to the 1980 election thrown by Duncan, then chairman of the House Appropriations Transportation Subcommittee. Duncan traditionally ran

shoestring campaigns against token opposition. In 1980, however, he faced a stiff primary challenge from Ron Wyden, a 30-year-old lawyer who was executive director of Oregon's Gray Panthers organization.

To put together an invitation list for his $250-a-head affairs, Duncan's executive secretary, Helen Burton, said she began with a variety of PAC mailing lists, including one from the American Trucking Associations. She added the addresses of officials of groups that had invited Duncan to speak at their conventions, business cards collected by Duncan from people who had come to see him on issues, and the names contained in a card file of contacts maintained by Thomas J. Kingfield, staff assistant of Duncan's subcommittee.

Among those making follow-up phone calls urging attendance were Duncan's legislative assistant on transportation Terry Scannell and lobbyists for the Marine Engineers Beneficial Association and the General Aviation Manufacturers Association.

Not surprisingly, about two-thirds of the proceeds from the 1979 event ended up coming from transportation PACs and individuals interested in transportation matters. "I guess it's pretty heavy with transportation people," conceded Burton, "although the transportation people did not come through as heavily as I expected they would." Duncan managed to sweeten the pot a bit with a third event, a

$1,000-a-plate dinner with transportation and timber representatives at the home of lobbyist and former Rep. Lloyd Meeds, D-Wash. (1965-79). Nevertheless, the aggressive, well-planned campaign of the youthful Wyden was successful and Duncan was defeated handily in the primary election.

Getting the Best Buy

When PAC officials or lobbyists try to decide whether to buy a ticket to a fund-raiser, they often act just like any other consumer: They try to figure out ahead of time what they will get for their money.

There are two basic reasons for purchasing a fund-raiser ticket. A group can base its buying decisions on the chance of winning future access to a member, or on the hope of an ideological return.

Those more interested in access buy tickets so that their candidates — if later elected — presumably will meet them at the door and welcome their future lobbying pitches.

Fund Raising for Profit or Politics...

Charlene Baker Craycraft does it for conservatives. Victor Kamber does it for labor. Thomas H. Boggs does it for friends. Nancy Cole does it for money. What all of them do is arrange fund-raising events, using their inside knowledge of Washington to help steer millions of interested dollars into the coffers of congressional candidates.

Tom Boggs is one of a handful of Washington lawyer-lobbyists who have become almost as legendary for their ability to corral dollars as for their knack at shaping federal law. This group of "superheavies," as one fund-raising expert described them, includes lawyers and lobbyists of such high-powered firms as Patton, Boggs and Blow; Williams and Jensen; Charls E. Walker Associates; and Timmons and Co.

Helping to arrange fund-raisers not only boosts their stock with members of Congress, but it also gives them a valuable status among their fellow lobbyists. Boggs was born into politics, the son of House Majority Leader Hale Boggs, D-La. (1941-43; 1947-73), and Rep. Lindy Boggs, D-La., who took her husband's place after he disappeared in an Alaskan plane crash.

Boggs' law firm lobbies for a string of clients that includes General Motors Corp., Chrysler Corp., Exxon Corp., Pepsico, Pillsbury and Ralston Purina. He also helped the Carter administration lobby for Senate passage of the Panama Canal and SALT II treaties.

Thomas H. Boggs

In a 1980 interview, Boggs said he was involved at the time as a coordinator or participant in the campaigns of 25 or 30 candidates, ranging from Sens. Russell B. Long, D-La. ("the easiest" to raise money for) to Patrick J. Leahy, D-Vt., and John A. Durkin, D-N.H. ("the toughest" — Durkin lost). For Senate candidates, Boggs will help arrange fund-raisers not only in Washington, but also in New York, Chicago, Los Angeles and Dallas.

Boggs "has the ability to convince his clients and his friends of their need to contribute to an individual or the party," Robert C. McCandless, a member of the Democratic National Committee's finance council, told *The Washington Post* in 1979. "You've got to be able to tell your clients that if they're going to do business in this town, they better make certain contributions to the party in power."

Boggs, however, said he does not solicit or receive much campaign money from his law firm's clients, because they usually are too conservative for the candidates he favors. Mostly, he raises money from other lobbyists and their political action committees. Federal records also show he had given more than $7,000 of his own money by mid-1980 for that year's election.

Boggs said "people like me frankly resent" the growth of for-profit fund-raising companies, especially when these professionals ask him to help out as a volunteer. "These are hard political dollars to raise, and you don't like seeing them going to people who basically are just getting a percentage."

J. D. Williams, whose law firm represents such clients as Litton Industries, Brown and Root, and American Medicorp, said there are "numerous, frequent" occasions when he will help a candidate with a bit of advice — or a few phone calls to his highly reputed list of lobbying contacts. "If it's somebody that I want to give to, I give to them personally and a lot of times we will make recommendations to clients, suggestions as to where they perhaps want to consider giving," Williams said.

Williams' firm also maintains its own PAC, financed by the partners, which donated to at least 22 candidates in the 1980 elections. And Williams gives liberally from his own pocket — more than $10,000 to 1980 campaigns as of mid-May 1980, according to FEC records.

Victor Kamber probably is the best known money raiser for organized labor, putting on 12 to 15 fund-raisers a year for House and Senate candidates. Formerly political operative for the AFL-CIO Building and Construction Trades Department, he opened his own office as a consultant in 1980 but said he would continue to do unpaid fund raising for friends — his own and labor's. His loyalties are mostly to Democrats, though sometimes he harvests campaign money for Republicans. He raised $40,000 for then-Sen. Jacob K. Javits, R-N.Y., at a $1,000-a-head dinner prior to the 1980 election. In 1979 he did one for Sen. Bob Packwood, R-Ore., raising some hackles among Oregon labor groups who were still waiting to see who the Democratic challenger would be. Kamber explained that the Packwood event was designed to alert Republicans that they, too, can reap financial rewards for helping labor on its major issues.

Kamber favors public financing of congressional elections to end reliance on special interest money, but "as long as that's the system we have, and as long as the other side is doing it, I'm going to do the best job I can."

Several fund-raising professionals offer their services only to candidates of one party. Bradley Sean

... The Experts Candidates Call for Help

O'Leary, president of the Response Marketing Group, works exclusively for Republican senators, and says they get a hefty discount from his usual commercial marketing work. Prior to the 1980 election, O'Leary stated as his goal "control of the U.S. Senate for the Republican Party. That's all I'm interested in. I make more money at the other things I do, but that's the only way I can afford to do the political things." O'Leary sees the Washington fund-raiser as one part of a two-year-long candidate marketing plan; his program for a campaign often will run to more than 400 pages and include mail solicitation and other techniques.

Among Democrats, the most experienced freelance arranger is probably Esther Coopersmith. Sen. William Proxmire, D-Wis., once called her "the den mother of all political fund-raisers." Coopersmith does not charge for her labors. In the 1980 elections, she raised money for Sen. Alan Cranston, D-Calif., as well as the unsuccessful campaigns of President Carter and Democratic Sens. Gaylord Nelson, Wis.; Birch Bayh, Ind.; and Frank Church, Idaho.

She boasts of "the great gift God has given me" for raising money. She first used that gift at the age of 17 in an Estes Kefauver campaign. Coopersmith came to Washington in about 1956, and was a pioneer of the use of political celebrities and rarely glimpsed private homes to lure donors. "If I went into this as a business, I'd really be paid very, very well," she said.

The Americans for Constitutional Action may be the foremost conservative political group in the field of fund-raising events. ACA Chairman Charlene Baker Craycraft will organize 20 or 30 events a year, usually upon request from candidates who score well in ACA's annual conservative vote rating.

ACA has a $100,000 annual budget for compiling its ratings and helping candidates find money, she said. In the 1978 election, it raised about $700,000 for conservative candidates, about 90 percent of that through Washington fund-raisers. Craycraft is inclined to scoff at "instant experts" who raise money only for pay (often they "can't get past the secretary" of a potential donor), and at members who rely on informal groups of lobbyists to drum up donations (they are too busy to devote full time to fund raising).

Several firms in Washington will arrange all or part of a fund-raiser for a fee. Nancy Cole of Fundraisers Unlimited is a 10-year veteran who will work for anyone, regardless of party. Her list of about 20 campaigns for which she worked in the 1980 election included those of Reps. Tom Bevill, D-Ala.; Matthew J. Rinaldo, R-N.J.; and Charles Wilson, D-Texas. She also worked for the unsuccessful campaigns of then-Reps. Bob Carr, D-Mich., and John Buchanan, R-Ala. She also said she prefers to

Lawyer-lobbyist J. D. Williams, center, and his wife at a party with Vice President Walter F. Mondale during the Carter administration.

handle the entire event, from preparing a mailing list and organizing a committee of lobbyist-helpers, to booking the caterer and collecting the checks. She charges about $2,000 on top of expenses.

Two newer entries in the field are PAC Associates and PAC Information Services, both organized within the year before the 1980 elections. They have computerized lists of PACs, broken down by area of interest and past giving, and offer services ranging from direct mail solicitation and targeted invitations to "full service" fund raising.

William P. Steponkus of PAC Associates, who has worked for Republicans in Congress and the White House, said his firm handles only GOP clients. The company was involved in a dozen 1980 campaigns, including those of Guy Vander Jagt, R-Mich., and Henson Moore, R-La. Steponkus said the typical price of preparing and sending invitations to an extensive, tailored list of PACs is around $5,000, including postage.

Michael deBlois of PAC Information Services said his group is non-partisan, a claim supported by his list of Senate clients in 1980. PAC Information Services also will arrange fund-raisers outside of Washington. "For a senator sitting on the Finance Committee, for example, there may not be much interest in that committee assignment in his state, but there would be in Chicago or New York," deBlois said. "We go where the greatest potential dollars are."

Crab Soup or Liz Taylor, In Fund Raising...

Walter Mondale may have been the vice president to you, but to a fund-raising expert during the 1980 campaign he was a great gimmick. Like crab soup, Liz Taylor or a day at the circus.

With hundreds of congressional candidates competing every election year to attract paying guests to Washington fund-raising events, it is no longer enough to offer tiny meatballs, watery cocktails and the over-familiar atmosphere of the Democratic or Republican clubs on Capitol Hill, say experts in the field.

While the biggest draw is still the opportunity to bend the ears of members of Congress and their staffs, fund-raisers say, it helps to have a celebrity, an exclusive location, an unusual menu or a bit of song and dance — a gimmick.

"On July 4 last year, Americans spent $610 million on fireworks," said Bradley Sean O'Leary, president of Response Marketing Group in Washington. "That's compared to about $400 million spent every two years to elect a Congress. I've got to say that cracking the entertainment dollar is easier than competing for the political dollar. If you give them more bang for the buck, you have a better chance at those dollars."

O'Leary is remembered in fund-raising circles as the man who had John Wayne enter a 1972 Nixon-Agnew fund-raiser riding shotgun on a stagecoach drawn by four white Belgian horses. Wayne's dramatic entrance brought the entire, formally attired crowd to its feet, jumping onto table tops and cheering wildly.

Regional Themes

Probably the most common gimmick in Washington these days is a party with a regional theme. Ted Miller, general manager of the Capitol Hill Club, said he would suggest ham and bourbon for a Kentucky congressman, salmon and crab for an Alaskan, and, of course, chili for a Texan. Nevada Democrat James Santini evokes the Wild West with an annual banquet of buffalo, quail, venison and other game,

while Louisianan John B. Breaux, D, feeds his contributors Cajun food.

Marty Russo, D-Ill., who is of Italian descent, featured Italian food. William H. Gray III, D-Pa., who is black, set one end of a banquet table with ribs, black-eyed peas and collard greens, the other end with roast beef. Barbara A. Mikulski, D-Md., served Maryland fried chicken and crab soup, while William Lehman, D-Fla., imports stone crabs from a famous Miami restaurant. In a more homey touch, Don Bailey, D-Pa., had various ethnic groups from his district bring in their traditional dishes for a fund-raising potluck.

Rep. Tony Coelho, D-Calif., topped the usual limits for freshman fund-raisers by distributing individual bottles of California wine, each labeled with the names of Coelho and the contributor.

Clowns, Midgets and Showgirls

One of the more unusual non-culinary gimmicks is Rep. Andy Ireland's, D-Fla., annual trip to the circus. When the Ringling Bros. and Barnum & Bailey Circus, which winters in Ireland's district, comes to Washington, the congressman books a block of tickets, puts up a tent beside the D.C. Armory, and arranges for clowns, midgets and showgirls to come over and entertain the crowd before showtime. At $250 for a lobbyist and his family, the event brings in about $20,000, according to an Ireland aide.

Rep. James J. Howard, D-N.J., once rented a boat and cruised his fund-raiser down the Potomac River. House Majority Leader Jim Wright's, D-Texas, annual, multi-candidates soirée, which Common Cause has dubbed "the Super Bowl of fund-raisers," is usually an opportunity to see members of Congress let down their hair. In 1980 Rep. Howard provided the entertainment, singing his version of the mining song "Sixteen Tons" — bewailing the "Sixteen Hours" in a congressman's workday.

When Rep. Bella S. Abzug, D-N.Y. (1971-77), ran for the Senate in 1976, she rented a theater and showed her husband's film of a trip 10 congress-

"This town works on personal relationships," fund-raiser Israel said. "Anytime there's an opportunity to develop those relationships, it's a plus.

"The most anybody figures they can get in this business is access. You can't buy a vote. What you can do is say, 'Listen, I've helped you. Now let me make my case, and then you can make up your mind at least having heard my side of the story.'"

Officials of the American Trucking Associations' PAC, for example, go to almost every fund-raiser they are invited

to. "We're not that interested in whether the man's a liberal, conservative, Democrat or Republican," said lobbyist John M. Kinnaird. "We're just interested in whether he is friendly or has an open mind on the issues we're concerned with."

On the other side are the groups hoping to funnel their contributions so effectively that the balance of thought in Congress eventually will be tipped toward their point of view. For example, BIPAC — the Business-Industry PAC — intended to dole out its 1980 campaign war chest of

...Candidates Find You Gotta Have a Gimmick

Poster for Rep. Andy Ireland's Circus Fund-raiser

women took to China — home movies at up to $100 a head.

Star Quality

A star of show business or politics, or an invitation to a rarely viewed home, usually will draw a crowd in Washington.

Sen. Edward M. Kennedy, D-Mass., can count on plenty of takers when he opens his home for a fund-raiser, as he has on a few occasions. Wealthy Washington socialite Anna C. Chennault sometimes opens her plush penthouse for Republican candidates. And few people turn down invitations to the home of Sen. John W. Warner, R-Va. Before their separation, his wife, actress Elizabeth Taylor, was a tireless fund-raiser for GOP causes.

"She must have a heart of gold," a political action committee director remarked. "Sure, she choked on a chicken bone. She must eat 6,000 chickens a year."

For Democrats, former national party Chairman Robert S. Strauss is close to the top as a fund-raiser. A June 1979 "Mo Udall Birthday Party" in Tucson, Ariz., featuring Strauss, raised about $50,000, more than double the take at a Udall fund-raiser five months later in Washington.

One of the more profitable Washington fund-raisers by a challenger was held by Democrat Gene Wenstrom of Minnesota, who advertised Mondale as his star attraction. The vice president canceled at the last minute, but was booked for a later date. The guests got rain checks.

Fund-raisers: No Fun

Despite all the efforts to find gimmicks, fun fund-raisers are the exception rather than the rule, say many of the lobbyists who attend them. More often than not, the food, surroundings and company are predictable, and the events are all in a monotonous day's work.

"The food is generally all the same," said a lobbyist for a major corporation. "I don't think people go for the food. If they think that's why a guy does or doesn't show up, they're nuts."

In his 1978 campaign, Sen. Mark O. Hatfield, R-Ore., sensed the general distaste for conventional fund-raisers and found a way to cash in on it. He staged a $100-a-plate dinner without the dinner. He simply sent donors an engraved china plate.

$250,000 based solely on which candidate was "more business-oriented," according to the PAC's president, Joseph Fanelli. Candidates are judged on the basis of business groups' vote ratings and consultations with local businessmen, he said. "Since we don't lobby, we don't even think about access."

More often, the decision whether or not to buy is based on a combination of ideological compatibility and access. For example, Rohm and Haas Co.'s $10,000-a-year PAC account will go toward the support of "members who sup-

port our point of view," said Kenneth E. Davis, the chemical and plastics firm's director of government relations. "For those who support our point of view, they don't need to ask. Our natural inclination is to give to their campaigns."

However, "some members from marginal districts might come to us and ask to see it their way, and half the time we'll sympathize with them. We might need access to a guy or a committee report or some information. There are a lot of off-the-book relationships we have with guys whose business record with the Chamber of Commerce is a zero," Davis said.

Although back in the district a member might charge as little as $10 or $25 for a fund-raiser, Washington ticket prices rarely go below $100 each and often are much more, reflecting what the market will bear. A typical ticket that was $100 in 1977-78 was running $200 to $250 in 1979-80, lobbyists reported. The price of admission to a fund-raiser for an incumbent senator can cost as much as $1,000 a head.

The cost of throwing a fund-raiser in the Republicans' Capitol Hill Club or the Democrats' National Democratic Club can run as low as $15 a person for a simple reception with a bar and hors d'oeuvres, or as high as $50 a head for exotic food and a fancier bar, according to Ted Miller, general manager of the Capitol Hill Club.

Though a freshman incumbent's fund-raiser may typically rake in $8,500 or less, the take for a more senior member generally ranges between $15,000 and $60,000.

Fringe Benefits

Many PAC officials and lobbyists buy tickets to fund-raisers and then do not show up. But those who do get more than just clam dip and a weak drink. They can see and be seen by the member throwing the event, make business contacts, meet other lobbyists — and maybe even get in some legislative lobbying on the side.

Most lobbyists agree that it is bad form to buttonhole a member at his own fund-raisers, although the practice is not unheard of. However, the other senators and House members in attendance — invited to the reception as window dressing — are considered fair game.

"On a matter of great importance, it's unlikely you would go to a guy at his own fund-raiser and tell him you need his vote," said Rohm and Haas' Davis. "It's really amateurish and not the way to win his respect. If you have to go to the guy's fund-raiser to ask him for his vote, then you're already too late. You should have known before buying the ticket that he would give you his vote."

For the other incumbents in attendance, on the other hand, the rule seems to be that that is what they are there for. "I can be as direct as I want with those fellows because it's just like meeting someone at a cocktail party," Davis said. "If a guy can get his entire state delegation, or a whole bunch of senators to attend, that sets up a great opportunity to get to meet a guy you've been trying to reach for three weeks but you can't get past his legislative assistant," explained a transportation lobbyist.

Joseph Miller, who lobbies for the Marine Engineers Beneficial Association, said perhaps one fund-raiser out of four will produce a lobbying opportunity or a tidbit of intelligence; more often, he said, attendance is simply "showing the flag. It's telling the guy you cared enough to come."

Canapés and Conflicts

In the view of some lobbyists and members of Congress, the fund-raising minuet of lobbyists and candidates unduly influences the making of the nation's laws and creates frequent opportunities for conflicts of interest. Exactly what a lobbyist buys for his $250 ticket to a fund-raiser is disputed. At the most, it appears to assure access; at the least, it seems to give some peace of mind.

But in many cases the relationship is more complex — especially when a lobbyist actually organizes a fund-raiser or works on a fund-raising steering committee. Such assistance often blossoms from a one-time favor into a perennial relationship. Thomas Boggs, the Washington lawyer-lobbyist, said most of the 25 to 30 fund-raisers he helped organize for candidates in 1980 were for people he had helped year after year.

Moreover, according to an FEC spokesman, so long as the lobbyist asserts he did the work on his own time, it does not count as an in-kind campaign contribution. Thus while Boggs, according to *The Washington Post*, earns $165 an hour for his services, the time he donates to candidates need not be disclosed in any way. "Put yourself in his shoes," a fellow lobbyist said of Boggs. "He is one smart dude. There is nothing in it financially for him, but when he calls that member, you can be sure he'll get good access. My surprise is not with Boggs, but with the congressman who would let him do this for him. It's not illegal, but it's surprising."

Boggs, however, maintains that his role is little different from an entertainer offering his talent to a campaign. "Under the campaign laws, Frank Sinatra can donate his services to Ronald Reagan, which is probably worth half a million dollars for a one-night concert, which is certainly a lot greater than the $1,000 maximum you can give to a candidate," Boggs said in an interview.

William E. Timmons, a former assistant to Presidents Ford and Nixon and now a Washington lobbyist, said, "If I were a member, I would be more appreciative of a fellow who spent some time and effort at it, as opposed to just giving some money, especially when it's usually someone else's money."

But Timmons does not feel such time and effort are rewarded with extra influence. "I just think the rising costs of a campaign mean politicians have got to appeal to those who generally agree with their philosophy. I don't think there's anything sinister in that. I think that's just democracy working," he said.

Lawyer J. D. Williams, another well-known fund-raiser, said the fund-raising partnership of candidates and lobbyists is beneficial because "you not only get people's financial support, but you can develop relationships where you can get a lot of advice on how to be an effective member of the House, and how to advance your career and your constituents' interests."

Others are not as comfortable with this relationship between candidates and lobbyists. One representative of a major corporation pointed out that lobbyists on a company payroll must either take time off without pay or risk violating the law against corporate campaign contributions. "I just don't think that's a valid thing for us to be doing. I don't mind putting in a good word for some of my friends ... but where do you stop?"

A lobbyist who fought for a bill to contain hospital costs in 1979 — and lost — complained that an opposing lobbyist, Lucinda Williams of the Federation of American Hospitals, was helping to arrange fund-raisers for key congressmen during deliberations on the bill. "I happen to believe it's a good way to buy votes and make friends," the lobbyist said. "But who's to say her clientele wouldn't vote that way anyway?"

"I'm not helping anybody that I wouldn't have helped anyway," Williams replied. Noting that fund-raisers may take months to set up, she added, "How am I to know if the vote on whatever issue will be the same week?"

The Goldschmidt Fund-Raiser That Wasn't

A fund-raiser thrown by Rep. James J. Florio, D-N.J., prior to the 1980 elections, illustrates why fund-raisers are so popular with members of Congress and lobbyists alike.

The members' influence in writing laws may help persuade lobbyists to buy tickets. Lobbyists often willingly buy the tickets because they feel this may give them a favored status with the member in the future. Sometimes, though, this hoped-for relationship can go awry. A lobbyist may send his money to the wrong man. Or, occasionally, an influential Washington name may be misused, accidentally or otherwise. The Florio episode is a case in point.

As chairman of the House Commerce (now Energy and Commerce) Subcommittee on Transportation, Rep. Florio had jurisdiction over several key aspects of national transportation policy. The invitation to his March 10 fund-raising reception featured the seal of the Transportation Department and the message: "The Secretary of Transportation, Honorable Neil Goldschmidt, cordially invites you to join him for a reception for Congressman Jim Florio."

To a lobbyist interested in transportation matters, the presence of Goldschmidt alone was a sure-fire draw. But the invitation also was good for Florio's image because it made him appear so powerful that the transportation secretary would want to sponsor a fund-raiser for him. In the world of Washington influence peddling, a transportation lobbyist would think twice before ignoring such an event.

The strategy apparently worked, for Florio. The fund-raiser brought in $26,900 for his campaign.

But it was less of a success for at least one lobbyist, Frank P. Gallagher, president of the New Jersey Bus Association. He heard about the fund-raiser from American Bus Association (ABA) Governmental Affairs Director David H. Miller, who got the invitation at ABA's Washington headquarters.

Florio's subcommittee at the time was considering legislation authorizing funds for the completion of the Northeast passenger rail corridor. The subcommittee planned New Jersey field hearings on the legislation and Gallagher wanted to testify because the bus industry competes with passenger rail service in the Northeast corridor.

Despite the ticket purchase, however, Florio turned down Gallagher's plea. Buses, Florio told Gallagher, were under the jurisdiction of the Public Works Subcommittee on Surface Transportation, chaired by fellow New Jersey Democrat James J. Howard. Gallagher wrote Miller to thank him for the information about the Florio fund-raiser. He then told him of his failure to change Florio's mind. Finally, he added: "If you receive any invitation for a Jim Howard fund-raiser, please let us know."

Goldschmidt was secretary of transportation during the Carter administration. Although it appeared that he had sponsored the Florio event, in fact he was only an invited guest at a function put on by Florio's campaign committee. "There was some confusion about the fund-raiser because it gave the impression that Mr. Goldschmidt was the sponsor," a Transportation Department spokeswoman said. "Mr. Goldschmidt has never given a fund-raiser."

Florio's office referred the matter to campaign treasurer Tom Cucinotta, who said he had never seen the invitation and had played no role in its design. When a reporter described the invitation to him, he said: "There was a picture of the Transportation Department seal at the top? That doesn't sound too cool." Cucinotta added: "There was never any intention to convey the impression that he [Goldschmidt] was sponsoring the event. I guess I'd have to offer an apology if this impression was given."

The Secretary of Transportation

Honorable Neil Goldschmidt

cordially invites you

to join him

for a reception

for

Congressman Jim Florio

on March 10, 1980

at

The Reserve Officer's Club

One Constitution Avenue, N.E.

6 - 8 p.m.

RSVP   Price
Envelope Enclosed $250 per person

While Incumbents Rake the Money In...

October 17, 1979 — A lively crowd circles the hors d'oeuvre table in the Presidential Room of Washington's Mayflower Hotel, paying homage (at $1,000 a head) to Sen. Warren G. Magnuson, D-Wash., then chairman of the Senate Appropriations Committee and Senate president pro tempore.

Many of the Senate's big names are here — Kennedy, Byrd, Cranston, Jackson — surrounded by a Who's Who of Washington lobbyists. Brock Adams, former secretary of transportation and Washington state congressman, and now a lobbyist, mugs for a Seattle TV crew, pulling out his checkbook and signing over $1,000 to the Magnuson campaign.

The take for the evening: About $125,000.

April 17, 1980 — Magnuson's challenger, Washington Attorney General Slade Gorton, waits with his wife at the doorway to the Republican Capitol Hill Club. The contributors, who have paid $100 a head, trickle in, perhaps 30 paying guests, a few Republican senators, and enough non-paying friends to put a small dent in a huge round of beef.

Later, one of the lobbyists in attendance will implore a reporter not to use his name because "I don't want the company to get in trouble with Warren Magnuson. And I want to keep my job."

The take: $3,525.

Although the incumbent Magnuson, an old-fashioned New Deal, pork-barrel politician, lost in the 1980 election to the moderate Republican Gorton, his fund-raising experiences still serve as examples of one of the advantages of incumbency.

High Card

If campaign fund raising is a deck stacked against challengers, the Washington fund-raiser is one of the highest cards an incumbent can hold.

According to a Federal Election Commission study of the 1978 elections, political action committees give $3 to incumbents for every $1 they give challengers. And while there are no official figures to measure it, incumbents almost certainly get the lion's share of the money passed out at capital fund-raisers.

"Non-incumbents who come to Washington are frequently disappointed and, indeed, to a degree embittered by the lack of interest in their efforts here, because this town is just geared toward incumbents," said J. D. Williams, a lawyer-lobbyist and one of the city's best-known fund-raisers. "It's not a town of gamblers. Or even speculators."

Charlene Baker Craycraft, who organizes fund-raisers for the conservative Americans for Constitutional Action, estimates that of the 250 PACs she can count on to help conservative candidates, perhaps 25 will assist a challenger. "Washington really is a city full of people who want to get a little bit of mileage out of their contributions," she said.

The most valued mileage is the chance to talk to a powerful incumbent, and to have him remember that you helped his campaign. Because the number of PACs has grown, experts say there is more money for everyone in the capital, including non-incumbents. And some PACs, perhaps an increasing number, are more concerned with a candidate's philosophy than his power.

The Business-Industry PAC, for instance, which does not lobby, gave two-thirds of its money in the 1978 election to non-incumbents. The National Conservative PAC organized about 25 fund-raisers prior to the 1980 elections, almost all for challengers because, explained Chairman John T. Dolan, "By and large, we're more interested in changing the Congress than preserving it. And we're not interested in access."

But traditionally, Washington donors have preferred to use their money to build up useful friendships with members who have proved their value.

Rule of the Game

"Our basic rule," said John M. Kinnaird, vice president for government relations of the American Trucking Associations, "is that we normally would support the incumbent unless he's been totally anti-trucking in everything he's done. Why? Well, you avoid a lot of political problems. And then, why not

Since fund-raising and legislating seasons coincide, the timing may be happenstance, but sometimes it can be convenient for the lobbyist. For example, former building trades representative Victor Kamber's $1,000-a-head fund-raiser for then-Sen. Jacob Javits, R-N.Y., a member of the Labor and Public Welfare Committee, came when the committee was mulling over an occupational safety bill the union hotly opposed.

One senior House Democrat, however, said most members are extremely sensitive to the possibility of seeming to be unduly influenced by lobbyist-contributors. "There is a

very fine line in this business between soliciting support and engaging in even jocular attempts to gain favors in exchange for campaign contributions," he said. "Most members would not want the contribution if they thought it meant they were guaranteeing their support for a particular position, even if they already held that position."

Pressure from Members

From the lobbyists' point of view, sometimes the lawmaker exploits their relationship. A lobbyist invited to Rep. Duncan's 1979 fund-raiser was chagrined that the

...Challengers Often Find It More Difficult

support him? He's been there. You've gotten to know him. You've got that relationship. You just don't want to gamble on it. I don't."

"Challengers definitely have to work harder because before you give him money he has to establish his credibility by giving you an idea of what he's interested in and his stand on the issues," said another Washington lobbyist. "But the main reason incumbents get the money as opposed to challengers is that you don't want to alienate the incumbents."

The Washington fund-raiser is especially important to incumbents because it is a card that can be played early in the campaign. PACs that normally make their major giving decisions later on, usually have enough loose money so their Washington representative can attend fund-raisers early in the off-election year. This gives the incumbent a head start on the money necessary to reserve television time, hire a direct-mail specialist, and get a campaign organized.

One Challenger's Story

By most conventional wisdom, Slade Gorton represented the most credible challenger Magnuson had had in his seven races for the Senate. He was popular in the state, an energetic campaigner facing a 75-year-old incumbent, a moderate conservative running against a man long identified with government spending and regulation.

But in the race for dollars, Gorton gave himself an early handicap by declaring he would not accept any money from PACs. His intent was to dramatize Magnuson's reliance on PAC money; and he probably realized he could not compete with the incumbent in soliciting such safe-money bettors. Nonetheless, when Dallas Salisbury, an old friend who now runs an insurance research firm in Washington, proposed a Washington fund-raiser, Gorton went along.

Salisbury followed standard procedure, borrowing a mailing list from the Republican Senatorial Campaign Committee and cross-checking it with a PAC directory purchased from a local press. He sent out about 3,000 invitations, then rounded up some friends — mostly lawyers and lobbyists — to make more than 800 follow-up phone calls.

He ran into two problems, neither one unexpected. First, many lobbyists were not willing to come if their PACs could not pick up the tab. And second, many said they did not want to take on the chairman of the Appropriations Committee unless they were pretty sure he was going to lose. "They said, 'Are you out of your mind?'" Salisbury recalled on the evening of the fund-raiser.

Gorton said even some of the Republican senators who showed up to lend credence to his event "say they can't walk by [Magnuson] without him chewing their ears off." Two lobbyists who did attend both stressed afterwards that they had paid from their own pockets, as a personal gesture, after meeting Gorton and liking him. Both said their firms were contributing to Magnuson.

Though the Gorton fund-raiser did not raise much money, Salisbury said that — along with a fund-raising lunch in New York that raised an equivalent amount — it made Gorton's trip worthwhile. And he said it established some future contacts, useful especially when Magnuson seemed to be in trouble.

Still, as of March 31, 1980, according to FEC reports, Gorton's entire campaign had raised $82,191, about two-thirds of Magnuson's haul that one evening in October 1979.

Magnuson's event — sponsored by about 30 senators and promoted by a group of aides and lobbyists — drew money from scores of PACs and executives with interests before Appropriations and the Commerce Committee he used to chair. Magnuson's administrative assistant, Michael Steward, nevertheless disparaged the notion that his legislative power gave the senator a fund-raising advantage.

"I would presume it's because Magnuson has a strong record and people that are contributing to his campaign think he's the best candidate," Steward said.

---

invitation arrived shortly after his group had testified before Duncan's subcommittee, requesting an increase in the annual appropriations bill. The subcommittee did not mark up the bill until after Duncan's event.

That "made it uncomfortable," the lobbyist said. "Whether or not there was any pressure, we felt we should go." Duncan's executive secretary, Helen Burton, said the fund-raiser unavoidably had been rescheduled from an earlier date and its time was "rather fortuitous.... If they didn't want to participate, they didn't have to," she said. "If that is a problem, no one told me about it."

Rep. James M. Hanley, D-N.Y., chairman of the Post Office and Civil Service Committee, staged a June 1979 fund-raiser a few weeks after his committee drafted a bill to increase federal postal subsidies. The lion's share of the $40,000 he raised came from representatives of postal unions, magazine publishers, direct mail outfits and other groups with a special interest in the postal issues.

Hanley later announced he would retire at the end of 1980. An aide said the congressman had not decided what to do with the $39,812 in his campaign account, although under existing law he could declare it as income and keep

Getting the Money for an Expensive Race

On a damp April evening in spring 1980, Rep. Robert K. Dornan, R-Calif., looked out at the faces crammed tightly into the McLean, Va., basement of direct-mail wizard Richard A. Viguerie, and was pleased.

"Because of people like Richard Viguerie, because of people like you," he told the admiring faces, "we have raised more money in the off-year than any other congressman in the history of America."

On Dornan's left stood singer Pat Boone, who came as a personal favor to Dornan. Next to Boone stood Viguerie, who had opened up his home for this fund-raiser as "just one of those things I try to do to help the conservative movement."

For the price of a $100 ticket, the several hundred guests were able to crowd the basement bar, snack at hors d'oeuvres' and oysters, and knock off prodigious quantities of smoked salmon, chicken curry on rice, salad, coffee and pastries. They were allowed to poke their noses into every corner of Viguerie's oversized suburban home, shake hands and chat with the candidate, and get a pep talk from Boone. The reward: an estimated $50,000 in campaign funds.

The fund-raiser was just one part of a strategy Dornan expected to produce $600,000 by the end of May 1980. Through March, Dornan said he had raised about $450,000, most of it from direct-mail campaigns by two firms — one of them Viguerie's. These donations were being augmented by at least four fund-raisers, Dornan said.

In 1978 Dornan's 27th District had been the site of the closest, most expensive race in California that year. Dornan spent $291,762 to squeak to a 51 percent to 49 percent victory over Democratic opponent Carey Peck. Peck had spent $308,017 on the campaign, much of it raised with the help of his actor father, Gregory Peck.

For 1980 Dornan said he wanted to be better prepared. "Peck said he's going to raise $600,000," Dornan said. "I said, 'Richard [Viguerie], let's get going.'"

If the 1978 race seemed expensive, the outlays were petty cash compared with the 1980 expenditures of the two candidates. Dornan's fund-raising efforts paid off handsomely: He brought in $1,947,190 and spent all of it. Peck raised about half as much, $564,582, and reported expenditures of $559,315. The 1980 election outcome was much closer: Dornan won with 51 percent of the vote to Peck's 47 percent. A third-party candidate picked up the rest.

Although the figures were high in both elections, they were not out of line with the costs of a close race for a House seat. Both the 1978 and 1980 Dornan-Peck contests illustrate the skyrocketing costs of federal campaigning.

Federal Election Commission figures show that House candidates in 1978 spent $88 million on the November ballot, a 44 percent increase over the $60.9 million in 1976 expenditures. Moreover, spending on House elections between 1972 and 1978 rose 34 percent over the increase in the Consumer Price Index, according to a Harvard University study.

Together Dornan and Peck spent $599,779 in 1978, an average of $299,889 each. Not long ago a campaign in which two House candidates spent even a quarter million dollars was considered expensive. In 1972, 24 districts had campaigns that large. In 1976, 63 campaigns passed the $250,000 mark. By 1978, nearly a third of the House contests — 129 — cost more than $250,000.

A principal reason is that close races cost a lot of money, particularly in suburban districts such as Dornan's.

In individual spending, the Dornan-Peck race also was part of the growing tendency toward expensive House races. In 1976 there were just 15 House general election candidates whose individual campaigns cost more than $250,000. In 1978 the figure was 81.

For Dornan, the re-election costs were moving in a direction opposite to those of many colleagues; as a rule, the longer a member is around the House, the less costly a re-election campaign becomes. Members who were first elected in 1976, as was Dornan, spent an average of $143,000 to win re-election in 1978. For the 216 representatives elected before 1974, the average campaign cost just $87,000.

Fund-raisers would seem to be a good way to raise campaign dollars. Ticket sales for the Dornan reception in Viguerie's home were brisk. The party cost Dornan nothing because Viguerie donated the food and drink, and the site. On the other hand, direct-mail campaigns have expensive printing and postage costs, and only a small percentage of the letters produce a cash return.

Viguerie maintained nonetheless that direct mail was working much better for Dornan than were the Washington fund-raisers. "One gosh-awful lot of work went into that reception compared to what was raised," Viguerie said. "The fund-raiser is the old way to raise money. Direct mail is one of the key components of the campaign of the future."

"I suspect that the average reception probably will raise only two to three dollars for every dollar spent," Viguerie said. By comparison, he maintained that Dornan's direct-mail campaign was netting six to seven dollars for every dollar spent. The reason, he said, was that direct-mail campaigns return again and again to the same contributors, asking for more money. The people who give once, Viguerie said, are likely to give every time they are asked.

it, or give it to a charity. Another congressman who retired, Commerce Committee Chairman Harley O. Staggers, D-W.Va., raised $72,095 in October 1979 at a Washington fund-raiser. An aide said Staggers mailed all the money back to contributors. Staggers' fund-raiser came at a time when his committee and its subcommittees were weighing major bills on railroads, communications and health, and when he was expected to be a conferee on a bill governing the Federal Trade Commission. His event was heavily attended by groups interested in all of those bills.

"There's always a little pressure" to buy a ticket, commented one business lobbyist. "On the few occasions when the incumbent himself calls, you are under a lot of pressure to ante up. . . . Sometimes, I've had to sell my whole [PAC] committee on switching its position and giving to a guy, if I've felt his pitch was so strong that I felt that to say, 'no,' would really harm our interests," he said.

Other lobbyists said it is not unusual for members of Congress to prime the pump before a fund-raiser with not-so-subtle reminders of their past favors for interest groups. Sen. Gravel, for example, preceded his 1980 election fund-raiser invitation with a series of letters, on official stationery, to energy PACs, reminding them of his staunch opposition to an oil windfall profits tax as chairman of the Finance energy subcommittee.

Rep. Charles H. Wilson, D-Calif., invited donors to an April 1980 fund-raiser with the assurance that he would be moving to a position of "even greater influence" in Congress — referring to his growing seniority on the House Armed Services and Post Office committees. The fund-raiser came a few days after Wilson's attorneys had won a two-week delay in House disciplinary proceedings against the congressman. Nevertheless, Wilson lost in the California primary.

An energy lobbyist recounted an even less subtle come-on from a high-ranking member of the House Ways and Means Committee when the lobbyist visited the member's office to discuss a tax issue. "The first question out of his mouth was, 'You guys got a PAC?' It was sort of like that was the entry fee. . . . We said, 'Yes, we do, and we're still making up our minds,' and then we dropped it. . . ."

Several lobbyists say they find fund-raising solicitations especially annoying when they come from members who face little or no opposition for re-election. Rep. Richard Bolling, D-Mo., who faced token opposition and had had no serious contest since 1964, held a fund-raiser at the Democratic Club in October 1979, and a fund-raising dinner hosted by lobbyist and former Rep. Lloyd Meeds, D-Wash. (1965-79), in February 1980.

"Because a lot of [a member's] friends in interest groups have been asking what they can do to help . . . sometimes he'll hold an event just to get them off his back," said labor political operative Victor Kamber.

Constituent Loyalty

As a central feature of the larger phenomenon of PAC giving, the Washington fund-raiser also is subject to another criticism — that "nationalization" of campaign financing weakens a lawmaker's loyalties to his constituents back home. According to a 1979 Harvard University study, "As Washington has become the best place to raise campaign funds, a concomitant concern is the increasing detachment of candidates from their constituents."

One lobbyist who has worked and raised money for members of the House said reliance on Washington money is an increasingly touchy issue with incumbents. "It's something most of them are very, very careful about," she said. "But the fact of life is that they cannot raise enough money back home to wage an effective campaign."

Fund-raiser Statistics Hard to Uncover at FEC

Federal election law makes it difficult for the public to learn key details about congressional fund-raisers — including when and where they take place, who organizes them, who supplies the mailing lists for the invitations, who attends them and even who pays for the food and drinks. An examination by Congressional Quarterly of hundreds of campaign spending reports filed with the Federal Election Commission (FEC) indicates that while many candidates make it their business to detail how they raise their campaign dollars, others do not bother.

The Federal Election Campaign Act Amendments (FECA) of 1971 required each candidate for federal office to report to the FEC on a special form "the total amount of proceeds from the sale of tickets to each dinner, luncheon, rally and other fund-raising event." However, because all major campaign donors had to be listed on another FEC reporting form as well, many candidates simply did not file the special fund-raising event form. Because of FEC's limited staff, the requirement was not vigorously policed. And Congress voted to drop the separate form in 1979 amendments to the 1971 law. "One of the reasons they were dropped is that the commission found very little use for them," commented FEC spokesman Fred Eiland. "We're more concerned with full disclosure than with how the money was raised."

Campaign law also permits an individual to spend up to $1,000 on a candidate's campaign for food, beverages and "invitations" — including the cost of mailing lists and postage — without that money being counted as a reportable contribution. The reporting threshold originally was $500 but was raised to $1,000 in the 1979 amendments. In-kind contributions by an individual — such as the donation of one's time or home — do not have to be counted at all in computing money spent.

The net effect of the law is that a lobbyist can organize and hold a fund-raiser in his or her home and provide guests with up to $1,000 in food and drink without the event appearing in the candidate's FEC reports and without the lobbyist appearing in the reports as a contributor to the candidate's campaign.

Because of the criticism Washington fund-raising sometimes attracts, it often is a sensitive subject with members of Congress and those who attend the functions. Frequently reporters are barred, or at least discouraged, from attending; members do not put out press releases to their hometown papers announcing their fund-raisers or boasting of their success.

Rep. Don J. Pease, D-Ohio, was embarrassed in his 1978 campaign when a reporter for his hometown paper attended his Washington fund-raiser and wrote about the lobbyists in attendance. Pease started thinking there might be something to the criticism, and in 1980 he decided to forgo a Washington fund-raiser and work harder to gain individual donations from his district.

"I know it is true in most cases when members say they can accept money from a PAC and then turn around and vote against them," he said. "But I think there's still sort of an unspoken *quid pro quo* of some kind. Whether it's lending an ear, or more than lending an ear, I don't know." Pease said he found many of his colleagues also feel "uncomfortable" about Washington fund-raisers, but view them as "necessary evils" in these days of high-cost campaigning.

Despite the problems, the Washington fund-raiser is an institution that promises to continue playing a major role in the political process, if only because there is no consensus for an alternative. Common Cause, organized labor and many liberal congressmen have long argued that the answer is public financing of congressional elections, similar to that now available for presidential campaigns. They argue public financing would reduce the reliance on "interested" money.

At the other end of the spectrum, some conservatives, such as John T. Dolan of the National Conservative PAC (NCPAC), argue that the solution is to lift limits on individual donations to reduce dependence on special interest money. Asked if he considered the growth of Washington fund-raisers — and PAC spending in general — a healthy thing, Dolan said: "No, I guess I really don't. By mandating artificially low campaign spending limits, we have mandated precisely the thing the reformers were opposing. Now, their solution [public financing] is more poison."

The Harvard study leaned a long way in Dolan's direction by proposing that the limit on individual donations be raised from $1,000 to $3,000 per election. "In effect, the current law forces candidates to turn to corporate and labor PACs as well as to their personal bank accounts for the needed funds no longer available through the parties and from individual contributors," the study said. "At the same time, the limits on amounts individuals can contribute directly to candidates have served primarily to divert money into channels of organized giving." The report said raising the individual donation limit "would provide the best means to limit the potential influence of political action committees and personal wealth while simultaneously improving the flow of money into campaigns."

8

Congressional Rating Game

Rep. George Miller's brief fling with the Chamber of Commerce of the United States was over almost before it began. In 1981 the California Democrat scored 65 percent on the Chamber's annual index of business approval, based on his votes in 1980. While not exactly magna cum laude, it was a passing grade, more than double his career average. In 1982 Miller plummeted to a score of 11.

Miller's short stay on the business honor roll reflected changes — not in his behavior but in the rating system. The Chamber had altered its scoring technique three times in as many years.

It was the sort of aberration that explains why group ratings are viewed with skepticism by many politicians and analysts, and why many of the raters themselves preface their annual score cards with warnings to the reader.

On the following pages are the highlights of scores compiled by eight interest groups based on what they saw as key votes in 1981. The ratings are those of the Americans for Democratic Action (ADA), the Americans for Constitutional Action (ACA), the Chamber of Commerce of the United States (CCUS), the AFL-CIO, Public Citizen Congress Watch (PCCW), the League of Conservation Voters (LCV), the National Federation of Independent Business (NFIB) and the National Taxpayers Union (NTU).

Each of the eight is widely circulated and frequently cited in campaigns and press reports. Yet each has been accused at one time or another of being biased, fickle or misleading.

Caveats

While ratings often are used as a political shorthand to depict politicians as "liberal" or "pro-business" or "pro-environment," what they actually show is a good deal more limited. They measure how often a lawmaker voted the way the interest groups wanted on an imperfect, subjectively selected sample of votes.

"Please remember," the League of Conservation Voters wrote in a preface to its latest rating, "that these votes do not reflect your representative's total record. They are the tip of the iceberg and the tip may be deceiving."

The league cited Robert T. Stafford, R-Vt., (score: 47) and William Proxmire, D-Wis., (56) as two senators who "cannot be judged merely by chart scores which show only floor votes and do not reflect their outstanding work in Committee or leadership on Senate floor fights."

The Chamber of Commerce warned that its report "covers only a small percentage of the hundreds of floor votes cast during the congressional session. A thorough evaluation of the position of members of Congress can be made by examining their total voting records, in the committees and subcommittees on which they serve and on the floor."

The Chamber noted, for example, that it had lobbied in 1981 on a variety of small-business issues, including creation of export trading companies, delinquent government payment of contractors, and inventory accounting methods, but all of those were dealt with by voice votes or lopsided margins and thus not included in the study.

"We put all sorts of caveats on [our rating]," said Chamber Vice President R. Hilton Davis. "I don't know if anybody reads them."

The caveats usually are forgotten when ratings are used as ammunition in political campaigns.

In his unsuccessful 1982 campaign for the Republican senatorial nomination in New Jersey, for example, Jeffrey Bell used Rep. Millicent Fenwick's past high ADA ratings in advertisements portraying her as too liberal.

Fenwick, who won the nomination, in turn put out press releases touting her relatively high scores from NFIB (100) to show her support for small business, LCV (79) to show her environmental record, and the National Alliance of Senior Citizens (70) to show her standing with the elderly.

Fenwick's legislative assistant, Robert Grady, conceded the limitations of the ratings, but added, "Obviously if we get a high rating from a senior citizens' group, we think that's something the senior citizens in New Jersey ought to know."

Understandably, Fenwick did not issue a press release on her rating from the rival National *Council* of Senior Citizens, which gave her 30 percent. The council is a lobby group affiliated with the AFL-CIO. The alliance is a conservative group created mainly to counter the impression that politicians on the right are anti-elderly. The two ratings usually are mirror images of one another.

As the two senior ratings illustrate, there are enough competing score cards around so that almost any incumbent can find something to crow about. Ratings have proliferated, with more than 70 interest groups, from farmers to fundamentalists, regularly measuring members of Congress based on a sample of votes. Their value depends in large

part on how much the reader knows about the interest groups and what their views are.

A case in point: Candidates can point to high scores from the Chamber of Commerce or the National Taxpayers Union as evidence of "fiscal conservativism." But while NTU's position on spending is uncompromising — any vote to spend tax money is a "wrong" vote — the Chamber strongly supports federal spending for business-oriented programs such as nuclear development and export subsidies.

And Public Citizen, which watches Congress from the perspective of consumer advocate Ralph Nader and publishes a rating generally viewed as liberal, contends that a true fiscal conservative should show well on many of its selected votes — opposing farm price supports, public works projects and export loan subsidies.

"A classic conservative would get pluses from us on the corporate subsidy issues," said Public Citizen attorney Jay Angoff.

Changeability

Another problem with ratings is that interest groups' interests change. The American Conservative Union (ACU), for example, traditionally counted a vote to raise the federal debt ceiling — necessary to pay for the programs Congress has previously approved — as a black mark against members of Congress. But in 1981 conservative President Reagan supported an increase in the debt ceiling, and ACU dropped the issue from its scoring. ACA, the other major conservative group, stuck to tradition and counted the higher debt-ceiling vote against members.

In the early 1980s the Chamber of Commerce score cards became a prime example of erratic rating behavior, as Rep. Miller's fluctuating scores showed. In 1980 the Chamber rated the Senate on the basis of 11 decisive votes on its priority issues. One senator who came out poorly, J. Bennett Johnston, D-La., loudly protested that the sample was too small. The Chamber rewrote its score card, adding a few votes. That boosted Johnston's score but tarnished the Chamber's reputation for independence.

The following year the Chamber tried a "catchall" rating, tallying dozens of business-related votes without assigning any priority to major issues, and without weeding out votes decided by lopsided margins. This time the protests came from the House, where the scores of some conservatives sagged while those of several liberal lawmakers (such as George Miller) soared.

"It was a weird mix of votes that probably gave more weight to some issues where the Chamber's position was not totally conservative," Chamber Vice President Davis said.

In 1982, he said, the Chamber returned to "the way we used to do it in the old days." The Chamber selected votes that reflected its legislative priorities, mainly those where the winning margin was fairly close. But because so many of its selected votes were decided along party lines, Democrats accused the Chamber of favoring Republicans.

Partisanship

Partisan bias is a common complaint about ratings; that was especially true of 1981, when Reagan's program polarized the interest groups as much as it did Congress. The Chamber's 1981 rating, because it reflected the group's active lobbying on behalf of the Reagan program, gave Democrats unusually low scores.

Even more controversial was NFIB's small-business score card, which used just four votes in the House to measure support for small business. Three of the votes were on Reagan's efforts to cut spending, and the fourth was on his tax cut. NFIB lobbied with the president on all four. As a result, 90 percent of the Republicans in the House received ratings of 100, while 70 percent of the Democrats, including many longtime favorites of the small-business group, scored zero.

In May 1982, 100 Democratic House members wrote NFIB an angry letter, calling on the group to withdraw its score card. Contributing to the Democratic distress was the fact that NFIB traditionally leaned heavily on its ratings in deciding whom to support with money and endorsements at election time.

NFIB Deputy Director John J. Motley defended the rating as an accurate reflection of the group's preoccupation with Reagan's economic issues. "We opted for consistency even though we knew the wrath of God would come down upon us," he said. "Of course I feel very uncomfortable with a four-vote voting record.... But as far as whether those votes reflect where NFIB members were, I think they're tremendously accurate." Motley added, however, that NFIB would be updating its rating, including votes taken in 1982, before plunging into re-election campaigns. The NFIB rating system also had aroused controversy in the 1980 elections. *(Box, p. 79)*

Rep. Charles Whitley, D-N.C., said the Chamber and NFIB ratings ignored the fact that, by the time budget and tax bills reached the House floor, there was little difference between the Republican and Democratic alternatives; nonetheless, business groups sided with the Republicans.

Small Business Lobby Plays Trick or Treat

Groups that rate Congress typically hope to reap fringe benefits of publicity and power, but none has carried that wish as far as the National Federation of Independent Business (NFIB). The small-business lobby has a rating scheme that combines polling, computers, campaign gifts and pewter statuettes in an elaborate effort to build legislative influence.

"I like to say we have a complete system," boasted John J. Motley, NFIB deputy director.

Some rival business lobbyists and members of Congress have said less flattering things about the NFIB formula. "An extremely unfair and slanted voting index," was the judgment of Sen. Russell B. Long, D-La., who scored 42 in 1980 and 88 in 1981. But many high scorers revel in the rewards.

NFIB begins with a periodic polling of its 620,-000 members on upcoming issues to determine the federation's position. Each member of Congress is sent a breakdown of the poll results, including a computer printout list of all businessmen who responded from his state or district.

As a measure approaches a floor vote, NFIB first sends all members of Congress a personalized letter stating the group position and then a green-edged, oversized post card indicating that the issue will be a "key small business vote" and probably will appear in the annual rating.

At the end of a session, NFIB counts up the votes and publishes the results with all the fanfare it can muster. A member who scores 70 percent or better is declared a "Guardian of Small Business" and receives a pewter minuteman trophy. The award is accompanied, if the member wishes, with a publicity blitz aimed at hometown press.

When Rep. Berkley Bedell, D-Iowa, won his 1980 "guardian" statuette, he was in the midst of an apparently serious race for re-election. NFIB distributed a press release that produced stories in half the newspapers in his district, according to a Bedell aide.

The final component in NFIB's "system" is a political action committee, which in 1980 gave $217,222 to candidates. A 70 percent rating entitles an incumbent to an endorsement and, if he is in a close race, a contribution. Conversely, a score lower than 40 percent sends a donation to the challenger.

NFIB's rating scheme evidently has made some impression on Congress. Late in the 96th Congress (1979-81), according to one House leadership aide, some members were watching closely for small-business votes that might boost their scores before the election and help them fend off conservative challengers. "More than a few people knew where they stood, and how much they would have to come up to make 70 percent," the staffer said.

NFIB's Motley said, "I think the fact that we are tying a political reward-versus-punishment system to the small-business movement has sped up that move-ment dramatically."

Herbert Liebenson, president of the National Small Business Association, questioned whether the rating added significantly to NFIB's influence in the Capitol. "Sure, it gets them in the door . . . ," he said. "But most doors are open to us anyway." *(Small-business lobby, case study, p. 113)*

In September 1980 Sen. Long, then chairman of the Finance Committee, took the Senate floor to denounce the rating as "a flagrant misrepresentation of the work we have done in this Congress to help small business . . . biased, superficial and deceiving."

Long made no mention of his own 42 score. His complaint was that NFIB had given Gaylord Nelson, D-Wis. (1963-81), chairman of the Small Business Committee, the lowest rating in the Senate — 22. To question Nelson's devotion to small business, Long declared, was as preposterous as "to challenge the credentials of Jesus Christ as a moral leader to us Christians."

Liebenson of the Small Business Association agreed the Nelson rating was "a total distortion. . . . Just about everybody else in small business supported him and recognized what he had done."

But NFIB was unrepentant. The group shot off a reply to its Wisconsin members defending the rating and pointing to its pre-vote polling as justification for its stands. The letter raked Nelson's record over the coals, concluding the senator had "not been an effective or true champion of small business."

John J. Motley

Whitley had a career average of 65 on the Chamber score card, but scored only 39 in 1981. Two NFIB trophies in his office reflected his past high scores in the group's rating, but in 1981 he collected a zero.

"Historically, business people have always said to conservative Democrats, 'The thing we like about you is, you're not so partisan. You examine the issues, you don't just vote a party line,'" Whitley said. "The business community didn't do last year what it admired us conservative Democrats for doing — looking hard at the issues."

1981 Group Ratings

Following are sketches of the eight groups listed above and names of the members of Congress who scored highest or lowest for 1981 on the groups' score cards.

Americans for Democratic Action

Since 1947 ADA ratings have been a standard, if sometimes disputed, measure of the term "liberal." Early ratings focused on lawmakers' support of New Deal-like programs, and gradually grew to include support for a non-interventionist foreign policy.

For 1981 ADA selected 20 votes each in the House and Senate. In the Senate, there were 13 votes on domestic issues. ADA opposed spending cuts in a variety of social programs, supported targeting tax cuts to middle- and low-income taxpayers, and fought new limits on busing and abortion. In seven votes on defense and foreign policy issues, ADA opposed the sale of advanced aircraft to Saudi Arabia and funding of chemical weapons, the MX missile and the B-1 bomber; it favored limiting U.S. military aid to El Salvador, Chile and Angolan rebels.

The House votes covered many of the same issues, in addition to support for extending fair housing laws and key enforcement provisions of the Voting Rights Act and opposition to a bill to punish those who disclose the names of U.S. intelligence agents.

The ADA said it generally found a "reactionary" trend in congressional votes on domestic programs, but Congress "resisted the conservative tide" on foreign policy issues such as human rights and nuclear proliferation.

Below are the ADA's 1981 high and low scorers.

Senate High Scorers. Two Northern Democrats, Edward M. Kennedy, Mass., and Carl Levin, Mich., received perfect scores.

The highest-scoring Southern Democrat was Dale Bumpers, Ark., with 95 percent.

Lowell P. Weicker Jr., Conn., and Mark O. Hatfield, Ore., were the highest-scoring Republicans at 55 percent.

Senate Low Scorers. Eight Republicans received a zero score: Jeremiah Denton, Ala.; Barry Goldwater, Ariz.; Steven D. Symms, Idaho; John P. East and Jesse Helms, both N.C.; Strom Thurmond, S.C.; Jake Garn and Orrin G. Hatch, Utah.

Among Southern Democrats, Russell B. Long, La., and John C. Stennis, Miss., were the lowest scorers at 15 percent. Independent Harry F. Byrd Jr., Va., who caucuses with the Democrats, scored 10 percent.

Edward Zorinsky, Neb., was the lowest-scoring Northern Democrat at 20 percent.

House High Scorers. Fourteen representatives, all Northern Democrats, scored 100 percent: George Miller, Calif.; Sidney R. Yates, Ill.; Barbara Mikulski, Md.; Barney

Frank and Gerry E. Studds, both Mass.; Peter W. Rodino Jr., N.J.; Charles E. Schumer, Ted Weiss, Jonathan B. Bingham and Richard L. Ottinger, all N.Y.; John F. Seiberling, Ohio; Ron Wyden, Ore.; Robert W. Edgar, Pa.; and Mike Lowry, Wash.

Highest-scoring Southern Democrats were Mickey Leland, Texas, 95 percent; William Lehman, Fla., and Harold E. Ford, Tenn., both 85 percent.

The highest Republican score was 75 percent, received by Harold C. Hollenbeck, N.J. Stewart B. McKinney, Conn., Bill Green, N.Y., and Claudine Schneider, R.I., each scored 70 percent.

House Low Scorers. Forty-five members received zero scores. Thirty-five of them were Republicans.

Southern Democrats Richard C. Shelby, Ala.; Doug Barnard Jr., Ga.; W. J. "Billy" Tauzin and John B. Breaux, both La.; G. V. "Sonny" Montgomery, Miss.; Phil Gramm, Marvin Leath and Charles W. Stenholm, all Texas; and Robert W. Daniel Jr., Va., also received zero scores.

Bob Stump, Ariz., a Northern Democrat who planned to run as a Republican in 1982 for re-election to his House seat, received a zero score.

AFL-CIO

The organized labor umbrella group, which began rating members of Congress in 1955, claimed its rating represented "votes for or against the interests of workers."

As the AFL-CIO saw it, those interests included federal public works projects and regulation of competing imports, job-safety rules, social programs for the poor and jobless, union wage and bargaining rights, civil rights laws, and tax laws that share the wealth.

The selection of 15 House votes and 19 Senate votes in 1981 showed the labor federation's ideals under harsh attack. Most of the AFL-CIO's selected votes opposed initiatives of the Reagan administration.

The AFL-CIO was more supportive of the administration in foreign policy, but it included no foreign policy or defense spending votes in its 1981 scores.

Over the years, Democrats generally fared much better than Republicans in the AFL-CIO rating. The average House score in 1981 was 73 for Democrats, 18 for Republicans; in the Senate, 69 for Democrats, 17 for Republicans.

Below are the AFL-CIO's 1981 high and low scorers.

Senate High Scorers. Democrats Alan Cranston, Calif., Christopher J. Dodd, Conn., and Levin, Mich., scored 100 percent.

The highest-scoring Southern Democrats were Bumpers, Ark., 84 percent and Walter D. Huddleston, Ky., 68 percent.

High-scoring Republicans were Charles McC. Mathias, Md., 67 percent, and Weicker, Conn., 65 percent.

Senate Low Scorers. Four Republicans — William L. Armstrong, Colo., Richard G. Lugar and Dan Quayle, both Ind., and Alan K. Simpson, Wyo. — received a zero score.

Independent Harry Byrd, Va., scored 16 percent. Stennis, Miss., was the lowest-scoring Southern Democrat with 28 percent.

Nebraska's Zorinsky, 26 percent, and Wisconsin's Proxmire, 32 percent, were the lowest-scoring Northern Democrats.

House High Scorers. Twelve representatives received perfect scores. Northern Democrats were Julian C. Dixon, Calif.; Ray Kogovsek, Colo.; Daniel K. Akaka, Hawaii; Gus Savage, Ill.; William D. Ford, Mich.; Robert A.

Roe, N.J.; Benjamin S. Rosenthal, Shirley Chisholm and Robert Garcia, all N.Y.; and Joseph F. Smith, Pa.

Southern Democrats with perfect scores were Claude Pepper, Fla., and Ford, Tenn.

Harold C. Hollenbeck, N.J., was the highest-scoring Republican with 73 percent.

House Low Scorers. A total of 29 Republicans received zero scores.

Larry P. McDonald, Ga., was the only Southern Democrat to receive a zero rating.

Among Northern Democrats, Stump, Ariz., received a low score of 13 percent. James D. Santini, D-Nev., followed with 23 percent.

U.S. Chamber of Commerce

The ratings of the nation's biggest business lobby reflected its outspoken support for the Reagan economic program. The Chamber used 18 Senate votes, 13 of them on spending and tax issues in Reagan's program. Of 19 House votes, 12 related to spending cuts and two to the tax program.

On all but one of these votes the Chamber's position was the same as the administration's. The exception was a Senate vote on exempting military construction projects from the Davis-Bacon Act, which requires government contractors to pay the locally prevailing wage. The Chamber wanted Davis-Bacon waived, claiming it inflates construction costs; the administration disagreed.

Not surprisingly, Republicans fared much better than Democrats — even Democrats traditionally rated as pro-business — in the 1981 selection of votes.

Below are the Chamber's 1981 high and low scorers.

Senate High Scorers. Republican senators who received perfect scores were Denton, Ala.; Ted Stevens, Alaska; S. I. "Sam" Hayakawa, Calif.; Mack Mattingly, Ga.; Symms, Idaho; Robert Dole, Kan.; Paul Laxalt, Nev.; Harrison "Jack" Schmitt, N.M.; East and Helms, both N.C.; Thurmond, S.C.; John Tower, Texas; Hatch, Utah; John W. Warner, Va.; Simpson and Malcolm Wallop, both Wyo.

The highest-scoring Southern Democrat was Stennis, Miss., with 93 percent.

Zorinsky, Neb., received the highest score among Northern Democrats with 78 percent.

Senate Low Scorers. Three Northern Democrats received zero scores: Dodd, Conn., Levin, Mich., and Thomas F. Eagleton, Mo.

The lowest-scoring Southern Democrat was Bumpers, Ark., who received 24 percent.

Mathias, Md., trailed among GOP senators with 46 percent.

House High Scorers. Thirty-seven Republicans received scores of 100.

Southern Democrats Andy Ireland, Fla., and McDonald, Ga., also received perfect scores.

Northern Democrat Stump, Ariz., scored 95 percent.

House Low Scorers. Sixteen representatives were given zero scores. Northern Democrats were John L. Burton, Calif.; Ronald V. Dellums, Calif.; Savage, Ill.; Floyd Fithian, Ind.; Joseph D. Early and Brian J. Donnelly, both Mass.; John Conyers Jr. and George W. Crockett Jr., both Mich.; William Clay and Richard Bolling, both Mo.; Frank J. Guarini, N.J.; Rosenthal, Chisholm and Garcia, all N.Y.; and Mary Rose Oakar, Ohio.

Henry B. Gonzalez, Texas, was the only Southern Democrat with a zero score.

Low-scoring Republicans were James M. Jeffords, Vt., with 53, followed by Schneider, R.I., with 63 percent.

Americans for Constitutional Action

ACA began publishing ratings in 1958 as a counterpart to ADA. It is a conservative group that prides itself on its consistent adherence to the principles of limited government, free markets and anti-communist foreign policy.

In 1981 ACA used 21 Senate votes and 24 House votes. The group favored budget and tax cuts; school prayer; restrictions on busing, legal aid and food stamps; decontrol of natural gas; funding for the MX missile and B-1 bomber programs and selling advanced aircraft to Saudi Arabia. ACA opposed a new tax break for lawmakers, funding of the Tennessee-Tombigbee waterway, funding for public broadcasting and higher farm subsidies.

Democrats averaged 36 in the Senate and 29 in the House, compared with 67 for Senate Republicans and 75 for House Republicans.

Below are the ACA's 1981 high and low scorers.

Senate High Scorers. High-scoring Republicans were North Carolinians Helms, 95 percent, and East, 94 percent.

Independent Harry Byrd, Va., scored 95 percent.

David L. Boren, Okla., was given a 76 percent score, the highest among Southern Democrats.

Northern Democrat Zorinsky, Neb., received an 80 percent score, followed by Proxmire, Wis., with 71 percent.

Senate Low Scorers. Dodd, D-Conn., was the only senator to receive a zero score.

Southern Democrat Bumpers received a 15 percent score, followed by Ernest F. Hollings, S.C., with 29 percent.

Low-scoring Republicans were Weicker, Conn., 17 percent, and Mathias, Md., 26 percent.

House High Scorers. Six Republicans received perfect scores: Carlos J. Moorhead and William E. Dannemeyer, both Calif.; George Hansen, Idaho; Philip M. Crane, Ill.; Jim Jeffries, Kan.; and James V. Hansen, Utah.

McDonald, Ga., scored 100 percent, the highest among Southern Democrats. He was followed by Gramm, Texas, with 88 percent.

The highest-scoring Northern Democrat was Stump, Ariz., 91 percent.

House Low Scorers. Northern Democrats Phillip Burton, Calif.; Savage and Paul Simon, both Ill.; Rosenthal and Chisholm, both N.Y.; Louis Stokes, Ohio; and William H. Gray III, Pa., received zero scores.

Lehman, Fla., and Ford, Tenn., were the only Southern Democrats to receive zero scores.

Jeffords, Vt., scored 24 percent, the lowest among Republicans. He was followed by Green, N.Y., with a score of 25 percent.

League of Conservation Voters

LCV is a political committee organized in 1970 to give environmentalists some clout in elections. It makes campaign contributions and has organized get-out-the-vote drives for sympathetic candidates.

A governing board including lobbyists for many leading national environmental groups picks the LCV's key votes. The 1981 rating counted 16 Senate votes and 14 House votes.

Lawmakers scored favorably for opposing Reagan nominees such as Interior Secretary James G. Watt and Assistant Agriculture Secretary John B. Crowell. The LCV also rewarded votes against spending on water projects, synthetic fuels and nuclear power, and votes supporting work-place safety regulation and federal aid for solar power and energy conservation.

The league opposed deployment of the MX missile, arguing that the basing mode would cause environmental damage.

The average score for House Democrats was 63, House Republicans 32.

Senate High Scorers. Northern Democrats Joseph R. Biden Jr., Del., and Patrick J. Leahy, Vt., were the top scorers with 99 percent.

Among Southern Democrats, Bumpers, Ark., received the highest score, 79 percent.

The highest-scoring Republicans were John H. Chafee, R.I., 75 percent, and William S. Cohen, Maine, 72 percent.

Senate Low Scorers. The lowest-scoring senator was Schmitt, R-N.M., at 5 percent.

Howell Heflin, Ala., and Long, La., were the lowest-scoring Southern Democrats with 6 percent.

The Northern Democrat receiving the lowest score was Zorinsky, Neb., at 12 percent. He was followed by Dennis DeConcini, Ariz., with 31 percent.

House High Scorers. Twenty-one Northern Democrats received scores of 100. Southern Democrat Mike Synar, Okla., also received a perfect score.

Millicent Fenwick, N.J., and Schneider, R.I., were given scores of 79 percent, the highest for Republicans.

House Low Scorers. Republicans William L. Dickinson, Ala.; Eldon Rudd, Ariz.; John Paul Hammerschmidt, Ark.; John T. Myers, Ind.; James H. Quillen, John J. Duncan and Robin L. Beard, all of Tenn., received zero scores.

Ralph M. Hall, Texas, a Southern Democrat, also received a zero.

The lowest-scoring Northern Democrat was Stump, Ariz., with a zero score, followed by Beverly B. Byron, Md., who was given 17 percent.

Public Citizen Congress Watch

Public Citizen Congress Watch, a group founded by Ralph Nader, styles itself a consumer advocacy group, but the ratings go beyond consumer issues. Its selection of 30 House votes and 40 Senate votes in 1981 covered a wide range of spending, regulatory, tax, environmental and "government reform" issues.

Subsidies for business were a particular bugaboo to the group. Eight of the Senate votes and five of the House votes, for example, were in opposition to various farm price supports. The group also opposed funding for a variety of energy development projects and for the Export-Import Bank.

Public Citizen gave points to lawmakers who supported social programs for the poor, strong regulations on corporate behavior in such areas as antitrust law and health and safety programs, and efforts to make the tax system more progressive. The group opposed new pay raises and tax breaks for members of Congress.

Public Citizen attempted to correlate each member's score with his or her campaign contributions from business political action committees. The campaign gifts are not listed here. In general, Public Citizen found that lawmakers who scored above 80 in its index received an average of $13,000 or less in the House, and $20,000 or less in the Senate from business PACs during their most recent election campaigns. Those scoring below 20 averaged more

than $62,000 in the House, $264,000 in the Senate.

Senate High Scorers. Only one senator scored over 80 percent: Kennedy, D-Mass., 83 percent.

Bumpers, Ark., scored 55 percent, the highest among Southern Democrats.

Cohen, Maine, and Chafee, R.I., were the highest-scoring Republicans with 50 percent.

Senate Low Scorers. The lowest-scoring senators were Republicans James A. McClure, Idaho, and Tower, Texas, with 8 percent.

Louisiana's two senators, Long and J. Bennett Johnston, scored lowest among Southern Democrats at 10 percent.

John Melcher, Mont., and Howard W. Cannon, Nev., were given 25 percent, the lowest score for Northern Democrats.

House High Scorers. Northern Democrats Studds, Mass., and William M. Brodhead, Mich., received the highest score, 97 percent — except for Speaker Thomas P. O'Neill Jr., Mass., who was given a 100 percent score on the basis of a single vote.

The highest-scoring Southern Democrat was Gonzalez, Texas, at 67 percent.

Schneider, R.I., at 70 percent scored highest among Republicans.

House Low Scorers. Nine members received the low score of 3 percent. Republicans were Dickinson, Ala.; William M. Thomas, Calif.; Joe Skeen, N.M.; John L. Napier, S.C.; Quillen, Tenn.; Tom Loeffler, Texas; Thomas J. Bliley Jr. and J. Kenneth Robinson, both Va.

A Southern Democrat, Ireland, Fla., also received 3 percent.

Stump, Ariz., received the lowest score for a Northern Democrat: 7 percent. Byron, Md., received the next-lowest, 17 percent.

National Federation of Independent Business

The National Federation of Independent Business is the largest lobbying organization of small businesses, representing 500,000 members. The group is a conspicuous participant in the rating wars, because it accompanies its ratings with ruffles and flourishes and campaign gifts. A member who scores 70 percent or better receives a "Guardian of Small Business" trophy for his office, and becomes eligible for a donation from NFIB's campaign war chest if his re-election race is close. *(NFIB awards, box, p. 79)*

In 1981 NFIB used only four House votes, three on spending and one on taxes. The group used eight Senate votes, all but two on spending and taxes. In addition to the Senate economic votes, NFIB supported exempting military projects from the Davis-Bacon Act requirement that government contractors pay the prevailing local wage. It also backed a resolution urging that the next vacancy on the Federal Reserve Board be filled by someone knowledgeable about small business.

Senate High Scorers. Thirty-five Republicans received perfect scores.

Southern Democrats receiving scores of 100 percent were David Pryor, Ark.; Sam Nunn, Ga.; Stennis, Miss.; Boren, Okla.; and Lloyd Bentsen, Texas.

Independent Harry Byrd, Va., also scored 100.

Only one Northern Democrat, Zorinsky, Neb., received a perfect score.

Senate Low Scorers. Northern Democrats Dodd, Conn.; Kennedy, Mass.; Eagleton, Mo.; and Bill Bradley, N.J., were given the lowest score: 14 percent.

The Trail of the Dirty Dozen

In 1970 a newborn lobby group, Environmental Action (EA), mated two time-tested publicity concepts, the group rating and the wanted poster. The result was a hit list — the "Dirty Dozen" — that in one stroke gave congressmen fits, Environmental Action a reputation and other interest groups something to think about.

Like most raters, Environmental Action began with a selection of "key" votes. Then it picked 12 powerful members of Congress who recorded low scores and appeared to be vulnerable to a campaign challenge. Posters, press conferences and, later, paid advertisements vilified the dozen as enemies of the environment.

EA consultant Peter Harnik, who worked on four Dirty Dozen campaigns, said the tactic "was very effective at making congressmen think twice about certain votes. There were numerous examples of members or their staff calling and saying 'Is the congressman close to being on the list?' 'Is this vote going to be used to determine the list?' "

The influence of environmentalists in most races was impossible to measure. In the course of five elections, 52 incumbents made the Dirty Dozen, and 24 were defeated the same year. The House Republican Research Committee called EA's impact "impressively chilling." But a Dirty Dozen congressman from pro-development Oklahoma once reported EA's expenditures as a contribution to his campaign, claiming it helped more than it hurt.

The Dirty Dozen, in any event, did catch the eye of many other groups, and probably helped set a fashion in tactics. Environmental groups in Illinois, Wisconsin, Georgia and other states set up Dirty Dozen lists of their own. An industry group tried to counter

the campaign one year by giving "environmental" awards to an industry-favored "Sweet Sixteen."

Hit lists also became a conventional weapon in the arsenal of the New Right. A leading anti-abortion group called its targets "the Deadly Dozen." The National Conservative Political Action Committee (NCPAC), which elevated attack politics to a high-priced art in 1980, also gave some credit to its environmental forerunner. NCPAC Chairman John T. "Terry" Dolan said of the Dirty Dozen campaign, "What they have done is given us legitimacy, certainly."

The Dirty Dozen campaign finally fizzled for several reasons. The novelty wore off. Environmentalists found themselves with an awkward choice between attacking enemies too secure to be beaten or targeting vulnerable members of Congress who earned less objectionable records.

Also, Harnik said, "We found that congressmen come and go, while the vested interests live on. The new congressmen we helped elect started to look like their predecessors."

In 1980 EA dropped the Dirty Dozen and took up the "Filthy Five" — aimed at corporations with big campaign bankrolls and allegedly unsavory environmental records. The group asked candidates to sign a pledge to accept no campaign contributions from the five companies: Amoco, Dow Chemical Co., International Paper Co., Occidental Petroleum Corp. and Republic Steel Corp.

The success in the first year was "not overwhelming," Harnik said. Only 67 candidates signed the pledge, and both corporations and candidates were bitterly critical of the ploy. But Harnik said he believed that "like the Dirty Dozen, it will grow."

Bumpers, Ark., and Hollings, S.C., received 63 percent, the lowest among Southern Democrats.

Low-scoring Republicans were Weicker, Conn., and Mathias, Md., both with 50 percent.

House High Scorers. A total of 173 Republicans scored 100 percent.

Southern Democrats with perfect scores were Bill Nichols and Richard C. Shelby, both Ala.; Ireland, Fla.; Charles Hatcher, Larry McDonald, Billy Lee Evans and Doug Barnard Jr., all of Ga.; Jerry Huckaby, La.; Montgomery, Miss.; Sam B. Hall Jr., Gramm, Leath, Jack Hightower, Stenholm and Kent Hance, all Texas; and Daniel, Va.

Three Northern Democrats — Stump, Ariz., Byron, Md., and Santini, Nev. — also received perfect scores.

House Low Scorers. Zero scores were given to 142 Northern Democrats.

Twenty-nine Southern Democrats also scored zero.

Among Republicans, Schneider, R.I., Charles F. Dou-

gherty, Pa., and Jeffords, Vt., received low scores of 50 percent.

National Taxpayers Union

NTU produces one of the most controversial, but most widely reported, ratings. The group's methodology is unusual: Any vote that would result in an increase in federal spending is counted as negative, any vote that would cut taxes is rewarded, and issues with no measurable impact on spending or taxes are excluded.

The 1981 rating counted 151 House roll calls, and 231 Senate roll calls.

The rating discounts motives — a lawmaker who votes against a spending cut because he feels it does not cut enough will still lose a point with NTU. The organization claims, however, that by compiling all of the spending votes for a year, it discovers a pattern that is "a truly unbiased picture of congressional spending attitudes."

NTU considers a score of 68 percent or higher in the Senate and 57 percent or higher in the House "good." A score of 38 to 58 in the Senate and 32 to 44 in the House is "average." Lower scores mark a "big spender."

With a few exceptions, such as Wisconsin Sen. William Proxmire, Democrats fare worse than Republicans. The average Senate score was 38 for Democrats, 61 for Republicans. The average House score was 32 for Democrats, 51 for Republicans.

Senate High Scorers. Northern Democrat Proxmire, Wis., was the highest-scoring senator at 83 percent.

Independent Harry Byrd, Va., scored 78 percent.

Boren, Okla., was the highest-scoring Southern Democrat with 58 percent.

High scoring Republicans were Don Nickles, Okla., and Helms, N.C. with 76 percent.

Senate Low Scorers. Three Northern Democrats received the lowest scores: Cranston, Calif., 21 percent; Daniel K. Inouye, Hawaii, 22 percent; and Kennedy, Mass., 23 percent.

The lowest-scoring Southern Democrat was Wendell H. Ford, Ky., with 31 percent.

Mathias, Md., received the lowest score among Republicans, 35 percent.

House High Scorers. Only one member scored over 90 percent: Ron Paul, R-Texas, 94 percent. Other high-scoring Republicans were Daniel B. Crane and Philip M. Crane, both Ill., with 75 percent.

Southern Democrat McDonald, Ga., received 81 percent.

The highest-scoring Northern Democrat was Stump, Ariz., with 63 percent.

House Low Scorers. Two Southern Democrats received the study's lowest scores: Gonzalez, Texas, 14 percent, and Pepper, Fla., 15 percent.

Northern Democrats Clement J. Zablocki, Wis., and Vic Fazio, Calif., received scores of 16 percent.

The lowest-scoring Republican was Benjamin A. Gilman, N.Y., with 31 percent.

Case Studies

Weapons Industry Lobby

On the patio of the Washington Sheraton Hotel, Army officers look over the latest in tanks to the tune of a tape-recorded sales pitch. Nearby, in the exhibit hall, visitors from the Pentagon or Capitol Hill can drive a helicopter simulator, test the heft of a submachine gun or watch fighter jets dance across a screen to disco music. Magicians perform card tricks and make rubber balls appear. ("Say the magic words, 'United Technologies.'")

A model in hip-hugging custom fatigues pours free coffee, but those with a nose for something stronger find their way upstairs to one of the corporate hospitality suites.

Welcome to the scene at the 1980 annual meeting of the Association of the U.S. Army, an organization of service alumni and civilians interested in Army activities. For defense contractors, the meeting and similar events sponsored by the other service associations were obligatory stops on the military hardware sales circuit.

Such razzle-dazzle was expensive (companies could pay as much as $8,000 just for floor space), and probably had a minuscule effect on U.S. military procurement. But as one exhibitor put it, between plugs for his company's tank-mounted anti-aircraft gun, in marketing weapons "everything counts." His competitor across the exhibit hall agreed: "Unfortunately, politics and visibility play a large part in decision-making."

In fiscal year 1981, Uncle Sam was a customer with a $61 billion budget for military procurement, research and development approved by Congress. The amount grew as members of Congress acceded to the Reagan administration's call for higher defense spending. The amount budgeted for fiscal 1982 increased to $85 billion.

Defense companies maintained substantial Washington offices, including large marketing and government relations staffs, to help steer that money their way. *(Top 18 defense contractors, box, p. 89)*

How Much Influence?

How much influence do defense contractors have over the way national defense money is spent? The answers range from those who believe there is a powerful defense cabal made up of arms lobbyists, hardware-happy military brass and pork-barreling congressmen, to the other extreme, such as the Senate specialist in defense budgets who called the industry's lobbying so "inept ... it's a miracle they ever get anything."

The New York-based Council on Economic Priorities (CEP), a group that considers current defense spending excessive, published a study of eight major aerospace firms in June 1981. Using such indices as lobbying staff, campaign giving, advertising and entertainment expenses, memberships on Pentagon advisory committees and the exchange of personnel between industry and government, the report concluded that the defense budget was caught up in a web of political influence. "It is this network that makes it almost impossible to have a debate about alternative weapons systems, defense strategy or defense priorities," said Gordon Adams, the group's director of research on government relations.

Yet many congressional defense aides and military contractors believed such studies exaggerated the clout of the industry. The consensus among those who handled defense legislation was that the industry's influence was probably marginal compared to other factors that shaped defense spending: conflicting views of what was good defense strategy; honest differences over the technical merits of various weapons; perceptions of public anxiety about national security; mistrust between Congress and the administration on defense issues; and partisan politics.

A defense contractor rarely got the ball rolling on a major weapons system; in tandem with members of Congress representing defense districts, the companies sought to exert influence on how much of a weapon the government bought, how quickly, and for how long.

Benign Role

Those who participated in the process often viewed the lobbyists' role as benign. Lobbyists were an indispensable source of technical information; although they tried to put the best face on their data, the smart ones usually were cautious to dispense reliable information, rather than jeopardize their credibility. "If they come in and try to b.s. their way through, they're dead ducks," said Rep. Jim Lloyd, D-Calif., an Armed Services Committee member and friend of the aerospace industry.

The arms lobby tended to avoid policy debates — such as the desirable size of defense spending overall or strategic arms limitation — but concentrated instead on marketing its own products. Except for profit-related issues, such as the debate over the need for a Renegotiation Board to police cost overruns, the industry shied away from collec-

Display at Washington Arms Exhibit

tive exercises of muscle.

Nonetheless, there was no shortage of critics who said the industry shared the blame, at least indirectly, for a number of apparent problems with the American defense establishment.

• To those who felt the defense budget was too big and larded with waste, the industry loomed as a logical culprit. Several aides to members of Congress skeptical of defense spending said industry lobbying made it difficult to kill programs past their usefulness, to oppose new weaponry or to challenge cost overruns.

Contractors replied that other factors — a well-entrenched civil service of a million employees, the high cost of a volunteer army, accelerating retirement rates, the soaring price of oil — were more to blame for the cost of defense. Another reason, according to Richard K. Cook, Washington vice president of Lockheed, was that budget politics and congressional scrutiny had stretched the development time of new arms; in 1980 it took an average of 10 costly years to bring a weapon from the drawing board to the assembly line.

• Supporters of heavier defense spending complained that because the industry was so preoccupied with carving up the pie it did not push for overall increases in spending. "We have 1,200 corporate members, 300,000 individual members, and you can count almost on one hand the ones that are defense contractors," said Richard Sellers, director in 1980 of the Washington office of the American Security Council, a leading lobby for bigger defense budgets; his comments echoed similar criticism from Capitol Hill defense boosters and the Pentagon itself. "They're so attuned to next week's allocation of government money that they're not looking to the long-range national security interests of the country," Sellers added.

Hal W. Howes, vice president of Fairchild Industries in 1980 (and an individual member of the American Security Council), pleaded guilty: "Most of the defense industry people, like myself, have a full plate just trying to look after their own company's interests."

• Some felt the industry helped focus military debate on "sexy" items, to the neglect of skilled manpower, spare parts, ammunition, maintenance and the other, less glamorous components of defense. The complaint had gained popularity as military readiness became a keen issue in the preceding years.

"Hardware and R & D [research and development] have an impressive constituency," said Robert B. Pirie Jr.,

assistant defense secretary for manpower, reserve affairs and logistics in the Carter administration. "They are highly visible and identifiable as to congressional district. Mundane matters such as keeping the lights lit, the floors swept and the spare-parts bins full get pushed aside." Said a Senate defense aide: "[Lobbyists] push for hardware, and they find a receptive audience for hardware."

"We have to be concerned with O & M [operations and maintenance] and manpower; in the past we have not," conceded Lockheed's Cook. But he said the Armed Services committees intended to begin scrutinizing operations and maintenance as a separate item in the authorizing process for fiscal 1982, which "will make it much harder to play that game of grabbing money out of the O & M account."

• American and allied defense producers, eager to protect their markets, resisted standardization of weapons that some believed might make NATO more efficient. They also fought purchase of foreign-made weapons that might be superior.

One hotly disputed example was the Army's decision to buy Chrysler's XM-1 tank over the German-designed Leopard. "Had the Leopard been American, I think there's no question but the Army would have picked up the concept," said Lloyd Preslar of DGA International, which represented the foreign tank.

One defense expert with long experience on Capitol Hill and in the domestic defense industry said the Army probably should have been buying European trucks for troops stationed there. But, he added, "We haven't reached the political point of transferring those dollars and those jobs to Europe."

Hunting Lodges

In addition to these criticisms, the defense lobby periodically had undergone bursts of public scandal for its activities. In the mid-1970s, for example, press reports based on internal Pentagon audits disclosed that some contractors courted military and congressional personnel with parties at hunting lodges, free rides on corporate jets, football tickets and yacht rides. In some cases, by means of military contracts which allowed companies to bill the government for a portion of overhead expenses, the companies then extracted the costs of their wining and dining and other lobbying activities from the government itself.

The stories provoked a flurry of investigations, a sweeping series of audits by the Defense Contract Audit Agency (DCAA) and an effort to write a stricter Defense Department policy governing the legitimate business costs that could be billed to government contracts. The quest for a new policy quietly died in the Defense Department acquisitions office in 1980 after vociferous protests from the industry that it would be burdensome. Instead, the amount of Washington-office costs that companies were allowed to charge to the government would be, in effect, "negotiated" with Defense Department auditors.

While it was likely that taxpayers ended up subsidizing some lobbying, entertainment of potential customers was sharply curtailed in 1980, according to contractors, Pentagon auditors and congressional aides. Lobbyists still paid for a lot of lunches and some companies still maintained their traditional open-bar hospitality suites at service conventions, but the more lavish partying was restrained. "High press and low influence," was the way Gordon Adams of the Council on Economic Priorities described such activities.

"I think there's a new breed of lobbyist around," said

an aide to a senator often critical of the industry. "There's less of the slap-on-the-back, 'I've been dealing with you for 15 years, let's go duck hunting' kind of approach. Now it's, 'Here's a 20-page paper full of technical slides, charts showing the budget impact, a table on how it meets the threat situation and some language in case you'd like to introduce an amendment.' "

Year-Round Cycle

The quest for arms contracts did not begin in Congress, although it was most visible there. One key to securing production contracts, arms-makers said, was to get in on the ground floor by winning research and development contracts. The company that designed a weapons system often, not coincidentally, was best suited to build it.

Adams said his group's study of eight top aerospace firms found they got 25 percent of the military contracts during fiscal years 1970-79; in the same period, they won 37 percent of the research and development contracts, assuring their future foothold in the list of top contractors. Clark MacGregor, senior vice president of United Technologies Corp., said a company's best chance to influence a contract was in the field, where contractor personnel work side by side with military technicians reporting to Washington.

The marketing and lobbying of weaponry is a year-round cycle. When the services make up their initial budget proposals in the spring, contractors vie to have their products given high priority. Then they follow the budget up through the Department of Defense and the president's Office of Management and Budget (OMB).

"You try to convince the customer it will give them additional capability and be the most efficient use of their dollars," said Gordon H. Ochenrider, senior vice president of Grumman Aerospace. "You continually build up a rapport and a credibility. That's important. You give them bad information once, and forget it."

Assistant Defense Secretary Pirie, who sat on the department's committee for acquisitions review, said by October 1980 he already had been lobbied by all the manufacturers of high performance fighter planes on procurement plans for fiscal 1982. He doubted such contacts made much difference in the selection of major systems, such as aircraft, but said they could influence decisions on smaller items, such as electronic components or munitions.

When contractors went to Congress for help, it was usually with the tacit support of one of the services, which were not supposed to lobby themselves — especially for a program the Defense Department or White House had rejected. "The main role [contractors] served was in helping the services get what they wanted in the budget process," said a congressional aide who followed the defense budget. "Contractors have told me, 'The Army . . . told me to call you so we can prevent our plant from being closed.' "

Cook said that to sell or protect a program in Congress, it was "fundamental" to have an ally in the service. "It's rare, if ever, a contractor can conjure up a program the customer doesn't want," he explained.

Constituency

The most important weapon in a defense lobbyist's arsenal was his "constituency relationship" with members of Congress whose districts included company facilities. The degree to which companies prized this relationship was evident in their campaign giving. Even the most outspoken critics of defense spending received gifts from defense companies in their home districts. (Defense PACs, p. 91)

Top Eighteen Defense Contractors

Following is a list of the top 18 defense contractors, the amount of their contracts and their products in fiscal year 1981.

1. McDonnell Douglas Corp. $4.4 billion. Aircraft, including Air Force F-15 Eagle, F-4 Phantom, KC-10 cargo plane, and Navy F-18 Hornet fighter; and Harpoon and Dragon missiles.

2. United Technologies Corp. $3.8 billion. Aircraft engines and helicopters.

3. General Dynamics Corp. $3.4 billion. Air Force F-16 fighter planes, nuclear submarines, high-performance missile and gun systems.

4. General Electric Co. $3.0 billion. Aircraft engines, including one for the Navy F-18 fighter aircraft, helicopter engines, Minuteman missile and nuclear submarines.

5. Boeing Co. $2.7 billion. Research and development on missile and space systems, aircraft, Airborne Warning and Control Systems (AWACS) and cruise missiles.

6. Lockheed Corp. $2.7 billion. Trident and Polaris missile systems, C-130 Hercules helicopters, space vehicles.

7. Hughes Aircraft Co. $2.6 billion. Research and development for missile and space systems, radar and navigational aids, and missile remote control for the F-14.

8. Raytheon Co. $1.8 billion. Patriot, Hawk, and Sparrow missile systems.

9. Grumman Corp. $1.7 billion. Navy F-14, E-2, A-16 and EA-6B aircraft, and electronics for Air Force F-111 aircraft.

10. Chrysler Corp. $1.4 billion. M1 and M60 tanks; research and development for tank and other engines.

11. Litton Industries Inc. $1.4 billion. Guided missile cruisers and parts, and electronics and communications equipment.

12. Martin Marietta Corp. $1.3 billion. Missiles, including principal subcontractor role on the MX, rockets and satellites.

13. Philbro Corp. $1.2 billion. Petroleum.

14. Exxon Corp. $1.2 billion. Petroleum.

15. Tenneco Inc. $1.2 billion. Newport News Shipbuilding and Dry Dock subsidiary did work on nuclear submarines, and aircraft carriers.

16. Rockwell International Corp. $1.1 billion. Research on the B-1 aircraft, fourth stage of proposed MX missile and space shuttle orbiter. Electronics and communications equipment.

17. Westinghouse Electric Corp. $1.1 billion. Aircraft, nuclear reactor electronic systems.

18. FMC Corp. $1.1 billion. Infantry fighting vehicles, guided missile launchers, guns, and research and development for tank engines.

Lawmakers, too, understood the importance of defending home territory. Sen. Alan Cranston, D-Calif., may have been a liberal on most scorecards, but he was the foremost advocate of the B-1 bomber, made by California-based Rockwell International Corp. Rep. Thomas J. Downey, D-N.Y., noted for his attacks on defense spending, also strongly defended the merits of the F-14, made by Grumman Aerospace Corp. near his district. After Rep. George E. Brown Jr., D-Calif., an outspoken dove, became a supporter of the B-1, he explained his conversion with unusual candor: "If the B-1 was being built in some other state, and if I didn't have two Air Force bases and a lot of retired military people in my district who feel strongly about the B-1, I'd probably have voted the other way."

Constituent service was not restricted to the congressional arena. It could begin before a proposal reached Congress and continue after it supposedly was out of legislators' hands. According to one Senate aide who requested anonymity, General Dynamics solicited letters to the Army from its congressional allies making a pitch for the company's tank-mounted anti-aircraft gun, called DIVAD, a system with little support in the civilian hierarchy of the executive branch. The letters urged the Army to put the system high on its list of 1982 budget priorities.

"The company is trying to gin up a lot of interest so the Army will recognize it has enough support in Congress to be worth fighting for," the aide said. "If there's someone [in the service] who wants it, they use the letters for ammunition. A couple of letters can make a difference, because nobody wants to get Congress upset."

When the stakes were high, members of Congress even attempted to sway the final award of a contract on an approved weapon. According to a Senate source closely involved in one such episode, senators from California and Washington both telephoned Defense Secretary Harold Brown before he awarded the prime contract for production of the cruise missile to impress upon him the industrial capacities of their states. After Washington's Boeing won, the source said, the department steered some non-competitive production contracts to California's General Dynamics as a "consolation prize."

Rallying in Congress

Once a defense debate reached Congress, constituency became a more dominant factor. Rep. Downey, a former member of the House Armed Services Committee, said, "You can identify almost all the members [of the committee] by who they're representing. . . . It's not always a good place to be reasonable."

The story of the A-7 attack plane provided an example of this. Although secretaries of defense had tried for years to stop production of the A-7 attack plane, which they considered dated, the plane remained in the budget until 1981. The main reason was that an LTV Corp. subsidiary manufactured the aircraft in Texas and the Texas congressional delegation usually rallied to the company's support. A-7 proponents were joined by the Air National Guard, which found the plane useful for training purposes.

Ultimately, two key A-7 supporters, Senate Armed Services Committee Chairman John Tower, R-Texas, and the manufacturer itself, restrained their advocacy in deference to the budget-cutting needs of the administration late in 1981. Notwithstanding the enthusiasm of the Air National Guard, the A-7 was struck from the budget.

Fairchild's A-10, a tank-hunting bomber sold to the Air Force, was another airplane that came under regular assault in Congress. When it did, Fairchild's Howes and friends worked with members of Congress from New York and Maryland, where the plane was made, feeding them technical information and helping convince undecided members from other states.

Grumman had worked each year with New Yorkers in Congress to keep the F-14 assembly line going. In 1980 the House added $123 million to the fiscal 1981 appropriation to increase the purchase of F-14s from 24 to 30; an additional 30 planes were ordered for fiscal 1982.

General Electric Co., working with the Massachusetts delegation, capitalized on dissatisfaction with the engine a United Technologies subsidiary built for the F-18 fighter plane and won federal money to develop a competing engine. Speaker of the House Thomas P. O'Neill Jr. and Sen. Edward M. Kennedy, both D-Mass., joined in what UT's MacGregor called a "spirited contest" each year to continue funding GE's engine. "The Massachusetts people think GE's engine is the greatest thing since shoe polish," said Rep. Lloyd. "Why? Because it's made there."

MacGregor said former Sen. Thomas McIntyre, D-N.H. (1962-78), once told him of visiting a GE plant in his home state. Though the plant had nothing to do with aircraft, he was met in the plant manager's office by three officials of GE's aerospace division, eager to discuss the merits of their proposed engine.

Constituency also could make life uncomfortable for defense critics. Downey, having left the House Armed Services Committee in 1979 after his first two terms in Congress, said he always worried that his attack on a weapons system would result in reprisals aimed at Grumman's F-14. "You run the risk at some point of having people take retribution against the weapons systems built in your district if you're not a get-along, go-along guy," the congressman said.

In fact, Downey said, Grumman lobbyists often lobbied him on behalf of aircraft built by other companies because of that fear. "I wanted to cut money for the F-18 and the Grumman lobbyist would argue against it, though they made the competing plane, because they were concerned that if I went after it the reverse would happen," he said. Downey added that the awkwardness of his position helped persuade him to leave Armed Services to take a seat on the Ways and Means Committee.

Lockheed's Cook contended that the industry's clout was limited because the major concentrations of weapons production fell in a few states. "I don't think that our industry can lay claim to being among the top five or 10 employers in more than 100 congressional districts and maybe 10 or 12 states," he said. "I don't think we can rely on very many members of Congress, or even members of the Armed Services committees, to respond to us based on political considerations."

On an important weapon, however, contractors also mobilized the subcontractors who made components. Fairchild, in lobbying to keep the A-10 in the budget, enlisted support from General Electric, which made the engines and guns, or other subcontractors. "For some contractors, it is a large portion of their business," said Fairchild's Howes. "For others, it's not. They usually act accordingly."

When Rockwell was defending its B-1 against President Carter's opposition in 1976 and 1977, it was able to call on subcontractors in 47 states. One congressional source involved in the pro B-1 fight said subcontractors actually were selected partly for geographical distribution,

Defense PACs: Watchword Is Pragmatism

A defense lobbyist, who also helps handle his company's campaign giving, was asked in 1980 about his preference in the presidential race. "That's a difficult subject," he replied. "We sit here with a lot of insight and access to the White House. A new president gets in and we have to start all over again.... On the other hand, Reagan says he would kick up defense spending, and that would be good for the industry. So I guess you'd say I've got mixed emotions."

So mixed were his emotions that his company's political action committee (PAC) gave money both to President Carter and his opponent Ronald Reagan. Back in the primaries, the company had contributed to other hopefuls, including Sen. Edward M. Kennedy, D-Mass., who was not known as a darling of the defense industry.

Investing in both sides of an election race, the lobbyist explained, was just good business. "If they don't win this time, they may be back later." He added that "money's not going to buy anyone, but you get their attention and you get the door open."

A 1980 review of federal campaign spending reports for 10 defense companies — all among the top 20 military contractors and each relying on the government for more than 25 percent of its sales in fiscal 1979 — showed a pattern of pragmatism. First in line for donations from most of the PACs were incumbents who sat on the committees of special interest to the industry, particularly the House and Senate Armed Services committees and the Appropriations subcommittees in charge of defense spending. Second, the arms PACs gave to members of Congress who had defense plants in their districts, cementing a constituency relationship. Finally, the PACs leaned toward candidates who campaigned on a pro-business, pro-defense platform.

However, this ideological leaning frequently was sacrificed to the more pragmatic goal of good relations. Clark MacGregor, senior vice president of United Technologies (UT), explained that his company's PAC had two longstanding aims: "To elect a more business-oriented and national defense-conscious Congress ... and to improve our relationship with the congressmen and senators from areas where we have plants and people." But the goals sometimes were in conflict.

"We frequently find people [in UT plants] urge us to support an incumbent or a challenger whose philosophy may not accord with our long-range objectives." Usually, he said, the PAC abided by their recommendation. "It's only natural for people to work with those who work with them," concurred Hal W. Howes of Fairchild Industries (not one of the 10 surveyed). "If you have a member who is absolutely unresponsive, you might support a challenger. By and large, our philosophy is to be loyal to our delegation members."

A striking contrast to these 10 PACs was the one representing Boeing Co., the seventh-ranked defense contractor. Boeing's PAC simply passed along contributions earmarked by the employees who gave them. The PAC itself made no decisions on campaign gifts.

Here are a few examples of the pragmatic investment strategies of the 10 defense PACs surveyed:

● Of the nine PACs that gave to presidential candidates in 1980, all contributed to the Carter-Mondale campaign. Seven also gave to Reagan. During the primary season, Republicans George Bush and Sen. Howard H. Baker Jr., Tenn., each got money from five of the PACs, Democrat Kennedy and GOP contender John B. Connally from four. Grumman Aerospace gave at least $2,000 each to seven presidential candidates.

● Some of the PACs also hedged their bets in congressional races of 1980. Grumman, headquartered in New York, gave the limit ($5,000) to Sen. Jacob K. Javits, R-N.Y. (1957-81), and his primary challenger, Alfonse D'Amato, who ended up winning the general election. An official of the company said in October the PAC had just contributed $2,000 to the Democratic nominee in that race, Rep. Elizabeth Holtzman (1973-81).

Litton Industries, based in California, gave to both sides in two heated races there: $500 to Sen. Alan Cranston, D, and $1,000 to losing challenger Paul Gann, R; $900 to Rep. James C. Corman, D (1961-81), and $1,000 to successful challenger Bobbi Fiedler, R. General Dynamics and Hughes Aircraft Co. both gave to incumbent Sen. John C. Culver, D-Iowa (1975-81), and his successful challenger, Rep. Charles E. Grassley, R.

● Several incumbents painted by their campaign opponents as soft on defense were among the biggest recipients of defense PAC money, either because of key committee assignments or because they represented districts with heavy defense employment. The 10 PACs reviewed, according to FEC summaries, gave $10,125 to Cranston; $6,500 to Javits; $6,200 to Corman; $6,050 to Sen. Gary Hart, D-Colo.; $5,500 to Sen. Charles McC. Mathias Jr., R-Md., and $3,825 to Culver. Some gave smaller amounts to such liberals as Reps. Norman Y. Mineta, D-Calif.; Thomas J. Downey, D-N.Y.; Timothy E. Wirth, D-Colo.; Patricia Schroeder, D-Colo.; Bob Carr, D-Mich. (1975-81), and Sens. Patrick J. Leahy, D-Vt.; John A. Durkin, D-N.H. (1975-80), and George McGovern, D-S.D. (1963-81).

● Apparently, most of the companies had not decided that one political party better represented their interests than the other. Only three of the PACs showed a strong (2-1 or better) preference for the candidates of one party: Raytheon Co. (for Democrats) and Litton Industries and United Technologies (for Republicans). UT's MacGregor described the evenhanded generosity as "a gesture of our continuing commitment to the two-party system."

to provide political leverage. Rockwell Vice President William L. Clark said, "I've heard the charge. I don't think it's true."

True or not, the B-1 was killed in a battle that demonstrated the real-life limitations of contractor lobbying. "They [Rockwell] did everything that anybody is supposed to do when they lobby, and they lost," said a participant in the fight. "Presidential politics meant more than any lobbyist." Rockwell's congressional allies, however, did not give up entirely. In 1980 Cranston added money to the budget, over administration objections, aimed at development of a new manned bomber. One candidate, Cranston had hoped, would be a revival of the B-1.

Revolving Door

Another bond between the arms salesman and the customer was the revolving door — in this case, mostly a one-way door — between the industry and the government. Each year since 1970 the Defense Department has sent the Senate Armed Services Committee a little-noticed list of former or retired military personnel or former Pentagon civilian employees (GS-13 or above) who have gone to work for defense contractors, or vice versa. The 1980 report listed 1,623 defense employees who had moved to industry between 1977 and 1979; 79 reported having moved from industry to defense posts. Corresponding figures from 1979 to 1981 were 1,824 and 21. Most were engineers or technicians, but the report included an assortment of former officials involved in procurement, government relations or planning of future weapons.

The report did not include those who moved to or from policy-making jobs outside the Defense Department. UT's MacGregor, for instance, joined the company after 10 years as a GOP representative from Minnesota and tours of duty as President Richard Nixon's White House counsel and director of his re-election committee. "Personal friendship and personal associations make it easier for you to do business," he said. "If you've known somebody for a period of time, whether you're selling vacuum cleaners or whatever, people are more likely to listen to you than to someone they don't know."

MacGregor noted that Hugh E. Witt, UT's director of legislative liaison, came to the company in 1977 from OMB, where he was administrator for federal procurement policy.

"Hugh has maintained his friendships" at OMB and they help the company make its case at budget time, MacGregor said. Cook, at Lockheed, also came to the industry from the Nixon White House, where he was a deputy assistant after eight years as a congressional aide. Fairchild's Howes, formerly a lobbyist for the Air Force, could recite in 1980 the names of several former colleagues in the Air Force's congressional liaison office who had come to work for industry competitors.

There also was a steady flow from Capitol Hill to the industry. Two of many examples were Frank Slatinshek, former staff director of the House Armed Services Committee, and former Rep. Elford A. Cederberg, R-Mich. (1953-79), who had been the ranking minority member of the Appropriations Committee. Each man established his own consulting firm, specializing in defense. Slatinshek was a registered lobbyist for Grumman, United Technologies and General Dynamics; Cederberg lobbied for Grumman, UT and Martin Marietta.

Conflicts?

The interchange of personnel led to instances of alleged conflicts of interest. In one celebrated case, Malcolm Currie, a vice president for research and development at Hughes Aircraft Co., became director of defense research and engineering in the Nixon and Ford administrations, then moved back to Hughes. While at the Pentagon, according to Rep. Les Aspin, D-Wis., Currie was involved in decisions to buy the Condor and Roland missiles, both projects partly performed by Hughes.

In 1980 John Stirk, defense adviser to Senator Robert Morgan, D-N.C. (1975-81), was hired away by General Dynamics at the height of debate over whether the military should adopt the company's FB-111 jet as a manned bomber. A reporter for the *Winston-Salem Journal* in North Carolina disclosed that Stirk, while on General Dynamics' payroll, continued to advise Morgan, who already had become a leading advocate of the FB-111.

Fred Kaplan, a defense specialist formerly on Aspin's staff, said a more serious consequence of this revolving door was that Defense Department planners all start to think alike. "They have been educated to believe that all problems are essentially technical problems. The companies exploit this sort of thinking," he said.

New Jobs for Old Members

The first phone calls came the morning after Rep. Herbert E. Harris II, D-Va. (1975-81), lost his seat in a narrow election defeat: Golly, Herb, callers said. That's a damn shame. A loss to the district and the country. You know, we could sure use a lawyer of your caliber. Let's have lunch and talk it over, hey? A week later, Harris had fairly firm offers of lobbying work from a government employees union and the mass transit industry, two interest groups he had defended energetically during his days in Congress. Harris prepared to step into one of Washington's dizziest revolving doors and emerge as a lobbyist. "Negligence work or divorce work is just not appealing to me," he told a reporter.

Harris' transition raised no eyebrows in the capital. Many members retired from service or cast off by their constituents found they could earn more, worry less and still inhale the heady fumes of politics by working *on* Congress rather than in it. In interviews and a review of public records, Congressional Quarterly turned up the names of more than 60 former members earning a living as counselors, strategists or persuaders for special interests in Washington in an election year that would augment their ranks. That list no doubt was incomplete.

The 95th Congress (1977-79) alone saw about a fourth of its 87 departing members remain in Washington working for corporations, trade groups, consulting companies or law firms with a legislative bent. Ex-members who discover a niche in Washington find they are surrounded by droves of former congressional staffers hiring out their Capitol Hill experience.

The gravitation of public officials into lobbying is nothing new, but two factors seem to have accelerated the revolving door. One is that today's Congress, with its demanding year-round schedule and ethics rules, cuts a member off from home and outside business interests. An ex-member may find he has little reason to go home, and little to sell (at least for his accustomed salary) but his knowledge of Congress. At the same time, businesses have steadily enlarged their Washington presence, responding to increasing government regulation, a dispersal of power in Congress and competition from public interest groups. That has expanded the demand for knowledgeable people to report on what the government is up to and attempt to influence it. "A former U.S. congressman, no matter how capable, is worth more in Washington than anyplace else —

considerably more," said Dan H. Kuykendall, a former Tennessee Republican representative (1967-75) with a string of lobbying clients. "Even those members who go to law firms back home end up getting sent back to Washington."

Mating Dance

The closing days of the 96th Congress (1979-81) were the occasion for a discreet mating dance between outgoing members and special interests. Members and senior committee staffers awaited the exploratory phone calls and luncheon invitations that might lead to job offers, or they extended feelers through friends already set up in business. More junior staffers sent out a blizzard of résumés and plaintive phone calls.

Though the change in administrations made Washington a tight job market, interviews with a sample of outgoing representatives and senators indicated that ex-members were still in demand. Rep. Robert Duncan, D-Ore. (1963-67, 1975-81), after losing his May 1980 primary was promptly enlisted to open a Washington office for a hometown law firm, a common move for ex-members who are lawyers. He said his duties would include some lobbying on transportation and natural resources, the issues that were the focus of his attention in Congress. "It will be not dissimilar from what I've been doing here: going down to the White House and trying to educate them on the problems of the West," Duncan said. Except, he noted, it will pay better.

Rep. William H. Harsha, R-Ohio (1961-81), retiring as the ranking Republican on the Public Works and Transportation Committee, planned to open a Washington consulting firm. He expected his clients to be truckers, airlines and other transportation interests. Rep. Bob Eckhardt (1967-81), a liberal Texas Democrat, said after being unseated that he was in "serious" discussions with two law firms about jobs that would include legislative advice and some lobbying in addition to litigation.

On the other hand, Rep. Lionel Van Deerlin, D-Calif. (1963-81), who was chairman of Commerce's Communications Subcommittee, declined invitations to talk over jobs in that field and decided instead to return to San Diego to teach and write. Van Deerlin, a former journalist, said a lawyer who stays in Washington "has something to sell other than influence. What do I have? All I have is the fact

Scores of Ex-Members Have Lobbied...

More than 60 past senators and representatives were watching the 96th Congress from the offices of law firms, corporations or trade associations in Washington. Here is a sample of those who went from Congress to the lobbying business, with varying success.

Carter Manasco

Back in February 1949, Congressional Quarterly surveyed the rolls of registered lobbyists and found 15 former senators and representatives. One of them was still at it at the end of 1980, his cigar-chomping visage a fixture on Capitol Hill.

"They say I'm the senior member of the lobbying racket," said Carter Manasco, an Alabama Democrat who lost his bid for a fifth House term in 1948. He spent 32 years consulting for the National Coal Association.

Manasco spent his days in the congressional press galleries and offices of committees with energy jurisdiction, swapping tales and absorbing intelligence. One Senate Energy Committee aide said Manasco almost never asked for anything, but was "kind of part of the wallpaper around here."

Manasco said part of the wisdom of lobbying was knowing when to lie low: "That gets a lot of lobbyists in trouble, just triple-hammering a guy that's already with him."

James G. O'Hara

As chairman of the House higher education subcommittee, a close friend of organized labor and a reputed legislative craftsman, James O'Hara, D-Mich. (1959-77), had several job prospects after he lost a Senate bid in 1976. His credentials were in order for a post in the new Carter administration or a college presidency. He could return to Michigan to practice law.

Instead, he took a partnership in the well-connected Washington, D.C., lobbying law firm of Patton, Boggs and Blow. "It became apparent to me that such skills as I had were more in the area of dealing with the bureaucracy and the Congress," recalled O'Hara. "I hadn't practiced back home in 18 years." The six-figure salary was also appealing.

O'Hara lobbied for General Motors on clean air legislation, Chrysler on its loan guarantee, California landowners fighting to protect irrigation subsidies, Alaska timbermen, the boating industry, the American Federation of Teachers and the Business Roundtable. He said he enjoyed the work and was "quite content" to be out of Congress because the issues there were no longer clear-cut and the work was thankless.

By contrast, O'Hara said of his fellow ex-member lobbyists, "there are guys around who have done very badly, and haven't made a connection, and are very unhappy with it." He added "they sort of fade from sight and end up back home."

John Y. McCollister

GOP Rep. McCollister (1971-76) intended to return to Nebraska after losing his Senate bid to Democrat Edward Zorinsky, he said, but the Firestone Tire and Rubber Co. persuaded him that with his business background and his free enterprise viewpoint he would be an ideal member of "the Business Roundtable environment" in Washington.

Wrong.

McCollister found the work of a Washington representative frustrating, and quit after two years to run his family's business.

One falling out with Firestone involved the Firestone 500 radial tires, which were ultimately recalled for safety defects. McCollister said he urged the company to be "more forthcoming" about problems with the tire, but corporate officials ignored his advice.

McCollister discovered that politicians and corporations sometimes make uneasy partners. A politician, he said, often does not know how to get access into corporate decision-making. Corporations, in turn, do not understand how to use someone like a former member; the corporate attitude toward government is likely to be "don't bother us, we're selling tires."

...Here Are the Experiences of Six

Frank E. Moss

After losing his seat to Republican Orrin G. Hatch, Sen. Moss, D-Utah (1959-77), joined a former aide in a Washington law firm. As a staunch defender of the Federal Trade Commission and other consumer-oriented agencies, "I can't say I was stampeded by people running me over looking for my services," Moss recalls.

And some of the clients his partners brought to the firm — such as Kellogg Co., then fighting a major battle against the trade commission — made him "slightly uncomfortable." In 1980 Moss moved to another law firm, where he continued to represent such clients as Thiokol Corp., a maker of propellants for spaceships and airbags; United Parcel Service; Applied Solar Technology; and a Utah TV station.

"It's largely advising them on strategy and reporting to them where matters stand," Moss said of his legislative work. "I don't have very much contact with members of Congress."

While many former members adjust to life after Congress, Moss said he did not. "You never get over missing it," he said. "Time just sort of hangs heavy."

Roger H. Zion

Before going to the House, Roger Zion, R-Ind. (1967-75), was a specialist in training salesmen and sales managers. After he lost a race for re-election in 1974, he picked up where he had left off. But he

added a Washington branch to his Evansville, Ind., consulting office, and an additional type of salesmanship to his repertoire — lobbying and legislative advice.

Zion came to advise a wide range of clients on how to sell their products to the public and their ideas to Congress.

His customers included independent oil producers in Indiana, Illinois and Kentucky; an asphalt refining company; a loan company; truckers; and a group opposed to collective bargaining by public employees.

The oil producers, he noted, may have been attracted by his congressional experience as chairman of a Republican task force on energy and resources, where he pushed for elimination of oil price controls. After his defeat, he sent out engraved cards offering himself to energy interests as "Resource Development Consultant to People, Industry and Government."

"I'm still working the same beat in a sense," he said. "I'm still trying to save the world for democracy, further the free market system and reduce government interference in the private sector."

Charles W. Whalen Jr.

One surefire place not to look for former members of Congress is among the lobbyists for public interest groups. The main reason is that the salaries cannot compete with the stipends for corporate lobbying.

Former Rep. Charles Whalen, R-Ohio (1967-79), is a rare exception. After retiring from the House, Whalen became the president of New Directions, a citizens group advocating arms control and increased foreign aid to developing countries. The pay was far more generous than in Ralph Nader's sphere — about $45,000 — but still well below what most ex-members command. The heir

to a clothing store fortune, Whalen said he could afford it better than other former members.

Being a graduate of Congress "certainly opened doors that might have been a little slower in opening," he recalled. "Frankly, after I got into it I felt a little uneasy about trading on friendships, even though I felt what I was doing was correct."

Whalen's experience lobbying for the SALT II treaty and for self-help programs in poor countries reinforced his impression of Congress as an institution in decline. The lack of leadership and the proliferation of amendments and roll-call votes, he said, forced members to take public positions with scant information. Rather than make educated decisions, he said, members avoid risk and "pander to the public's emotions."

Whalen left New Directions in 1980 to write a book about the House and foreign policy.

I worked on legislation and access to my colleagues. I really think I can hold my head a little higher if I'm doing something else."

Retiring Rep. Charles A. Vanik, D-Ohio (1955-81), who headed the Ways and Means Subcommittee on Trade, said he had several offers to work as a trade consultant in Washington. He said he refused to discuss them before adjournment and that, in any case, he would not feel comfortable returning to Congress as a supplicant for special interests. With the Republicans coming into power, "I would think there's less of a market for liberals," said Vanik, who was one. But his own experience indicated otherwise. Several of his business inquiries came from people who frequently disagreed with his performance as a lawmaker. "Some [call] because they like what you did," he said. "Some because they like how you did what you did."

How It Works

Former members who lobbied asserted that connections count for much less than popularly believed. "People think, erroneously, the way you get something through Congress is to go up to your old pals and say, 'Hey, do this for me, will you?'," said former Rep. James G. O'Hara, D-Mich. (1959-77), a partner in the lobbying law firm of Patton, Boggs and Blow. "I don't think in four years I've ever asked anyone for a favor."

"The secret is knowing how the system works, how to get your issue to one committee instead of another, how to see that it gets acted on first instead of second, how to see that the amendments you don't want are non-germane and the amendments you do want are germane," he added.

"A very, very small percentage of your work is really dealing with members," said former Sen. Robert Taft Jr., R-Ohio (House 1963-65, Senate 1971-76), whose clients included the American Hospital Association, Family Leisure Centers, Grocery Manufacturers of America, Hanna-Barbera Productions and Penn Central Corp. "You deal mostly with staff, and most of them I did not know [while in Congress]; many of them were not there," Taft said.

He said a typical legislative activity for him was the passage of an amendment in 1977 that protected amusement and theme parks — his clients — from minimum wage and hour laws. In that case, Taft mapped out the strategy and prepared material for executives from theme parks around the country, who came to Washington and fought their own fight. Taft himself contacted no members, he said, knowing from experience that constituents make a stronger impression than ex-senators.

Former members said that, having been on the receiving end of lobbying appeals, they know how to tune their pitch to a member's ear. In most cases that means a brief, factual, non-hysterical presentation that shows an awareness of the member's district and political situation.

Connections

Even if connections are not a substitute for ability, that does not mean they are without value, especially if a former member is willing to exploit them. Ex-members generally agreed that, as a matter of courtesy, they got quicker access to sitting senators and representatives, a higher place on hearing agendas if they wished to testify, and more ready answers to questions about vote counts, proxies or likely amendments.

Former House Ways and Means Chairman Wilbur D. Mills, D-Ark. (1939-77), for instance, capitalized on congressional courtesy when he represented Encyclopaedia Britannica Co. in its efforts to ease a Federal Trade Commission rule governing the behavior of its door-to-door salesmen. Mills would set up appointments with his former congressional colleagues, make a brief introductory speech, then introduce Britannica lawyers to make the case in detail.

Mills seemed only "roughly familiar" with the specifics of the problem, said a House aide who sat through one such briefing. "My assumption is his name was being used to gain the appointments." When the issue came before the Senate Commerce Committee, Chairman Howard W. Cannon, D-Nev., let Mills sit on the dais with committee staff and contribute informally to the proceedings. Mills did not get the law changed as he wanted, but congressional interest helped win his client a new hearing at the trade commission, according to commission sources.

Ex-Rep. Donald G. Brotzman, R-Colo. (1963-65, 1967-75), vice president of the Rubber Manufacturers Association, told of another residual benefit of public service. While in Congress, he said, he was an author of an amendment that required U.S. trade negotiators to have an industry advisory committee. After he went to work for the rubber-makers, Brotzman was appointed to the advisory committee and represented his industry at Tokyo trade talks.

Congressional Fraternity

Former members also have the privilege of access to the floor, the members' gymnasium and dining room and other sanctuaries closed to civilian lobbyists. House rules forbid lobbying on the floor, but Senate rules do not and staffers said they had seen ex-senators circulating while the Senate considered legislation of interest to their clients. Exploiting this privilege to lobby is rare and risky, because many members consider it improper.

Special access, however, helps ex-members maintain their status in the congressional fraternity. Quasi-official events, social gatherings and political fund raising also keep alive a degree of camaraderie some ex-members feel gives them a short leg up on other lobbyists.

Mike McKevitt, a one-term GOP congressman from Colorado (1971-73) and lobbyist for the National Federation of Independent Business, went sailing with members on the Chesapeake Bay, attended Super Bowl games with Rep. Jack F. Kemp, R-N.Y., and dined in the homes of former colleagues. Roger H. Zion, a former Indiana congressman (R, 1967-75) who lobbied for a variety of clients after leaving Congress, continued to attend a weekly House prayer breakfast.

"When you're talking to somebody you've played paddleball with or played in the Republican-Democratic golf tournament with, or seen regularly in the Capitol Hill Club, there's no question that helps," Zion said. "I think most sitting members go out of their way to be helpful to former members."

Some former members remain politically involved, too, which keeps them on familiar terms with congressional incumbents. The most common activities are attending fund-raising events and helping former colleagues round up donations at election time, but some ex-members become more full-fledged campaign participants. Ex-Rep. O'Hara, for example, was a vice chairman of the Kennedy for President campaign and a prominent participant in the effort to force open the Democratic convention.

On the Republican side, Ronald Reagan's presidential campaign enlisted several ex-member lobbyists in campaign and transition roles. One of them, Kuykendall, helped handle liaison with Congress and the planning of inaugural festivities. Asked if his participation would be good for his lobbying business, Kuykendall exclaimed, "Hell, yes. People will hire you just because of who you know. This is the first time since I left Congress it was a good time to be a Republican."

Reservoir of Credibility

Finally, if a member has built up reservoirs of trust and credibility during his public career, he may be able to tap them as a lobbyist. O'Hara, for instance, established himself in Congress as a leading advocate of organized labor. When the Business Roundtable hired him to argue the corporate viewpoint on a regulatory reform bill, O'Hara was able to approach the AFL-CIO and conduct one-on-one negotiations. The AFL-CIO was allied with consumer advocates in support of regulations the business community wanted relaxed. O'Hara attempted to win labor away from that alliance with a compromise, and consumer advocates say he nearly succeeded.

Most former members who lobby specialize in areas they handled while in public service. Frequently they end up selling their skills to the people they used to oversee and regulate. A few prominent examples:

● Eight-term Rep. Fred B. Rooney, D-Pa. (1963-79), made his name in Congress as an advocate of the railroads. When the voters retired him, his first client as a newly established consultant was the Association of American Railroads.

● Rep. Philip E. Ruppe, R-Mich. (1967-79), went from the ranking minority position on Interior's Mines and Mining Subcommittee to Amax Inc., a metals company.

● Another Interior member, Lloyd Meeds, D-Wash. (1965-79), who was the author of much public lands legislation, has subsequently lobbied for the state of Alaska and timber interests on public lands issues.

● Rep. Brock Adams, D-Wash. (1965-77), was particularly well suited for his representation of truck and railroad users interested in legislation to deregulate those two modes of transportation. Besides handling transportation issues on the Commerce Committee, Adams served as President Carter's first secretary of transportation.

A Transportation Department official said Adams, as a lobbyist for commercial rail users, played a major role in selling the House on a rail deregulation bill he helped devise as a Cabinet member. He opposed his former Transportation Department colleagues on the trucking bill; representing grocery manufacturers, he tried, without success, to keep price controls for grocery stores that transported their own goods.

Few Restrictions

There are few restrictions on former members of Congress returning to reshape legislation they handled while on the public payroll. The 1978 Ethics in Government Act requires a one-year cooling off period before certain ex-government officials can lobby their former agencies on matters they handled, but the law does not apply to members and Capitol Hill aides. The Senate has incorporated a similar one-year hands-off period into its rules, but the

effect is largely psychological: Senate rules are only binding on current members and staff.

While some outgoing members of Congress said they found the revolving door distasteful, Congress was leery of tightening restrictions on the flow between government and the lobbying trade, fearing barriers that would discourage qualified people from entering government. In 1979, the ethics law was loosened because of that fear. "I've always looked at the revolving door argument with great skepticism," said Eckhardt, who as a House member was is well regarded by reform groups. "It's one of those apparent reforms that is not a reform at all."

"Look, everybody in this life essentially sells their knowledge and experience," said Rep. Bob Carr, D-Mich. (1975-81) "I don't see why members of Congress ought to be excluded from that club." Carr lost his 1980 re-election bid.

Odd Couples

Most former members seem to pick work compatible with the views they held in Congress. But sometimes the marriage of ex-members and clients seems a bit unusual. Liberals who go into the lobbying business seem especially likely to hear charges that they have "sold out."

Adams said in an interview that he did no "substantive" work on the Japanese account, though he briefed members of the firm who were presenting congressional testimony for the Japanese. He said his firm was hired to deal with the purchase of fish caught within America's 200-mile fishing zone. "We don't have anything to do with whales at all," he said.

Former Rep. James W. Symington, D-Mo. (1969-77), known as a civil rights advocate during his public career, later lobbied for the government of South Africa. Human rights advocates contended that Symington was hired to lend credibility to a government that practices racial discrimination.

Symington said his job was not to defend apartheid, but to "open lines of communication" that could change South Africa's separatist system. He also argued that commerce with South Africa was good for American employment and hence good for blacks here. "There's nothing that I have done or would agree to do on that particular account that I don't deem to be in the interest of the United States and of peace in the world," Symington said.

Environmentalists were particularly resentful of ex-Rep. Meeds, who was seen as a conservationist for most of his career in Congress. In his last term, Meeds broke with environmentalists — for example, sponsoring Alaska lands legislation that would have allowed oil and mineral development favored by state officials. Meeds went on to represent the Alaska government as a "legislative advocate" (the job description he prefers), along with other development-minded concerns such as Northwest lumber mill operators.

"What a turnaround in a career!" said an aide on Meeds' old Interior Committee. "A lot of people here are bitter about him." Meeds, in an interview, said he split with the environmentalists because they became too extreme, not because he was looking forward to soliciting pro-lawyer, "You represent clients. It may not in all instances be a position which you would have philosophically had as a member."

To a man, former members who lobbied said they would not represent an interest that clashed with their conscientious beliefs. But as O'Hara pointed out, only a small portion of a member's votes grow out of deep personal conviction. "God knows, I didn't feel strongly about 90 percent of the stuff I voted on [in Congress]," he explained. "It was just a matter of going along with what the district wanted or what the party wanted."

O'Hara said his clientele sometimes had led him into positions he might not have taken as a liberal Democrat in Congress. For example, he worked for timber interests trying to maintain logging rights in the landmark Alaska lands bill. While in Congress, O'Hara probably would have voted with the bill's conservation-oriented sponsors, he said. On the other hand, he added, "If somebody asked me to repeal [the Occupational Safety and Health Act], I'd say 'I think you need some other firm.' "

The Right Credentials?

Being a former member does not doesn't automatically make a person a saleable lobbyist, and there were some who found it a disadvantage. "I tend to find a former member doesn't make all that good a lobbyist," said Kenneth E. Davis, a former Senate aide who represented Rohm and Haas Co. "A lobbyist has to do the grunt work. Members of Congress have staff to do the grunt work."

Partners in three Washington law firms — all former congressional staffers — said they looked over the 1980 crop of outgoing members and decided they were not interested. The lawyers all asked not to be identified.

"A lot of former members of Congress don't understand the mechanics of the procedure well enough to get very far," said one. "A lot of them just like to float around seeing their old buddies, hanging out in the Speaker's lobby." "The last thing a small law firm needs is a former member of Congress who thinks he's still running the show," concurred another.

"It's a little hard to absorb some of these people," added the third. "You don't want them unless they're going to bring in some business, and it's hard to imagine how much business some of these guys could attract." He explained that "you don't hire an ex-member to sit in the library and draft [legislation]: a) it's not economical, and b) he probably couldn't do it."

One lawyer-lobbyist told of a senior Republican senator who, upon retirement, was snapped up by the Washington office of a home state law firm in the anticipation that he would bring in lucrative clients. The law firm later learned that the senator was not regarded as terribly bright by his former colleagues or the business community, and he did not bring in enough clients to pay his hefty retainer.

Former Rep. John Y. McCollister, R-Neb. (1971-76), who worked for the Firestone Tire and Rubber Co. after losing a Senate race, said ex-members often do not understand how decisions are made in corporations, and corporations do not don't understand Washington, or want to. "I believe a lot of companies find the employment of a former member of Congress is a handicap rather than a benefit," he said.

A Saner Life

For former members who make the transition to lobbying, it can be a comfortable life. The money is better (roughly from $75,000 a year for a trade association job, to $200,000 or more at a high-powered law firm). The pressure is reduced.

"It's a much saner life," said former Rep. McKevitt. "You're not barreling to National Airport every Friday night to catch the last flight to Denver. Your weekends are your own. You can spend time with your family. You don't have to keep saying goodbye to your friends."

Some ex-members, like former Sen. Frank Moss, D-Utah (1959-77), admit they miss Congress deeply. Most of of those who lobby left Congress against their will and some admit to feeling, as one put it, "like a firehouse dalmatian when the alarm bell goes off" each time an election approaches.

But many, after the initial separation pangs, say they are relieved to be out of an institution they see as declining in prestige, hamstrung by special interests and simply not much fun anymore. Fred Rooney, for one, recalls a carping press, demands to explain every vote to one special interest or another and pressure on his time and attention. "I wouldn't take that job if I were appointed and the salary was doubled," he said.

Symington, a third generation member of Congress who learned about the institution at the table of his grandfather, lamented that with power so decentralized, "It's so tough up there to get things done that you're proud of."

And another ex-member, who asked not to be identified, agonized out loud over the fact friends were urging him to make a comeback attempt. His main concern was the "posturing and role-playing" necessary to get and hold office. "I just can't get myself geared up to endure all that punishment again," he groaned. "It's a real pain in the ass. It just erodes the inside of you."

New Federalism

Within shouting distance of the U.S. Capitol in Washington, D.C., stands a marble edifice labeled the Hall of the States. Between 1976, when the National Governors' Association moved in, and 1981, the group gradually leased more than three acres of floor space, subletting 60 offices to the representatives of governors, state legislatures, and associations of state bureaucrats.

A block west is the new $12 million headquarters of the National Association of Counties (NACO). NACO moved its lobbyists, researchers, newsletter and several affiliates there in March 1982 from rented offices downtown, giving the group a permanent staging area near Capitol Hill. Less than a mile away, the National League of Cities also has a new office complex, housing league staffers, lobbyists for many individual cities, and several allied organizations. The league's sister group, the U.S. Conference of Mayors, occupies suites in a building nearby.

Before 1981 these headquarters of the state and local government lobbies — or "PIGs" as they call themselves, an acronym for "public interest groups" — would have been viewed as formidable barriers to the sort of assault President Reagan conducted on federal aid programs that year. Having come to Washington to cope with the red tape of federal aid, the groups became, in varying degrees, dependents and persuasive defenders of that aid.

With the advent of a new administration and philosophy, economic and political tremors shook those buildings to their foundations. When Reagan drove through Congress early in 1981, whacking at state and city aid programs, most of the PIGs put up little fight. Many of them saw additional cuts as inevitable — if not in that year, then in 1982 and thereafter.

The reality of federal aid cutbacks and the prospect of further wrenching changes in the federal-state relationship provoked intensive internal debate between city and state, small city and big city, Frost Belt and Sun Belt, Republican and Democrat about how to cope with an era of retrenchment. Questions that in fat times were mostly academic took on real urgency: Which programs most deserved to be kept intact? How should responsibility be apportioned among states, counties and cities? What was to be done about the unfulfilled promises of Reagan's "new federalism" — relief from federal regulation and a handing over of some new revenue-raising powers to states and localities?

For individual cities and states represented in Washington, there was also a more down-to-earth question: How to grab a piece of the federal aid that remained? "They see the handwriting on the wall. The long bull market in federal aid is over," said John Shannon, assistant director of the Advisory Commission on Intergovernmental Relations, a federal agency. "Now that the great federal withdrawal is taking place, it's more or less every man for himself."

Washington Explosion

State and local governments were hardly the only interests to have built a high profile on the Washington skyline, but they were the only ones to have done so almost entirely at taxpayers' expense. The groups were financed primarily by dues paid out of state and local government treasuries and by federal grants. And from the new buildings and the frantic activity inside, it was clear Washington representation was one service hard-pressed state and local governments were not cutting back.

True, there had been minor casualties. Most of the PIGs relied heavily on federal grants and contracts, which dwindled during the early months of the new administration. This money paid for studies and training rather than lobbying, but it touched at least indirectly on lobbying as well. (Grants, box, p. 100)

In addition, a few crisis-ridden localities had economized at the Washington end. San Francisco dropped out of the League of Cities due to the pinch of California's tax-limiting initiative, Proposition 13. Minnesota shut its state office in 1981 as an economy measure. Michigan closed the Washington office of its state Legislature in April 1981 because of a fiscal crisis back home. (The Legislature still retained a lobbyist to handle social service issues, and the governor maintained a separate office in the Hall of the States.)

But for the most part, Washington representatives said their services were in demand more than ever before as states and localities tried to absorb the shocks from the White House and Capitol Hill.

As with most interests that had converged on Washington, the state and local lobbies boomed after federal programs bloomed in the mid-1960s. Until 1967, for example, the governors relied on a tiny, three-person Washing-

Federal Aid's Special Risks

The U.S. Conference of Mayors had two distinctions in 1981 among the groups that lobbied for state and local governments. Its lobbying staff was the most outspoken in derision of Reaganomics. And its research and education staff was hit hardest by cutbacks in federal grants. Coincidence? Or reprisal?

Melvin Mister, the mayors' deputy executive director, said he traced one lost grant up through the bureaucracy after a mid-level official told him the White House was "out to get" the mayors. His conclusion: While he believed there probably was "a political component" to the mayors' bad luck, too many other factors were involved to prove it.

Innocent or not, the mayors' loss of grants was a reminder that reliance on federal aid carried special risks for a lobbying organization. 1981 was full of such reminders for state and local lobby associations. The five leading state and local lobby groups had relied on federal aid for 30 to 60 percent of their budgets. The money was used for surveys of how federal programs were working, training local governments in making the best use of federal aid, and other educational pursuits. While all of the organizations took pains to separate grant employees from those who assisted the lobbying efforts, grant money helped pay the "overhead" for the entire organization. When grants fell off, all of the groups' activities were jeopardized.

1981 Cutbacks

In 1981, four of the five major state and local lobbies experienced cutbacks in their grant aid, though not as severe as had been expected a few months earlier.

- The U.S. Conference of Mayors expected $2.1 million in grants (60 percent of its budget), a drop from $3.7 million in 1980. The decline forced the conference to cut its staff from more than 100 to about 70, with additional layoffs expected.
- The National League of Cities received $3.1 million (43 percent of the association budget), down from $3.6 million. Spokesman Randolph Arndt said the group laid off about 25 people as a result.
- The National Governors' Association expected $2 million in grants in 1981 (42 percent of its budget), compared to $3.5 million in 1980. However, spokesman Joseph P. McLaughlin Jr. said most of the loss resulted from the normal expiration of a grant being passed along to subcontractors. The association lost six of its 85 staffers.
- The National Conference of State Legislatures got $2 million in federal money (36 percent of its budget). That was about $500,000 less than the year before, and resulted in some layoffs, mostly in the group's Denver office.
- The National Association of Counties (NACO)

had $1.5 million in federal grants (30 percent of its budget), a slight increase over 1980. NACO's grant receipts trickled in slowly early in the year, but the association picked up about $800,000 in federal contracts after mid-September, according to Chuck Oglebay, director of administration and finance.

Spokesmen for the various groups said some disruption of grant funding was not unusual at the start of a new administration, especially an administration that vowed to be hard-nosed about "non-essential" spending. Also, some of the grants came from agencies the administration wanted to abolish or diminish, such as the Law Enforcement Assistance Administration.

Some state and local representatives suspected their grant income was influenced by the positions the recipients take. The suspicion was enhanced in 1981 by demands of conservative groups, like the Conservative Caucus, that the White House use its grant power to "defund the left." But Mister said he believed the influence was in the minds of timid program managers, not orders from on high. "If I were a mid-level bureaucrat, I'd certainly have been a little leery about aggressively making a grant to the Conference of Mayors," he said.

At NACO, where a grant windfall arrived after the organization supported Reagan's budget cuts, Oglebay said there was no reason to believe the grants were a political reward. "I genuinely don't know whether that's an element or not," he said. "We'd like to think it isn't."

Influencing Judgment?

On the opposite side of the coin, some critics contended that federal grants compromised a group's judgment, whether the grant-givers intended it that way or not. Three lobbyists who represented local governments but received no grants told Congressional Quarterly they believed federal aid colored the judgment of the associations that received it. "I think it's a clear conflict of interest," said Floyd H. Hyde, who represents Denver, Colo., Gary, Ind., and other cities. "How can you look at a program objectively when you get millions of dollars in grants from the program?" Another city lobbyist said grant money "really causes them to pull their punches. The government audits their grants, and they always have that hanging over their heads."

The grant recipients all adamantly maintained that federal money did not influence their lobbying. Positions on legislation were decided by the member mayors, governors or county officials, not by the lobbyists, they pointed out. In fact, most groups were able to point to instances where they had sued or lobbied against an agency that was paying them to do a study.

ton office of the Council of State Governments to keep them up-to-date on federal activities. In March of that year, the governors opened their own Washington office, with a staff of five. "The Great Society was hitting them like a whirlwind," said Jim Martin, one of the first staffers in that office, and later the governors' top lobbyist. "They opened the office to cope with the confusion."

By 1981 the association had a staff of 79 lobbyists, researchers, administrators and secretaries. The association assessed its member states a 50 percent dues increase and stepped up the involvement of its most effective lobbyists, the governors themselves. "The governors are here, I think, more than they've ever been," said Martin. His calendar for the first week of October listed six governors who were in Washington to lobby on various issues. Martin added that state and local representation expanded to keep up with all the other interests competing for the ear of Congress, such as businesses that want Congress to preempt local authority. In 1981, for example, the National League of Cities out-lobbied cable TV operators who wanted Congress to limit city regulatory power.

In 1975 the state legislatures decided that, with the increased professionalism of state legislative bodies, they needed their own voice in Washington. The National Conference of State Legislatures in 1981 had a staff of 35 in Washington and another 90 in Denver. City and county groups had longer histories — the U.S. Conference of Mayors dated back to 1932 — but for them, too, the real explosion had come in the 1970s.

The principal local government groups in 1981 were:

● The U.S. Conference of Mayors. A product of the federal-city partnership constructed by President Franklin D. Roosevelt, the conference represented 470 mayors of cities over 30,000 in population; the group tended toward the views of big-city Democrats, whose cities relied most on federal aid. It had a staff of about 70.

● The National League of Cities. The league represented 1,000 cities, plus state municipal leagues comprising another 14,000 localities. It was seen as somewhat more conservative than the conference, reflecting the political leanings of small- and medium-sized cities. It had 109 employees.

● The National Association of Counties (NACO) represented 2,190 counties. NACO had 130 people working for it, plus a host of affiliated groups representing county health officials, parks and recreation directors, welfare directors and so on.

The governors, legislatures and three local groups — plus the International City Management Association and the Council of State Governments, two groups that lobby little —met regularly as the "Big Seven" to discuss mutual interests.

In 1976, the National Association of Towns and Townships joined the crowded PIG community. The association in 1981 claimed to speak for 13,000 small communities, and had a Washington staff of six. "Our feeling was that small towns have tended to get only the crumbs at the federal level," said Barton D. Russell, executive director.

When these groups brought in their legions to lobby Congress, the lawmakers tended to be warily attentive. As Richard Williamson, Reagan's assistant for intergovernmental relations, wrote in a September 1981 report sizing up the clout of local officials: "Every state legislator or county official is a potential congressional opponent. Every mayor or governor is a potential Senate opponent."

Proliferation

These groups, however, were only the front line. They had been joined by dozens of associations representing specialized state and local government functions. A sample: the American Association of State Highway and Transportation Officials, the Council of Chief State School Officers, the Federation of Tax Administrators, the National Association of Attorneys General, the National Association of State Budget Officers, the National Association of State Mental Health Program Directors, the State and Territorial Air Pollution Program Administrators, the Council of State Housing Agencies, the National Association of State Aviation Officials and the National Association of State Auditors, Comptrollers and Treasurers. Most of these groups were in Washington principally to keep an eye on regulations that could affect their professional duties, but many of them also lobbied both Capitol Hill and the agencies that implemented the laws.

By 1975, the National Governors' Association was so concerned about the proliferation of state executive branch associations that it commissioned a study of the phenomenon. The study concluded that these associations were costing taxpayers millions of dollars in dues, travel costs and lost work time; that they were often "captives" of the federal bureaucrats involved in their specialties; and that they sometimes worked at cross purposes with the governors.

Following the report, the governors attempted, with some success, to harness this disparate community. Many of the leading groups were consolidated in the Hall of the States, and more closely coordinated with the governors and legislatures. But conflicts persisted, according to state lobbyists. In the 1981 budget fight, for example, groups of health and highway officials fought to preserve programs that the governors and state legislatures did not consider high priorities.

And That's Not All

Many individual states and cities, convinced that national associations could not tend to their unique or regional problems with the federal government, had hired their own Washington representation. In 1966, the League of Cities and Conference of Mayors spawned a "man-in-Washington program" catering to the special needs of individual cities, primarily in pursuit of federal grants. That program, later called the National Center for Municipal Development, grew to include 15 lobbyists representing 48 cities. Other cities and some counties hired independent consultants, usually former government officials, who specialized in such problems. Most of the governors maintained their own offices in the Hall of the States, and others had contracts with free-lance consultants.

The Illinois, New York, California and Michigan state legislatures hired their own Washington help, rather than rely on an office answerable to the governor. Bill Holland, who opened an office for the Illinois legislature in 1980, explained that leaders of the state Assembly "felt the information that was being supplied to them from the governor's office was executive-slanted." The legislature had a staff of five in Washington in 1981. New York state had separate lobbyists serving the governor, the Democratic-controlled state Assembly and the Republican-controlled state Senate. During the 1981 debate over block grants, the New Yorkers lobbied in opposite directions, the Assembly opposing the block grants, the Senate supporting them.

Altogether, 30 states and more than 100 cities and counties had offices or had hired agents in Washington in 1981. Some were grants-chasers. Others primarily monitored the outpouring of new laws, regulations and judgments that affect how their sponsors operate at home. Most of them did some lobbying, especially to influence the formulas by which federal aid is distributed. "In a world of shrunken resources, going after those resource dollars is becoming a far more competitive effort," noted Robert E. Gordon, director of the National Center for Municipal Development.

Another activity that seemed to keep city and state representatives busy was the internal politics of the PIG community. Lobbyists said they spent a lot of time in meetings with other lobbyists, exchanging information, trying to recruit allies, or attempting to influence the positions of the national associations.

Efficient Government?

To some observers, the "intergovernmental lobby" resembled a huge machine for the recycling of public money. "Millions of your state tax dollars are being spent every day in efforts to affect how your federal tax dollars are spent, while millions of your federal tax dollars are spent fending them off," writer Michael Kinsley jibed in *The New Republic* in March 1981. "This is efficient government?"

That question was echoed by some lawmakers. "Why should the state of Utah have to have an office here?" Sen. Jake Garn, R-Utah, wondered in an interview. "I've got a staff here, and a staff in the state. The governor and I are good friends. If he has a problem, all he has to do is call." Karyn Severson, Utah's representative in Washington, responded that members of Congress often do not have the time and interest to follow the "75,000 picayune things" the federal government does that affect state programs.

Most congressional offices viewed their local, state and city representatives as useful sources of information, and sometimes as valuable allies. Elizabeth Robbins, a social services lobbyist whose clients included the Michigan Legislature, worked closely with Rep. John D. Dingell, D-Mich., to help save Medicaid funding worth about $30 million to his state. She used her contacts to round up representatives from other states, moving around with more liberty than a congressional staffer. Robbins' service cost the state about $80,000 a year, but if she helped influence just that one decision — and participants agreed she was an important player — then, she pointed out, "The state's return was pretty good."

Are They Greedy?

Probably the most common criticism of the PIGs was that they deserved their acronym: That they were greedy to expand programs, but almost never willing to offer any up in the interest of budget-balancing. Garn, a former Salt Lake City mayor who was active in the League of Cities, recalled that in the early 1970s mayors said that if they were given revenue-sharing money without federal strings attached, they could get by with less "categorical" aid earmarked for housing, sewers or playgrounds. "Then they got revenue-sharing and wanted to keep all the categorical programs as well," Garn said. "I don't have a great deal of sympathy on categorical aid. I don't believe they followed through on their part of the bargain."

Floyd H. Hyde, a former mayor and federal housing official who in 1981 represented eight cities and counties, blamed the city associations in part for a backlash against federal spending. The big cities, especially, demanded more and more categorical aid because they had large staffs adept at wheedling grants, he said. "It seems to me they've become identified as just another interest group," he said. "A congressman will say, 'Today I'm seeing the sugar lobby, and next week the oil lobby's coming in, and in between I'm seeing the city lobby.' "

Even the governors, who came to Washington skeptical of aid programs that bypassed their authority, muted their criticism of categorical aid after they got a piece of revenue-sharing in 1972, according to Joseph P. McLaughlin Jr., director of public affairs for the governors' conference. "After 1972, these groups became collaborators in expanding the federal role," McLaughlin said.

PIGs and their supporters, however, pointed to two other factors in the push for federal aid programs. One was the belief of local officials that they were not getting enough help from the state level, where legislatures were reluctant to raise taxes. The other, and perhaps greater, force for federal aid was Congress, whose members like showing off the bacon they bring home.

'Divorce' Under Stress

The days of easy pickings at the federal level ended well before Reagan arrived in town. In cutting local programs, President Carter brought changes in degree while Reagan wanted a change in direction, said NACO Director Bernard F. Hillenbrand. Dolefully reciting the programs he had lobbied to put in place, he likened the situation to "a divorce."

Early in 1981, faced with Reagan's evident popularity and the acquiescence of Congress, most of the PIGs issued general endorsements of the Reagan budget cuts, manfully vowed to accept their fair shares, and focused their attention on rescuing a few top-priority programs. The governors and legislatures, for example, led a successful drive to prevent a cap on Medicaid payments, then pitched in — over the angry dissent of some individual states — to lobby in support of the budget reconciliation measure that forced Reagan's other cuts into law. The states were particularly enticed by Reagan's block grant proposals, which were designed to consolidate power at the state level. They lobbied hard for block grants even though the price was a cut of 20-25 percent in the consolidated programs.

City and county groups were less enthusiastic, but too divided and disheartened to put up a strong resistance. Also, they were tantalized by Reagan's promises of less regulation and new taxing power for them. They considered themselves fortunate to save the framework of such programs as the Economic Development Administration (EDA) and the Urban Development Action Grants (UDAG), although these funds were reduced drastically.

The only unabashed disapproval of Reagan's proposals came from the Conference of Mayors. Mayor Richard Hatcher of Gary, Ind., then president of the conference, criticized the Reagan cuts so derisively that, according to conference officials, the White House stopped inviting Hatcher to meetings on city issues. "The more they didn't invite him, the more outspoken he became," said John J. Gunther, executive director. "We were fighting a losing battle." (Relations became more cordial after Lincoln, Neb., Mayor Helen Boosalis took over in the summer of 1981.)

While the mayors' group had a large (65 percent) Democratic majority, internal disputes over the president's programs were loud and bitter. At the mayors' annual conference in June 1981, which Gunther recalled as "the most partisan I've ever seen," Republicans and Sun Belt Democrats split with liberals to effectively neutralize the group.

Reagan's drive was helped, too, by the re-emergence of old divisions within the PIG community. Some officials at the U.S. Conference of Mayors and the National League of Cities resented the states for promoting block grants. The governors' association felt bitterness toward the League of Cities for refusing to help out in 1980 when President Carter sought to cut the states' portion of revenue-sharing.

County leaders sniped at urban programs; NACO President Richard Conder, for example, told a press conference in September 1981 that he personally would like to see the UDAG program scrapped.

The net result, according to White House aide Williamson, was that the PIGs ended up serving the White House in selling the initial budget cuts. "They saw a momentum," he said."They were not sure they could stop it, even if they had wanted to."

Fighting Back

Reagan's announcement in September 1981 that he wanted Congress to squeeze another $13 billion from the fiscal 1982 budget drove the PIGs back together for a time. Even those most supportive of Reagan — the state and county groups — reacted with cries of betrayal, complaining that the administration failed to consult them on the cuts and that the additional economies were too much to absorb so suddenly.

On certain cuts the lobby groups were united and some lobbyists suspected Reagan's second assault on the budget would reinvigorate the PIGs as an effective resistance for the long run. "I think most of the people who were disposed to go along then now believe we are taking an unfair share of the cuts, and they will oppose further cuts as applied to our programs," said George Gross, director of federal relations at the League of Cities. "There are now creeping doubts about whether this whole thing will work," said NACO's Hillenbrand.

But other representatives pointed out that local governments were surrounded by powerful forces, not just a popular president. The pressures for lower taxes and stronger defense, and the difficulty of cutting such entitlement programs as Social Security left Congress little option besides more cuts in state and local aid.

For the same reasons, few people seriously expected Congress to turn over any of its revenue-raising power to states and localities soon. "It may be some [of the PIGs] think the good old days will come back," said McLaughlin. "But I personally would be very skeptical that they will."

The Christian Right

When conservative Christian lobbyists were rounding up congressmen for a House petition to force a floor vote on school prayer, Rep. John Buchanan, a moderate Alabama Republican, balked at signing. Buchanan is a Baptist minister and was an author of an unsuccessful constitutional amendment to permit prayer in schools. But he had serious misgivings about the complex legal strategy conservatives had come up with to tie the hands of the Supreme Court. To leaders of the Christian political groups Moral Majority and Christian Voice, that was no excuse. They branded Buchanan an opponent of school prayer and began denouncing him in his congressional district.

Facing a difficult Republican primary race against a conservative challenger, Buchanan gave in and signed the petition. "I just decided that, while I don't think it will work, I was not willing to be put down on the wrong side of an issue where I have a strong feeling," Buchanan explained. "Ironically, it has not made any difference. The Moral Majority, or someone, has continued to flood my district with material showing me to be on the wrong side of school prayer."

Buchanan also was castigated by the Christian right, from platform and pulpit, for his liberal votes on such issues as the Equal Rights Amendment (ERA) and busing. On Sept. 2, 1980, he lost his primary. "I'd say they did a rather thorough job of beating my brains out with Christian love," he said the day following his defeat.

Blunt Instrument

At a time when the Christian right was imposing itself on the public conciousness — more than 250 press and broadcast representatives covered the movement's August 1980 revival meeting in Dallas — Buchanan's story illustrated that this was a force to be reckoned with. But it was the force of a blunt instrument, not a surgical scalpel.

The evangelical right is a loose alliance of groups attempting to enlist strict Bible adherents — mostly Baptists and independent evangelical sects, but also theological conservatives within Catholic, Mormon and Protestant denominations — as the new troops of political conservativism. Within weeks of their Dallas meeting, these groups already were making impressive claims about money raised, voters registered, newsletters circulated and pastors mobilized. *(box, p. 107)*

Perhaps the most impressive was the claim of Moral

Majority, the largest Christian right organization. The group boasted it had registered 3 million voters, most of them newcomers to politics. The figure was widely reported, but appeared to have little factual basis. Though Moral Majority President Jerry Falwell said the number was based on estimates from state affiliates, Moral Majority directors in two of the more active states — California and Alabama — said they merely sent out voter materials to pastors and made no effort to keep a count of new registrants.

Moral Majority claimed a part in many congressional races of 1980, with its clearest influence in Oklahoma and Alabama Senate contests. In Oklahoma, Don Nickles, R, prevailed over conservative Democrat Andy Coats and in Alabama former war hero Jeremiah Denton, R, beat the well-known Jim Folsom Jr. Moral Majority participated in several House races other than Buchanan's, including successful assaults on Reps. John Brademas, D-Ind. (1959-81), Bob Eckhardt, D-Texas (1967-81), John G. Hutchinson, D-W.Va. (1980-81), and the nearly successful challenge to Rep. Marc L. Marks, R-Pa., who planned not to run in 1982.

As a result of their successes, the evangelical groups expected Congress to look more favorably than it had in the past on a number of Christian New Right Crusades such as voluntary school prayer, a ban on abortions and stiff penalties for drug peddling and pornography. However, even the architects of the movement conceded they had not yet achieved their ultimate goal — the ability to bend Congress to their will — nor had they distinguished themselves as a durable political factor beyond the conservative surge of 1980.

Networks

The evangelical right drew its strategists from secular conservative lobbies and single-interest forces such as the right-to-life and stop-ERA movements. The American Conservative Union, the National Conservative Political Action Committee and the hawkish American Security Council were secular groups closely associated with the movement. Two of the principal consultants to the evangelical right were Paul M. Weyrich of the Committee for the Survival of a Free Congress, a New Right group; and

Howard Phillips, a former Nixon aide who founded the Conservative Caucus.

What separated the Christian right from these groups was its focus on churches as the precincts for organizing campaign and legislative activity, the use of TV and radio preachers as a motivating force, and the emphasis on the Bible as the validation for political activity. Despite this distinction, however, evangelical groups were increasingly shedding the confining religious orientations with which they began.

In 1980 Phillips called this movement, "The most significant development in American politics since organized labor discovered the ballot box." Proclaimed Weyrich, "We are talking about Christianizing America."

The four principal Christian right organizations — Moral Majority, The Religious Roundtable, The Christian Voice and the National Christian Action Coalition — all had Washington offices to monitor legislation and lobby, employing the traditional techniques of glad-handing and arm-twisting, the mass mail-in and the telephone blitz. Sometimes they warned members of Congress that a wrong vote would hurt their scores in the new "moral" or "family" vote ratings. *(box, p. 109)*

The evangelical presence in Washington was small, many representatives in the Capitol were temporary, and their lobbying activities still were largely unsophisticated. But veteran conservative strategists said that seasoned lobbyists were secondary to local organizing; grass-roots efforts had remained the preferred technique of political persuasion. "We have to fight a political guerrilla war, not a fixed battle in Washington, D.C., but hundreds of skirmishes in congressional districts around the country," said Phillips in an interview. "We will create a climate where it's not necessary to lobby in Washington, but where the appropriate course is obvious [to members of Congress]."

Inside Allies

Their two most concerted lobbying efforts in 1980 were the battle for voluntary school prayer and passage of an amendment restricting federal intervention in private schools to stop racial discrimination. Evangelicals also joined other conservative groups in legislative fights against abortion, homosexual rights, the Equal Rights Amendment and creation of the Department of Education, and in favor of budget-balancing, an anti-communist foreign policy and heavier defense spending. School prayer remained a contentious issue in 1982 and the matter of tuition tax credits for private education was a high priority. Some Christian groups projected that legal infanticide and euthanasia would become important concerns in the future.

The Christian right had assisted in getting churches exempted from a bill requiring disclosure of lobbying activities. Pulpit politicos in 1980 found their inside allies at the right tip of the political spectrum — men like Sens. Jesse Helms, R-N.C., and Gordon J. Humphrey, R-N.H., and Reps. Robert K. Dornan, R-Calif., Philip M. Crane, R-Ill., Larry P. McDonald, D-Ga., John M. Ashbrook, R-Ohio (1961-82), and George Hansen, R-Idaho. "George Hansen calls me so many times a day, I wonder if he's a congressman or a used car salesman," said Moral Majority Vice President Ronald Godwin.

Heavy-Handedness

The school prayer fight brought the most intense lobbying from Christian right crusaders. The battle was over a complex and legally controversial bill to deny Supreme Court jurisdiction over voluntary prayer. Most of the great bulk of postcards and letters Bible believers launched at Rep. Robert W. Kastenmeier, D-Wis., who chaired the House Judiciary subcommittee dealing with the bill, portrayed the issue as clear-cut: Either you are for prayer in schools, or against it. Members like Buchanan, who balked at signing a discharge petition to wrest the bill from Kastenmeier's subcommittee, were marked as opponents of school prayer and blasted in their home districts.

Another target of this strategy was Rep. Mickey Edwards, R-Okla., a staunch conservative who "is with us 90 percent of the time," said the Rev. Robert J. Billings, a founder of Moral Majority. According to Billings, when Edwards did not sign promptly, William C. Chasey Jr., a lobbyist for The Roundtable, phoned a television preacher in Oklahoma who agreed to castigate the congressman on the air for failing to toe the fundamentalist line. The TV sermon brought Edwards a flood of unhappy letters from prayer supporters, Billings said.

Billings said the ploy worked — Edwards signed the petition — but it left conservative Christians with a reputation for heavy-handedness that could hurt them next time they needed a favor. "In our enthusiasm, we sometimes do or say things that we wouldn't do if we were a little more experienced and mature," said Billings, who was also Republican presidential candidate Ronald Reagan's liaison with church groups. The school prayer bill remained in the House Judiciary Committee in July 1982.

Legislative Agenda

The evangelical right celebrated a sort of public debut in Dallas on Aug. 21 and 22, 1980, with a political revival meeting called the National Affairs Briefing. The affair attracted crowds ranging from 7,000 to 15,000, at least a fourth of them ministers. Of equal interest to the organizers was the crowd of reporters drawn to the affair, many of them compiling stories about what seemed to be that year's most colorful political phenomenon.

Who's Who In The Christian Right

Moral Majority. In late 1978 the Rev. Robert J. Billings borrowed $25,000 from a Texas believer and used it to buy the mailing list of television's *Old Time Gospel Hour*. The resulting "educational" group, which *Gospel Hour* star Jerry Falwell and Billings called the Moral Majority, had semi-autonomous chapters in all 50 states by 1980; a newsletter mailing list, including non-paying recipients, of more than 400,000 in 1982 (80,000 of them pastors or preachers); and an annual budget of $7 million. "I think it's safe to say Moral Majority has become a household word in a little over a year," said Ronald Godwin, vice president in charge of Washington headquarters.

To preserve tax advantages, Moral Majority carefully set up separate structures to handle lobbying and campaign giving. But all of the legal entities were Falwell satellites, and all worked toward a single purpose: "To create a moral climate in which it is easier for politicians to vote right than wrong," as Godwin put it.

Moral Majority initially had high hopes of influencing elections through a political action committee (PAC). But the Moral Majority PAC, according to its mid-1980 report to the Federal Election Commission, raised only $22,089, and was left dormant. Moral Majority had three full-time workers in Washington. In addition to lobbying (none of the staff previously had been a professional lobbyist), the group concentrated on enlarging state affiliates, training political activists and setting up such "grass-roots" machinery as telephone banks.

The Religious Roundtable. The brainchild of Edward E. McAteer, a former Colgate Palmolive marketing man and field operative of the Conservative Caucus, and James Robison, a fiery Baptist preacher from Dallas, The Roundtable was envisioned as a top-level alliance of prominent, politically minded evangelicals. The group held several political seminars, by far the largest the National Affairs Briefing, which drew audiences of up to 15,000 in Dallas Aug. 21 and 22, 1980.

McAteer and Robison planned to begin state chapters, and began distributing a newsletter, *The Roundtable Report*, in September 1980. Some evangelicals privately saw this as a battle of egos between Robison and Moral Majority's Falwell.

But McAteer, who was also on the board of Moral Majority, said in an interview The Roundtable would concentrate on training leaders, while Moral Majority would mobilize troops. The Roundtable also claimed to have a broader religious base than Moral Majority, which drew most heavily from Baptists. The two groups, at any rate, shared an identical political outlook: bedrock, Bible-based conservative. The Roundtable's funding came primarily from donations.

The group's lobbying arm, called Roundtable Issues and Answers, hired William C. Chasey Jr., former director of special interests for John B. Connally, to lobby in Washington in 1980. Chasey was also paid as a consultant for The Roundtable and, as a volunteer, ran a "Christian Voter Program" for Reagan. By 1982 Chasey had left the Roundtable and the Washington office was undergoing reorganization.

Christian Voice. Based in California, Christian Voice was a lobby group best known for its "report card" on Congress. Gary Jarmin, formerly an official with the Rev. Sun Myung Moon's Unification Church and legislative director for the American Conservative Union, was the Voice's Washington lobbyist. Jarmin claimed Christian Voice had 300,000 members, including 37,000 ministers, who received a monthly newsletter and occasional legislative alerts.

Jarmin ran the group's PAC, the Moral Government Fund, which he said planned to spend $1 million in 1980; the PAC reported at the end of June 1980 it had raised only $78,214, and incurred debts of $82,380, most of it in an independent campaign for Reagan. Christian Voice fell short of its intended lobbying budget as well. In 1982, the operating budget for the whole organization was $ 1.3 million.

Christian Voice had a hit list of 36 incumbent members of Congress it hoped to help unseat in 1980, 40 in 1982. A lobbyist for one rival evangelical group said Christian Voice was considered "a little bit radical" for its willingness to attack. "They tend to have more of a knee-jerk reaction," he said.

National Christian Action Coalition. The coalition was founded by the ubiquitous Robert Billings as a lobby group for Christian schools, and was taken over by his son, William. William Billings said when his father and Falwell started Moral Majority, "They went up front and we kind of went into the background."

The coalition became both a small "think tank" for the evangelical right, and the Washington representative for an assortment of Christian morality-in-politics groups. Billings, formerly of the National Conservative Political Action Committee, ran an office with a full-time staff of five.

He said the coalition's material — including legislative alerts and political organizing tips — went to thousands of churches and Christian schools. Billings did little direct lobbying, but hired a professional on occasion to press Christian school concerns.

The group produced a movie featuring conservative lawmakers like Sen. Jesse Helms, R-N.C., telling Christians to get politically active. Also, the Christian Voters' Victory Fund issues a congressional "scorecard" rating members of Congress on family issues.

The crowds listened to a tag team of preachers and politicians who delivered hellfire sermons about moral decay and high-pitched denunciations of the liberal establishment in Washington. The persistent theme was that Bible believers were to blame for the national condition, because they had sat out the political process. "It's time for Christians to crawl out from under the pews," Texas evangelist James Robison, one of the sponsors, exhorted the crowd.

Falwell, star of television's *Old Time Gospel Hour* and president of Moral Majority, recited what he called a "laundry list for the Eighties" — the evangelicals' ambitious legislative agenda. Among the top items: constitutional amendments to ban abortion and permit voluntary prayer in schools; the death of ERA; opposition to "socialized medicine" in the form of national health insurance; stiffer penalties for pornography and drug peddling; and world superiority in weaponry. "The things that I've been talking about tonight, preach them in your pulpit," urged Falwell. "...America is waiting for leadership, preachers, and you're it."

One item high on the agenda of evangelical lobbyists was Sen. Paul Laxalt's, R-Nev., Family Protection Act, a collection of 38 "pro-family" titles touching on school desegregation, homosexual rights, "sex-intermingling" in school sports, child abuse, school prayer, sex education, distribution of contraceptives to minors, tax status of private schools and other talismans of the right. Like the school prayer bill, however, the Family Protection Act had not been much advanced by July 1982.

Though they were not on Falwell's "laundry list," lobbyists for the evangelical right also held strong views on economic matters, supporting tax and spending cuts that sounded remarkably like the Republican Party platform. Charles Cade, director of state organizing and former legislative specialist for Moral Majority, said the group had commissioned polls and hired marketing consultants to find out what issues "the most people are likely to get involved in." One was the economy. "Abortion, pornography, homosexuality — those are hard for average Christians to relate to," Cade said. "They don't read *Playboy*, their daughters aren't pregnant, they don't know any queers. But when people's life savings are deteriorating at 15 to 20 percent a year, that is *evil*."

Critics of the evangelical right observed that the movement's agenda excluded the more traditional watchwords of Christian concern — peace, care for the needy, human rights. "It's all scare," said Tom Getman, an aide to Sen. Mark O. Hatfield, R-Ore., an evangelical with a liberal voting record. "It's all playing on people's dark side. They say nothing about social justice. Nothing about the nuclear arms race. Nothing about our militarism or materialism."

Tactics

The legislative tactics of the evangelical right were outlined for about 300 participants who stayed after the Dallas conference for a morning of political hints:

• Massive voter registration drives centering on the churches. The Roundtable was trying to persuade ministers to preach and conduct voter registration in their churches and to deliver get-out-the-vote sermons for the November elections.

• Church-level "layman's leagues" or "moral action committees" to study candidates and legislation.

• State and regional training seminars in political tactics; both The Roundtable and Moral Majority said these were being planned with an eye to the 1982 elections.

• An already-thriving network of newsletters that "simplified" and "clarified" political issues from a scriptural perspective. Weyrich noted the Christian right sometimes was criticized for its stark and uncompromising portrayal of complex issues, but he told the crowd not to listen to such criticism. "Frame [issues] in such a way that there is no mistaking who is on the right side and who is on the wrong side," he urged. "Ultimately, everything can be reduced to right and wrong. Everything."

• A communications network of "telephone trees" that could bring a hail of Christian opinion down on Congress at critical points in the legislative battle. Weyrich, noting that press attention in Dallas had given the movement immeasurable new credibility, added, "I suggest you go out of your way to court the media."

Conservative strategists said that by adopting these tactics they were simply following the lead of organized labor, environmentalists, consumer advocates and other liberal groups, which won their way by making themselves impossible to ignore. "The question is, whose issues are going to be debated?" said Gary L. Jarmin, lobbyist for Christian Voice. "Who's going to take hold of the high ground? What we do is take an issue, build a constituency around it, and then the politicians can't ignore it."

A dozen ministers interviewed at the Dallas gathering

James Robison of The Roundtable welcomes Ronald Reagan to Dallas.

Christian Vote Ratings: Study in Absolutes

Don't tell Houston preacher Harold L. Champion that politics is not all black or white. In the concourse of the Dallas Reunion Arena, where Christian conservatives held a political revival meeting in 1980, Champion was selling thousands of copies of a $3.95 book that provided black-and-white pie charts for each member of Congress, purporting to summarize the member's views on family, business and farm issues. "The blacker the chart, the more anti-family they are," he told an attentive crowd of delegates one afternoon. "Look at Sen. [John] Glenn of Ohio. If you follow the media, he always comes across as Mr. Clean. But just look at his charts — all black!"

The book Champion was hawking was just the most graphic of several new Christian conservative voting guides that claimed to give a clear picture of where incumbents stood on "moral issues." The evangelicals thus had joined scores of secular special interests who published annual score cards on the voting performances of members of Congress.

Saints and Sinners

The most widely distributed evangelical right rating was the Family Issues Voting Index, published by the Christian Voters' Victory Fund, and used by both Moral Majority and The Religious Roundtable. Author William Billings said he intended to circulate one million copies for the 1980 elections.

A more heavily publicized rating was the Christian Voice "Report Card" of "14 Key Moral Issues." Author Gary Jarmin said thousands had been distributed in 1980, with plans to disseminate millions of report cards in 1982.

Jarmin said the "major objective" was to get "a lot of press," which succeeded. He had a collection of newspaper clippings with headlines like "Lawmakers Given 'Christian' Ratings" and "Morality Score Low For Local Congressman." One paper ran pictures of lawmakers under the headings "Saints" and "Sinners." Jarmin said many of these stories "misinterpreted" the purpose of the report cards arguing that they were "not intended as a statistical evaluation of the moral character of members of Congress."

Billings and Jarmin used a common pool of issues for their ratings. Lawmakers won points for opposing extended ratification time for the Equal Rights Amendment; government legal aid to foster homosexual rights or abortion; busing for racial balance; sex education; creation of the Department of Education; and penalties for segregated private schools. They scored plusses for supporting a balanced budget and restoration of prayer in public schools. Christian Voice added foreign policy to its report card, applauding lawmakers who supported a vow to defend Taiwan ("from an attack by Godless Communist China") and opposed sanctions against

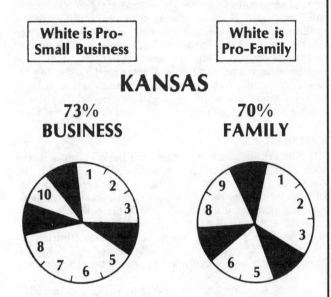

A portrait of Sen. Robert Dole, R-Kan., in black and white, from a congressional scorecard aimed at Christian conservatives. Each slice represents a "key vote" selected by the rating organization.

Rhodesia (a "pro-American nation under attack by atheistic Marxist forces").

Christian Positions?

Jarmin said issues were picked for their "significant moral implications." In some cases, he conceded, the correct moral stance may have been "a little obscure." Creation of the Department of Education was immoral, for example, because it would "increase federal intervention and bureaucratic humanist regulation over public education," and because it was supported by the National Education Association, "which espouses a radical, secular-humanist philosophy."

The ratings provoked criticism that the evangelical right was equating Christianity with right-wing politics, and ignoring such apparently "moral" concerns as arms control and feeding the hungry. "Some of the votes that they called distinctly Christian positions, I can't call distinctly Christian positions," said Robert Dugan of the National Association of Evangelicals. "Its unfair to insist that politicians fit into a certain Christian mold." Conservative leader Paul M. Weyrich, however, defended this approach, noting "It is not going to do any good to register millions of voters and then not tell them who the good guys are and who the bad guys are." "We believe in absolutes," said Champion. "The Bible is a book of absolutes."

said they would follow the advice at least as far as voter registration. Most said they would encourage their congregations to read literature put out by the evangelical right groups because the secular media could not be trusted, and many planned to discuss the issues in church. "I will never name a candidate from the pulpit and say you must vote this way," said Dana Halstead, pastor of a 250-member evangelical congregation in Shawnee, Kan. "But when an issue comes up, I will encourage our people to write letters to congressmen and express their convictions." Halstead said he already had conducted a voter registration day in his church, and asked a lawyer in his congregation to help set up a committee to discuss legislative issues. "We are a group that's going to have to be contended with," he said.

Potential

Numerically, at least, organizing evangelicals was an idea with tremendous potential. A poll conducted by George Gallup's Princeton Religion Research Center in 1979 found that 20 percent of Americans, about 30 million voters, considered themselves strict Bible believers of the type the evangelical right considers its natural constituency. Another 21 million voters met a looser definition of "born again" Christians. Other polls showed this group to be one of the least politically active segments of the electorate.

Politicians have been impressed by the enormous audiences of the TV preachers who galvanized the movement — and their proven ability to raise huge sums of money. Falwell, for example, said he grossed $56 million in donations in 1979 from *Gospel Hour* viewers, and expected $70 million in 1980. The money supported his broadcast ministry and school complex in Lynchburg, Va., and only indirectly advanced the cause of Moral Majority. Its operating budget for 1982 was $7 million, $750,000 of which was earmarked for Washington activities.

The four leading evangelical groups reported raising roughly $4 million in 1980 for their national lobbying and "educational" activities. Their efforts to be a big financial force in election campaigns, however, were not so successful. Moral Majority's political action committee — which reportedly was designed to raise a million dollars for 1980 campaign offerings — reported at midyear it had raised only about $22,000. Falwell said he lost interest in the PAC because it was a drain on resources and diverted attention from issues to candidates.

Christian Voice, which had ambitions of spending $1 million through its Moral Government Fund, mostly on independent activities for Reagan, reported at the end of June 1980 it had raised $78,214 and incurred $82,380 in debts. The group's goals for 1982 were more modest; having raised $250,000 by July, Christian Voice hoped to spend $500,000 by the end of the year.

Spreading the Word

According to the Rev. Benjamin L. Armstrong, executive director of the National Religious Broadcasters Association, airwave preachers ran 1,360 radio stations and about 35 full-time television stations in 1980. Another 700 radio and TV programs were distributed to secular broadcasters, of which 80 percent, Armstrong estimated, were evangelical Christian. While in 1982 the number of radio stations leveled off at around 1,300, 30 more TV stations had been established.

Polls and industry estimates for 1982 said that 10 million to 15 million Americans were regular, faithful viewers of several religious shows, and as many as 115 million may have tuned in one of the broadcasts each week. In the late 1970s and early 1980s, many of the most popular shows — Falwell's *Gospel Hour* and the Rev. Pat Robertson's *700 Club*, for instance — acquired an openly political tone. Armstrong said many of the smaller outlets followed suit. He suggested that anyone who doubted the influence of the electric church need only ask the Federal Communications Commission (FCC).

In 1974 two men petitioned the FCC for a rule that might have subjected FM religious broadcasters to commercial competition. By August of the following year, when the FCC dismissed the petition, a million letters of protest had rolled in, generated by distressed religious broadcasters. Over the ensuing five years, the FCC received another 11 million pieces of mail from religious listeners apparently unaware that the issue was long dead. An FCC official in 1980 said the letters were still "trickling" in at the rate of 100 a day.

Presidential candidate Ronald Reagan accepted an invitation to address the religious broadcasters' convention in October 1980 where an unprecedented 400 radio stations and 3 religious networks were plugged in, reflecting their new attention to politics. "They never had any interest in these things in the past," Armstrong said.

Seeking Support

Carter and Reagan both added church liaisons to their staffs in acknowledgement of the movement's potential. On Aug. 5, 1980, President Carter held a secret meeting with several evangelical churchmen to discuss how he might combat the attacks made on him by groups like Moral Majority. He also met separately with such church luminaries as Southern Baptist Convention President Bailey Smith, in an effort to put himself right with the Bible-believers. "As noisy as some of the leaders are, you have to take this seriously," said the Rev. Robert Maddox, a Baptist minister Carter named in 1979 as his liaison with church groups.

Reagan made an open play for the evangelical vote, typified by his statement to a thunderously friendly crowd in Dallas that "I endorse you and what you are doing." Moral Majority's former director Billings, an unpaid "coordinator for church voter groups," helped Reagan set up five advisory panels of churchmen who were promised quick access to the candidate. Reagan's committees included leaders of Moral Majority, The Roundtable and the National Christian Action Coalition.

Groups such as Moral Majority and The Roundtable, because they take tax-deductible donations, were prohibited from endorsing candidates except through separate political arms. But, in practice, because individual leaders were free to make strictly personal political statements, there never was much doubt about which politicans were favored. In anticipation of the 1980 presidential election, Billings pointed out that "where the rubber hits the road, the Moral Majority is pro-Reagan, ex-officio."

In congressional races, the evangelicals made a push to unseat endangered liberals. Christian Voice in August 1980 released a formal list of 36 incumbents "targeted for defeat." Jarmin said the group's PAC planned mass leaflettings outside churches in the disputed congressional districts, focusing on the "anti-family/moral voting

Established Churches Also Lobby Congress

Next door to the Supreme Court and a short stroll from the Capitol is an Italian Renaissance-style building owned by the United Methodist Church. It is not a place of worship, but a strategically located place of lobbying — headquarters for groups that press a variety of liberal and humanitarian causes.

The United Methodist Building is just one of the more conspicuous signs that the established churches have long had an active place in the midst of government. For all the fanfare that accompanied the arrival of the evangelical conservative lobby, it was small compared with the more liberal church lobby already settled here. "For years, the liberals have had a monopoly on representing the Christian viewpoint in this city," complained Gary Jarmin of Christian Voice.

Interfaith Council

One rough indicator of the church presence in the capital was the Washington Interfaith Staff Council, an informal association of church lobbies that met twice a month to talk over legislation. The council included representatives of 39 major denominations and religious groups — Catholic, Protestant and Jewish — each of which maintained its own Washington presence. The Christian members ranged in outlook from the free-thinking Unitarians to the more dogmatic Baptists.

The political spectrum of this group embraced the liberal National Council of Churches and the more conservative National Association of Evangelicals. The latter group was this establishment's closest link to the burgeoning Christian conservative movement. Though churches could jeopardize their privileged tax status if they devoted a "substantial" portion of their wealth and manpower to lobbying, "substantial" was a vague enough word to leave major churches plenty of room to testify, persuade and cajole.

Most of the established denominations had newsletters and magazines to get their message out to the grass roots, though they were not so unabashed as the new Christian right in mobilizing mass-letter campaigns and phone-ins. The established churches generally steered clear of election campaigns.

Human Dignity

Churches have been at the center of political debates from the American Revolution to the abolition of slavery to Prohibition to the Vietnam War. Except for such emotional issues as abortion and homosexuality, which have split the mainline denominations, most church lobbying is in alliance with liberal groups.

Religious lobbyists, for example, have been credited with a major role in creating and protecting the food stamp program and with helping link U.S. foreign aid to human rights issues. In contrast to conservative religious newcomers, most of the established denominations also have testified against legitimizing prayer in public schools, fearing a threat to the separation of church and state.

The U.S. Catholic Conference, which ran one of the largest religious lobbying operations, published handbooks on "Political Responsibility" in 1976 and 1980. Its legislative positions, said to be derived from papal encyclicals and rulings by the synods of bishops, were based on a central theme of "human dignity and human rights." They included support for comprehensive national health insurance, food stamps, employment subsidies and SALT II. The Catholics would side with conservatives in opposition to abortion and support for tuition tax credits.

The Catholic conference opened a Washington office to cope with immigration issues after World War I, and has since multiplied like the proverbial loaves and fishes. The church's government liaison in Washington was staffed by five lobbyists in 1982.

The United Methodist Board of Church and Society had nearly a dozen full-time legislative specialists. The Methodist political agenda was somewhat more liberal than that of the Catholics. Methodists supported the legal right to abortion, the civil rights of racial minorities and homosexuals, restraints on defense spending, and a foreign policy based on human rights.

Straying From Scripture

These traditional church lobbyists "don't represent my part of the country," said Dallas preacher James Robison, a founder of the conservative Religious Roundtable. Robison contended the established church lobby had strayed from the Bible: "Political liberalism has been spawned by theological liberalism."

Leaders of the new Christian right claimed the only thing they were doing differently was expounding conservative views, which they believed to be more accurately in line with scripture. But Charles V. Bergstrom, executive director of the Lutheran Council Office for Governmental Affairs and chairman of the interreligious council, argued that the evangelical right was not just conventional church lobbying with a different point of view.

"First, they mix revivalism and evangelism with political issues," Bergstrom said. "You're a sinner and an immoral person if you vote against them. Second, they claim to be called by God with this political mission. . . . When you start feeling you've been selected by God, there's a strong danger. Third is the establishment of hit lists. . . . They have every right to get involved, but it ought to be clearly on the issues."

records" of the liberal incumbents. The only ambiguous issue in the Christian Voice campaign was the degree to which the group really influenced elections; other established conservative groups and, in many cases the Republican Party, had targeted the same districts.

In addition to such formal aid, some of the evangelicals' favored candidates seemed to be getting valuable exposure through conservative churches. The activity was reminiscent of the role some Southern black churches played in assisting liberal candidates. The Rev. Dick Vignuelle, pastor of Shades Mountain Independent Church near Birmingham and head of Alabama's Moral Majority chapter, said he had two conservative Senate candidates attend services in his church and answer questions about their views "on moral issues." He said 1,000 believers were in attendance for each. The two men were vying for the right to oppose Sen. Donald Stewart, D-Ala., a target of the evangelical right, in a contest eventually won by the movement's preferred candidate, Jeremiah Denton.

Moral Majority held a Birmingham rally Aug. 26, 1980, one week before the primary, at which Falwell plugged the group's local heroes, and took swipes at the local congressman, Buchanan. Buchanan said Vignuelle also had denounced him from the pulpit as "un-Christian," which the pastor denied. Vignuelle said, "I have mentioned his name [from the pulpit] but not in the light of trying to cast influence one way or the other." Buchanan said conservatives fired up by Moral Majority also conducted door-to-door campaigning and a get-out-the-vote crusade that "almost certainly" was the deciding factor in his defeat. "If you ever have to choose between facing the lions and getting involved with these Christians," the congressman advised, "I'd follow Daniel right into the lions' den."

Pitfalls

A serious problem for the evangelical right was that it had begun to produce a backlash among the established churches and moderate evangelicals, not to mention Jews, who worried that slogans about "Christianizing America" sounded dangerously close to a state religion.

Church involvement in politics was not new to history or exclusive to the right wing. Most of the mainline churches maintained lobbying operations in Washington. (box, p. 111)

But the "hit lists" and "moral" vote ratings, and the tendency to equate Christianity with conservatism, sent a tingle of alarm through members of Congress who were theologically conservative, but politically liberal. An aide to

one such member, in the course of an hour-long interview, used the terms "fascist," "witch hunt," "inquisition" and "Big Brother" in connection with the fundamentalist fringe.

"I believe you have to allow a person to differ from you politically and still be a Christian," said Bailey Smith, president of the 13-million-member Southern Baptist Convention. Smith was invited to speak at The Roundtable rally in Dallas, but he admitted in an interview backstage, "I don't even know what I'm doing here."

"Generally it is a good movement," he said of the evangelical right. "I think we have to really be careful, though, in identifying all conservative political views as synonymous with Christianity.... The way some of these men talk here, I think they're more excited about missiles than about the Messiah."

Savior in the White House?

While the 1980 elections constituted a clear triumph for conservatives, it was not clear how much the Christian Right contributed to those results on its own. In 1982 conservative religious leaders could not afford to rest on their laurels.

Evangelical right leaders were at least able to draw from the experiences of 1980. They had become concerned that they had focused too much on elections, which could have two devastating results. If the candidates they chose lost, disappointed Christians could abandon the movement in dismay. And if the candidates they supported won, leaders saw a serious danger of disillusionment.

Billings said that after Reagan used the word "damn" in public, he was swamped with phone calls and letters from anguished evangelicals. Christians do not swear, he was told. Later, when a news magazine carried a lighthearted item about Reagan consulting his horoscope, Billings got another barrage of protests. Christians do not consult horoscopes. "You have to understand our folks," Billings said. "They have been preacher-led. So anyone we promote is up there on the same platform with the preacher."

Complacency could also prove deadly. If religious leaders in Dallas betrayed their concern for missiles, many believers thought the Messiah had come in the form of Ronald Reagan. William Billings of the National Christian Action Coalition feared that such a perception could cause a slackening of efforts at the grass-roots level.

Thus, the recurring admonition at Dallas, and in the movement at large, had become: Focus on issues, not candidates. "People let you down," said a Moral Majority official. "Principles are eternal."

Small Business Lobby

Organizing on the national level and using their natural grass-roots constituency, the nation's 10 million small-business owners employed aggressive lobbying tactics to influence legislation and government policy in the 1980s. While some groups traditionally regarded as representing "big business" worked to take advantage of this movement, and in the end may have derived its greatest and most lasting benefits, the small-business lobby increasingly carved out its own niche in Washington.

Only in the late 1970s had independent small businesses made serious efforts to organize and influence federal policy. While achievements attributable principally to small-business influence were not yet numerous by 1980, the lobby could point to several developments that showed government was listening. The White House Conference on Small Business, an event that culminated Jan. 14-17, 1980, in Washington after a series of regional meetings, produced a 60-item agenda of priorities and increased small-business visibility early in an election year. President Carter, other high administration officials and members of Congress spoke at the gathering, hoping to persuade delegates that they understood small business problems.

The Small Business Administration (SBA), which often had been rocked by charges of scandal and inefficiency, began to exercise more effectively its role as an advocate for the small-business executive. The SBA's Office of Advocacy began to actively participate in federal rulemaking proceedings on behalf of small businesses. In addition, a task force put together by the SBA office drafted a proposal to promote increased innovation by small businesses. The plan served as the basis for bills introduced in the fall of 1979 by the Senate and House Small Business committee chairmen. Finally, and perhaps most importantly, small business began to rack up some legislative victories in Congress. Legislation specifically intended to help small businesses, such as the Regulatory Flexibility Act of 1980, was regarded as a barometer of the lobby's increasing political clout.

However, in other instances — defeat of labor law "reform," for example — the victories may have been more the result of effective lobbying by organizations representing larger corporate interests than the clout of small business. While small business continued to press its own legislative agenda, only on occasion did it strongly advocate positions opposed by big business interests.

Economic Role

A principal reason for the growing political power of small businesses was their significant impact on the nation's economic health. Small business means jobs. "Jobs are gut issues. Jobs are votes. And where are the jobs coming into? They're coming into small business," said Bill Anderson, co-chairman of the Council of Small and Independent Business Associations (COSIBA), an umbrella advocacy group.

Government statistics support this view. The more than 10 million non-farm small businesses in the United States constituted 97 percent of all U.S. non-farm enterprises, according to the SBA in 1980. Their share of the gross national product was 43 percent.

There is no universally accepted view of what constitutes a small business. SBA, and even small business organizations, use many measures in attempts to provide a definition. SBA looks upon a small business as an enterprise privately owned and operated, not dominant in its field. Depending on the industry, the dividing line between large and small businesses is determined by annual earnings or the number of employees. In certain industries, such as rubber production, a "small business" may have as many as 1,500 employees. In others, such as merchandise wholesaling, annual receipts may reach $22 million.

A profile of small business can be pieced together from these 1980 figures:

- About 80 percent of U.S. non-farm businesses employed fewer than 10 people.
- Most small businesses were in either the service or retail trade industries.
- Minorities owned only 4.4 percent of U.S. businesses; nearly all minority businesses were small.
- Women owned 4.6 percent of U.S. businesses, and 5.7 percent of small enterprises.

Thus small business could claim greater federal attention than had hitherto come its way. In addition to providing employment for 58 percent of the U.S. business work force — excluding farms — small business historically had created more jobs than big corporations. Between 1969 and 1976, small- and medium-sized businesses generated six million of nine million new jobs. Most of the three million other new jobs were created by state and local governments. There was virtually no increase in employment over that period among the 1,000 largest U.S. corporations, ac-

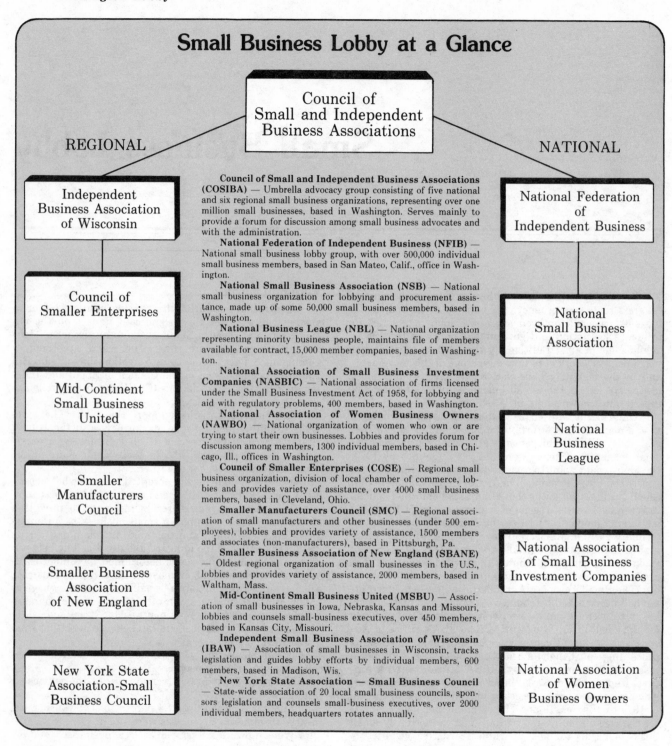

Small Business Lobby at a Glance

Council of
Small and Independent
Business Associations

REGIONAL

NATIONAL

Independent
Business Association
of Wisconsin

Council of
Smaller Enterprises

Mid-Continent
Small Business
United

Smaller
Manufacturers
Council

Smaller Business
Association
of New England

New York State
Association-Small
Business Council

National Federation
of
Independent Business

National
Small Business
Association

National
Business
League

National Association
of Small Business
Investment Companies

National Association
of Women
Business Owners

Council of Small and Independent Business Associations (COSIBA) — Umbrella advocacy group consisting of five national and six regional small business organizations, representing over one million small businesses, based in Washington. Serves mainly to provide a forum for discussion among small business advocates and with the administration.

National Federation of Independent Business (NFIB) — National small business lobby group, with over 500,000 individual small business members, based in San Mateo, Calif., office in Washington.

National Small Business Association (NSB) — National small business organization for lobbying and procurement assistance, made up of some 50,000 small business members, based in Washington.

National Business League (NBL) — National organization representing minority business people, maintains file of members available for contract, 15,000 member companies, based in Washington.

National Association of Small Business Investment Companies (NASBIC) — National association of firms licensed under the Small Business Investment Act of 1958, for lobbying and aid with regulatory problems, 400 members, based in Washington.

National Association of Women Business Owners (NAWBO) — National organization of women who own or are trying to start their own businesses. Lobbies and provides forum for discussion among members, 1300 individual members, based in Chicago, Ill., offices in Washington.

Council of Smaller Enterprises (COSE) — Regional small business organization, division of local chamber of commerce, lobbies and provides variety of assistance, over 4000 small business members, based in Cleveland, Ohio.

Smaller Manufacturers Council (SMC) — Regional association of small manufacturers and other businesses (under 500 employees), lobbies and provides variety of assistance, 1500 members and associates (non-manufacturers), based in Pittsburgh, Pa.

Smaller Business Association of New England (SBANE) — Oldest regional organization of small businesses in the U.S., lobbies and provides variety of assistance, 2000 members, based in Waltham, Mass.

Mid-Continent Small Business United (MSBU) — Association of small businesses in Iowa, Nebraska, Kansas and Missouri, lobbies and counsels small-business executives, over 450 members, based in Kansas City, Missouri.

Independent Small Business Association of Wisconsin (IBAW) — Association of small businesses in Wisconsin, tracks legislation and guides lobby efforts by individual members, 600 members, based in Madison, Wis.

New York State Association — Small Business Council — State-wide association of 20 local small business councils, sponsors legislation and counsels small-business executives, over 2000 individual members, headquarters rotates annually.

cording to SBA statistics. Also, small business had been responsible for more than half of all United States patented inventions since World War II.

Using these statistics, the small-business lobby mounted increasingly aggressive efforts to influence government action. Small-business groups armed themselves with detailed position papers, promoted grass-roots letter-writing to Congress, met frequently with members of Congress and executive branch officials, and reached for a greater role in initiating legislation and securing support for measures.

Small-Business Lobbies

Two major national groups lobbied primarily for small business — the National Federation of Independent Business (NFIB) and the National Small Business Association (NSB). NFIB, founded in 1943, spent about $500,000 in 1979 in Washington lobby-related activities, about half of its total Washington budget, according to John Motley, the group's deputy director. Its funding came from dues, paid by individual members "based on what they think the organization is worth to them," according to Motley. The dues payment ranged from $35 to $500 — although few paid the top figure.

NFIB's growing national presence resulted from a decision made in the early 1970s, to give greater support to Washington operations, which previously had been sparsely staffed and inactive in lobbying. By 1980 NFIB was compiling voting records of every member of Congress and rating them on issues affecting small businesses. It testified or provided position papers on small-business-related proposals, secured cosponsors for bills, did "head counts" of members' positions on bills, and urged members to write to Congress. All this was done with an extensive computer operation and a 20-member Washington staff, including 11 full-time, registered lobbyists. NFIB, composed of individual small businesses, had grown from fewer than 300 members nine years earlier to some 600,000. Lobby operations, carried out in 24 states in 1980, were expanded to all 50 states by 1982.

The NFIB's resources were small when compared with those marshaled by organizations usually identified with larger corporate interests. For example, the Chamber of Commerce of the United States had a national budget of more than $55 million and employed about 45 registered lobbyists in 1980. Five were full-time lobbyists; others were "issues managers" who coordinated lobby efforts and sometimes personally contacted congressmen or testified at hearings.

The NFIB's purpose, said Motley, was purely to get legislation passed that would help the small-business executive. "We will shift coalitions with the issues. We don't care who we fight with as long as we win," he said.

NSB and SBLC

NSB, headed by Herb Liebenson, was made up of about 50,000 small-business executives in 1982. The organization, founded in 1937, was based in Washington where it had 3 lobbyists on a staff of 12. Its budget, estimated at nearly $1 million, was derived from dues paid by members. Payments ranged from $40 to $500.

NSB's major lobby efforts were in conjunction with the Small Business Legislative Council (SBLC). NSB formed the council in 1977 with about 20 trade associations to provide a broader base for determining policy and directing lobbying on issues affecting small business. In the past, NSB had formed ad hoc coalitions with trade associations on specific issues.

SBLC was made up of 75 national trade associations and several state trade associations, representing some four million small businesses. Both SBLC and NSB published newsletters for members, and took positions on issues of particular interest to small business.

COSIBA

NFIB, NSB, the National Association of Small Business Investment Companies, the National Business League, the National Association of Women Business Owners and six regional groups made up the coalition COSIBA, the Council of Small and Independent Business Associations. COSIBA members, representing more than a million companies, regularly met to swap information on legislation. The group also met frequently with presidential advisers, Cabinet members, and other top-level executive branch officials to talk over small business concerns and solutions.

In 1980 COSIBA tackled few legislative issues because a consensus of members often was difficult to achieve.

Instead, the organization primarily provided a forum for contacts between small business interests and administration officials.

A certain tension existed between NFIB and NSB, the only two national, general small-business organizations. "There is a small business lobby," said one observer, "[but] it is not monolithic." In 1980 the typical NFIB member was a retailer grossing $100,000 to $200,000 a year, according to an NFIB spokesman. Seventy-five percent of the members employed fewer than 10 persons. But NFIB had no cutoff for determining eligibility. Thus, for instance, if a business expanded in size while a member of the NFIB, it was not subject to rejection for renewed membership because of its growth. By contrast, NSB tended to be more rigid in membership standards, athough it also avoided a single definition of "small business." Businesses with more than 500 employees, for instance, were not considered eligible to belong to NSB. An NFIB spokesman suggested that NSB members were more likely to be "very small" businesses. An NSB spokesman said the organization had no statistical profile of its members.

The two organizations admitted that they competed for constituents, although there always had been some overlap in membership. Some observed that lobbying by the NFIB generally was more effective than that by NSB because NFIB's membership was much larger and its lobby efforts were better organized, staffed and financed. Also, NFIB frequently was perceived as more effective in achieving legislative aims. But some observers, including Dan Bicker of Congress Watch, a Ralph Nader-affiliated organization, said the NFIB leaned too much toward cooperating with big-business interests to obtain congressional victories.

According to NFIB's Motley, at one time there had been talk of merging the two groups because NSB's finances were shaky. But when NSB regained a certain stability, the idea was rejected.

Grass-Roots Efforts

Because small businesses literally are everywhere, they have a natural grass-roots constituency. Long-established regional groups such as the Smaller Business Association of New England (SBANE) were comprised of individual small businesses in target areas. Regional organizations tended to concentrate as much on informing members and providing business education programs as on levying pressure to influence government action.

Following the example of SBANE, the oldest regional organization in the country, several similar groups organized and were beginning to make an impact on government decision-making by 1980. These included the Council of Smaller Enterprises (COSE) in Cleveland, the Independent Business Association of Wisconsin (IBAW), and others. On the whole, small-business spokesmen said that their power and ideas came from the local level.

NFIB, for instance, regularly polled all its individual members, using questionnaires called "mandates." Positions attracting the most support automatically became the organization's official line. NSB, with monthly newsletter "action alerts," encouraged members to write Congress on specific issues at critical points in the legislative process. Letters from individual business execuitves had an important effect on policy-makers. "Basically, the small-business man in the past [would] catch the congressman when he's

Chamber Lobbying Takes To The Air

Already a lavish practitioner of "grass-roots" lobbying techniques, the U.S. Chamber of Commerce has introduced satellite telecommunications into the battle for the hearts and minds of Congress.

In April 1982 the Chamber began beaming custom-made television programming to business subscribers around the country. The broadcasts — including legislative and political news with a business slant, call-in shows starring government officials and features tailored for small businesses, corporate lawyers or exporters — were designed mainly to enhance the business community's political sophistication and clout.

According to the Chamber's satellite network manager Doug Widner, the new TV system, called "The American Business Network," or "Biznet" for short, would enable business executives to respond instantly to developments in Congress rather than having to wait for a more conventional call to action sent out by mail or telegram.

"Biznet has the potential on paper to become one of the most powerful lobbying tools in the country," Widner declared. "We can disseminate to the business community information about government while there's still time to do something about it."

In private, some allied business lobbyists said the Chamber's network represented a costly gamble. They questioned whether there was a market for the programming that was being promised to subscribers — about four hours each workday. But they agreed that it would enhance business influence mightily if it worked.

Union lobbyists at the AFL-CIO, watching the Biznet developments from their Washington headquarters near the Chamber offices, set up a committee to discuss the possibility of nationwide "teleconferences" for organized labor. But labor representatives said unions could not afford anything near the scope of Biznet.

Millions in Hardware

Biznet, according to Chamber sources, was the brainchild of the group's president, Richard L. Lesher, a former official of the National Aeronautics and Space Administration. The Chamber spent $6 million for new television studios and a satellite dish at its Washington headquarters. Widner said the cost of producing and sending the programming — estimated at an additional $3 million a year — was to be reimbursed by subscription fees charged to local recipients.

The recipients would be corporations, local chambers of commerce and trade associations willing to invest $15,000 in a satellite "Earth station" plus a $5,000 annual subscription fee to receive the Chamber broadcasts. Chamber officials contended the lo-

cals could recoup this expense plus a profit by selling tickets to Chamber "teleseminars" and other broadcasts.

Representatives from the Chamber expected to have about 50 subscribers using the system by the time it was working to its planned capacity of four hours each workday in October 1982. In May of that year nearly 25 customers had signed contracts and were having their systems installed; another 25 were working out the details of their agreements with the U.S. Chamber.

The Chamber already was well known for its efforts to mobilize business executives on legislation. During President Reagan's 1981 crusade to cut budget and taxes, the Chamber's "action call network" helped generate thousands of letters and phone calls to swing legislators urging support of the White House.

Sherry Rusbuldt, who was in charge of marketing Biznet, said the new network would speed this dramatically. For example, she said, the Chamber was considering sending out live coverage of a congressional committee debate on tax legislation, allowing business viewers to size up their lawmakers and respond instantly. "If they see their congressman is voting in a way they don't like, they can pick up a phone and before the congressman gets back to his office there will be a message waiting on his desk," she said.

Campaign Tool

Chamber officials had other plans for Biznet. On major lobbying efforts, the Chamber could expand its audience by buying time on cable television networks or other satellites. The Chamber talked to executives of the Holiday Inn chain, for instance, about occasional broadcasts to its hotels equipped with satellite receiver dishes. This enlarged network could be used for nationwide "business rallies," such as those the Chamber staged in Washington to push for President Reagan's tax cuts earlier in 1981.

The network also could be a two-way lobbying tool, Widner said. Outside of regular broadcasting hours, the system could be reversed by selected clients, such as business executives in one city or state who wanted a "teleconference" with their congressional delegation. (The viewers would grill the lawmakers through the Chamber's toll-free phone lines.)

The network also would be used, Widner said, to help elect "pro-business" congressional candidates. Because Biznet was a private system, it would not be subject to regulations, such as the Fairness Doctrine, that govern the public airwaves, Widner said. Occasionally, the Chamber planned to turn over the network to its political action committee to lend a forum to favored candidates, officials said.

doing Main Street. Now, they seem to have gotten in the habit of writing their congressmen and personalizing their concerns," said Rep. James R. Jones, D-Okla., a House Ways and Means Committee member and later chairman of the House Budget Committee.

The result of mass mail, said one House Small Business Committee staff member, was that "when a congressman has heard enough times from enough different people back home ... the problem of proving the case [for small business] is not a hurdle." One example was the 1978 defeat of the proposed Consumer Protection Agency, strongly opposed by business. NFIB estimated that some 30,000 of its members wrote Congress against the measure. Others who urged small-business persons to send letters in that effort included NSB, the U.S. Chamber of Commerce and the National Association of Manufacturers (NAM).

According to Motley, critics claimed the number of letters from small-business people on the issue totaled some 60,000. The measure was defeated by a 36-vote margin in the House. As a result of these organizing efforts, it was thought that small-business concerns would be taken more seriously in Congress.

"Small businesses are becoming more sophisticated as a lobby," said Robert Dotchin, staff director of the Senate Select Small Business Committee. *(see Congressional Committees, p. 118)* "They're getting beyond the emotionalism and offering concrete suggestions."

Michael Gildea of the AFL-CIO's Legislation Department, frequently confronted small business on the opposite side of issues. "They are making their presence felt by contacting their congressmen. That kind of constituent pressure is most effective," he said.

But Gildea added that on a number of issues, particularly labor law reform and efforts to restrict Federal Trade Commission activity, small-business people were "more or less being used by big business." He said labor had been hesitant to approach small business to seek alliances because "their interests are split, or the Chamber [of Commerce] has co-opted them. So we wouldn't waste our time." Dan Bicker, of the public interest lobby Congress Watch, said, "When small business combines with big business ... then you have some influence. When they come up *against* big business, big business wins hands down."

Bicker said NFIB was influential, but "not as prominent" as organizations associated with larger corporate interests. The reason, he said, was that NFIB simply could not match the spending done by groups representing big business.

Diversity: Curse or Blessing?

One of the biggest assets the small-business lobby could claim in wielding influence was its size. But its vast membership was a disadvantage also. Because the community was so large, it was diverse and difficult to assemble. As a result, it sometimes failed to present a united front on congressional proposals.

One example of this occured in the 1980 debate over capital cost recovery proposals — legislation to rewrite the tax rules and speed up the depreciation of business equipment. When a business depreciates the value of its equipment, it writes off the lost value as a business deduction, lowering the amount of income subject to federal taxation. NFIB, regional groups, and big business groups supported the "10-5-3" proposal to permit business depreciation of buildings in 10 years, equipment in five years and cars and

light trucks in three years. But NSB adamantly was opposed to the bill. Spokesmen said the plan was a "giveaway" for big business, with a total cost so high that the resulting inflation would hurt small businesses more than the bill would help them.

One congressional staffer complained, "There's a lack of unity among the various [small-business] interest groups. ... [T]hey all have their own viewpoints, and they don't speak with one voice." Anderson of COSIBA countered, "You're dealing with the largest single unorganized constituency in the country ... a loose-knit coalition. We're not organized like labor ... like the farmers. These are independently operating guys." Anderson also pointed out that many small-business problems were parochial, and thus ill-addressed in a national forum. Daniel A. Cronin, SBANE president, added "It's not in the nature of small-business people to organize a lobby. We resent special-interest government."

Even when the unity hurdle was surmounted, some congressional staffers said small business lobbyists diluted their influence by tackling too many issues. "Some of them get into issues that aren't really small business. I've seen some get into abortion," said Tom Powers, majority council of the House Small Business Committee.

Big or Small Business?

Some groups traditionally identified with big business also took steps to speak up for smaller merchants. But their motives and commitment were questioned by some small-business advocates. The U.S. Chamber of Commerce, for instance, had an established reputation for favoring big commercial interests that belied its mostly small-business membership.

In 1982, approximately 90 percent of Chamber members were businesses with fewer than 100 employees. But because it generally was perceived as being a big-business lobby — so much so that it was scrutinized in a report on corporate-interest lobbying — the organization had been working to alter its image. In 1976 the Chamber established a staff unit and advisory group to focus exclusively on small business concerns — the Center for Small Business and the Council of Small Business.

The Council was empowered only to recommend positions on small business issues; final policy was determined by the Chamber's 65-member board of directors. These in-house bodies produced a ripple effect — some 700 local chambers were said to have units handling small-business problems in 1980. There were 300 such units in 1977.

Ivan Elmer, director of the Chamber's Center for Small Business, said the changes simply made the organization's small-business advocacy efforts more easily identified. "We realized so many things we were routinely doing for small business were not being recognized," he said.

By contrast, the National Association of Manufacturers, another organization traditionally linked with big-business interests, neither set up organs to voice small-business concerns nor assigned staffers to deal specifically with these issues. NAM's membership was similar to that of the Chamber; of a membership of about 12,000, some 11,000 were small businesses. Jim Carty, an NAM vice president, said NAM lobbyists routinely were expected to consider small-business views. "We're just all more sensitized to the problems that small-business men have," he said.

Observers took different views of these efforts to side with small business. "Small business has gathered a lot of

Congressional Committees

Congressional committees devoted particularly to the concerns of small business were not established until after World War II. In 1947 select small-business committees were created for investigatory purposes by each chamber. Even by 1980, Small Business panels in both the Senate and the House had limited jurisdiction. While they had the authority to consider and report some legislation, the small-business committees often were obliged to share that power with other standing committees. Much comittee work consisted of providing a sounding board for small business issues. Urged by small-business lobbies, the committees launched investigations into issues from export assistance to antitrust policy.

The House Select Small Business Committee was upgraded to a standing committee in 1974, when the House gave it the jurisdiction of the former House Banking and Currency Small Business Subcommittee. An early working draft of the reorganization plan had proposed abolishing the Select Small Business Committee. Congressional proponents of abolition feared they might lose their seats on the panel because of restrictive rules on committee membership, and they opposed creating the standing panel. The final reorganization plan, however, contained a provision allowing those members already serving to remain on the committee. The panel had 40 members in 1982.

In the Senate, a reorganization plan of 1977 threatened the existence of the Senate Select Small Business Committee. Early proposals would have merged it into either the Agriculture or Finance committees. Small-business advocates fought the reorganization, arguing that their concerns would be ignored on the larger committees.

Letters from thousands of reorganization opponents flooded Senate offices in what David Voight of the Small Business Administration (SBA) recalled as "a classic lobby effort." The Senate Small Business panel was saved. Later, the committee became so popular that its membership was expanded from 14 to 17 in the 96th Congress (1979-80) to accommodate the many requests by senators for assignment to the panel. In 1981 the Senate Small Business Committee was made a full committee.

As standing committees, while primarily concerned with legislation affecting the SBA and certain narrow small-business problems, the Senate and House Small Business panels have been freer to make proposals concerning taxes, trade policy, and regulatory reform — matters previously assigned to other committees or jointly referred to Small Business panels.

steam in the last two years. And there are a lot of people that are trying to piggyback on the ride, now that it's a force to be reckoned with....," said Dave Kromarsky of NSB. David Voight, an assistant to the SBA's advocacy chief counsel, said that "the big-business organizations and companies are fairly adept at aligning their issues with small business ... and sort of hiding behind them...."

One small-business lobbyist rated NAM's efforts at representing small business as "non-existent," and the Chamber's as "far from a vital force." The proof, according to some observers, was the way in which these organizations determined stands on issues with conflicting small-business/big-business interests. Because larger businesses in advocacy organizations contributed hefty financial support, positions were likely to be modified in their favor, said Powers of the House Small Business Committee. "You don't have views presented with what's good for smalls," he contended. "It's got to be meshed. They can't alienate the other [big-business] members."

To charges that the Chamber merely sided with small business to achieve big-business goals, the Chamber's Elmer replied, "I think we're pulling the bandwagon. We were in this, in relative terms, quite a long time ago. Our visibility has increased because [of] the White House conference."

In many cases, said Carty of NAM, consensus could be achieved on policy. But if small- and big-business interests seemed unalterably opposed, he said, "sometimes you don't take any position." NAM got more dollars and a greater percentage of financial support from larger businesses, said Carty. He would not disclose specific figures.

Larry Kraus, general counsel and chief financial officer for the Chamber, said the organization received only about 25 percent of its dues from big businesses. The Chamber defined big businesses as those among the 1,300 largest U.S. corporations, grossing an average of $80 million a year. Dues made up about half of the Chamber's national budget, with remaining revenues coming from the sale of its magazine, *Nation's Business*.

But small-business lobbyists were quick to point out that even though small- and big-business interests occasionally differed, they had many interests in common. "Our big fight has not been with big business," said COSIBA's Anderson. "Our big fight has been with government treating all business the same. Big businesses are our customers. We need big business to be healthy."

Activist Origins

Most observers trace the origin of small-business activism back to efforts to create and maintain House and Senate Small Business committees. *(box, this page)* But the intense efforts of the 1970s by small-business executives to make their voices prominent in Washington was almost universally attributed to a favorite target of opposition: government regulation.

Small business contended that Congress and federal regulators frequently failed to consider the impact of their actions on small businesses. Small business "had a non-reputation in Washington," said one House Small Business Committee staff member. NSB's Liebenson agreed. "In the past, especially on broad economic issues — labor, Social Security — there was literally no input from small business because none of the associations had the money or the staff...."

But increasing government regulation, based on measures such as the Occupational Safety and Health Act

(OSHA) of 1970 and the Employee Retirement Income Security Act (ERISA) of 1974 strengthened their resolve to work at influencing government. OSHA required businesses to abide by detailed safety standards. ERISA set down strict rules for private pension plans, requiring businesses offering them to submit voluminous paperwork. Small businesses found themselves for the first time confronting detailed and stringent government rules that affected their everyday operations. "The more they got hit over the head, the madder they got," said Liebenson.

Congressional Attitudes

In general, members responded positively to small business' legislative overtures, in the view of lobbyists, congressional staffers, and members themselves. Sen. John C. Culver, D-Iowa (1975-81), author of regulatory reform and product liability proposals favored by small businesses told one small business trade association, "Small business' growing capacity to speak up is being matched by a new willingness on the part of Congress to listen." Culver presided over two Senate subcommittees handling regulatory reform bills considered vital to small business.

It is easy to see why Congress listened to small business. Due to small business' pervasive nature, it was a large part of any member's constituency. Census Bureau statistics of 1979 that classified some 4.5 million businesses by industry and size showed nearly 4.4 million businesses throughout the 50 states with fewer than 100 employees. The sheer numbers involved underscored small business' natural grass-roots constituency. For example, even in a state like Nevada with a relatively low population, the census figures showed that 13,875 of 14,139 businesses in the state were literally "small businesses," employing fewer than 100 people.

A less visible factor was that many members of Congress had been engaged in small enterprises themselves. Another consideration was that open support of small business was less likely to be frowned upon by the public than alignment with major corporate interests, particularly on business versus consumer issues. Congressional support for small business was "a motherhood kind of thing," said NSB's Kromarsky.

Nonetheless, when it came to specifics or controversies pitting small business against big business or labor, members of Congress were cautious in choosing sides. "I wouldn't say any member of Congress is anti-small business," said Powers. "But they've got other interests."

Many small-business advocates pointed to 1978 as a watershed year in which small business first began to win significant legislative victories. On a number of the issues — reduction of corporate income tax rates, defeat of labor law "reform" and defeat of a consumer protection agency — small business found itself aligned with larger corporate interests. But on other issues small business was the primary beneficiary. For instance, a provision in Labor-HEW fiscal 1979 appropriations extended widespread small-business exemptions from OSHA rules and penalties. The exemptions also had been enacted in fiscal 1978 Labor-HEW appropriations, and were aimed to reduce what supporters of the provision called "nit-picking" by OSHA inspectors.

Another example was congressional approval of a bill extending SBA programs. The bill later was pocket vetoed by President Carter, who said it was too rigid in allocating spending. But the veto did not affect most fiscal 1979 programs, since they had been authorized by an earlier law. The bill would have provided higher authorizations for some programs and expanded the role of SBA's advocacy office.

Electoral Politics

The small-business lobby hoped to enhance its influence by delving into electoral politics, an arena used by other major interest groups to influence government. NFIB set up a political action committee (PAC) to dole out contributions to congressional candidates rated highly by the organization for their support of small business. NFIB also planned to target contributions to opponents of legislators with low ratings. "[We] have the beginnings of a political reward-punishment system, similar to what other lobbies have had for years," said NFIB lobbyist Motley.

NSB, by contrast, rejected the idea of a PAC. "The problem with PACs is that frequently you'll make an enemy where there's a potential friend," said Kromarsky. But he said that NSB financially supported some members of Congress without establishing a PAC. In one instance, the organization sent representatives to a campaign fundraiser, and encouraged NSB members to attend. In 1982, NSB was still without a PAC.

It was thought unlikely that small business as a whole would begin fielding individual political candidates. Small business is "a cross-section of America," said SBANE's Cronin. "They're not very predictable." Yet small business was beginning to believe it could effectively shape legislative and administrative decisions in Washington. As Tim Wittig, minority counsel for the House Small Business Committee, noted, "There's a lot of things they haven't gotten yet. But they've started to fight. And that's half the battle."

Fast-Food Lobby

The operators of McDonald's, Burger King, Kentucky Fried Chicken, Pizza Hut and other fast-food outlets in 1981 began a concerted effort to convince Congress that — to paraphrase a familiar jingle — they deserved a break today.

The break they had in mind was an extension of the targeted jobs tax credit, which allows employers to write off part of the cost of hiring young, disadvantaged workers. For companies that employ vast numbers of minimum-wage youngsters, the targeted credit had emerged as the year's best hope of cutting the high cost of labor.

The fast food lobby got its break. In 1981 the tax credit was extended for one year and efforts continued in 1982 to increase the extension again, this time to five years.

Fast-food lobbyists seeking tax legislation in the early 1980s were a sight as familiar as golden arches. But the 1981 stirrings of the fast-food lobby on the tax credit and just before that on government milk-price supports marked a new level of activism for an industry that traditionally had kept a low political profile.

"The maturing of the industry is just now starting to take place," said Clayton C. Taylor, manager of congressional relations for McDonald's Corp. At age 27, McDonald's was the senior citizen of modern fast food in 1982.

"It's kind of a sleeping giant, as it were," said Ronald Platt, vice president of Miami-based Burger King, the No. 2 fast-food purveyor. "It has not realized any significant degree of its potential." Platt said the industry had just begun to realize the effect government policies had on its operations and the power it had to influence those policies.

A Ready-Made Lobby

In an era of grass-roots lobbying, imagining the lobbying potential of 68,000 small businesses located in virtually every American neighborhood was easy. "We've got at least one [Burger King] restaurant in every congressional district in the country," said Platt. "Our franchisees are independent, local businessmen, who pay local taxes and provide local jobs."

Burger King was just one regiment. As of 1980 fourteen fast-food companies had chains with more than 1,000 units each, according to the National Restaurant Association. Most had ready-made communications networks initially designed for product uniformity and quality control. Chain eateries, moreover, had built their success on marketing, a skill also important in politics.

"The potential for a franchisor-to-franchisee grass-roots program is absolutely incredible," said Jerry C. Wilkerson, director of government relations for the International Franchise Association. The association represents fast-food chains and other franchised industries, from muffler shops to day-care centers.

The awakening of the fast-food chains, Wilkerson said, was not the only evidence of the clout waiting in franchised business. He pointed to the 1980 lobbying victory of soft-drink bottlers, another franchised industry, in a battle over antitrust legislation. Hotel and motel chains are organized for lobbying, and there was a growing franchise component in the politically active real estate industry.

'Like Pulling Teeth'

Yet for an industry that went overseas to market hamburgers in Hong Kong, pizza in Puerto Rico and chicken buckets in Beirut, fast-food retailers were relatively slow to expand their political franchise. With the exception of a rather discreet 1977 campaign to influence the minimum wage law, fast-food companies tended to avoid the legislative fray. In their explosive early years, companies said, they had little time for dickering with the government.

Until inflation and soaring gasoline prices dampened the industry's growth in 1979, fast-food entrepreneurs had little to complain about. A slump that year showed the industry how susceptible it could be to economic pressures. "I suppose the reason some of the fast-food people are getting active all of a sudden is they're finding out what some of these government regulations and programs are costing them," said Peyton George, a lawyer-lobbyist representing Pizza Hut.

The industry also was very image-conscious, which probably created misgivings about plunging into politics. When the Senate Select Committee on Nutrition held hearings on American dietary habits in 1979, persuading McDonald's to testify "was like pulling teeth," one organizer of the hearings said.

"They have establishments on every street corner," explained Andrew Lawrence, director of government relations for the National Restaurant Association, discussing McDonald's wariness of public conflict. "They're easy-to-identify targets, like the oil companies, for anyone who wants to throw criticism."

Leading Fast-Food Chains

Chain (Parent Company)	1980 Food Sales (Est.)	Number of Outlets (Est., end 1980)
McDonald's	$6,360,000,000	6,247
Burger King (Pillsbury)	2,250,000,000	2,766
Kentucky Fried Chicken (Heublein Inc.)	2,000,000,000	4,150
Wendy's	1,250,000,000	2,018
Dairy Queen	1,019,000,000	4,905
Hardees	1,005,000,000	1,321
Pizza Hut (Pepsico)	1,000,000,000	4,000
Marriott*	970,000,000	1,570
Arby's (Royal Crown)	500,000,000	928
Church's	450,000,000	1,270
Jerrico	415,000,000	1,050
Jack-in-the-Box (Ralston-Purina)	403,000,000	775

* Includes Big Boy, Roy Rogers, Hot Shoppes and Farrell's chains.

Source: Nation's Restaurant News

In 1981 McDonald's, Kentucky Fried Chicken and Burger King, the industry sales leaders, did not maintain offices in Washington, preferring to have their lobbyists commute from corporate headquarters. Other companies were even more detached from Washington, relying on trade groups to keep them informed and express their views.

Burger Chef, a subsidiary of General Foods Corp., had no separate division to follow government activities, handling legislative matters out of its legal department. The chain rarely participated in legislative issues.

Marriott Corp., which owns the Roy Rogers and Big Boy burger chains, also demonstrated little sense of urgency about congressional affairs. The company's vice president for government relations retired early in 1981, but the company decided it could wait until January 1982 to replace him. W. Don Ladd, assistant to the director of the Science and Education Administration at the Agriculture Department, eventually was picked for the job but stayed with the government until he amassed the necessary length of service for his government pension.

Sterling D. Colton, Marriott vice president and general counsel, said efforts to interest franchisees and managers in legislation had been "rather sporadic, and I'm not sure how effective.... A manager of a Roy Rogers restaurant is so busy he just doesn't have much time to write letters to his congressman." Besides, he added, "We just don't visualize ourselves as lobbyists."

Beefing Up

By the early 1980s, however, several of the big chains had overcome any ambivalence about lobbying and had inaugurated their own governmental affairs programs. They were, for the most part, grass-roots operations; the

companies monitored legislation and, when an issue arose that affected corporate interests, encouraged local franchisees to take the case to their own member of Congress, with little visible evidence of the corporation's role.

Franchise lobbying could only work, industry sources agreed, on issues of immediate concern to the small-business executive. The top priorities were food and labor costs, the two largest items in a restaurateur's budget. Those were the issues where fast-food lobbying took place in 1981 and where its potential was expected to grow.

Here are some of the more active restaurant chains as of June 1981:

● McDonald's had the oldest legislative department, formed in the mid-1970s. Three full-time executives, based outside of Chicago, handled both state and federal affairs.

The company had a network of 1,400 owner-operators, most of whom owned more than one unit. Congressional relations manager Taylor said about half of them could be counted on to respond with calls, telegrams or visits when Congress needed a push on legislation that affected them. Taylor said the company mobilized its entire franchisee system "a few times a year." More often, as in the case of milk prices, the company only called on franchisees who had access to a few key legislators.

Taylor, who worked in several Capitol offices and the 1976 presidential campaign of Sen. Lloyd Bentsen, D-Texas, said the company viewed legislative action as a service it performed for its franchisees, like management training or quality control.

McDonald's conducted workshops to train its franchisees in how government works and even offered courses in government affairs at its "Hamburger University" in Oak Brook, Ill.

● Burger King had a three-year-old government relations office based in Miami. The office included two full-time staffers who tracked state legislation. Platt, who organized and directed the office, said Burger King had elevated government affairs to a top corporate priority. The owners and managers of the company's 2,800 outlets were organized into 10 regional councils and encouraged to cultivate friendships with their lawmakers. "We're probably another three to five years away from where I'd like to be, but we'll get there," said Platt.

● Kentucky Fried Chicken, the third largest fast-food retailer, had no government affairs division, but it had a grass-roots network called the Franchisee Legislative Action Group (FLAG). FLAG began in 1977, during congressional debate of the minimum wage law, but only in March of 1980, at the company's convention in New Orleans, was it expanded to include all 800 store owners.

Jim Beckett, who coordinated the FLAG operation from the company's Louisville headquarters, said the company had long depended on the Kentucky congressional delegation to help with legislative problems. But FLAG "gives us a broader base" in appealing to Congress.

"Some of our strongest FLAG supporters are small operators," he said. "Out of their own pockets they'll hop on an airplane and come to Washington to talk to their congressman. It's really kind of heartwarming, the enthusiasm they show, and the level of sophistication."

● Pizza Hut, based in Wichita, Kan., formed its governmental affairs operation in January 1981. The impetus was the arrival of the company's new chief executive, Donald N. Smith, who had encouraged similar efforts during jobs at McDonald's and Burger King, according to Larry Shauf, director of governmental and public affairs.

Pizza Hut and sister company Taco Bell, both owned by Pepsico, had a total of 5,300 outlets. Pizza Hut made a quick impression within the industry and Congress when it cooked up a lobbying effort that helped beat the dairy industry on milk-price supports.

• Jerrico, the Lexington, Kentucky-based company that ran Long John Silver fish restaurants, started a government affairs office in 1976. The company's lobbying network called on 100 franchise-holders in 40 states who in turn owned 1,100 restaurants. Thirty to 40 percent of the franchisees and shop managers would write to Congress on request, vice president Bruce Cotton said, and the letters were chock-full of persuasive personal experience. "There's probably grease stains on the letter," he said.

Like many other businesses, fast-food chains established political action committees (PACs) to reinforce their legislative interests. The PACs pooled donations from company executives and franchisees and parceled them out at election time, either to help ensure access to key incumbents or to support candidates sympathetic to business.

Restaurant chain PACs and their reported contributions in the 1980 elections, included: McDonald's ($98,650), Burger King ($40,000), Marriott ($38,550), Steak and Ale Restaurants ($103,500), Jerrico ($9,050) and Red Lobster ($11,775). Where the chains did not have PACs, their parent companies could; the Pepsico PAC served for its Pizza Hut subsidiary, the Heublein Inc. PAC for Kentucky Fried Chicken. Beckett said Kentucky Fried Chicken's franchisee group expected to set up its own PACs for the next election at the federal and state levels.

Trade Associations

The trade associations serving fast-food chains also reflected the new political awareness and the interest in grass-roots lobbying techniques. The National Restaurant Association, which represents "mom and pop" restaurants as well as fast-food chains, had tilted sharply toward Washington to accommodate the growing political interest within the food service industry. The association moved its headquarters to Washington from Chicago in 1979, and in 1981 hired two top executives with Capitol Hill experience.

The association had assembled its own network of 900 restaurateurs who would write to Congress on request, and had an "action task force" of 60 government affairs executives of restaurant chains that coordinated lobbying efforts "so we're all singing from the same songbook," said governmental affairs director Lawrence. Lawrence was a Washington veteran who worked in the Senate office of Robert Dole, R-Kan., chairman of the Finance Committee, and in the campaign of Sen. Orrin G. Hatch, R-Utah.

The association had its own PAC, which contributed $70,650 in the 1980 campaign. Chain restaurants also received Washington help from the Foodservice and Lodging Institute and the International Franchise Association. Officials of both groups confirmed the dramatic increase in attention to government by their members.

Milk Prices

The first sign of the industry's awakening in 1981 came when the Reagan administration proposed to skip an increase in government milk-price supports scheduled for April 1 of that year. The proposal was meant to cut the budget and keep down the cost of milk.

While that battle received widespread attention as an early test of the Reagan administration's mettle, House Agriculture Committee aides said the fast-food industry gave the administration a vital backup. The campaign was the first legislative foray by Pizza Hut, which, according to a competitor, "saw this as a way to cut their teeth."

Peyton George, a former Agriculture Department official retained by Pepsico, lobbied members and committee staffers, while Shauf mobilized franchisees in a phone-in and letter-writing campaign focused on the Agriculture panels. Shauf said Pizza Hut's "action alert" to franchisees generated 1,100 letters to Congress (the company collected copies of franchisee letters and responses), not counting the support of other chains.

According to George, the franchisees had good reason to respond with a passion; Pizza Hut uses about 56 million pounds of cheese annually. George calculated that the April 1, 1981, price increase would have cost the average franchise $1,500 a year.

John Bailey, a House Agriculture Committee aide, said George "was instrumental in the milk thing. When nobody thought we could do it, he pushed for it." Bailey said the Pizza Hut campaign helped convince the administration's supporters in Congress that constituent support for bucking the vaunted dairy lobby existed.

The milk issue was the first time anyone could recall this major food-consuming industry getting so deeply involved in a food issue. But it was not expected to be the last. The restaurant association and several chains closely watched legislation affecting sugar prices, beef imports and casein, an imported milk extract used in artificial cheese and non-dairy "shakes." "The fast-food industry is defi-

nitely becoming more and more interested in commodity prices," said Sheila Bamburger, who lobbied on those issues for the National Restaurant Association.

Subminimum Wage

Ironically, the industry got more public attention for an issue it chose not to support. The issue was the youth sub-minimum wage, which attracted reporters in early 1981 when Sen. Hatch, the chairman of the Senate Labor Committee, announced he would push it.

Although the proposal never reached a committee vote in 1981, it would have allowed employers to pay three-fourths of the minimum wage — $3.35 at that time — to workers age 19 and younger during their first six months of employment. Hatch argued that the lower wage would lead to more young, unskilled workers being employed. In 1977, a youth differential was viewed in the fast-food industry as panacea for labor costs, which make up nearly a third of operating expenses.

But if Hatch thought fast-food chains would back him, he was in for a surprise. Fast-food entrepreneurs huddled with other business groups and calculated that the political price for a youth subminimum might be an increase in the basic minimum wage, a price they considered unacceptable.

And they were admittedly unhappy about the public perception that the bill was a windfall for their industry. McDonald's was distraught about news stories describing the subminimum wage as "the McDonald's amendment." Bruce Cotton of Jerrico said if the industry pushed the bill, "People would say, 'They're just salt-mine operators out to rape youth.' "

While the National Restaurant Association, mostly at the urging of small members, supported the bill, McDonald's and other chains declined an invitation to testify when Hatch held hearings. Hatch responded scornfully, remarking that now he knew why so many fast-food chains were introducing chicken into their menus.

"The senator has been a little teed off about it," said Hatch aide Kristine Iverson. "We went out on a limb to push this legislation, which we feel is important to them. Now that all of a sudden we have a chance to follow through, they're chickening out."

Tax Credit

After that, the industry focused on an alternative way of relieving labor costs. "Instead of the subminimum wage, we're pushing very strongly for the targeted jobs tax credit," said William G. Gierry of the Foodservice and Lodging Institute.

The targeted jobs tax credit, created as part of the 1978 tax cut bill, was designed to give employers a tax credit worth up to $3,000 the first year and $1,500 the second year for each worker hired from various "target" groups, including work-study students, handicapped persons and economically disadvantaged youth. The program was scheduled to expire in December 1981, and the Reagan administration had recommended that it not be extended on grounds it was little-used.

According to testimony by Labor and Treasury Department spokesmen at Senate hearings in April 1981, the credit was claimed for only 112,000 new workers in 1980, out of an estimated 1.6 million who were eligible. Moreover, about two-thirds of those claims were for workers found to be eligible after they had already been hired. "The financial incentive provided by the targeted credits has not greatly affected the decisions of employers to hire eligible individuals," asserted John E. Chapoton, assistant secretary of Treasury.

Supporters of the tax credit said employers did not use it to its full extent because Labor, Treasury and state employment agencies did not promote it — and in some cases, discouraged claims with barriers of red tape.

The tax credit was supported by a wide variety of organizations interested in employment of low-income young people, especially in light of budget cutbacks in federal employment and training programs. The National Urban League and groups of corrections officers, vocational rehabilitation counselors and reform schools were among the members of a coalition supporting an extension.

But the business clout behind the bill came largely from the fast-food industry, which singled out the tax credit as a top legislative priority for 1981. The diverse coalition composed of business and social interests was successful in gaining a one year extension for the program that year.

Work continued on another extension in 1982. Most of the major chains as well as the National Restaurant Association and the Foodservice and Lodging Institute alerted their members to begin writing, calling and visiting lawmakers, urging them to cosponsor a bill introduced in 1982 by Sen. John Heinz, R-Pa., to extend the bill 3-5 years. As of mid-1982, no action had been taken on this extension.

Lobbying State Governments

Because their outlets exist almost everywhere, fast-food companies become embroiled in political battles on many fronts other than Washington.

In 1980, for example, fast-food chains helped lobby a bill through the Maryland Legislature to allow their franchisees to participate in promotional contests, according to Burger King's Platt. Pizza Hut pushed legislation in Pennsylvania to relax limits on liquor licenses (the chain, which serves beer, is the nation's largest holder of liquor licenses). Kentucky Fried Chicken promoted a bill in Missouri to change laws governing the job references employers give departing workers. In 1982 legislation was passed guaranteeing that employers could not be sued for punitive information put into a service recommendation.

Shauf of Pizza Hut said the company anticipated that the reduction of federal spending and regulation under the Reagan administration likely would bring a resurgence of state government activity, and the fast-food industry planned to be there to influence it. But the promised rollback of the federal government did not inhibit the industry's determination to move to Washington, industry officials said. "Reagan is simply not going to be able to do it by himself," said Shauf.

The Bank Lobby

In 1981 the public relations people at America's largest bank holding company, Citicorp, produced a tongue-in-cheek guidebook for bank robbers. Forget banks, the booklet advised; knock over a brokerage house, an insurance company, a retailer or a travel agent.

Citicorp was pointing to a revolution in the financial services industry, the aggressive entry of "non-banks" such as Merrill Lynch and Co., American Express Co., Prudential Insurance Co. and Sears, Roebuck and Co. into banklike business. These and other companies are the adoptive parents of money market mutual funds and similar devices that, free of the interest limits and other rules governing banks, have lured savings away from traditional depository institutions. "In Ma Barker's day Sears was 'Where America shops,' " jibed Citicorp. "Today, Sears is where America banks."

Citicorp and other major banks were pressing in 1982 for a measure of deregulation that would free them to fight back with mutual funds of their own. Like many of the non-banks, the banks envisioned a future in which most financial services — checking and savings, lending and investing, mortgages and insurance — would be handled by diversified, electronically sophisticated financial supermarkets.

This vision had some well-placed believers. Sen. Jake Garn, R-Utah, chairman of the Senate Banking Committee, vigorously promoted a first step toward massive restructuring of the financial industry in 1982. His bill was intended to dissolve some of the distinctions between banks and savings and loans (S & Ls), allow these traditional depository institutions into the blooming business of money market funds, ease mergers within the industry and relax various consumer protection rules. Garn stressed that his something-for-everybody bill could combine a variety of provisions. As of June 1982, the legislation remained in the Senate Banking Committee awaiting markup.

The Reagan administration endorsed most of this, along with some longer strides down the same road. The administration was prepared to let banks loose in such forbidden territory as insurance and data processing, as long as they set up subsidiaries to run the new activities. Garn promised a full review of other major rules, including restrictions on interstate banking.

But a constellation of reluctant and influential lobbies, determined to protect their members and to avoid giving competitors an edge, stood in the way. Some of them feared that the decades of regulation they previously lobbied into place to protect their pieces of turf could be rendered obsolete by the economy and non-bank enterprises. They also worried about getting trampled in the rush to deregulate. The ailing thrift industry, many smaller banks, the new money market funds, the real estate industry, home builders, and consumer groups all, for different reasons, saw deregulation as a dangerous proposition.

In search of compromise, Garn exhorted industry lobby groups to come together and recognize their shared circumstances. He promised to address each faction's special problems, but only if it was willing to swallow some things it didn't like. "If the traditional depository institutions don't get their act together and stop the intermural warfare ... there won't be any legislation," Garn told the National Association of Federal Credit Unions Jan. 25, 1982, in what became his standard refrain.

The industry was listening. One noteworthy development was an unprecedented, closed-door summit meeting Jan. 14 and 15, 1982, of more than 75 officials from all of the major depository trade groups. While the meeting produced no consensus, participants emerged with informal proposals to take back to their respective organizations. Continuing through March, virtually every segment of this diverse industry held legislative meetings, with "the bank bill" at the top of the agenda.

"The signs are very good," said M. Danny Wall, Garn's committee staff director. "There has been significant movement already." Privately, Wall added, the factions admitted they were closer to compromise than they appeared.

But the disagreements of that year were of long standing, and were felt acutely in the House, where all members faced elections. In an election year, candidates look for legislation that will produce quick results while antagonizing as few people as possible.

Donald J. Crawford, senior vice president of the Securities Industry Association, one of the trade groups representing the non-banks, observed that freeing the banks of regulatory restraints "is not an issue that's going to get a congressman one additional vote back home. Yet it carries with it a very substantial political liability. No matter how you vote, you've made some segment of the financial industry angry at you."

The Thrift Problem

The most powerful motive for legislation was not Citicorp's passion to compete, but the wobbly condition of the thrift industry. The thrift industry includes S & Ls, credit unions and mutual savings banks — institutions designed to collect savings deposits and loan the money back out for non-commercial purposes such as home mortgages.

The economy had walloped the thrifts from two sides. Inflation-minded savers pulled out of low-interest passbook accounts in favor of better-paying money markets, certificates of deposit and other savings devices. Thus, the thrifts rapidly lost assets — and paid much higher rates for assets they had.

At the same time, many thrifts held portfolios of old, fixed-rate mortgages they made when interest rates were lower. Those mortgages had not produced income equivalent to what the companies had to spend to attract new funds. According to William B. O'Connell, president of the U.S. League of Savings Associations, at the end of November 1981 S & Ls were paying depositors an average of 11.66 percent for use of their money, but earning only an average of 9.92 percent on outstanding loans. The figures explain why that year the federal government was required to step in and arrange a record 23 mergers to prop up collapsing S & Ls.

On the part of the industry, O'Connell remarked in an interview that "we don't plan to stand aside and let the business be, in effect, semi-liquidated." In 1982 the thrift lobby advocated three steps to recovery:

● First, legislation to create an orderly merger process, so that the failing thrifts could be absorbed by more solvent institutions.

● Second, some sort of federal bail-out of their old, low-yield mortgages.

● Finally, once these measures had set them back on their feet, the thrifts sought legal authority to compete in new ways — some of the checking and commercial lending authority of banks, plus a crack at the new money market funds.

The 4,400-member U.S. League, the largest of the thrift trade groups, endorsed Garn's bill because it was intended to help with the mergers and give thrifts new powers. At the same time, the group and its allies pushed for a bail-out of low-yielding mortgages. Without it, they insisted, commercial banks would be in a much stronger position to use Garn's new freedoms than would the S & Ls.

Various forms of bail-out were discussed, including tax write-offs or repackaging the old mortgages as collateral for new securities, but they all had the same basic result: The government would pick up the difference between the old, face value of the mortgages and their current market value. This proposition had many foes, including Garn and the Reagan administration. "We just feel that's too costly," said a Treasury Department spokesman. "We believe interest rates will come down, and that'll be the real solution."

Late in 1981 the House passed one piece of the thrift package, the so-called "regulators bill," aimed at easing emergency mergers of troubled institutions and providing an infusion of financial aid. House Banking Committee Chairman Fernand J. St Germain, D-R.I., said that more ambitious changes should be postponed until hearings had been held, and perhaps until the economy had settled down.

The Bank Factions

Bankers — despite the poor-mouthing of Citicorp's booklet — had not done so badly due to their reliance on commercial loans for which interest rates are flexible. The industry generally had been profitable and, though some analysts in 1982 saw trouble ahead, there was less urgency about the banks' condition in Congress. Therefore, if the banks were to get legislation ridding themselves of some regulations, their best chance was to hook it onto a bill rescuing the struggling S & Ls.

"Our basic view is that Congress will probably in some way be needing to deal with the problems of the thrifts," said Fritz M. Elmendorf of the American Bankers Association. "But as they do it, it's important that they not *just* focus on the thrifts."

But the bankers themselves were divided deeply about reshaping their industry. Many big banks and bank holding companies considered the securities industry their competition. Relatively sanguine about competition from street-corner S & Ls, bankers were eager to diversify into innovative financial services. "We see the Garn bill as an essential first step," said John S. Rippey, legislative director of the Association of Bank Holding Companies, whose 180 members included most of the companies salivating at the prospect of money markets. The association had its own draft of a proposed next step, which included letting banks operate across state lines. "Market forces should dictate where banks operate, rather than lines drawn in the 18th or 19th centuries," Rippey said.

On the other hand, many smaller banks, such as the 7,300 members of the Independent Bankers Association of America (IBAA), were suspicious of sudden change. One worry was that liberated big-city banks would gobble them up. Another was that if S & Ls gained commercial lending powers they would have built-in advantages; in some states, S & Ls had been allowed statewide branches while commercial banks had not.

IBAA favored the regulators bill, and backed up the S & Ls in endorsing a bail-out of the thrifts. (Many small banks also were stuck with old, low-interest mortgages.) But IBAA lobbyists criticized Garn for holding thrift legislation "hostage" to win broader legislation. "The changes should be made carefully, so that as many people as possible can be survivors," said Jeanne Marie Murphy, Senate liaison for the IBAA.

The American Bankers Association, embracing 13,200 banks of all sizes, was dancing in the cross fire between big and small banks. Though eager to have its big members allowed into the money-market competition, the group hesitated to share its commercial lending authority with the thrifts, in deference to smaller members.

In informal negotiations, the ABA and U.S. League of Savings Associations focused on the new powers for thrifts. S & Ls indicated they would settle for limited power to make commercial loans — say, up to 20 percent of their assets. ABA still balked, preferring a different approach that would make it simpler for an S & L to change into a bank.

ABA does not take positions on legislation until it has reached a broad consensus through its "banking leadership process." The cumbersome machinery involves a committee of about 400 bankers, split into groups representing small, medium and large banks. At a meeting of the ABA in Washington on Feb. 10, 1982, the bankers agreed in principle to allow limited commercial loans by thrifts if the restrictions on interest rates imposed by Regulation Q were relaxed. *(Deregulation, box, p. 128)*

Yet, according to Fritz Elmendorf of the ABA, such specific compromise terms were an expression of the increasing urgency felt by bankers for the long-term health of their own industry. The real terms of any trade off between deregulation for thrifts and banks would be left to comprehensive legislation.

Togetherness

Garn aide Wall and U.S. League President O'Connell both noted increasing interest in accommodation in 1982. "The banks are realizing that while the thrift industry is what the alligators are eating now, when they're done eating the thrifts the banks are next," Wall said. Echoed O'Connell: "Are we moving any closer to agreement with the banks? I suspect so, because we have a common competitive problem out there."

One piece of the Garn bill that was expected to unite the banks and thrifts was a provision permitting due-on-sale clauses banned in some states. In effect, the Garn bill was designed to allow a lender to demand full payment of an outstanding mortgage before a house could be sold, rather than letting the seller pass on a cheap mortgage.

A critical factor in the fate of Garn's bill was the prospect of his welding the ABA and the U.S. League into a common front, yielding substantial political clout behind his legislation. Bankers and thrift executives alike had cultivated good relations with their hometown members of Congress. They tended to be civic leaders, chamber of commerce officials and campaign contributors — active in both state and federal politics. *(Bank political action committees, box, this page)*

Their trade groups had conducted a continual courtship of the bank-writing committee, both through routine lobbying and invitations to speak and socialize at conventions. (Usually for a price. Garn, for example, even before he became chairman in 1981, was collecting about $12,000 a year in honoraria for speaking to banking and related groups. The ABA consistently was among the dozen or so biggest honoraria spenders.)

When cued by ABA or the U.S. League, bankers and thrift executives made up an impressive lobbying machine. In 1981, for example, bank and thrift executives persuaded Congress to establish tax-exempt All Savers Certificates and to expand the use of Individual Retirement Accounts, two Treasury-subsidized efforts to win depositors back from the money markets. They repeatedly resisted presidential attempts to force withholding of income taxes from interest on savings — an issue that President Reagan continued to raise.

But even if ABA and the league reached accord, Garn's proposal would still face major obstacles. The independent bankers seemed adamant, and enough prospective opposition existed outside the industry to give skittish House members fits.

New Entries

One source of opposition was the securities industry, the proprietors of the booming money market mutual funds and other investments, whom Garn called "the new boys on the block." Two trade groups had been the principal guardians of this group's interests. The Investment Company Institute (ICI), representing 650 mutual funds,

Bankers Deposit Big Political Money

As befit an industry whose business was money, banking and thrift executives were prolific donors to congressional campaigns. The financial world's two largest political action committees — the American Bankers Association (ABA) Bankpac and the U.S. League of Savings Association PAC — were expected to disburse more than $1 million between them for candidates in the 1982 elections.

Bankpac, with a spending goal of $650,000, was designed especially to cement the ties between lawmakers and their local bankers. While a portion of the money was used by ABA lobbyists for admission to Washington fund-raising parties, the bigger gifts were delivered in person by selected local bank executives back home. The U.S. League of Savings Associations expected to put about $400,000 into 1982 congressional races.

If the pattern of the 1980 political season held true, candidates were expected also to reap more than $100,000 from each of several other industry PACs, including those representing the Credit Union National Association, Inc., the Mortgage Bankers Association of America, savings and loan leagues in Ohio and Florida, California bankers, and Citicorp.

Another measure of the industry's campaign activities was the number of much smaller PACs that were organized, like branch banks, to help political candidates. A scan of Federal Election Commission (FEC) records disclosed more than 280 separate PACs affiliated with individual banks and thrifts, their state and national associations, or bank holding companies. Many of these planned to spend only a few thousand dollars on federal races, concentrating more on governors and state legislatures.

Depository institutions accounted for roughly one out of every seven corporate or trade association PACs registered to give money to federal candidates. The pervasive PACs, however, told only part of the story. Bankers were generous donors as individuals, especially to members of the banking, commerce or tax-writing committees. Many of them participated in the local fund-raising activities of their favorite candidates. And when a candidate needed seed money for a campaign or an extra boost in the closing days, he could go hat in hand to his local banker for help.

In 1982, according to the FEC, a bank or thrift institution could make unlimited loans to a campaign as long as it met the normal requirements for business lending.

Deregulation Committee Makes First Moves

In 1980 the bank overseers in Congress thought they had found a way to duck one of the fiercest intramural lobbying battles between banks and thrift institutions — the fight over Regulation Q, which limits the interest they can pay on deposits. Congress set up an independent panel of officials plucked from other financial regulatory bodies, called it the Depository Institutions Deregulation Committee (DIDC), and told it to phase out interest ceilings by 1986.

But far from bringing peace, DIDC itself became a second front in the battle over deregulation, with members of Congress continually drawn into the fray. On one side were commercial banks, urging a speedy end to interest ceilings so banks could compete with the high-paying money market funds. On the other side were the savings and loan associations (S & Ls), fighting to keep interest ceilings in place. They said raising the interest rates would force them to pay more for funds held in low-paying passbook accounts, without encouraging any inward flow of new deposits.

In 1981 the S & Ls successfully froze the deregulation process, primarily by doing just what they did before DIDC existed — bringing hundreds of local savings managers to Washington to appeal to Congress. In October, for example, a blitz by thrift lobbyists convinced DIDC to reverse itself and cancel a .5 percent increase in passbook interest rates that had been scheduled for Nov. 1. Then in November, with executives of the U.S. League of Savings Associations and the National Association of Mutual Savings Banks in Washington for a conference, the thrifts marched to Capitol Hill to assure that no deregulation would take place at a December DIDC meeting.

Several key lawmakers agreed to intervene on their behalf — including Senate Banking Chairman Jake Garn, R-Utah, and House Banking Chairman Fernand J. St Germain, D-R.I. — and DIDC deferred further action.

The bankers also put the squeeze on DIDC, though mostly on the defensive. While the S & Ls were derailing the December 1981 meeting, the American Bankers Association (ABA) was busy trying to make sure DIDC would not back away from an earlier decision authorizing new, unlimited-interest retirement accounts.

When more than 300 bankers came to Washington for a legislative meeting in November, the ABA had them bring copies of their local bank letterheads. The association sat the bankers down to write letters supporting the retirement account decision, collected the letters and delivered them to DIDC. DIDC stuck by its decision. "People at DIDC had said volume of letters did count," said ABA's Fritz Elmendorf. "So we gave them volume."

The pummeling of DIDC prompted hearings in a House Banking subcommittee, and left some DIDC members exasperated. William M. Isaac, chairman of the Federal Deposit Insurance Corporation and a DIDC member, sent Garn and St Germain a letter in December complaining of "conflicting signals, as evidenced by the scores of congressional letters received during the past week urging no action at the DIDC meeting." The substance of Isaac's message to Congress: Make up your mind whether you want deregulation or not.

In March 1982 the DIDC began to act on the original congressional mandate and instituted unrestricted interest ceilings on time deposits.

tried to protect the funds' hold on the money market business. The Securities Industry Association (SIA), representing 550 investment broker-dealers, placed more emphasis on keeping banks out of the business of underwriting municipal revenue bonds.

Both groups argued that banks have huge assets and that certain tax and legal advantages would make them instant goliaths in the new business. They warned that banks could end up using depositors' savings to bail out faulty investments — as commonly happened before banking and securities were separated by the 1933 Glass-Steagall Act. "The securities industry would probably applaud [Citicorp Chairman] Walter Wriston if he wanted to get rid of his bank and become a broker-dealer," said SIA's Crawford. "But not if he wants to enter the field with his $120 billion in assets."

Crawford also questioned the underlying assumption that the trend had been toward financial supermarkets. He

said that may have been an overreaction to the heated climate of high interest and inflation. "Some of what is going on right now has a certain mob psychology to it," Crawford said.

The securities industry did not have the same strong, indigenous ties to members of Congress that banks and thrifts had, but brokers rivaled bankers for influence on Wall Street and in Washington. (In the Reagan administration, Treasury Secretary Donald T. Regan, the former chairman of Merrill Lynch, was perhaps the most prominent alumnus of the securities industry.) Moreover, computers — the nervous system of the securities industry — made a dandy lobbying device, as the industry demonstrated in 1981.

In the spring of that year, congressional supporters of the depository institutions attempted to rein in the money market funds by requiring that money fund managers set aside large cash reserves. The U.S. League of Savings Associations and the ABA supported the effort. But, coached by the ICI, money market managers across the country sent their shareholders letters warning in dire terms that the assault would cut yields for savers. "The only way you can prevent this legalized theft from occurring is to write your senators and congressman and let them know what you think of this blatant piracy," said one letter, from The Reserve Fund Inc., of New York City. "Politicians need two things to survive in office — votes and contributions. Bankers make contributions, but you have the vote."

The crusade was an enormous success — the proposal disappeared without a trace. Several congressional offices said the outpouring from constituents rivaled the flow of mail on President Reagan's economic plan. In addition, the victory convinced ABA and the savings league to shift strategy, from regulating securities to deregulating themselves.

Securities lobbyists doubted they could duplicate that success on an issue such as deregulation, since it was not a direct threat to their shareholders. Even some managers of money market funds were not enthusiastic about lobbying to keep banks out of the field. Thomas C. Miller, executive vice president of Government Investors Trust, a small mutual fund in Arlington, Va., said he felt his industry should accept competition from banks and focus on preserving its head start. To fight the entry of banks into mutual funds, he said, would be "illogical and contradictory for an industry based on the free market philosophy."

Yet if the securities lobbyists threw their weight against a deregulation bill, ABA's Elmendorf figured they would have a strategic advantage. "It's a relatively easy thing to *stop* a bill," he said. "You don't have to have the resources of the banks or thrifts to stop a bill." Garn added: "They don't have to oppose the legislation, because the banks and the thrifts have been doing such a good job of cutting each other up."

Remaining Difficulties

Another source of trouble for the Garn bill was the housing lobby. Realtors and home builders said they would support a bail-out of the thrifts, but not measures to let S & Ls turn their attention from mortgages to other investments. "It's almost as if they're all trying to walk away from housing," said Peter E. Knight, assistant director of mortgage finance at the National Association of Realtors. "I don't think we disagree that the Garn bill would make thrifts more profitable. But at what cost?"

The Garn bill drove two additional wedges between the thrifts and the housing lobby. The Realtors worried that due-on-sale clauses would inhibit home sales. Also, the home builders were "unalterably opposed" to a provision that would let banks or thrifts get directly involved in development and real estate.

In early 1982, however, both housing groups signaled some willingness to negotiate. "Originally [the Garn bill] was something we would like to see just go away," said James H. Schuyler, legislative counsel for the home builders. But after a January convention in Las Vegas, he said, "Now we are accepting the notion that some changes are needed."

Consumer groups — supported by organized labor, state government groups and others — also had complaints about deregulation. Garn's bill, in the name of a free marketplace, would override a variety of state laws aimed at protecting consumers. Perhaps the most controversial provision would extinguish state usury laws that limit interest charges on consumer loans for cars, furniture and other purchases.

"We fondly refer to it as the loan shark revitalization act of 1982," said Ellen Broadman of Consumers Union. "The bill grossly intrudes on the ability of the states to protect the consumer in financing." Garn aide Wall countered that usury laws make it tough for consumers to borrow in times of high inflation. "The question is, do you want to be able to get a loan, or do you not?" he said.

John Brown, of Ralph Nader's Public Interest Research Center, said letting banks into the securities business would invite conflicts of interest, and would set a dangerous precedent for the ultimate unbridling of large corporations. "Garn and the administration have been very effectively stroked and fed information by the lobbyists for some of the big banks," Brown said.

While consumer groups may not have carried the weight of bankers and thrift managers, their message was one element of this complicated issue that may have had some appeal to the general public — creating one more reason for the House to shy away from doing anything. "This is an election year," noted Broadman, "and it is going to look real bad for people to be voting against laws that protect the consumer."

NRA: Top Gun in Washington

The National Rifle Association has worn the adjective "powerful" like a bayonet, fixed to its name. Rarely, in the popular literature on gun legislation, have the initials NRA occurred far from some reference to the group's image as an influential — if not the single most influential — lobbying force in Washington. The NRA itself has encouraged this reputation. A brochure described the NRA Institute for Legislative Action as "the strongest, most formidable grassroots 'lobby' in the nation."

Despite polls showing a majority of Americans favoring some strengthening of gun controls, and despite periodic waves of revulsion brought on by the shooting of public figures, gun control legislation was consistently pistol-whipped following the hard-fought, heavily compromised Omnibus Crime Control and Gun Control Acts in 1968. In the 97th Congress (1981-83), an NRA-backed bill weakening the 1968 laws was thought more likely than one establishing new controls on firearms. All of this was attributed to the stopping power of the NRA and its allied defenders of firearms freedom, with their imposing arsenal of direct-mail computers, free-spending campaign committees and uncompromising lobbyists.

Why was the gun lobby apparently able to do things that other lobbies, just as big and rich, could not? Was its power diminished since the publicized handgun shootings of music star John Lennon and President Reagan? Or was the NRA, as one handgun control advocate put it, really "like the Wizard of Oz" — an enormous bluff that Congress was afraid to call?

"The reason we are so successful — you can snicker if you want to — is because we are right," contended NRA's legislative chief in 1981, Neal Knox. In fact, many members of Congress did seem to believe, as NRA said at every opportunity, that curbing firearms was an impossible task, would not help reduce crime and could interfere with the "legitimate" sporting or self-defense of law-abiding citizens.

But many lawmakers who were personally sympathetic to some restrictions on guns shied away from any involvement. Some were afraid of the political consequences. Others saw such efforts as futile as long as the NRA stood in the way.

If lobbying power could be defined by a formula, it might be something like this: size plus organization multiplied by passion, divided by scope of interest. The NRA had all of the variables going for it — a large, well-organized, passionately concerned constituency, concentrated on a single issue. The group claimed 2.4 million members by 1982, dramatically increased in previous years by an aggressive promotional campaign. The $15 annual dues provided most of a $36 million budget. (Another 10 percent of the budget came from advertising, mostly by the weapons industry, in NRA magazines.)

NRA frequently was cited as a model of lobbying organization, with a network of state and local gun clubs hooked up to a ganglion of sophisticated computers. NRA could target mass mailings overnight to any state, congressional district or state legislative district.

But computers were standard weaponry in modern lobbying. What distinguished NRA was what lay at the receiving end of its network — a body of gun lovers linked by a common activity that continued even when the legislative front was quiet. The NRA did not have to gear up for action. It was inherently geared up.

A Long Tradition

Little thought was given to the political potential of this network when NRA began 110 years ago, as an effort by Yankee officers to improve citizen marksmanship they felt had been put to shame by the superior shooting of Southerners in the Civil War. Ulysses S. Grant was an early NRA president, and military men led NRA throughout its first century.

Over the years, NRA's status as the shooters' establishment, and hence its lobbying clout, were bolstered by a variety of official sanctions. A 1903 law, for example, declared that surplus military arms could be sold to civilians only if they were NRA members. When Detroit police wanted surplus army carbines for riot control in 1967, 400 members of the police department had to send in $5 apiece for NRA memberships. A 1979 court ruling, in a lawsuit filed by the Coalition to Ban Handguns, ended NRA's special deal with the Pentagon. In the course of the lawsuit, NRA released documents acknowledging that the special access to military guns had contributed to huge leaps in membership.

The rifle association also had seats on the U.S. and International Olympic committees, where it was the official overseer of shooting competition. Through its marksmanship and firearms safety programs, it had close ties with police departments, fish and wildlife officials, and the Boy Scouts of America.

Though its members were peppered with magazine articles and fund-raising letters warning of "threats" to gun ownership, NRA did not play a heavy political theme in recruiting new members. Mike Gretschel, president of an advertising firm that ran NRA membership promotion, said solicitations stressed "goods and services" — magazines, free gun insurance and premiums such as discounts at Avis Rent-a-Car. NRA's defense of "Second Amendment rights" was cited only as another fringe benefit.

The nature of the organization, its weekend role in the life of many members, helped explain the response of gun owners when NRA issued a political call to arms. NRA was associated with guns as a cultural phenomenon, not just a political cause. According to James D. Wright, a University of Massachusetts sociology professor who was conducting a study of weapons and crime for the National Institute of Justice, opponents of the gun lobby misjudged their enemy when they envisioned gun owners as right-wingers or paranoiacs. In most cases, he said, guns were a cultural value instilled from childhood. "The single best [statistical] predictor of whether somebody owns a gun is whether his or her father owned a gun," Wright said.

Guns are widely regarded as a totem of American manhood (NRA membership was overwhelmingly male). And in the one-time frontier states of the West and South, guns are still a nostalgic token of independence. "The gun is ... a symbol of freedom to these people. It has a lot more significance to people than a job," said John M. Snyder, lobbyist for the Citizens Committee for the Right to Keep and Bear Arms, a rival gun group.

All of these things gave NRA members more than a political bond and made them extraordinarily responsive. "You ask NRA membership to do something, they do it," marveled Bill Pickens, a former NRA legislative director who later lobbied for the Edison Electric Institute. "You ask them to write, they write. You ask them to get involved in a campaign, they get involved. You ask them to give financially, they give."

Political Education

By the early 1960s, when a gun-weary Congress was moving toward passage of the 1968 Gun Control Act, the gun lobby was a formidable, if still unsophisticated force. Gun owner protests succeeded in gravely weakening the 1968 law. But NRA leaders subsequently sought to make passage of that bill their last major defeat. In time, tension built up between the "old guard" NRA leadership and a more militant faction wanting a professional, uncompromising political organization.

In 1975 John Snyder, an editor at one of NRA's magazines, left to become the lobbyist for the Citizens Committee for the Right to Keep and Bear Arms. The same year, the Gun Owners of America was formed in California with the aim of defeating gun critics in the next election. The Citizens Committee and the Gun Owners, unlike NRA, eschewed the sporting aspects of gun ownership for pure politics. The birth of these strident rivals strengthened the hand of hard-liners within NRA by proving gun owners were willing to play tough politics. A few months after Snyder set up shop, NRA established its lobbying arm, the Institute for Legislative Action. *(Organization, box, p. 135)*

In 1977 the rift within NRA broke into the open at a convention in Cincinnati. The old guard proposed to sell the group's eight-story Washington headquarters and move to Colorado, there to refocus attention on marksmanship and wildlife conservation. The militants organized enough of the voting life members to squelch this proposal and take over leadership of the association. "The membership did not want to be 'reasonable' anymore; they wanted to stake out a clear legislative position and stick to it at the federal, state and local level," NRA board member Joseph P. Tartaro recalled in a history recently published in *Gun Week.*

NRA chief executive Harlon B. Carter, a one-time head of the U.S. Border Patrol, and legislative director Knox a former gun columnist and a leader of the militant NRA faction, were among the beneficiaries of the coup. In the wake of their takeover, NRA's lobbying institute grew to a 55-employee, $4.1 million effort, and those urging "moderation" were purged from the Washington ranks.

In 1980, three of NRA's top five lobbyists left, complaining that Neal Knox took an unrealistically hard line with Congress. "Neal's attitude is that we can put a congressman or a senator to the wall and stick it to him any time," said one of the departed lobbyists, who asked that his criticism be anonymous. "They don't feel you have to compromise on anything." Knox would not discuss the reasons for the exodus, except to say, "It was just a matter of who's going to run the place."

However, by the late spring of 1982, Knox himself was replaced, along with his executive assistant, James Norell, and general counsel, James Featherstone, in an apparent dispute over legislative goals and coordination with the Reagan administration. The new lobbying chief would be Jay Warren Cassidy, an insurance company president from Lynn, Mass.

Control or Confiscation?

As any lawmaker knows who has set out to promote a "compromise" gun control bill, NRA's policy recognized no such thing. NRA portrayed any restriction on owning a pistol as a step down the slippery slope to confiscation of deer rifles and shotguns. "They misrepresent my stand completely," charged Rep. Robert McClory, R-Ill., voicing a familiar complaint of handgun control advocates. "They invariably charge that I'm trying to take their guns away, and I'm not."

But the gun lobby insisted that confiscation would be the ultimate result of even a moderate gun control measure, whether proponents admitted it or not. Due perhaps to skillful packaging of the issue or to popular mistrust of Uncle Sam, gun advocates preached this message to a receptive audience. A 1978 poll conducted for the Center for the Study and Prevention of Handgun Violence, a pro-control group, asked people if they agreed with this statement: "Requiring all handgun owners to be licensed is just the first step in confiscating all guns, including shotguns." Thirty-nine percent of those polled agreed.

A favorite variation on this theme was the alleged villainy of the Treasury Department's Bureau of Alcohol, Tobacco and Firearms (BATF), which enforced existing federal gun laws. Congressional supporters of the gun lobby repeatedly dragged the agency before House and Senate committees to answer charges of harassing innocent gun dealers and collectors.

Some BATF officials conceded that the agency had, in the past, had a tendency to go after small-time violators of the gun law, occasionally with a heavy hand. But officials said such abuses were corrected years ago. BATF told *The Washington Star* that in 1980 the agency conducted only 103 investigations of firearms sellers and revoked only 10 of 180,000 dealer licenses — statistics the agency said hardly suggest harassment. "I think the NRA set them up as a bogeyman" to rally support and raise money, said Richard J. Davis, who was the Carter administration's assistant Treasury secretary overseeing BATF.

Davis became an NRA arch-enemy in 1978, when BATF proposed regulations centralizing records of gun sales to ease tracing of weapons used in crimes. The gun lobby, calling this a backdoor registration scheme, seeded the clouds, and 350,000 letters rained down on the agency. "They called me a perjurer, a liar, a scoundrel, a skunk.... There were letters calling for me to be fired," said Davis.

In Congress, NRA allies amended BATF's appropriations bill to forbid implementation of the regulations, and then slashed $4.2 million from the agency's enforcement budget just to be sure the order would not be circumvented. The Carter administration never brought up the idea again.

NRA's top priority in the 97th Congress was a bill introduced by Sen. James A. McClure, R-Idaho, and Rep. Harold L. Volkmer, D-Mo., to limit some powers given BATF under the 1968 gun control law, including the power to inspect records of gun dealers. In the previous Congress the bill had attracted 182 House and 62 Senate cosponsors but failed to clear procedural obstacles. President Reagan supported the bill, a White House aide told NRA members in Denver in May 1981, yet by July 1982 it remained in the House Judiciary Committee.

Meanwhile, Reagan proposed a significant rollback in BATF manpower in a reorganization plan that came to mean a shift of gun control responsibilities from BATF to the Secret Service. While NRA continued to support the McClure-Volkmer bill, it opposed the reorganization plan. The group feared that the Secret Service, as a law enforcement rather than regulatory agency, would find it easy to ignore the demands of gun owners. Reorganization awaited a Treasury appropriations bill in Congress in 1982.

Ballot Leverage

NRA said its leverage rested on the fulcrum of the ballot box. The group, and many candidates, saw NRA members as a one-issue constituency. The only scientific effort to prove that — a survey in the mid-1970s by two University of Michigan researchers — found opponents of gun control no more likely to cast their vote on that basis than supporters of controls.

But the antennae of members of Congress received different signals. "In politics you learn to identify the issues of the highest intensity," said Rep. Dan Glickman, D-Kan., a member of the Judiciary Committee who leaned toward limits on cheap handguns but opposed broader gun registration. "This issue is of the highest intensity. Those people who care about guns, care very strongly, almost to the exclusion of other issues."

NRA and like-minded groups helped channel the passion of their members at election time by spending generously, especially on races where gun critics seemed vulnerable. "Our polls show that on a close race we can go in and deliver several percentage points of hard vote," said Wayne R. LaPierre Jr., NRA director of governmental affairs.

In 1980, only the second election since NRA inaugurated its Political Victory Fund, the group reported spending $1.1 million, with equal amounts going for direct donations to favored candidates and for independent mailings and advertisements telling NRA members whom to support.

The largest share went to the presidential race — about $205,000 attacking arch-enemy Sen. Edward M. Kennedy, D-Mass., and another $171,000 for Ronald Reagan and against his general election opponents. Gun advocates claimed they made the difference in several hotly contested congressional races, including the Senate victories of Charles E. Grassley, R-Iowa, (for whom NRA spent $56,950) and Thomas F. Eagleton, D-Mo., ($26,444), and the House win of Jack Fields, R-Texas, ($22,327).

"We knew in Iowa when their mailing hit the state because all of a sudden, across the state, cars were splashed with these bumper stickers saying, 'Sportsmen for Grassley,'" said Beverly Hubble, Grassley's press secretary. She said Grassley was sure NRA helped turn the election his way. Fields, too, credited gun groups with making a decisive difference in his race. While the man he defeated, Rep. Bob Eckhardt, D (1967-81), also argued against gun controls, NRA official LaPierre said Eckhardt's loyalty had been only "room temperature."

Gun control advocates disputed NRA's reputation as an electoral powerhouse. As an example, they pointed to NRA's persistent, costly, but unsuccessful efforts to unseat Rep. Abner J. Mikva, D-Ill. (1969-73, 1975-79), a longtime gun control advocate whom President Carter later nominated for a federal judgeship. "They are the best example of that old political axiom that the appearance of power is as good as the reality," claimed Sandy Horowitt, a former Mikva aide who worked for the Coalition to Ban Handguns. But, he added: "No one wants to see if I'm right."

Does the Gun Lobby Defy Public Opinion?

Students of the gun control issue often marveled that the gun lobby had sold Congress something the general public did not seem to buy. As early as 1972, a writer in *Public Opinion Quarterly*, summing up public opinion polls on gun control, remarked that "it is difficult to imagine any other issue on which Congress has been less responsive to public sentiment for a longer period of time."

But a closer look at the polls on gun control showed that public attitudes were not all that simple. A review of nationwide samplings by eight national polling organizations, including one poll commissioned by the National Rifle Association and one by the pro-control Center for the Study and Prevention of Handgun Violence, provided ammunition for both sides in the great gun fight.

Among the things polls generally agreed on:

● A strong majority of the public, usually between 60 and 75 percent, favored the general proposition of "stronger" or "more strict" controls on firearms. Similar majorities supported the concept of registration of firearms and licensing of firearms owners. The polls were quite consistent on this point, going back as far as a 1938 Gallup survey.

Polls that offered the choice of rolling back existing gun control laws found very little public support for that position. Even the NRA-sponsored poll, conducted in 1978 by Decision Making Information (DMI), found only 13 percent agreed there were "already too many" gun laws.

● A majority, usually about two-thirds, opposed banning the sale or manufacture of all handguns.

● The public was not well informed about state and local laws already on the books.

"The fact is that a substantial portion of the populace exists in [state and local] jurisdictions where registration, permits to own or permits to carry guns are already in effect," said James D. Wright, a University of Massachusetts sociologist who had reviewed the opinion research on gun control. That

lack of knowledge, he said, made it impossible to figure out from polls precisely what new policies the public would support.

● While people felt the need for some controls, they were doubtful gun laws would curb violent crime. Typical was a 1978 poll conducted for gun control advocates by Cambridge Research Inc., which found that people agreed, 78 percent to 13 percent, that: "Gun control laws affect only law-abiding citizens; criminals will always be able to find guns." The question was not included in a publicly released summary of the poll.

A *Washington Post*-ABC News poll taken after the Reagan shooting in March 1980 found 78 percent agreement that "no gun control law, no matter how strong, could prevent an assassin from getting a gun and shooting a president."

Wright said his own "hunch" was that most people thought of guns as something, like automobiles, that the government "ought to keep track of," but they did not expect these controls to prevent mishaps.

● The public strongly supported stiffer criminal penalties for crimes committed with firearms — a proposition long advanced by NRA as an alternative to gun control, and favored by some gun control proponents.

Wright said the few polls that had probed gun control attitudes in detail — such as the DMI and Cambridge Research polls — were untrustworthy, because questions were tilted in favor of the group that paid for the poll.

Pro-gun lobbyists criticized the Cambridge poll, for instance, because it prefaced gun control questions with a long chain of questions referring to handgun "attacks," "violence" and "accidents." Handgun critics, on the other hand, challenged the DMI poll because of "loaded" questions such as: "Would you favor or oppose the Federal government's spending $4 billion to enact a gun registration program?"

'Don't Talk to Me'

Whether NRA's power at the polls was real or not, gun control was an issue that made many members squirm in their seats. "When they see Rodino, they throw their hands up and say, 'Don't talk to me about [gun control],' " said an aide to Rep. Peter W. Rodino Jr., D-N.J., a leading handgun critic.

Even lawmakers with liberal records on other forms of government regulation steadfastly opposed gun controls. Eagleton, a frequent ally of gun critic Kennedy on other issues, voted a straight NRA line. Sen. Mark O. Hatfield, R-Ore., was an ardent critic of military weapons but cosponsored the NRA-backed McClure-Volkmer bill.

Former Sen. Birch Bayh, D-Ind. (1963-81), once a supporter of gun regulations, shifted to NRA's side prior to his 1980 election campaign. As a result, the rifle association stayed neutral in his unsuccessful effort. (The Gun Owners, calling his shift "a deathbed conversion," opposed him anyway.)

Rep. James J. Florio, D-N.J., an independent-minded liberal on many issues, was a seemingly incongruous member of the congressional "advisory council" of the right-wing Citizens Committee for the Right to Keep and Bear Arms.

Doubts about how much good gun laws accomplish were genuine and widespread. But they were intensified by

Pro- and Anti-Gun Groups in 1982

The National Rifle Association

Founded: 1871, by Yankee Civil War veterans, to promote marksmanship. Chartered in New York, moved to Washington in 1908.

Members: 2.4 million, paying $15 dues. Of these, 300,000 were life members, who paid $300. Members included Ronald Reagan (after 1972) and 14 members of Congress, one of them — Rep. John D. Dingell, D-Mich., — on NRA's board of directors.

Budget: $30 million, for a wide range of firearms-related projects, as well as legislative activity.

Lobbying: In 1982, the legislation of primary concern to the NRA was a bill introduced by Sen. James A. McClure, R Idaho, and Rep. Harold L. Volkmer, D Mo., which would revise the Gun Control Act of 1968 and circumscribe the authority of such regulatory agencies as the Bureau of Alcohol, Tobacco and Firearms. Five full-time lobbyists led by chief lobbyist Jay Warren Cassidy plus consultants Timmons and Co. Inc. represented NRA's lobbying branch, the Institute for Legislative Action. The Institute had a staff of 55 and a budget of $4.1 million.

Campaign Arm: The NRA Political Victory Fund reported spending $1.1 million in the 1979-80 campaign. Campaign gifts went to liberal and conservative opponents of gun control.

Legal Arm: The Firearms Civil Rights Legal Defense Fund provided legal counsel to gun dealers and owners accused by the government of violating gun laws.

Citizens Committee for the Right To Keep and Bear Arms

Founded: 1971, in Bellevue, Wash., by Alan Gottlieb, an officer of the American Conservative Union and promoter of conservative causes. Washington office opened in 1975.

Members: 300,000 "contributors, members and supporters."

Budget: About $1.2 million in 1982.

Lobbying: One full-time lobbyist, a former NRA magazine editor, John M. Snyder, who also produced the Citizens Committee newsletter, *Point Blank.* The committee had an "Advisory Council" of about 145 members of Congress.

Campaign Arm: Right to Keep and Bear Arms Political Victory Fund. Reported spending about $90,000 in the 1979-80 election period; the largest expenditure was a $25,000 civil penalty for soliciting contributions from non-members and for accepting corporate money. Spending on the state and local level for the 1982 congressional elections came to $50,000 by mid-summer of that year. The federal PAC had spent $15,000.

Research Arm: The Second Amendment Foundation, which published pro-gun books and tracts.

Gun Owners of America

Founded: 1975, in California, by arch-conservative state Sen. H. L. "Bill" Richardson. Originally a campaign group to defeat pro-gun control candidates, with lobbying added later.

Members: 50,000. Policy was set by Richardson assisted by Congressional and National (industry) Advisory Boards.

Budget: About $500,000 for legislative activities.

Lobbying: One registered lobbyist, Lawrence Pratt, a Virginia state legislator. Minimal presence on Capitol Hill, but reputedly very active in California.

Campaign Arm: Gun Owners of America Campaign Committee. Reported spending $1.4 million in 1979-80. The bulk of the money was for operating expenses or mass mailings not aimed at specific races. The rest went to conservative challengers. The group also participated in state races and referendum campaigns in California.

Handgun Control Inc.

Founded: In 1974. Later headed by Nelson T. Shields, a former chemical company marketing executive whose son was a handgun murder victim.

Members: 160,000, paying $15 a year.

Budget: $1 million in 1980; $2 million in 1982.

Lobbying: Three registered lobbyists. Favored the Kennedy-Rodino bill banning "Saturday Night Specials" and requiring a waiting period and police check before any handgun purchase. Opposed the McClure-Volkmer bill.

Campaign Arm: Handgun Control Inc. Reported spending $164,000 in 1979-80. Direct contributions to congressional candidates for 1982 totaled $37,000 by July of that year.

Coalition to Ban Handguns

Founded: In 1974, by the Board of Church and Society of the United Methodist Church.

Members: Thirty-two national civic associations and religious organizations, the largest being the American Civil Liberties Union. Over 125,000 contributing members.

Budget: About $700,000.

Lobbying: Favored a ban on the sale, manufacture, distribution (and ultimately private possession) of all handguns. Favored the Kennedy-Rodino bill, opposed the McClure-Volkmer bill.

Two registered lobbyists. More active in state legislatures, where it was affiliated with 26 state and local gun control groups.

the explosiveness of the issue. Gun owners "operate with such vehemence, such high emotion, that to have them as an enemy is unpleasant," said former Treasury official Davis. Though the bulk of gun owners are normal folks, he added, gun lobby appeals also "bring out the nuts," some of whom mailed him vile letters or bits of used toilet tissue.

On the other hand, lawmakers who sympathized with NRA were assiduously courted and lionized in gun lobby publications, not just at campaign time but year-round. When freshman Rep. Wendell Bailey, R-Mo., mentioned in an April speech about the Reagan shooting that he believed gun controls would not stop violence, NRA lobbyist Wayne LaPierre shot off a thank-you note, promising to "make sure our members in your district are well aware of your willingness to stand up for their views during difficult times." Bailey was so delighted he issued a press release about NRA's note.

Some gun control sympathizers who had little apparent reason to worry about the gun lobby nonetheless kept a low profile because they were convinced fighting guns was a waste of energy. House Judiciary member George E. Danielson, D-Calif., for one, said he thought registering guns and licensing gun owners "would work quite well" in controlling crime and would be popular with his constituents. But he declined to cosponsor such measures. He said the reason was not fear of the gun lobby, which he believed had little influence in his secure Los Angeles district, but simple futility. "You'd never get enough votes for it," he said.

Many lawmakers, eager to satisfy both the NRA and constituents who wanted something done about violence, backed bills to impose a mandatory penalty for federal crimes committed with a firearm. Though such a measure would do nothing to restrict gun possession — and would not touch the majority of gun crimes, which are violations of state law — mandatory sentencing was NRA's alternative to controls and also was endorsed by some handgun control champions.

Notches on the Gun

As proof the gun lobby could be beaten, critics cited NRA's all-out (losing) 1979 crusade to block Mikva's judgeship confirmation. They also pointed out that, despite heavy lobbying, NRA did not get as much land opened to hunting as it wanted in the 1980 Alaska lands bill; in part this was because the National Wildlife Federation, which also counted many hunters among its members, lobbied in the other direction.

Nonetheless, the gun lobby got its way quite decisively most of the time. All of the major handgun control ideas before the 97th Congress had been attempted in more liberal Congresses since 1968, without success. The last time a gun control bill raised its head had been in 1976, when the House Judiciary Committee adopted a ban on new "concealable" handguns. One week later, after gun owner protests, four committee members changed their votes, and the bill was recommitted to a subcommittee.

Proposals that may seem to outsiders minor inconveniences for the gun world were usually quickly snuffed out by gun lobby friends in Congress. A few examples:

● In 1975 both houses overwhelmingly ordered the Consumer Product Safety Commission not to meddle with ammunition, even by requiring safety labels such as "Keep Out of the Hands of Children."

● In 1976 the U.S. Fish and Wildlife Service restricted the use of lead shot for hunting, because it was poisoning waterfowl. NRA failed to overturn the regulation in court, but in 1979 NRA stalwart Sen. Ted Stevens, R-Alaska, amended an appropriation bill to forbid enforcement of the lead shot ban without state approval.

● In 1980 NRA helped kill a bill that would have required traceable "taggants" in explosive powder as an aid to law officers chasing bombers. NRA said the taggants were unsafe and would raise the price of power for guns hobbyists.

Anti-Handgun Groups

The National Rifle Association's image was enhanced by the comparative ineffectiveness of groups that lobbied for handgun controls. NRA's competition was always outspent and out-organized. Most important, its members tended not to have the single-minded concern of pro-gun voters.

Michael Beard of the Coalition to Ban Handguns said: "I would guess most of our supporters continued to support [defeated Sen. George] McGovern, even though he was wrong on gun control, because he was right on 10 other issues they care about."

The pro-control lobby also was divided on what it supported. The coalition argued that all handguns, because they are concealable and of little use for hunting, should be restricted to police and other security officers. Handgun Control Inc. put its limited weight behind a Kennedy-Rodino bill to ban only the relatively cheap handguns called "Saturday Night Specials," with lesser restrictions on other pistols. While chairman Nelson T. Shields had once advocated a ban on all handguns, he later changed his view, causing gun lobbyist Knox to scoff that "They're going for whatever the traffic will bear." David J. Steinberg, director of the Council for a Responsible Firearms Policy, said both of these views were "unreal" and believed that rifles and shotguns also should be subject to licensing and registration.

Renewed Interest

The shooting of musician John Lennon in December 1980 brought an invigorating surge of new donations to both the coalition and Handgun Control Inc. But it also firmed up the resolve of the gun lobby; as Snyder put it, gun owners "who might have been getting a little complacent are now aware that the monster is still out there."

Lobbyists on both sides generally agreed that passage of a gun control bill was extremely unlikely before 1983. "We're basically convinced that this Congress is not going to go very far on the issue," said Beard. "The anti-government trend of the last [1980] election has just frightened away any proponents who want to expand the role of government in the individual's life." The coalition concentrated its attention on state legislatures, where it also was routinely defeated by the gun lobby. Handgun Control Inc. professed only slightly more optimism.

At best, most gun control lobbyists said, the assassination attempt on Reagan in March 1981 had diminished NRA's chances for rolling back laws already in place. McClure and Volkmer introduced their bill to rein in gun enforcement in April 1981 with only half the cosponsors of the previous Congress. Glickman, a cosponsor in the past, said the Reagan shooting made him "forgive the pun, a little gun-shy" about signing up again.

Lobbying for the Poor

Time magazine columnist Hugh Sidey, often a barometer of conventional wisdom in Washington, spent his space in the March 30, 1981, issue disparaging a lobbying campaign by "special pleaders ... camouflaged in three-piece numbers from Brooks Brothers and armed with computer print-outs, artful charts and direct mail lists."

His particular targets were not the lobbyists of corporate America, but the traditional advocates of the downtrodden — the National Conference of Catholic Bishops, the National Low Income Housing Coalition, the Food Research and Action Center and others defending programs for the poor against President Reagan's budget cuts.

The message: Lobbyists who claim the poor as their constituents may once have merited deference, but these days they are just special interest groups, like all the others.

Sidey's column was a reminder to defenders of the poor that more than their programs were under attack. The philosophy underlying government help for the poverty-stricken and the political network that supported it also were being challenged by newly powerful conservatives, and with a fair measure of success.

On Capitol Hill, as in *Time* magazine, hearts were not bleeding as readily as they used to.

Many Republicans viewed social spending that exceeded the Reagan budget as verging on the unpatriotic. Many Democrats viewed it as politically suicidal. On both sides of the aisle, lobbyists for the poor were greeted with the Reagan-inspired refrain: "What are *you* willing to give up?"

Against that, advocates for poor people threw back a concerted effort to build influence where it counted — back home in the congressional districts. The immediate goal was to persuade Congress that it had misread the Reagan mandate, that there was popular support for food stamps, Medicaid, welfare and the like, and that it was backed up by votes. But with the congressional budget process barrelling along at a record pace, most lobbyists for the poor figured the best they could do was minimize the losses and brace for a grim future.

Lobby by Proxy

Their accouterments may include computer printouts, charts and direct-mail lists — perhaps even an occasional Brooks Brothers suit — but advocates for the poor are in some respects different from most lobbies in Washington. For one thing, they represent a constituency that, unlike the businessman, farmer or veteran, lacks an effective voice of its own.

The poor stay away from the polls in larger numbers than the rich or middle class. They rarely write letters, let alone the sort of letters that penetrate to the desk of a member of Congress. They are not usually on the congressman's back-home circuit; few food stamp recipients attend Kiwanis Club lunches, and it takes a special effort for a welfare mother to visit a congressman's district office. Many of the poor are children.

The more cynical among the poor believe their programs were cut for those very reasons. "It is easy to cut Medicaid, since few nursing home residents are able to speak out," said Joan E. Knowlton, a 66-year-old Minnesota nursing home resident who testified in March 1981 before the House Commerce Subcommittee on Health and the Environment. "We have no money, no high-paid lobbyist, no media campaigns."

Her own visit to Washington was financed by the subcommittee, which budgeted about $1,000 to help Medicaid recipients speak for themselves. More often, the poor participate in legislative debate by proxy. Their champions can be grouped roughly into three categories:

• The churches, charities, civil rights groups, philanthropic foundations and liberal activist organizations whose members support benefits for the poor out of moral obligation or ideology, rather than vested interest. In addition to their own lobbying, they help underwrite specialized advocacy groups in nutrition, health, housing and other areas, which in turn sound the alarm bells when programs are threatened.

Most of these groups are non-profit and tax-exempt, so their direct efforts to shape legislation are limited by law. But, in practice, the line between educating and lobbying is not rigid.

• Organized labor. Unions have a class kinship with the poor dating back to the early labor stirrings in the 19th century sweatshops. That kinship may have diminished as union pay scales moved a healthy distance from the poverty line; certainly, Reagan believed he had substantial blue-collar support for his cutbacks. But national union leaders continued to support social programs as a historical commitment, and they contended the majority of the rank

FOOD STAMPS

MEDICAID

Legal Services

LOW-INCOME HOUSING

Education for the Disadvantaged

and file was with them.

● Program administrators, poverty lawyers and providers — those with a professional interest in the programs. Examples of groups hard at work in opposition to Reagan budget cuts included public hospitals whose emergency rooms would handle patients deprived of Medicaid, cafeteria operators backing federal school lunch programs, Legal Services lawyers whose agency was marked for extinction, teachers supporting aid to disadvantaged students and the milk producers who profited from child nutrition programs.

Within each of these categories there was a measure of self-interest in preserving federal programs for the poor. Many civil rights groups, for example, received large federal grants to help operate job training, housing and other anti-poverty projects. In 1980 the National Urban League and its local affiliates received about $97 million in federal and other government grants.

For labor, too, the protection of the poor was not pure altruism. Some anti-poverty programs, such as food stamps, were an important lifeline for workers in times of unemployment.

Some unions had an even more direct interest in programs they protected; thus the United Food and Commercial Workers International Union, representing grocery clerks and other food industry workers, was one of the most tireless advocates of nutrition programs, and the American Federation of State, County and Municipal Employees, representing many hospital employees, was in the forefront of the battle for Medicaid.

Hanging Together

Champions of the poor assemble and reassemble in coalitions tailored to current events, pooling resources, sharing information and preparing strategy.

In the budget battles of the early 1980s the master coalition-builder was the AFL-CIO. Its National Budget Coalition pulled together an impressive array of 157 disparate groups, generally in agreement that President Reagan's budget gouged the poor and spared the rich.

Following a crowded press conference in February 1981, the coalition's steering committee continued to meet sporadically to exchange information and to harden lobbyists against the temptation to offer up each other's programs for sacrifice.

This massive gathering, however, like a similar one organized by the AFL-CIO in 1980 to fight President Carter's budget cuts, faced a short-lived usefulness. Once Congress had set its mind on cutting the budget, it was not especially receptive to lobbyists who simply said, "Don't cut anything."

Year in and year out, the real lobbying action revolves around more specialized coalitions, which can concentrate expertise and political clout on relatively narrow areas of policy, often attracting participants who might disagree on a broader sweep of public policy. *(Coalitions, box, p. 139)*

Lobbyists for food programs were among the best organized of those fighting Reagan budget cuts. They created two tightly knit coalitions, one emphasizing food stamps, the other child feeding programs.

They were reinforced by a coterie of leaders with long experience in government and the consumer movement. One example was Robert L. Greenstein, who acquired a reputation as one of the foremost food stamp experts while writing a newsletter for the Community Nutrition Institute. He later ran the food stamp program for the Carter administration. After Reagan took office Greenstein, with a grant from the Field Foundation — which advanced the 1960s' War on Poverty by exposing malnutrition in Appalachia and the South — set up a Project on Food Assistance and Poverty to prepare backup information for the war on Reagan's economics.

Greenstein's analysis of the Reagan budget was partly responsible for the first press reports showing that the administration's "safety net programs" primarily served those above the poverty line.

The anti-hunger lobby also was a favorite of churches because they often see the results in their own soup kitchens or charity outlets when federal feeding programs fall short. One of the two food alliances, the National Anti-Hunger Coalition, was financed by the Catholic Campaign for Human Development.

Another example of religious interest in anti-hunger programs was Bread for the World, an interdenominational Christian group that ran a "grass-roots" lobbying network out of an office near the Capitol. By a chain of phone calls to some of its 36,000 members, the group could quickly generate a few hundred letters or phone calls to key legislators on the eve of a crucial food vote.

Most programs for the poor, however, did not have that level of resources and organization. At the other end of the soup line was Aid to Families with Dependent Children (AFDC), the benefit most people mean when they say "welfare."

Welfare advocates rely on low-income advocacy groups such as the Children's Defense Fund and the Center for Community Change to monitor AFDC legislation and its impacts. But there had been no lead group for welfare lobbyists since the National Welfare Rights Organization dissolved in the mid-1970s following the death of founder George A. Wiley.

One handicap, according to lobbyists and congressional staffers, was that, unlike food stamps and other programs, AFDC had very few participants among the working poor. Most of its constituents were children and mothers in the poorest and most powerless niche of society.

The Poor Lobby: Alliances of Advocates

Almost any social program on the Reagan snip list had an alliance of advocates. Here is a sample of collective efforts on behalf of programs for the poor.

Food Stamps. The focal point was the National Anti-Hunger Coalition, organized in late 1979 by the Food Research and Action Center (FRAC) and later joined by six other national groups, including the Community Nutrition Institute (CNI). FRAC and CNI, in their own right, were influential regiments in the Washington "nutrition lobby." Each had a million-dollar budget from government and foundation grants to conduct studies and training programs, besides lobbying on government food policies.

The anti-hunger coalition, financed by a 1980 grant from the Catholic Church's Campaign for Human Development, was an effort to mobilize state and local anti-poverty groups in support of government hunger programs, especially food stamps.

The coalition bused about 400 local advocates and recipients to Washington in March 1981 to confront lawmakers on the subject of budget cuts.

Child Nutrition. The consumer-oriented Community Nutrition Institute and the National Milk Producers Federation lobbied on opposite sides whenever Congress debated dairy prices. But they laid aside their differences as members of the Child Nutrition Coalition, lobbying for programs such as school lunch and breakfast subsidies and the supplemental feeding program for women, infants and children (WIC).

The coalition leadership also included FRAC, the National Congress of Parents and Teachers; the Children's Foundation; and the American School Food Service Association, representing school cafeteria supervisors. Besides the milk producers, the group received farm help from egg, turkey and chicken growers, whose conservative members might have shied away from a food stamps lobby.

The coalition was much less formal than the anti-hunger alliance. Most of the members worked independently on their special budget concerns.

Education. The Children's Defense Fund, a foundation-supported group interested in programs that affected low-income and minority children, was the clearinghouse for a loose coalition opposing cuts in education for the disadvantaged. Principals included the National Association for the Advancement of Colored People and the Federal Education Project of the Lawyers Committee for Civil Rights Under Law, sponsored by the Carnegie Foundation.

Missing from that coalition were all of the major educator groups, which refused to single out low-income aid for special attention. Charles W. Lee, director of the educators' Committee for Full Funding of Education Programs, contended that all education programs make "a seamless web," with any cuts likely to pain the poor.

Betty Hamilton of Children's Defense Fund disagreed. She said her group was "not well-liked" by educators because it would cut some programs — such as impact aid to school districts serving federal employees — to preserve poverty programs.

Low-Income Housing. Headed by longtime housing activist Cushing Dolbeare, operating out of her Capitol Hill garage, the Low-Income Housing Coalition had a shoestring budget paid by a membership of church, labor, civil rights and tenant organizations. Dolbeare also headed a budgetary "strategy group" that included homebuilders and other interests who were not in the coalition.

The coalition, with conservative Sen. Jake Garn, R-Utah, as its unlikely champion, helped kill a 1980 effort to divert government housing aid to middle-income families.

Dolbeare was not optimistic, however, about a similar coup in the Reagan budget battle. She said the best the coalition hoped to do was to "come out with the Reagan level."

Medicaid. Medical aid for the poor had supporters ranging from the National Governors' Association to the National Gray Panthers, but consumers, providers and state and local officials often disagreed on how programs should be operated. Governors, for instance, generally supported greater state control over Medicaid, but beneficiaries worried about how some states would run things.

A coalition-building effort by the American Federation of State, County and Municipal Employees and a consortium of local consumer health groups rounded up 33 organizations to sign a letter opposing Reagan's proposed cap on Medicaid spending. But one organizer called that coalition "a one- or two-shot effort."

Probably the most influential lobbyists against the cap on Medicaid were the governors, who feared they would not be able to make up the difference from their own revenues. Other groups active on their own were county officials, public hospitals (the providers of last resort when Medicaid falls short), the Children's Defense Fund and the National Health Law Center.

Legal Services. The Legal Services Corporation, which Reagan wanted to abolish, had defenders inside and outside government. The Coalition for Legal Services represented the insiders — poverty lawyers and program alumni who hired a former House staffer to help save the program.

Outside, the 250,000-member American Bar Association made the corporation its leading legislative cause for 1981, and it brought more than 100 lawyers to Washington to argue the case.

Spread Thin

Owing to the breadth and magnitude of Reagan's proposals and their apparent momentum on Capitol Hill, many defenders of the poor found themselves spread thin in the job of defense. Other potential advocates decided to support Reagan out of sympathy with the general direction of his economic policy, or at least they withheld opposition in hopes the president would spare other benefits they received.

Medicaid lobbyists, for example, initially hoped the booming voice of the American Medical Association (AMA) might be raised in their behalf. But the AMA decided to back the president's program, specifically including his cap on Medicaid. Private physicians were more concerned about Medicare, which Reagan left largely intact. Medicaid serves the poor, regardless of age; Medicare serves the elderly, regardless of income.

Nutrition lobbyists similarly expected a boost from the Food Marketing Institute, representing 1,100 grocers and food wholesalers. The grocers had issued a position paper strongly endorsing food stamps as an efficient and valuable program.

But when the group's members flocked to Washington for a winter conference and sensed the feeling on Capitol Hill, they decided not to lobby for food stamp budget hikes. "They overwhelmingly support the president's economic program," explained the institute's vice president, Jeffrey R. Prince. "We are not about to say that the one area that affects us directly should be spared from cuts."

Organized labor found itself somewhat distracted from the battle for the poor by conservative assaults on many flanks, from job-creating federal construction projects to occupational safety and health rules.

"As our basic programs are threatened, we will have to spend a great deal more time on those, and perhaps be more of a supplement on food stamps and so on, rather than playing a leadership role," said AFL-CIO lobbyist Peggy Taylor. "There is no diminution of cooperation, just a diminution in the number of hours we can spend on it."

Under Democratic rule, advocates of the poor could count on substantial help from the agencies and congressional subcommittees responsible for the programs. Such sources of inside help were dwindling.

In the House some committees provided sanctuaries for the resistance, calling hearings to dramatize the impact of cutbacks, compiling statistics showing the effects on individual congressional districts, giving lobbyists advice on the proper approach to recalcitrant colleagues.

Among the Democratic chairmen who made their units important House resources in the battle against budget cuts were Carl D. Perkins, Ky., of the Education and Labor Committee, Henry A. Waxman, Calif., of the Subcommittee on Health, Fortney H. "Pete" Stark, Calif., of the Subcommittee on Welfare, and Fred Richmond, N.Y., of the Subcommittee on Nutrition.

But nationally known allies such as Hubert H. Humphrey, D-Minn. (1949-64; 1971-78), and George McGovern, D-S.D. (1963-81), were gone from the Senate, and remaining champions, such as Edward M. Kennedy, D-Mass., were greatly outnumbered.

Within the executive branch, some of the agencies set up to help the poor also continued to assist, directly or indirectly, in lobbying for anti-poverty programs (including, of course, their own).

The Community Services Administration (CSA), the Legal Services Corporation, the domestic volunteer agency VISTA and the public service jobs program of the Comprehensive Employment and Training Act (CETA) were major sources of money or manpower for projects that were helping poor people to influence government. The administration wanted to liquidate all four of those programs, and it succeeded in the cases of CSA and the CETA jobs program. Congress, however, gave at least a temporary reprieve to Legal Services and VISTA.

To critics, the involvement of government-funded activists in defense of these programs was additional evidence that the War on Poverty had become, in the much-quoted phrase of Reagan budget director David A. Stockman, a vast "social pork barrel."

Stockman questioned the concept that people were entitled to a government-subsidized minimum standard of living. He argued that social programs had been perpetuated by a mix of self-interested lobbyists and vote-hunting lawmakers. Conservatives echoed that theme on Capitol Hill.

"Virtually all of the lobbying has come from people who are involved directly or indirectly in administering these programs," contended conservative Phil Gramm, D-Texas, in one of the blunter versions of a familiar refrain. "They seem more worried about the benefits being cut than the people who receive the benefits."

Defenders bristled at the implication that the poverty lobby consisted mainly of people doing well by the government's doing good. "The president has personally warned Americans to beware of 'special interests' working to unravel his entire economic package," said Rep. Waxman. "But if the term 'special interests' under the Reagan administration has become the sick, the poor and the helpless, I am proud to defend them."

Poverty program supporters with a clear economic stake said their interest was not confined to their pockets. "Yes, we have an economic interest," said Susan Fridy of the National Milk Producers Federation, a supporter of child nutrition programs. "But our involvement has gone beyond that. We're there to support the concept of a balanced diet, not just to say how much cheese they should eat and how much milk they should drink."

Charles Bosley, lobbyist for a group of poverty lawyers defending the Legal Services program, said that "Legal Services attorneys obviously are wrapped up in the program and work for it and care about it. But they are not getting rich at it. These are storefront lawyers in ghettoes and rural poverty pockets."

To combat the "special interest" theme, advocates tried to get lawmakers face-to-face with people who needed the programs. The National Anti-Hunger Coalition raised money to bring about 400 people, including food stamp recipients, to testify and meet their representatives — the sort of activity that was an annual routine for auto dealers, librarians or veterans.

The Food Research and Action Center (FRAC) had a $10,000 foundation grant in 1981 to pay the expenses of low-income people visiting Congress. "I hate to say this, but I really think congressmen don't know the needs of the people," said Delton Ponder, a Hattiesburg, Miss., hospital maintenance man who came to Washington on FRAC's grant and told the Senate Agriculture Committee how food stamp cutbacks would hit his family. "Oh, I know they have some paperwork on it, but they don't know the bills and the expenses."

Ponder returned home optimistic from his first experience as a congressional witness: "I just feel in my heart that

The Politics of Poverty Programs

Besides cutting programs that delivered food, housing, health care and cash, the Reagan administration proposed to eliminate agencies that in the past supplied the poor with another, more controversial commodity: power.

Government-sponsored advocacy agencies such as the Community Services Administration (CSA) and the Legal Services Corporation had long been unpopular with conservatives for their political activities, from city halls to Capitol Hill. Frequently congressional critics alleged that these agencies and their projects overstepped legal bounds in lobbying with federal funds.

CSA and Legal Services

The General Accounting Office, at the request of 20 members of Congress, investigated the Food Research and Action Center (FRAC) in 1980 and charged that it illegally had used government money to lobby against a federal "workfare" project. FRAC relied heavily on CSA grants, which, by law, could be used for "purely informational and educational activities" but not to urge passage or defeat of legislation. CSA's general counsel said FRAC's activities had been "educational" and thus within the law.

In late March 1981, Rep. Steve Gunderson, R-Wis., demanded an investigation of a rural Wisconsin community action project, West CAP, that received money from CSA. West CAP had mailed out fliers declaring "Reagan Says 'No' to Human Needs...," urging citizens to write their legislators and to attend West CAP meetings on the budget cuts.

West CAP information director Doug Drake said the staff and directors had chipped in $270 of their own money to have the brochure printed. But the postage and other costs, he said, had been paid from CSA funds, because the budget meetings themselves were to be "informational."

"What's that, compared to the resources the administration and the people behind the administration are bringing to bear on this issue?" Drake said.

Congress tried to tighten up on CSA-funded lobbying in the agency's 1980 appropriation. But, on the last day of the Carter administration, the outgoing CSA director published an "interpretive ruling" that found nothing new in the tightened restriction. The ruling said Congress had "merely legislated a prohibition that CSA already abides by."

In 1981 Congress went further and carried out President Reagan's plan to wipe out the agency altogether.

While Congress balked at abolishing the Legal Services Corporation, legislation was introduced to curtail the agency's lobbying in 1981. Legal Services lawyers could lobby legally, so long as they were representing specific clients.

Moving With Caution

With conservatives in power, some groups reliant on government funds were exercising special care. "We're being a little more cautious, a little more discreet," said Judith G. Waxman, a staff attorney at the National Health Law Program, a Legal Services center in Washington. "We're paranoid, that's for sure."

Contributing to the poverty lobby's jitters were rumors and fears that the administration might punish experts who supported anti-poverty programs.

For example, in early 1981 the University of Chicago Center for the Study of Welfare Policy issued a report showing that Reagan's budget cuts would hit poor people. At about the same time, the center was told that the Department of Health and Human Services (HHS) was "altering the scope" of an unrelated grant dealing with health programs for the elderly and disabled. HHS Secretary Richard S. Schweiker ordered that a series of regional conferences planned by the Chicago center be cut from 10 meetings to one.

That sounded like a reprisal to anti-poverty lobbyists, but the administration said that it merely wanted to avoid sponsoring conferences until it had a clear policy on the subject of long-term health care. Cheryl Rogers, an analyst at the center, said there was no indication from federal officials that the change was related to the poverty study. "There are a lot of rumors going around," she said. "Unfortunately, we can't substantiate any of them."

I did some good."

Angela Sosnowski, a rural Minnesota farm woman who supplemented her $400-a-month earnings with welfare, was a little more experienced at testifying in Washington. She said that on a 1981 visit she found Congress much more hardened than in past years to "horror stories" about life on poverty.

"They didn't want to hear that," she said, after making the rounds of several offices, courtesy of a grant from a Catholic charity. "The only thing that made a difference is if you were representing a lot of people that were going to vote against them. I think that's the bottom line now."

When three low-income women testified at Medicaid hearings, Gramm demanded to know how they would solve the nation's economic problems. Chairman Waxman cut him off, saying "that is our job, not theirs."

The question, however, was not about to go away. Even loyal liberals frequently demanded of lobbyists for the poor where to look for budget savings and refused to accept the standard litany of alternatives — cutting business subsidies, defense spending and tax "loopholes."

"People should try to identify places in their own programs where cuts can be made with less impact," said Sen. Carl Levin, D-Mich., when asked what he tells lobbyists for the poor.

Some program advocates rejected that advice. "I don't have to tell them where to cut the savings out of my programs, because I don't think there are the kind of savings they want in my programs," said Nancy Amidei, director of the Food Research and Action Center. As for identifying other budget alternatives, she added, "The organizations I work with don't have a staff of economists. We don't have computers. We can't do Mr. Levin's job for him."

Grass Roots

Like most other lobbyists, advocates of the poor saw salvation in "the grass roots."

The National Anti-Hunger Coalition, stepping beyond its interest in food programs, assembled a long list of poverty advocates to sponsor a "Nationwide Action for a Fair Budget." Town meetings with congressmen, rallies, teach-ins and press conferences were scheduled in numerous communities during the 1981 Easter congressional recess.

The Americans for Democratic Action, a liberal group, dispatched its officers to 18 cities to address local budget meetings and encourage creation of budget coalitions.

In several states, disparate groups banded together in lobbying partnerships such as the Illinois Coalition Against Reagan Economics and Washington state's Alliance for Education, Welfare and Other Human Services. Most of these efforts were aimed not just at the current budget crisis, but at something more lasting.

The anti-poverty network had no shortage of local chapters, but the groups tended to have no central rallying point for political activity. When they did, the binding force often was a poverty law center or community action agency funded by one of the programs Reagan wanted to cut.

Charity and foundation officials said they were hearing desperate pleas for financial aid to make up for the anticipated loss of these government programs. But in many cases it was possible just the opposite would happen: foundation money pulling out on the heels of government money.

"Much of our giving is supplemental, usually supplemental of government grants," explained Bernard McDonald, a program officer at the Ford Foundation. "If there is nothing there to supplement. . . ."

In the longer run, the frenzy of local organizing had a second purpose. Reagan was pushing to give more authority over social programs to states, through block grants. If he succeeded, the sponsors of the poor would have to fight over funding and operation of their programs in an arena where they customarily had little clout: state legislatures.

Local activists in Chicago, Pittsburgh, Seattle and other communities said they feared that poverty advocates would be at each others' throats when the states parceled out their block grants — and those programs that were politically weak or unpopular with the party in power were dumped.

Bracing for the Future

As the poverty network passed along the alarms about proposed budget cuts, members of Congress began to see a shift in their mail away from the early, uncompromising support of the president, according to congressional offices.

"A couple of weeks ago, the mail was decidedly 'We support the president,' " said Mike Hernandez, press secretary to Senate Budget Committee member Ernest F. Hollings, D-S.C. "Now it's decidedly 'We support the president, but. . . .' "

However, poverty lobbyists, like most interests dissatisfied with the Reagan program, were chasing a juggernaut. The quick budget timetable, the large population of new lawmakers with no attachment to existing programs and the fear instilled by conservative groups who planned to make each spending vote a political test, all helped propel Reagan's cuts through Congress almost unscathed.

Already, lobbyists were looking ahead to the ensuing years. Reagan's budget anticipated deep, additional, unspecified spending cuts in the remainder of his term, even if his forecasts for an economic recovery came true.

"If you look at the out-year cuts, and if you believe Reagan's economics won't work, things are going to be even worse next year," said Peggy Taylor of the AFL-CIO.

"By that time," added the Children's Foundation's Margaret Lorber, "the public will be painfully aware of what's going on. I'm sure there's going to be some kind of backlash."

The Environmental Movement

For a "counter-inaugural" party marking the start of Ronald Reagan's presidency, one environmental activist wrote a skit depicting a television talk show the day after the 1992 elections. The fantasy had a panel of commentators marveling over the sweeping victory of the Vegetarian Party. As the skit progressed, it became clear that this surprising event had its roots, so to speak, in the 1980 elections, when environmentalists lost their foothold in the government. The only jobs they could find were in health food stores, where they built a new political base.

In real life, the 1980 elections did expel a large number of environmental advocates from influential positions in Congress and the Carter administration. But they were not going to work in health food stores. Indeed, many of them were reabsorbed into a community of environmental thinkers, organizers and lobbyists that had matured into a solid part of the establishment.

In the Washington offices of the Audubon Society, the Wilderness Society, the Natural Resources Defense Council and the Conservation Foundation, these activists may have been out of government, but they would not be out of power. Despite a post-election period of hand-wringing and black humor ("How much energy does it take to stop the environmental movement? One Watt."), the environmental movement seemed, upon examination, to be in reasonably good health.

There even were indications the election of pro-business conservatives would jar the movement out of a period of complacency. Roger Craver, a fund-raising consultant whose clients included the Sierra Club, the Wilderness Society and the Natural Resources Defense Council, said the response to mail solicitations for the three groups had increased about 30 percent after the elections, because donors were "spooked" by the environmental pronouncements of President Reagan, his interior secretary, James G. Watt, and Sen. James A. McClure, R-Idaho, new chairman of the Senate Energy and Natural Resources Committee.

Craver said that in 1980 the groups' memberships had been "plateauing." "Now it appears they may take off again because of these fears," he said.

New Tactics

Even before the election, environmental groups had undergone an intense internal debate over how to adjust their focus for the 1980s. During the 1960s and 1970s, these groups sparked a legislative explosion, lobbying through Congress a menu of environmental laws and the regulatory apparatus to interpret and enforce them. The laws governed air and water pollution; forest, range land and coastal land management; strip mining; pesticides and toxic substances; and endangered species.

The lawmaking process continued up to the final days of the 96th Congress, which created a $1.6 billion "superfund" for cleanup of toxic waste dumps and protected from development 104 million acres of Alaska. With most of the major objectives written into law, many environmentalists said the new decade promised to be a period of holding the line and seeing that the existing laws worked.

Interviews with the lobbyists and leaders of Washington-based environmental groups indicated several trends, including:

● An increased emphasis on technical expertise, especially the language of economics, as the debate shifted from general environmental mandates to questions of "how" and "at what cost." One sign of this was the Wilderness Society's announcement in January 1981 that it had received a $620,000 Richard King Mellon Foundation grant to establish a department of resource economics. Ex-Rep. Joseph L. Fisher, D-Va. (1975-81), an economist, was hired to run it.

William A. Turnage, executive director of the 45,000-member group, said the new department would "for the first time allow conservationists to have equal footing with development interests in the debate over the wisest use of our natural resources."

● A turning away from Washington. Many environmental activists in Washington conceded they had neglected their political base as the movement entered middle age. They argued for rebuilding popular support to enhance their lobbying credibility. Moreover, because the major environmental laws relied on state implementation plans, and because Reagan had vowed to accelerate the transfer of authority to the states, some environmentalists favored shifting resources to fortify local groups working on environmental issues.

● An increased interest in conciliation. Even friends like Carter Interior Secretary Cecil D. Andrus and House Interior Chairman Morris K. Udall, D-Ariz., had chided environmentalists for being uncompromising.

"What we've got to do is not play confrontation games,

Millions of acres in Alaska were protected from development by the Alaska lands bill of 1980.

not be purists," Udall warned a symposium at the National Wildlife Federation in December. "Identify allies, play up the fact that conservation is a bipartisan issue."

Diversity

There was a tendency, even among environmentalists, to talk about the environmental movement as a crusade that sprang up on Earth Day, April 22, 1970, and had marched in step ever since. Of course, it was neither so new nor so uniform.

The American conservation movement began in the 1800s as an effort to protect land, mostly in the West, from unregulated and rapacious use. In the 1960s and 1970s, due in part to a number of widely publicized environmental disasters such as the pesticide poisoning of wildlife and the Santa Barbara oil spill, the older "conservation" movement began to embrace broader issues of public health and safety. New groups sprang up, expanding the litany of causes and the repertoire of tactics.

A directory compiled by the Congressional Research Service in 1980 listed 60 "environmental organizations" in Washington, from the Alaska Coalition to Zero Population Growth. National groups concentrating on the environment — even the dozen or so usually counted as "major" — were diverse in size, age, constituency and style.

At the more conservative end were organizations like the National Wildlife Federation (founded in 1936), with 4.6 million subscribers and contributors, many of them blue-collar workers interested in preserving hunting and fishing habitat. The federation had become the informal moderator of the Washington conservation community, sponsoring conferences and strategy sessions aimed at increasing harmony.

At the other end were groups like Environmental Action (founded in 1970), with 20,000 members and a focus on more urban-oriented issues such as air pollution, toxic substances and alternative energy. Environmental Action created campaigns against the "Dirty Dozen" members of Congress and the "Filthy Five" corporate polluters.

The wide middle ground was occupied by groups as

generalized as the 180,000-member Sierra Club, founded as a California hiking club in 1892 and by the 1980s a visible participant in every major legislative fight; as specialized as the 35,000-member Solar Lobby, which promoted renewable energy sources; as middle-of-the-road as the Conservation Foundation, a think tank sponsored by foundations, corporations and the government; and as combative as the environmental law firms, Natural Resources Defense Council and Environmental Defense Fund.

A survey of members of five groups, conducted in 1978 by Robert Cameron Mitchell of Resources for the Future, found them to be more well-to-do, highly educated and ideologically liberal than the general public.

Rather than the "radicals" or "extremists" portrayed by some critics, Mitchell found "a reformist movement which harbors a vision of an 'appropriate' society but which presses for reforms that are neither too deep nor too left to alienate . . . its middle class constituency."

Flash Gordon

Environmentalists tended to portray themselves as an underdog Flash Gordon in lone combat with the merciless Ming of American industry. Yet while the environmental lobby in Washington still included some starvation-wage, storefront participants, on the whole it was an increasingly slick and professional operation.

The National Wildlife Federation, by far the most affluent member of the community, actually employed 500 people in its Washington-area offices, about the same number as the American Petroleum Institute, the oil industry's umbrella group. Fund-raiser Craver said despite the leveling off from their mid-70s heyday and the soaring cost of fund raising, the major groups were on a fairly firm financial footing.

As with most public interest lobbies, the strength of the movement lay in the concept of "membership." Donors did not just contribute, they "belonged" — which, for dues of $15 to $25, guaranteed them regular magazines and newsletters, an occasional exhortation to write their congressmen, and pleas for more contributions. In addition to some financial security, substantial membership gave the groups legitimacy when they lobbied Congress.

Groups that were facing financial troubles seemed to have recovered. The Environmental Defense Fund and Natural Resources Defense Council, law firms once reliant on grant money, had built up memberships to support them. The Wilderness Society, bouncing back from two years of leadership disorder and tumbling membership, not only added a new economic section but expanded its lobbying staff from four to seven people, and added more staff for community organizing and publicity.

Though the salaries in most groups remained well below the market for industrial lobbyists, the people being hired often were experienced lawyers, scientists, journalists or lobbyists. "When we hire a writer or a lobbyist now, it's generally somebody with some professional experience. We hire virtually no one right out of school," said an editor at Environmental Action, which paid each employee an egalitarian $16,000 a year. "The interns who interview here say the same is true for public interest jobs all over Washington."

Techniques employed by the environmental lobby were the same modern practices used by business and organized labor: computerized direct mail and phone banks to mobilize constituents, mass mailings and visits from constituents to impress Congress, and coalition-building to increase lobbying effectiveness.

All of these were practiced to perfection by the Alaska Coalition, a tightly knit consortium of environmental groups that pushed the Alaska lands bill through Congress in 1980. At one point, this coalition even hired an "organizational development specialist"— an expert in helping corporations run smoothly — to teach the member groups how to work together efficiently.

Like business and labor (though on a smaller scale), the environmental movement had political action committees (PACs) to make campaign contributions to sympathetic politicians. The League of Conservation Voters, the movement's oldest and biggest PAC, spent about $460,000 on the 1980 campaign, more than double its spending in the 1978 elections.

Much of the money was spent independently to pay door-to-door canvassers not affiliated with the candidates' official campaigns, thus avoiding legal limits on direct donations. In 1980 the League spent about $50,000 in this way to assist Sen. John C. Culver, D-Iowa (House 1965-75; Senate 1975-81), and $30,000 for Rep. Robert W. Edgar, D-Pa.

The Sierra Club also registered a small, but growing PAC during the 1980 campaign, as did the Solar Lobby. Leaders of several environmental groups took leaves from their jobs to work in campaigns. "It is not something which can be done everywhere — it is too costly for that — but by demonstrating that it can be done for some of their most important friends, environmentalists can increase their clout in Congress," said League of Conservation Voters Director Marion Edey.

Experienced Insiders

The professionalism of the environmental lobby was bound to be enhanced by the influx of experienced insiders from Congress and the Carter administration. Following are some notable government alumni:

• Former Sen. Gaylord Nelson, D-Wis. (1963-81), the author of several environmental laws, became chairman of the Wilderness Society in December after being defeated for re-election, and began his new job by testifying against Watt's nomination.

• David G. Hawkins, whom Carter appointed to handle clean air regulations at the Environmental Protection Agency (EPA), returned to the Natural Resources Defense Council (NRDC) to help defend the clean air law during its reauthorization.

• M. Rupert Cutler, a former Wilderness Society executive who was an assistant secretary of agriculture, became senior vice president of the National Audubon Society, overseeing the group's Washington operation from its New York headquarters.

• Gus Speth, an NRDC attorney Carter named as chairman of the Council on Environmental Quality, moved to the Conservation Foundation to think and write.

After a teaching stint at Georgetown University Law Center, he would become president of the Institute for World Environment and Resources Inc. — established by a $15 million grant from the MacArthur Foundation of Chicago — in October 1982.

"These people are likely to be more effective in opposition than they were in power," said Lawrence Silverman, Executive Director of the American Clean Water Association."They have access to money and media, and they know where the bodies are buried."

Cause for Alarm

Environmental groups expected to need this expert help. While no one read the election as a referendum on the environment (candidates who advertised pro-environmental records generally did well), the balloting brought to power a lot of people who believed the business claim that environmental regulation hurts productivity.

Foremost among them was a president whose closest personal friends and advisers were rich businessmen, and who campaigned with blood-raising bromides about "environmental extremists." The appointments of Watt, Office of Management and Budget Director David A. Stockman and Council of Economic Advisers Chairman Murray L. Weidenbaum, all preachers of diminished government regulation, sent shivers through the movement. In addition, reports that industry consultant James R. Mahoney had been considered to head the Environmental Protection Agency, brought rumbles of foreboding.

Adding to the case of nerves was a voluminous report by a self-appointed Reagan advisory group, the unswervingly conservative Heritage Foundation, recommending a major rollback of environmental protection rules. The supervisor of that report, Louis J. Cordia, served on Reagan's EPA transition team.

In Congress, environmentalists lost several champions at a time when some of their legislative achievements were up for reauthorization. Among the major statutes up for debate would be the Clean Air Act, laws governing clean water, strip mining and a number of public land issues. In each case, a formidable business lobby was licking its chops. "I think there's adequate cause for alarm, to say the least," said Thomas L. Kimball, vice president of the National Wildlife Federation, a group not known for alarmism.

"What harm can Reagan do?" asked Marion Edey of the League of Conservation Voters. "He can appoint people like James Watt. He can refuse to enforce regulations. He can try to get Congress to change the laws. He can generally spend four years fooling around and wasting time while basic problems get worse."

In implementing the laws already passed, particularly brand new ones like the superfund bill, environmentalists said Reagan could do grave damage by doing not much at all. "Changing laws is difficult and slow," Kimball said. "But regulations are another matter. An awful lot of discretionary power is given by law to the agencies. Within the framework of the law, you can make or break our environmental objectives."

A Silver Lining?

Environmentalists were able to find some silver linings on a cloudy horizon. One was the tendency of executives to move toward the middle once in power. Reagan's environmental record as governor of California, for example, was considered progressive for its time.

Kimball noted that Reagan also had invited moderate Republicans into his advisory circle — former EPA chiefs Russell E. Train and William D. Ruckelshaus, former CEQ Chairman John Busterud, Audubon Society Director Nathaniel P. Reed and others. But Kimball, who knew most of these men personally from 21 years with the federation, said the moderates "are not being listened to at all" in the Reagan camp.

In Congress, environmentalists were reassured by the presence of moderates such as Sen. Robert T. Stafford, R-Vt., who chaired the Environment and Public Works Com-

The Cleanup Industry Lobbies Little

One dream of environmentalists in the 1970s was that new companies would be born to mop up the messes of civilization, and this industry would itself become a lobby for environmental protection. Moreover, some environmentalists hoped, business in general would relax its stiff opposition to environmental regulation when it saw that cleaning up went hand-in-hand with modernization and good public relations.

The cleanup industry was a reality by 1981, a multibillion-dollar business sector built on coal stack scrubbers, catalytic converters and the like. But its financial success had not been translated into a formidable political force in Washington. And businesses that, in their advertising, touted the joys of environmental consciousness, continued to question the laws that required it.

Low Key

The most visible of the groups that lobbied for the cleanup industry was the Environmental Industry Council, founded in the mid-1970s at the urging of Russell Peterson — then chairman of the Council on Environmental Quality and an early believer in the notion that industry would see the light. The industry group was supported by 25 companies and several trade associations. Director Esther Foer said the group represented about 80 percent of the pollution control industry.

As industry lobbies go, the council was tiny. Its budget of about $150,000 was less than many medium-sized companies spent lobbying against environmental laws. And unlike many other industry trade associations, it had no political action committee (PAC) to contribute to favored candidates.

The council made itself available to Congress as an expert witness on the capabilities of pollution control equipment, but it had not lobbied actively for stronger laws, Foer said. Some member companies were subsidiaries of larger firms that polluted; lobbying would have risked uncomfortable conflicts. As members of the business fraternity, they tended to share business' resentment of government. Cleanup companies were also leery of antagonizing their customers.

"We've generally been an industry that is very low-key," Foer explained. "In part, we're conservative because we're in the middle. We're caught between environmental regulations, which keep the industry alive ... and our customers." For example, a lobbyist for one company that made auto pollution control equipment noted that the major auto makers might resent his lobbying for stricter exhaust control deadlines. The lobbyist favored stricter deadlines, but generally kept that opinion to himself. Every environmental equipment maker's "customers wish

to hell he would dry up," he added. "You are very much inhibited in how overtly you fight against the people who put the bread in your mouth."

At the American Clean Water Association, which had attempted to mobilize the makers of water pollution technology to lobby for strong federal clean water programs, Executive Director Lawrence Silverman said industry support had been painfully slow in coming. "There are a lot of people in industry who wish us well and someday will join us, but they don't want to be first," he said.

Silverman said one promising sign was that some big companies, including Dow Chemical Co., Union Carbide Corp. and Campbell Soup Co., were divesting themselves of pollution control divisions. Newly independent, these divisions might feel freer in their marketing and political activities, Silverman speculated.

No Economic Incentive

Some companies saved money — and made headlines — by imaginative solutions to their own pollution problems. But those companies generally continued to lobby against anti-pollution laws.

Russell H. Susag, director of environmental operations at 3M Co., for example, estimated that the company had saved $20 million in the late 1970s through a widely praised program of preventing pollution at the source. But he said the saving simply meant that preventing pollution was cheaper than cleaning it up later; the company would save even more without any pollution control laws.

Those who tried to get business to take a more moderate stance in environmental battles said that even that idea met with strong resistance. "The traditional approach of industry has been to approach environmentalists as though this was some form of collective bargaining situation, where the best strategy is to come in with the most extreme position and hang onto it as long as possible," said John R. Quarles Jr., a former deputy administrator of the Environmental Protection Agency who headed an industry group advocating compromise between environmentalists and business hard-liners on clean air laws.

"From a lobbying or political strategy viewpoint, the more moderate voices within industry are subordinated," Quarles said. The result was that business acquired an unyielding image.

William K. Reilly, president of the Conservation Foundation, which sponsored "dialogue groups" between industry and environmentalists, said many companies were reluctant to break with the party line set by their trade associations. "Those convoys are forced to move at the pace of the most recalcitrant companies," Reilly said.

mittee. Stafford said in an interview that the new administration and a "more business-oriented" Congress would not be a fertile ground for new initiatives. But he doubted that the Reagan administration would prove to be "the menace to the existing environmental programs that some environmentalists fear."

Strengths

There were other reasons many environmentalists felt more secure than a casual viewer might have thought. First, the laws were in place. This placed limits on what Reagan could do, and provided the basis for court challenges if he exceeded the limits. "The old rapist days are over," said Brock Evans, Washington director of the Sierra Club. "Even the worst that could happen is not as bad as the worst that could have happened 10 years ago. We're all expecting to be in court a lot more."

Second, the government was equipped with built-in alarm systems designed to inject Mother Nature's voice into arguments over policy: the Environmental Protection Agency to administer environmental laws, the Council on Environmental Quality to advise the president and a whole network of bureaucrats to measure the environmental impact of government activities. Even if Reagan chose to stifle or ignore these voices, they would provide ammunition for defenders of the environment.

In Congress, the Environmental Study Conference existed specifically to raise and debate the environmental issues that revolved around pending legislation. This informational body, founded by a handful of House members in 1975, received financial support from the office accounts of 245 representatives and 73 senators in the 96th Congress (1979-81).

"The environment has been institutionalized," said Charles M. Clusen, conservation director of the Wilderness Society. "It's part of our prevailing set of attitudes. I don't think a Reagan administration or a new Senate can dislodge that."

A 1980 study of public attitudes toward the environment, conducted for the Council on Environmental Quality by Robert Mitchell, concluded that the movement was built on a firm foundation of public support. Comparing his own extensive poll with similar surveys taken through the 1970s, Mitchell did find a decline, from the excitement of Earth Day, in the public's willingness to sacrifice economic growth for a clean environment. But he also found that a plurality still believed "continuing improvement [in environmental quality] must be made regardless of cost."

Arousing the Public

Mitchell added that "the trick for environmental groups in the 1980s is to translate the continued support into action — to mobilize these people."

The question was, "How?"

One theme popular in Washington environmental circles was that environmentalists should be more attentive to their constituents, rather than viewing them merely as troops to be called on for financial support and an occasional barrage of letters to Congress.

William K. Reilly, president of the Conservation Foundation, described a conference his group sponsored in Estes Park, Colo., in early 1980. Some 250 environmentalists from around the country were there, and leaders from Washington were surprised to hear them voice the same complaints about government intrusion and red tape that popped up in conservative preaching. Local environmentalists, Reilly concluded, were "a community too easily assumed by many of us to be pro-big government, pro-regulation."

Several Washington environmental leaders also conceded that easy access to government during the Carter years made them lazy about selling their case to the general public. "While most of the public interest movement contentedly writes newsletters to itself, conservative groups are developing the most effective propaganda machine in history," Sam Love, former coordinator of Environmetal Action, wrote in that organization's January 1981 magazine.

Love urged an expanded use of radio and television to "rebuild a constituency for progressive programs." The Solar Lobby planned to take a step in that direction by opening a Los Angeles office to urge television writers and producers to feature alternative energy themes in their programs, according to the group's coordinator, Richard Munson.

Dollars and Sense

Washington environmentalists also admitted they had not done enough to frame arguments in dollars and cents. Paul Portney, who left a job as chief economist at CEQ to work for Resources for the Future, said environmentalists had been uncomfortable with the debate over costs vs. benefits, because so many environmental benefits — avoiding lung disease, or leaving a piece of the Earth for future generations — are hard to price.

By 1981, he said, there was a growing proficiency in the language of economics. He pointed to the Environmental Defense Fund's 1978 study demonstrating that energy conservation and renewable sources could cost less than new conventional power plants. The study helped persuade some Western utilities to launch expanded programs of conservation and renewable energy.

The Natural Resources Defense Council later did a "white paper" on the health effects of fine particulates, an issue in the Clean Air Act debate. "I don't like the idea of trying to put a price tag on clean air," Portney said. "But we have to realize we can't do everything. Comparing costs and benefits is one way to determine priorities."

Compromise

There was less agreement among environmentalists about the prospects for compromise with business. But a growing number of environmental leaders believed it was something worth trying — not just because the election strengthened industry's hand, but because it could result in more effective environmental protection. William A. Butler, an Environmental Defense Fund lawyer who took over the Washington office of the Audubon Society in early 1981, called the new decade a time for "fine-tuning, collaboration and compromise."

In the few years before the 1980 election, there had grown up a narrow demilitarized zone between the combatants of industry and environmentalism. Outside of Washington, it could be seen in the increasing use of professional negotiators to resolve local environmental disputes over such things as siting of a dam, power plant or waste dump.

In Washington, the Conservation Foundation ran "dialogue groups" to search out areas of accord between industry and environmentalists. In the summer of 1980, for example, one such group, made up of lawyers and scientists from business and the environmental movement, sent EPA a list of recommendations on classification of new toxic chemicals.

The Conservation Foundation expanded this "dispute resolution" program in May 1981 by absorbing the California-based Center for Environmental Conflict Resolution. The Ford Foundation, which had given many environmental law firms their seed money, was planning a major mediation project as well.

"I don't think environmentalists would have wanted to sit down with industry in 1968, when there were very few charters for the environment, and a diffuse and largely unprofessional environmental community," said foundation President William Reilly. "Now there's a much more equal balance of power."

Another sign of this new mood was that at least two of Carter's in-house environmentalists went to work for industry. Joseph Browder, a veteran of the Audubon Society, Friends of the Earth and the Environmental Policy Center before Carter tapped him to handle public land issues in the Interior Department, opened a consulting business. James W. Moorman, a former Sierra Club Legal Defense Fund lawyer who headed the natural resources division of the Justice Department, joined a Washington law firm.

Both said their ambition was to help industry obey the law. "It is in the environmental movement's interest that industry be able to comply with these laws," said Moorman. Some environmentalists do not seem to realize, he said, that business "is not the Mafia."

On some points environmentalists were thought to find kindred spirits in a more conservative administration and Congress — at least theoretically. Silverman, a former Ralph Nader associate who directed the American Clean Water Association, contended that in water policy Republicans had been natural allies. For example, Rep. Don H. Clausen, R-Calif., who consistently earned rock-bottom ratings from environmentalists for his voting, had "a distinguished record" of pushing small-scale water cleanup programs, Silverman said. After the election, Silverman wrote Clausen a nine-page memo laying out an environmental program he said would be consistent with past Republican initiatives.

Conservatives sided with environmentalists in opposition to synthetic fuels subsidies, highway programs and other large public works projects. Many environmentalists shared the Republican goal of decontrolling energy prices, though the movement was sharply divided on the question. "Democrats have done a better job of taking credit," Silverman said. "But the Republican Party has a lot of closet environmentalists." Agreed Edey: "If Reagan is an honest, smart conservative, he could do us a lot of good." But she added a note of suspicion. "Being an honest conservative is not the same as being a shill for big business."

If such suspicions were confirmed, environmentalists promised, the era of conciliation would be short-lived. "If they're going to forget these environmental objectives," warned Kimball, "we're going to take out the biggest ball bat we can muster and work 'em over."

El Salvador Interest Groups

In the spring of 1981, a poll of the public, the press corps or Congress on the subject of El Salvador might have produced a lot of shrugs and blank looks. One year later some of El Salvador's political personalities were as familiar to the attentive American newspaper reader as, say, some U.S. Cabinet members. The country's March 1982 elections and their immediate aftermath received the sort of study usually reserved for the New Hampshire primary. The House Subcommittee on Inter-American Affairs, once a black hole into which politicians disappeared, met in a room jammed with spectators and TV cameras.

Events, of course, forced American eyes toward El Salvador. But dozens of lobby groups of the right and left, human rights advocates, peace and "solidarity" networks, business and labor organizations — and, above all, churches — encouraged the interest and shaped it.

A post-election lull pushed El Salvador to the back pages, but only temporarily. As a new government organized there and indicated its direction, Congress prepared again to review growing U.S. involvement. Every six months the administration, if it wished to continue military aid to the El Salvadorans, was obliged to provide Congress with certification that the regime in power was protecting human rights and pursuing social reforms.

The events in El Salvador had consequences beyond the borders of that country. Liberal critics of the Reagan administration had gotten a heady whiff of success from the El Salvador experience, which they expected to invigorate their activities in related areas of foreign policy, military spending and nuclear arms control. Many critics saw a growing interest in other Latin American trouble spots such as Nicaragua, Guatemala, Honduras and Costa Rica.

Several congressional aides and lobbyists noted that the simultaneous drive for a nuclear arms freeze, while not directly related, involved many of the same interest groups. "El Salvador cannot be separated from the military budget issue, the nuclear freeze and the general perception of the direction of American foreign policy," said Rep. Jim Leach, R-Iowa, a prominent human rights and arms control advocate.

Who Has Influence?

In 1981-82, new names were added almost monthly to the inventory of American groups watching El Salvador. Some — the Committee to End U.S. Intervention in El Salvador, the Citizens Committee on El Salvador, the Coalition for Free Elections in El Salvador — were little more than short-lived alliances of like-minded people, with no staff, track record or firm future plans.

Even long-established and well-known groups involved with Latin America, some lawmakers said, were limited in their actual influence on the formation of U.S. policy. "All of these groups more or less talk to their friends," said Victor C. Johnson, staff director for the Inter-American Affairs Subcommittee, which was chaired by Rep. Michael D. Barnes, D-Md. "They don't so much influence as backstop."

Thus, he said, he frequently talked to the Washington Office on Latin America (WOLA), a church-sponsored human rights group that shared Barnes' perspective on Latin America. But representatives of the rightward Council on Inter-American Security rarely visited his office, and when they sent material, Johnson said, "I just throw it in the wastebasket." Some conservatives on Capitol Hill just as quickly shut out WOLA, considering it too leftist.

Rep. Jim Coyne, R-Pa., said he believed lobbying on El Salvador had been far less influential than press coverage that tended to awaken memories of Vietnam. Like many moderates and conservatives, Coyne said early reporting of the conflict was woefully simplistic, portraying the U.S. as backing murderous generals against Robin Hood rebels.

The one lobbying force that almost everyone agreed had a formative influence on U.S. policy toward El Salvador was the church community. By pressing lawmakers directly and by keeping a fire going under the boiler of public opinion, churches raised congressional interest in human rights, expanded the opposition to military aid, and backed the Reagan administration away from its early inclination to make El Salvador a global test of will.

Efforts to cut off U.S. military aid to the civilian-military junta in El Salvador — the major legislative objective of most church groups — were unsuccessful. But the churches and church-supported organizations were widely credited with the 1981 congressional action making military aid conditional on certain social and human rights reforms.

Several congressional aides also believed the pressure had made the Reagan administration far more cautious in its approach to other Central American flash points. "The fight over El Salvador has had a real dampening effect with respect to the administration's adventurism down there," said William Woodward, who worked for administration critic Rep. Gerry E. Studds, D-Mass. "That surprises us. To be honest, we thought we'd be steamrollered from Day One."

The biggest outpouring was from the Roman Catholic Church. According to many sources, involvement of the church hierarchy — represented by the U.S. Catholic Conference — was unprecedented for a foreign policy issue.

The National Council of Churches, an activist Protestant umbrella group, was another early critic of U.S. involvement in El Salvador. Among the individual Protestant denominations that were particularly visible were the United Church of Christ, United Methodists, Presbyterians, the American Baptists and several pacifist churches such as the Mennonites and Friends.

Their common themes were allegations of human rights abuses by the Salvadoran military, alarms about U.S. involvement becoming a larger, Vietnam-style engagement, and pleas for negotiations with the rebel Farabundo Marti National Liberation Front (FMLN) and Democratic Revolutionary Front (FDR). Some religious leaders, however, went further and endorsed the rebel cause outright.

Most of the churches sent missives to their clergy and believers urging letter-writing campaigns to end U.S. military aid. Many also testified or lobbied on Capitol Hill, arranged contacts for lawmakers and aides visiting El Salvador, and kept up a drumbeat of anti-administration arguments in their church publications and sermons.

In addition to individual church activities, two loosely affiliated networks dispensed a flow of El Salvador information, collected from human rights and other groups and repackaged for a churchgoing audience. The Inter-Religious Task Force on El Salvador and Central America, operating out of the National Council of Churches' office in New York, began circulating El Salvador messages in 1980 and later tried to broaden its focus to include other Central American countries. Beverly Keene, the task force coordinator, said the group's official policy was a cutoff of U.S.

military aid and negotiations with the rebels, but she said most of the task force's individual members "would clearly support the Democratic Revolutionary Front and the FMLN" as the legitimate voice of El Salvadorans.

The Religious Task Force, a less active group based in Washington, sent material to Catholic clergy and lay people.

El Salvador was a touchier issue among Jewish groups. Some, such as the Union of American Hebrew Congregations, joined the cry to cease sending arms. But others, such as the American Israel Public Affairs Committee, sent Congress material expressing concern about friendly links between the Salvadoran rebels and the Palestine Liberation Organization.

Church Critics

Church lobbying on El Salvador provoked bitter criticism from supporters of U.S. aid. "The most effective in lobbying are the church groups, because they wear a cloak of legitimacy," said Michael D. Boggs, assistant director of international affairs at the AFL-CIO, which backed the administration on El Salvador. "They get folks to write letters who don't have the faintest idea what they're talking about."

In 1981 supporters of "democratic values" organized the Institute on Religion and Democracy to provide a counterweight to the church activism on foreign policy. According to Penn Kemble, a consultant employed by the institute, it raised $200,000 from individual donations and conservative foundations to disseminate material to clergy and prominent laymen and to provide seminars.

Perhaps most infuriating to conservative critics, the churches provided money, credibility — and an audience — to a host of other groups critical of U.S. policy, ranging from liberal "human rights" organizations like WOLA to a network of organizations further to the left that were overtly sympathetic to guerrilla movements in Latin America. "So many left activists are linked up with church groups that it's hard to know what is a real church group," Kemble said.

Thomas E. Quigley, Latin American specialist of the United States Catholic Conference.

One church group, the United Methodists, played landlord to what was probably the busiest center of El Salvador lobbying in Washington. The Methodist Building, a block from the Capitol, housed the social action offices of the Methodists, Presbyterians, United Church of Christ, National Council of Churches, the Unitarian Universalist Association, plus WOLA and the Coalition for a New Military and Foreign Policy.

Against Involvement

Following are sketches of some of the participants in the liberal effort to brake U.S. involvement in El Salvador, most of them at least partially church-backed:

● The Washington Office on Latin America was founded in 1974 and supported by 40 groups, mostly churches. It funneled human rights information to lawmakers and aides, published newsletters, and escorted visiting dissidents from Central America (including, in 1977, José Napoleon Duarte, who later became president of El Salvador).

"The private sector and the governments in Latin America have a whole apparatus up here which amplifies their views," said Director Joseph T. Eldridge. "There are potent law firms and public relations outfits and the embassies and the military attachés. The question is, what about the poor peasant who has had his rights trampled on?"

WOLA had a $250,000 budget, a full-time staff of nine, and entrée to many (mostly liberal) offices on Capitol Hill. Aides to several congressional liberals said WOLA was "indispensable" but "predictable" and too leftish for many moderate and conservative members. "Even by a lot of liberal aides, they're perceived as too willing to give the benefit of the doubt to the FDR, the FMLN or the [Nicaraguan] Sandinistas," said a foreign policy specialist who worked for an administration critic.

● The Coalition for a New Foreign and Military Policy, started in 1976, was the nerve center of the liberal grass-roots network on Latin America. Most of the other groups opposed to U.S. policy on El Salvador — from liberal labor unions and mainstream peace groups such as the American Friends Service Committee to far left "solidarity" groups — relied on the coalition for up-to-date information on legislation, the voting records of members of Congress, and advice on how to approach lawmakers in letters or visits.

The group had a broad interest in disarmament, foreign policy in the Third World and military spending, but Co-Director Cynthia Buhl said Central America was the number one issue in 1981-82.

● The Council on Hemispheric Affairs was founded in 1975 by liberal academics, churchmen and union officials to counter industry influence on Latin America. Director Laurence R. Birns frequently was interviewed by reporters when they needed a spokesman for the liberal viewpoint on regional affairs. However, according to several congressional aides, the group had little presence on Capitol Hill.

● The Unitarian Universalist Service Committee, based in Boston, had its most significant impact by underwriting five congressional "study missions" to El Salvador. The trips usually included visits to rebels and other dissidents not on the agenda of officially sponsored tours. Most of the trips were for liberal lawmakers — including Rep. Studds, who credited his January 1981 visit with making him one of the most outspoken House activists against aid to El Salvador.

Subsequent trips aimed for a bipartisan cast. Rep. Thomas E. Petri, R-Wis., traveled to El Salvador with the Unitarians in August 1981. Republican moderate Coyne went in February 1982. Coyne said in an interview he realized the trip was "a political exercise" for his hosts, and he chided them for playing down abuses by the Latin American left. But the trip also strengthened his own opposition to U.S. military aid, and he wrote Reagan a letter saying so.

Unitarian human rights director John McAward, who escorted the study trips and planned several more, said he believed they had a ripple effect on congressional opinion, especially when the participants were not all ardent liberals. "If you bring back a couple of Democrats and they beat up on the Republicans, it doesn't have the same effect as if you bring back a bipartisan delegation and they make the same points, maybe in a softer tone," he said.

● Americans for Democratic Action (ADA), the traditional liberal lobby, became significant on El Salvador primarily because ADA's longtime foreign policy lobbyist, Bruce P. Cameron, moved to the inside as an aide to Rep. Tom Harkin, D-Iowa. Cameron helped arrange study trips for lawmakers and served as a link between liberals and outside groups.

ADA also played host to a former El Salvadoran land reform official, Leonel Gomez, who had visited several lawmakers to argue against military aid.

● Amnesty International, the London-based human rights monitoring agency, was highly visible on El Salvador. Amnesty directly contested Carter and Reagan administration claims on human rights and declared that U.S. military aid was contributing to rights abuses. Members of many of the group's 240 U.S. chapters wrote or visited lawmakers, following guidelines sent to them by the organization.

● The Committee in Solidarity with the People of El Salvador (CISPES), formed in October 1980, was openly sympathetic to the guerrilla opposition FDR and FMLN. It had success organizing marches and demonstrations, call-

Catholic Church Is a Major Influence...

The Roman Catholic Church toiled in the political vineyards of Washington for years, but it never was well known as a missionary of foreign policy. Abortion, tuition tax credits for parochial schools, civil rights and poverty programs — those were the issues tended by the lobbyists in Roman collars.

The violence in El Salvador, however, may have changed that with a jolt. "The Catholic Church has unquestionably had the most influence of any group" on El Salvador policy, asserted Rep. Michael D. Barnes, D-Md., chairman of the House Inter-American Affairs Subcommittee.

"I've never seen anything like it," said Bruce Cameron, a House aide and former foreign affairs lobbyist for the Americans for Democratic Action. "Members of Congress who have had trouble with the Catholic hierarchy in their districts because of abortion have suddenly found re-entry on this issue."

'Peace and Justice'

The center of Catholic activity on El Salvador was the Department of Social Development and World Peace run by the United States Catholic Conference, the administrative agency of the more than 300 U.S. bishops. The department maintained a staff of eight government relations professionals (they avoid the word "lobbyist"), evenly divided between domestic and foreign affairs.

The Rev. J. Bryan Hehir, director of the international division, dated the swell of U.S. Catholic interest in El Salvador to February 1980, when Archbishop Oscar Romero took to the pulpit of the cathedral in San Salvador to read a letter to President Carter. Romero urged Carter to revoke his planned transfer of $5 million in "non-lethal" aid to the El Salvadoran military, saying it would align the U.S. with abusers of human rights.

Romero's letter was representative of a major shift in the Catholic world view that churchmen trace back to the Vatican II conference of 1962-65. Catholicism was once known as a bulwark of anti-communism and bastion of the establishment — illustrated by church support for the U.S. war in Vietnam and by long alliance with oligarchies of Latin America. Later, however, the establishment ties gave way to a close sympathy with the downtrodden of the Third World — an emphasis on what the church called "justice and peace issues." "I think there is a growing sense in the modern Catholic church that the Christian is engaged in seeking a more just world," said Hehir's deputy, Thomas E. Quigley.

A month after his public call for U.S. non-intervention, Romero was gunned down at the altar while saying mass. The killing, blamed on the right wing, galvanized Catholic clergy and parishioners. "They may not know where El Salvador is, but they know killing a bishop while he's saying mass is not something they ought to be passive about," said Hehir. The subsequent killing of four Catholic missionaries in December 1980 sent a second wave through the church that never completely subsided.

After that, the bishops repeatedly voted their condemnation of military aid and called for negotiations with the rebels. Several ranking clerics testified before congressional committees, and bishops were urged to contact their local members of Congress.

One figure who helped keep El Salvador high on the Catholic agenda was Archbishop James A. Hickey. As bishop of Cleveland, Hickey was the overseer of a missionary team in El Salvador, including two of the women killed in 1980. He later became archbishop of Washington, a position that enhanced his influence within the bishops' conference and his political contacts.

The bishops' views on El Salvador were preached from pulpits in some parishes and given enormous coverage in the Catholic press, helping generate an outpouring of mail from priests, nuns and parishioners. "We don't push a button that turns on all the dioceses," Quigley noted. But, Hehir added, "When the bishops take that kind of leadership, there's bound to be a response."

Quigley said the church was careful not to make a point of the fact that many of the policy-makers involved in U.S. foreign affairs were Catholics, in-

ing on more than 300 local affiliated campus and activist groups.

In February 1982 CISPES demonstrators were arrested at a sit-in in the office of Rep. Silvio O. Conte, R-Mass. CISPES also was the linchpin of a March 1982 demonstration in Washington.

The group, however, was widely shunned on Capitol Hill. Studds, for example, backed out of a promised appearance at the March rally because "it was a little bit too left for him," said Rob Costa of CISPES.

McAward of the Unitarian Universalists, citing FDR President Guillermo Ungo as his source, contended CISPES was established to be an FDR mouthpiece in America. "CISPES is great people, they have a very effective grass roots, but they were formed by the FDR and FMLN and they get their marching orders from Ungo," McAward said.

Costa said CISPES kept in close touch with the FDR, but insisted, "We have no structural ties.... We are an independent organization."

...On U.S. Policies Toward El Salvador

cluding former Secretary of State Alexander M. Haig Jr., Assistant Secretary of State for Inter-American Affairs Thomas O. Enders, and House Foreign Affairs Chairman Clement J. Zablocki, D-Wis. "That's a delicate issue.... When we talk to officials, we pay no attention to where they spend their Sunday mornings," Quigley said.

The Reagan administration was alert to the Church opposition, though not very successful in dampening it. Before the State Department released its "White Paper" in February 1981, alleging Soviet interference in El Salvador, senior Catholic prelates were invited in for a three-hour briefing, in which Haig participated.

In addition to the formal activities of the bishops, Catholic officials participated individually in a wider community of activists. Quigley, for instance, was on the boards of the liberal Washington Office on Latin America and Council on Hemispheric Affairs, worked closely with the Protestant National Council of Churches, and helped start the Religious Task Force, which disseminated El Salvador information to a variety of Catholic clergy and laity.

Quigley said the bishops did not necessarily endorse all of the views of these groups, which tended to have more overt sympathy for the rebels, but many church officials did. "I think many in the church would go farther and say the FDR and FMLN are the embodiment of the legitimate aspirations of the El Salvadoran people," he said.

The activism of the church hierarchy was supplemented by many individual orders of priests and nuns, roused by attacks on missionaries in Latin America. Maryknoll priests and nuns (formally known as the Catholic Foreign Missionary Society of America) had a large Catholic audience in the United States. The group's publications, widely circulated in American Catholic schools and churches, prominently featured El Salvador. Two of the four Catholic missionaries slain in the 1980 attack were Maryknoll nuns.

The order also contributed to several groups opposing U.S. policy. The Maryknolls, for example, pro-vided two grants to help produce a film, "El Salvador: Another Vietnam," that was nominated for an Academy Award in 1982. The movie portrayed the civilian-military regime as the culprit in El Salvador, and U.S. aid to El Salvador as a step toward deeper involvement.

The Jesuits, an international order of priests, operated a university and seminary in El Salvador and were the target of official attacks there after 1977 because of their activism. Latin American Jesuits kept close contact with their counterparts in this country, most of them located at the order's 28 U.S. colleges and 47 high schools. Jesuit letter-writing campaigns, teach-ins and campus demonstrations were a mainstay in Catholic opposition to U.S. involvement.

The Catholic lobbying brought stern disapproval from supporters of the administration and conservatives. They contended that the church had developed a "liberation theology" — a blend of gospel and Marxism — in Latin America, and had been swept up in hysteria because of the killings of Catholics working in El Salvador. L. Frances Bouchey, Jesuit-educated director of the right-wing Council on Inter-American Security, scornfully described Hehir and Quigley as "clerical bureaucrats" who "politicize the spiritual mission of the church."

'Selective' Hearing

Penn Kemble of the Institute on Religion and Democracy, a group formed to counter liberal activism by church groups, said the U.S. Catholic position on El Salvador was "selective" in the cues it took from the clergy in El Salvador, ignoring those Salvadoran bishops who were more conservative. He and other critics also charged that U.S. bishops had paid scant attention to the military aid supplied by Cuba and the Soviet Union.

Quigley countered that the church deplored military aid from all sides, but that U.S. bishops considered U.S. policy their immediate responsibility. "We speak to Washington. We don't speak to Moscow or Havana," Quigley said.

Administration Allies

The selling of the Reagan administration's policy relied primarily on the administration itself. "I think a lot of the business and conservative groups felt that with the change from Carter to Reagan, the administration was going to carry the ball; it wasn't up to them," said Joseph H. Blatchford, a former Peace Corps director under President Nixon who represented El Salvadoran businessmen in Washington. But Blatchford contended the administration had been "on the defensive.... In my opinion, they have failed to mount an effective lobbying campaign to convince Congress and the American people of the rightness of their position."

El Salvador itself never had a large or sophisticated foreign service to make its own case, congressional sources said. In 1981 the Duarte government hired Michael Finley, a former congressional and State Department specialist in Latin America, to advise it on making the case for aid. Finley's contract ended in December of that year.

But the administration was not without allies. Perhaps the most significant political counterweight to human rights groups was the American Institute for Free Labor Development (AIFLD). Although the institute was financed primarily by the U.S. Agency for International Development, it was an affiliate of the nation's largest labor organization, the AFL-CIO.

AIFLD promoted anti-communist trade unions in Latin America, and assisted a program to turn over land to small farmers in El Salvador. Director William C. Doherty Jr. tried to impress lawmakers with the importance of strengthening the centrist Christian Democrats — with arms as well as economic aid — to protect the land reforms.

"The AFL has really been key in keeping some Democrats, who might just have reflexively opposed administration policy, from going overboard," said Penn Kemble. "If there's an issue that keeps the moderate members hanging in there with the administration policy, it's the agrarian reforms," agreed a House aide. "There you have to credit AIFLD's position as maintaining the member's faith."

Several liberal unions, such as the United Auto Workers, the Machinists and the Amalgamated Clothing and Textile Workers, organized a counter-lobby against Reagan policy, but they did not come close to matching the clout of the AFL-CIO-backed group.

Charges From the Left

AIFLD constantly battled charges from the left that it was a front for corporate or government interests. Writer Penny Lernoux, in her book *Cry of the People,* called the institute "a Trojan horse for the multinationals," because it was begun with financial aid from a number of major corporations. (Michael Boggs of the AFL-CIO said the corporate ties were severed two years ago.) Philip Agee, the renegade CIA agent, charged that AIFLD was funded by the Central Intelligence Agency and that director Doherty was a CIA agent. (Boggs denied any CIA connection.)

McAward, whose group ran some small projects in El Salvador, said AIFLD had been "discredited" in many Salvadoran circles because of the CIA allegations and its U.S. government source of funding. But he added, "They have a lot of clout with Congress because of the AFL."

The Reagan administration also was reinforced by business groups that brought up Salvadoran businessmen to meet with U.S. policy-makers. The Association of American Chambers of Commerce in Latin America, housed at the U.S. Chamber of Commerce in Washington, was the conduit for visitors from 19 local Latin American chambers representing Latin and U.S. businessmen. Keith L. Miceli, the association's executive secretary, said he had arranged Capitol Hill visits for several businessmen from El Salvador.

After a March 1982 visit, the members of the American Chamber of Commerce of El Salvador sent members of Congress a letter saying they were "astonished" at congressional misunderstandings of El Salvador. The businessmen urged lawmakers to shun all dealings with the guerrillas, continue aid to the military, and embrace the results of the Salvadoran elections.

Miceli was sometimes joined by Joseph Blatchford, who was the Washington agent for the Asociacion Nacional de Empresas Prividad, an El Salvadoran private sector group, and an adviser to the "free enterprise" Salvadoran umbrella group, the Productive Alliance. The businessmen generally argued that the Salvadoran Christian Democrats, portrayed in this country as centrists, were actually left-leaning advocates of communal land ownership. Blatchford contended the United States should be less hostile to the conservative El Salvadoran parties holding the balance of power after the election.

Two other groups considered influential on Central American policy-making generally steered clear of the El Salvador dispute, except for general exhortations to work with the private sector there. The Council of the Americas, a group of 200 corporations that played a lobbying role in support of the Panama Canal treaties and aid to Nicaragua, took no official stand on military aid to El Salvador. A newer corporate alliance, called Caribbean-Central American Action, devoted most of its attention to trade aspects of Reagan's Caribbean Basin plan.

On the Right

Nipping at the administration from the right were several groups that felt Reagan should be friendlier to the conservative parties in El Salvador. One was the Heritage Foundation, a conservative think tank that contributed several people to the administration. Richard Araujo, a former journalist who was the Heritage specialist on Central America, testified and wrote papers aimed at discrediting liberal groups active on El Salvador.

Araujo contended that "much of the debate in Congress has centered on charges of human rights abuses, usually leveled by organizations which have little or no direct contact with the situation in El Salvador or which have largely used guerrilla sources for their information."

Jeffrey Gayner, head of international affairs at Heritage, said he and Araujo often were consulted by officials in the State Department and National Security Council. "Clearly they have not followed all of our recommendations, but we certainly feel they've been receptive," Gayner said.

The Council for Inter-American Security, a six-year-old conservative group that lobbied against the Panama Canal and strategic arms limitation (SALT) treaties, was rated a fringe group by some moderates on Capitol Hill. But it counted 16 members of Congress as "advisers" and two of its founders were well placed within the administration: Roger Fontaine was a National Security Council adviser on Latin American policy, and Lt. Gen. Gordon Sumner Jr. was a State Department special adviser on Latin America.

The American Security Council, a pro-defense lobby that played a leading role in the SALT debate, produced a 26-minute film, "Attack on the Americas," aimed at raising public alarm about Soviet influence in Latin America. However, the film got little attention compared with the council's anti-SALT efforts, and was two years out of date by the spring of 1982, according to ASC Director Richard Sellers.

While groups on the right had personal pipelines into the administration, they were not able to mobilize the sort of public outpouring they orchestrated in the Panama Canal and SALT debates. Except for pro-administration marches organized by a campus group associated with the Unification Church and some demonstrations by Central American exile groups in Florida, conservatives were not able to muster public displays of support in their battle for control of U.S. foreign policy.

Foreign Agents

As members of Congress peered into the world of foreign agents during their 1980 investigation of Billy Carter's Libyan connection, some of them may have been gazing into their own future.

A review of files at the Department of Justice showed that at the time of the inquiry at least 18 former members of Congress were registered as agents for foreign governments or firms. The list also contained the names of a number of other former high-ranking officials, among them ambassadors, governors, Cabinet members and a one-time CIA director. *(Names, box, p. 157)*

Some of the the registered agents, like Billy Carter, represented unpopular or controversial clients. Some of them, also like Billy Carter, may have been hired more for their connections to power than for their skills.

The General Accounting Office has told Congress that because of loopholes and ignorance or evasion of the law, the names filed may be "only the tip of the iceberg." *(Foreign Agents Registration Act, box, p. 160)*

Justice Department records and interviews with several registered agents and government sources suggested that representing foreign interests is a business that is increasingly commonplace, usually lucrative, rarely glamorous and largely misunderstood.

Carter Probe

Congressional interest in the foreign activities of President Carter's brother Billy was sparked in mid-1980 when the Justice Department disclosed that Carter — after negotiating with Justice officials — had registered as a foreign agent representing Libya.

The registration statement showed that Carter (formally William A. Carter III of Buena Vista, Ga.) accepted $220,000 from the Libyan government of Col. Muammar al-Qaddafi. The statement also disclosed that Carter had helped set up a deal with Charter Oil Co. to help the company obtain more Libyan oil. Carter characterized the $220,000 as a loan, but Justice officials maintained it was for services rendered.

A special Senate subcommittee investigated and concluded that Carter's relationship with Libya did not influence U.S. government policy or involve any criminal wrongdoing. However, the 249-page report said that Billy Carter's conduct "was contrary to the best interests of the president and the United States and merits severe criti-

cism." The report also criticized the president and several officers of his administration for their actions in the affair.

While the episode quickly faded from the front pages, it drew rare public attention to the little-known world of foreign agentry and the equally obscure statute that regulates it.

Weighty Names

The Justice Department calculated that by mid-1982 713 agents had active files at the department. This compared with 453 at the end of 1970. Counting partners and associates who could participate in representing overseas clients, 6,810 individuals were listed as being in the service of foreign "principals." The roster of men and women enlisted to represent foreign interests was heavily studded with weighty names and impressive credentials.

Australian meat producers, looking for someone to defend them against high tariffs, hired the law firm of former Defense Secretary Clark Clifford and former Arms Control and Disarmament Agency chief Paul C. Warnke. The firm also represented the government of Algeria until late 1978.

The Government of South Africa, seeking to counter American condemnation of its apartheid policies, employed the law firm of former Sen. George Smathers, D Fla. (House 1947-51; Senate 1951-69), and former Reps. James W. Symington, D. Mo. (1969-77), and A. Sydney Herlong, D Fla. (1949-69), in April 1980 for an image building campaign.

The Political Public Relations Center of Japan snapped at a proposal by former CIA Director William E. Colby and his law partners to analyze Japan's public image problems in America and suggest what the Japanese could learn from other nations' lobbying efforts.

Japan and Japanese firms appeared to have more American representation than any other country; the embassy alone retained at least two former senators and a former congressman, in addition to Colby.

The French nuclear power industry received advice here from the law firm of R. Sargent Shriver Jr., the former Peace Corps director, ambassador to France and running mate to 1972 Democratic presidential nominee George McGovern. Through 1978 the firm also represented Zambian copper interests.

Former Sen. J. William Fulbright, D-Ark. (House

1943-45; Senate 1945-74), who as chairman of the Foreign Relations Committee headed an investigation of foreign agents, himself became a registered agent in 1976, representing Saudi Arabia and the United Arab Emirates. "It is understood you will personally be in charge and handle the work done for us," the Saudi ambassador stressed in a letter to Fulbright.

The list goes on. In addition to the most prominent names, the records included scores of former administration deputies, agency lawyers and congressional aides, often specializing in areas where they built their expertise in government service.

Former Civil Aeronautics Board members and aides represented foreign airlines; former Treasury Department and Senate Finance Committee staffers handled tax matters; former officials of the trade agencies dealt with import problems.

Some such as former Sen. Birch Bayh, D-Ind. (1963-81), chairman of the subcommittee investigating the Billy Carter affair, objected to former government officials acting as foreign agents. "We have to consider not only impropriety but the appearance of impropriety," Bayh said. "What does the average citizen perceive if a former Cabinet member is representing a foreign country?"

Value of Insiders

The value of hiring an insider was evident from some of the registration reports. As former Peace Corps director and Commerce Department official Joseph H. Blatchford boasted in a letter laying out his credentials to the government of El Salvador, his experience gave him a " 'feel' for the difficult passages which one must chart to understand and receive fair treatment from the U.S. government."

That "feel" may have been what the British tobacco and retailing conglomerate B.A.T. Industries Ltd. had in mind when it hired the law firm of Cook, Purcell, Hansen and Henderson to help get the company congressional hearings on a tax matter. The firm was headed by former Sen. Marlow Cook, R-Ky. (1968-74), who long had a home-state interest in tobacco and legislation affecting it.

The law firm reported that partner Graham Purcell, a former Democratic congressman from Texas (1962-73), arranged meetings with fellow Texans Bill Archer, a Republican, and J. J. Pickle, a Democrat, both Ways and Means Committee members, and House Majority Leader Jim Wright, D-Texas. Another partner, former Rep. Orval Hansen, R-Idaho (1969-75), arranged a meeting with Frank Church, D-Idaho (1957-81), who was then still in the Senate.

In addition, the law firm hired former House Ways and Means Chairman Wilbur D. Mills, D-Ark. (1939-77), to advise them on how to get hearings before the House tax panel. Mills' New York-based law firm, Shea and Gould, also was hired to represent the New Zealand Wool Board in a matter relating to tariffs on wool yarn. Mills said in an interview he did not personally lobby Congress, though he dealt with officials of the president's special trade representative.

In 1977 the Canadian pipeline firm of Foothills Ltd. hired the firm of Duncan, Brown, Weinberg and Palmer to promote its interest in a planned natural gas pipeline from Alaska. A few days later, former Interior Secretary Stewart L. Udall registered as counsel to the firm; partner Edward Weinberg had been Udall's solicitor at the department in the 1960s. The firm reported contacts with several members of Congress, including Udall's brother, House Interior

Chairman Morris K. Udall, D-Ariz. Stewart Udall told *The Washington Post* that "it wasn't me" who contacted Morris Udall. "I've never lobbied my brother."

Waste of Money?

John Martin Meek, president of the consulting firm Edelman International Corp., said foreign clients — even more than domestic clients — sometimes seek out the cachet, the connections, or the credibility they believe come with a former prominent insider. "Foreign clients are very susceptible to hiring someone who has had a position in government or has that kind of connection," said Meek, a one-time congressional liaison for the Democratic National Committee. He added that, while former officials usually are "very capable," shopping for an insider does not always pay off.

"I've seen people hired just because they had a name or a connection, and it proved to be just a waste of money," he said. He recalled watching a client pay a man $20,000, based on a five-minute interview, just because the man knew Sen. Everett M. Dirksen, R-Ill. (House 1933-49; Senate 1951-69); a week later, Dirksen died.

Individuals who register as foreign agents are not necessarily exiled from government service as a result. The best known examples are Clifford and Warnke, who both have interrupted their legal and lobbying work to serve in prominent government roles. During the Carter administration Clifford was a presidential envoy to Cyprus and India; Warnke headed the arms control agency on a leave from his firm.

Peter Hannaford, of the consulting firm of Deaver and Hannaford, was a top adviser in Ronald Reagan's presidential campaign, though his firm was a registered agent for the government of Taiwan.

Routine

Despite the glamour of the names connected with foreign interests, much of the work appears to be routine, and even boring. Agents say the time spent attempting to sway members of Congress or administration officials is small compared with the time spent collecting and recycling information, performing routine legal work such as paying taxes and purchasing property, arranging press conferences, and writing reports and position papers for foreign clients.

Fetching papers is one of the unglamorous but typical chores of a foreign agent. A former representative of the Japanese government said one of his jobs was to pass on every mention of Japan in the *Federal Register*, the *Congressional Record* and other government publications.

Once, when he cabled Tokyo the text of a federal report, the government congratulated him profusely for his great industry and initiative. He had beaten the Japanese Embassy by an hour.

Meek said Edelman International's contract with the government of Haiti was intended principally to promote business investment, but much of the firm's time was taken up with unexpected interruptions. In May 1980, President for Life Jean-Claude Duvalier got married, in an opulent ceremony that cost his poverty-stricken nation an estimated $3 million to $5 million; Edelman helped arrange press coverage, which was almost universally hostile. During the flood of Haitian refugees, the firm put on a slick public relations campaign to persuade America that the Haitians were fleeing economic hardship, not political repression.

Ex-Officials and Their Foreign Clients

Following is a listing of prominent former government officials and congressmen who have been hired to represent foreign interests. The list is necessarily incomplete because individuals who register as foreign agents do not usually include biographical information. An asterisk (*) denotes cases where client-termination notices were on file at the Justice Department, but other agent-client relationships listed here may no longer be current.

Former Members

- John W. Byrnes, R-Wis., House (1945-73): Government of the Philippines.
- Marlow Cook, R-Ky., Senate (1968-74): B.A.T. Industries Ltd. (Great Britain; tobacco and other products); CSR Ltd. (Australia, sugar); Patson PTY Ltd. (Australia, cattle).
- William C. Cramer, R-Fla., House (1955-71): Comite Nacional de Emergencia (Government of Nicaragua under Anastasio Somoza). *
- J. William Fulbright, D-Ark., (House 1943-45; Senate 1945-74): United Arab Emirates; Government of Saudi Arabia; Embassy of Japan; Council of European and Japanese National Shipowners Assocs.
- Charles Goodell, R-N.Y., (House 1959-68; Senate 1968-71): Kingdom of Morocco; Airbus Industrie (France); European Aerospace Corp.; Rheinmetall GMBH (Germany, weapons); Thompson CSF (France, weapons); Sofreavia (France, aircraft); Atlantic Container Line.
- Orval Hansen, R-Idaho, House (1969-75): B.A.T. Industries Ltd. (Great Britain; tobacco and other products); CSR Ltd. (Australia, sugar); Patson PTY Ltd. (Australia, cattle).**
- David N. Henderson, D-N.C., House (1961-77): B.A.T. Industries Ltd. (Great Britain; tobacco and other products); CSR Ltd. (Australia, sugar); Patson PTY Ltd. (Australia, cattle).
- Thomas H. Kuchel, R-Calif., Senate (1953-69): Korean Textile Manufacturers Association. *
- Robert L. Leggett, D-Calif., House (1963-79): Government of Somali Democratic Republic. *
- Wilbur D. Mills, D-Ark., House (1939-77), New Zealand Wool Board; B.A.T. Industries Ltd. (Britain).
- James G. O'Hara, D-Mich., House (1959-77): Central American Sugar Council; Korean Marine Industry Development Corp.; The Metal Market and Exchange Ltd. (London).
- Graham Purcell, D-Texas, House (1962-73): B.A.T. Industries Ltd. (Great Britain; tobacco and other products); CSR Ltd. (Australia, sugar); Patson PTY Ltd. (Australia, cattle).**
- George A. Smathers, D-Fla., (House 1947-51; Senate 1951-69): Embassy of the Republic of South Africa.
- James V. Stanton, D-Ohio, House (1971-77): Government of Bermuda.
- James W. Symington, D-Mo., House (1969-77): Embassy of the Republic of South Africa.
- Stewart L. Udall, D-Ariz., House (1955-61), Secretary of Interior (1961-69): Foothills Pipeline Ltd. (Canada).*

Others

- William McC. Blair Jr., ambassador to Denmark (1961-64), ambassador to Philippines (1964-67): Government of Zaire.
- Joseph H. Blatchford, director of Peace Corps (1969-72): Asociacion Nacional de Empresas Privadad (El Salvador businesses); Australian and French cheese manufacturers; Constructa Nacional de Carros de Ferrocarril (Mexico, maker of railroad cars); Government of El Salvador *; Danish Cake and Biscuit Alliance. *
- Clark Clifford, secretary of defense (1968-69): Australian Meat and Livestock Corp.; Government of Algeria. *
- William E. Colby, director of Central Intelligence, (1973-76): Political Public Relations Center (Tokyo).
- Frederick G. Dutton, special assistant to the president (1961-62), assistant secretary of state (1962-64): Embassy of Saudi Arabia.
- A. Linwood Holton, R, governor of Virginia (1970-74): United Arab Emirates *; Government of Saudi Arabia *; Embassy of Japan *; Bahamas Ministry of Tourism *; Council of European and Japanese National Shipping Associations. *
- Fred Korth, secretary of the Navy (1962-63): Government of Nicaragua under Somoza. *
- Endicott Peabody, D, governor of Massachusetts (1963-64): Government of Haiti. *
- William P. Rogers **, secretary of state (1969-73): Air France *, Republic of Indonesia. *
- Donald E. Santarelli, administrator of Law Enforcement Assistance Administration: Embraer S.A. (Brazil, aviation products).
- R. Sargent Shriver Jr., director of Peace Corps (1961-66), director of Office of Economic Opportunity (1964-68), ambassador to France (1968-70), Democratic vice presidential nominee (1972): Societe Franco-Americaine de Constructions Atomique (France, nuclear power plants) *, Zambian mining and metals companies. *
- Paul C. Warnke, director of Arms Control and Disarmament Agency and chief SALT negotiator (1977-78): Australian Meat and Livestock Corp.; Government of Algeria. *

* Client relationship terminated.
** Partner in a law firm registered under the Foreign Agents Registration Act, but not personally registered.

Lobbying

When foreign agents do turn their attention directly to the government, two of their most common concerns are arms sales and foreign aid. The *modus operandi* is similar for both, according to government aides.

First, the agents lobby the executive branch. During the Carter administration, with its reluctance to deal with repressive regimes, that often meant trying to bolster the case of the Pentagon and trade-minded bureaus of the State Department, and trying to calm the objections of State's human rights bureau. "You can't get anywhere if the administration is opposed to you" on arms sales, said a congressional aide.

That accomplished, the next step usually is to prevent Congress from passing a resolution of disapproval. This job begins with the House Foreign Affairs and Senate Foreign Relations committees. Lobbyists seem to work first on members who might be opposed to their wishes, trying to cut off opposition before it begins. Then, they move to the chairmen and ranking members, who usually are more inclined to support the administration.

One foreign agent often mentioned as having great impact on Capitol Hill was former Sen. Charles Goodell, R-N.Y. (House 1959-68; Senate 1968-71). Goodell and his colleagues were credited with an important role in two successes for foreign clients: reversing a U.S. ban on the sale of anti-guerrilla arms to Morocco and winning valuable American landing rights for the Concorde supersonic passenger jet.

In one of the most detailed reports on file at the Justice Department, Goodell itemized 253 meetings, lunches and phone calls he and his associates made to promote the sale of arms to Morocco. The recipients included all of the major congressional players in the debate over Morocco's war against Polisario guerrillas in the Sahara Desert.

On the Morocco arms sale, Goodell and company "did probably the most active job I've ever seen on African issues," said Pauline H. Baker, then a Senate Foreign Relations staff member. "Maybe the Israelis are more active on really big cases, and maybe the Saudis." A congressional aide said one tactic Goodell used effectively was emphasizing links between the Polisario and the Palestinian Liberation Organization, thus cementing the support of pro-Israel lawmakers.

Nicaragua

One of the more dramatic successes of foreign agentry was the campaign by two lobbyists for the former Nicaraguan regime of Anastasio Somoza — former Florida Rep. William C. Cramer, R (1955-71), and former Secretary of the Navy Fred Korth — to force Nicaraguan military aid on a reluctant Carter administration.

Korth told the Justice Department he accepted no money for his role, but decided after a visit to Nicaragua to "contact friends of his in the Congress and in the executive branch to acquaint them with the true facts" about the country. Cramer reported making about $150,000 a year at the peak of his activity.

Lars Schultz, a professor at the University of North Carolina, credits Korth with convincing fellow Texan Rep. Charles Wilson, a Democrat, to champion the Somoza government in the House. With Korth and Cramer helping to line up support, Wilson pushed through a $3.1 million military aid authorization in 1977, and then in 1978, held

Foreign agent lobbying helped win American landing rights for the Concorde supersonic passenger jet.

the foreign aid bill hostage until President Carter agreed to spend the money.

"Miracles are not the stock-in-trade of Washington lobbyists, but sophisticated tactics, plentiful supplies of money, and access to strategically placed friends can occasionally create one, as was demonstrated by the Nicaragua lobby in the late 1970s," Schultz wrote.

When U.S. relations with Somoza later deteriorated prior to a successful revolution, Cramer tried furiously to keep Congress behind the government in power. His final filing, on Oct. 1, 1979, reported that he met with 59 members of the House and Senate and 18 staffers, including House leaders and most key foreign policy players, while Somoza's government was in its death throes.

Well-paid Work

Whether they are successful or not, foreign agents usually are well paid for their efforts, and provided with generous expense accounts for air fare, first-class hotels and entertainment. Goodell's firm, DGA International, for instance, reported income of $927,855 from Morocco in the 12 months ending Oct. 28, 1980. Its other revenues included $306,678 from Airbus of France, which was trying to sell its A-300 passenger jet to U.S. airlines. Smathers, Symington and Herlong expected to receive a $300,000 annual retainer, plus expenses, for representing South Africa.

Clifford and Warnke reported they billed their Australian clients for $168,992 in the year ending Sept. 26, 1980, including a dinner that cost $1,003.89.

The governments of poor countries are not exempt from the high cost of a Washington presence. In the year ending Sept. 29, 1980, the government of Haiti, the most impoverished nation in the Western Hemisphere, paid former Massachusetts Gov. Endicott Peabody, D, $211,378 in fees and expenses for legal and government relations work, according to his reports. Peabody once reported billing the Duvalier government $331 for meals at the elegant Washington restaurant, Lion d'Or. Haiti paid an additional $105,398 to Edelman International for public relations, a bill Meek called "very modest . . . for this kind of work."

The government of poverty-stricken Zaire paid the law firm of Surrey and Morse $193,961 in fees and $27,658 in expenses in the 12 months ending July 5, 1980, to plead the country's case for foreign aid, according to the firm's report. The former U.S. ambassador to Denmark and the Philippines, William McC. Blair, was among the Surrey and Morse lawyers registered to represent Zaire.

Drought-stricken Somalia paid a more modest $20,000 to former Rep. Robert L. Leggett, D-Calif. (1963-79), for a year of work on the country's behalf. Leggett convinced Somalia to hire him to seek a trilateral development project involving Saudi Arabia and the United States.

Price Agents Pay

One price foreign agents pay for this employment is a requirement that they file detailed reports explaining who they have contacted, what materials they have disseminated (cited in disclosure forms as "propaganda"), how much they were paid and reimbursed for expenses and even what political campaigns they have contributed to.

Agents say that, in contrast to the loophole-ridden law requiring disclosure of attempts to influence Congress, the foreign agent reports are costly and time-consuming to prepare, and closely policed by the Justice Department.

The foreign agent reports "are very exacting and very tedious, much more so than the others" said former Rep. Mills. Representing a foreign client is "hardly worth it, it takes so much time," he added. Goodell complained about being labeled a "foreign agent" at all. "That sounds rather ominous and sinister, as if we're spies," he said. "I'd rather be called a 'foreign representative.'"

Controversial Clients

Billy Carter's flirtation with Libyan strongman Qaddafi was not the first affair between a well-known American and a controversial overseas client. South Africa, Iran, Nicaragua, the Philippines, South Korea, Haiti and other nations charged with violating human rights all have prominent Washington representation.

In some cases, foreign governments seem to have deliberately sought out representatives who might have been their critics during their official careers.

The government of South Africa, according to a Senate aide, considered it a "coup" when in April 1980 it signed up Smathers and Symington as agents. Symington, in particular, left government with a liberal reputation on civil rights, including a role in shaping President Kennedy's anti-poverty programs. Because of its racial apartheid policy, some lobbyists considered the country untouchable.

Goodell was widely known for his anti-Vietnam War views during his term in the Senate, but afterwards his clients included not only the king of Morocco but several foreign firms marketing military hardware.

Goodell defended his work for Morocco, saying King Hassan was "a friend of the United States," who generally supported U.S. foreign policy and desperately needed American arms to fight rebels armed by Algeria and Libya. "Here we have a friendly country that is being attacked by a group which is supplied with modern weapons by our enemies," he said. "Are we going to just sit by and fold our hands and say, 'Sorry, we won't even try to match them [Algeria and Libya] so you can stabilize your country and negotiate a peace?'"

Former Sen. James Abourezk, D-S.D. (1973-79), has been widely cited as a representative of Iran's Ayatollah Khomeini. Abourezk refused to comment on his relationship with the Iranian government, but friends of the ex-senator said his employment was confined to legal work, such as assisting in the lawsuits relating to American seizure of Iranian assets in this country. Abourezk was not registered as a foreign agent, and was not required to if he provided only legal counsel.

When the Central African Empire was ruled by the brutal Emperor Bokassa I, it contracted briefly with the well-connected Washington firm of Ragan and Mason to help keep America from withdrawing its Peace Corps volunteers. The firm was paid $25,000, but it reported "before being able to proceed, the representation was terminated due to a change in government."

One human rights lobbyist said he was shocked to see Peabody, known as a liberal in his days as governor of Massachusetts, representing the government of Haiti. "Here is the great liberal governor of Massachusetts, now carrying water for Baby Doc [Duvalier]," lamented Bruce Cameron of the Americans for Democratic Action.

Peabody said in an interview that when the Haitian ambassador first approached him in 1977 he expressed deep misgivings about the country's reputation on human rights. "'Well, my dear governor,'" Peabody quoted the Haitian envoy as saying, "'that is one reason I came to see you. We want you to assist us in that area.'"

Foreign Agents Registration Act

The Foreign Agents Registration Act was enacted in 1938 to keep watch on Nazis and other subversive groups in the United States. Since then, however, the law's focus has changed from identifying persons trying to subvert the government to identifying those seeking special influence. Major changes came in 1966 when Congress — after five years of consideration — amended the act to beef up enforcement mechanisms.

Who Is Covered

Under current law, a person must file with the Justice Department as a foreign agent if he 1) acts under the request or control of a foreign principal as an agent, employee or servant; and 2) engages in at least one of four specified types of activities. These activities include:

• political activity in the United States on behalf of the foreign principal;

• public relations counsel, publicity agent or political consultant for the principal;

• collecting or disbursing contributions, loans, money or other items of value in the United States for the foreign principal; and

• representing the foreign principal before any U.S. agency or official.

Exemptions are provided for several activities, including diplomatic personnel engaged exclusively in diplomatic work and so recognized by the State Department; persons engaged in private and non-political activities to further the foreign client's trade; those soliciting funds in the United States for medical aid or for food and clothing, and those engaged in activities to further religious or educational pursuits.

The exemptions also cover anyone representing a disclosed foreign principal before any U.S. court or government agency, so long as the legal representation does not include efforts to influence or persuade court or agency personnel beyond the scope of the legal proceeding.

The law also authorizes the attorney general, through regulations, to exempt persons from registering when the attorney general determines registering is not necessary to carry out the law's purpose of disclosure.

The law requires that a person file as an agent within 10 days of taking on a foreign client. The filing statement, which must be supplemented every six months, must include the agent's name, a "comprehensive statement" of the agent's business, a complete list of the agent's employees, if any, and the name and address of every foreign principal the agent is representing.

Every 60 days, an agent must file a statement showing the type and amount of compensation he received, how the money was disposed of, and what activities the agent engaged in on behalf of his client.

Enforcement

The law provides for a fine of up to $10,000 and imprisonment of up to five years, or both, for willfully making a false statement or willfully omitting any "material fact" on a registration.

A lesser penalty — a fine up to $5,000 and imprisonment for not more than six months — is provided for other violations, including failing to correct a deficient statement or failing to label properly propaganda information.

Prior to 1966 the act had no civil enforcement mechanisms. But that year Congress authorized the attorney general to seek an injunction preventing a person from violating the act or to require compliance with the registration law.

Law's Weaknesses

In 1980 testimony before a special Senate subcommittee, Justice Department and General Accounting Office (GAO) officials noted a number of weaknesses in the law, including inadequate enforcement tools.

Their major recommendations called for new Justice Department authority to subpoena records, new civil fines for minor violations, stiffening existing fines and giving the Justice Department's foreign agent registration unit a permanent inspection staff to review agents' activities and records.

Peabody said that as a result he believed he "had a part" in persuading Duvalier to release political prisoners, ease strict censorship laws and make other improvements in the country's treatment of its citizens. The State Department's 1979 human rights report praised the Duvalier government for reducing the practice of torture and allowing the creation of political parties. But the report noted that in the same year the militia was strengthened, a prominent political leader was arrested and the trend toward free speech and press was reversed. Peabody's law firm later in 1980 terminated its client relationship with the government of Haiti, according to the Justice Department's annual report on the Foreign Agents Registration Act.

John Meek, whose company competed for its Haitian public relations contract at Peabody's suggestion, said the firm had turned down several other foreign clients because of their human rights records, and looked upon some foreign governments as beyond consideration. "I definitely would not represent Libya," Meek said. "That's one, like South Africa, I don't even have to stop and think about."

In the Family

While Billy Carter apparently was the first presidential brother to engage in foreign agentry, at least two other agents have caused embarrassment for high-placed relatives. In 1976 Marion Javits, wife of Sen. Jacob K. Javits, R-N.Y. (House 1947-54; Senate 1957-81), gave up her vice presidency of a public relations firm following widespread negative publicity about her representation of the Iranian national airline. Critics said it was possible her $67,500-a-year consulting assignment could influence her husband, who at the time sat on the Foreign Relations Committee.

Michael Moynihan, brother of Sen. Daniel Patrick Moynihan, D-N.Y., and the proprietor of a public relations firm, suffered similar criticism for signing up to represent South Korea during the Koreagate furor.

But embarrassment is not the sole risk of representing foreign clients. Among those who have had contracts terminated by a sudden change in government are former agents for the late shah of Iran, General Anastasio Somoza of Nicaragua and Emperor Bokassa of the Central African Empire.

After a revolution deposed the Nicaraguan government of Somoza, Cramer reported he was stuck with a check for $33,806, which was "not honored by the drawee."

The check was received July 17, 1979, the day Somoza was forced to flee the country.

Selected Bibliography

Books

Adams, Gordon. *The Iron Triangle: The Politics of Defense Contracting.* New York: Council on Economic Priorities, 1981.

Ashworth, William. *Under the Influence: Congress, Lobbies, and the American Pork-Barrel System.* New York: Hawthorn/Dutton, 1981.

Backrack, Stanley. *The Committee of One Million: The China Lobby and U.S. Policy, 1953-1971.* New York: Columbia University Press, 1976.

Bauer, Raymond A., and others. *American Business and Public Policy: The Politics of Foreign Trade.* Chicago: Aldine Publishing Co., 1972.

Berry, Jeffrey M. *Lobbying for the People: The Political Behavior of Public Interest Groups.* Princeton, N.J.: Princeton University Press, 1977.

Braam, Geert P. A. *Influence of Business Firms on the Government: An Investigation of the Distribution of Influence In Society.* Hawthorne, N.Y.: Mouton Publishers, 1981.

Broder, David S. *Changing of the Guard: Power and Leadership in America.* New York: Simon & Schuster, 1980.

Chelf, Carl P. *Public Policy Making In America: Difficult Choices, Limited Solutions.* Glenview, Ill.: Scott, Foresman & Co., 1981.

Cook, Constance E. *Nuclear Power and Legal Advocacy: The Environmentalists and the Courts.* Lexington, Mass.: Lexington Books, 1980.

Crawford, Alan. *Thunder on the Right: The 'New Right' and the Politics of Resentment.* New York: Pantheon Books, 1980.

Crawford, Kenneth G. *The Pressure Boys: The Inside Story of Lobbying in America.* New York: Arno Press, 1974.

Deakin, James. *The Lobbyists.* Washington, D.C.: Public Affairs Press, 1966.

Dickson, Douglas N. *Corporate Political Action Committees.* Cambridge, Mass.: Ballinger Publishing Co., 1982.

Eastman, Hope. *Lobbying: A Constitutionally Protected Right.* Washington, D.C.: American Enterprise Institute for Public Policy Research, 1977.

Epstein, Edwin M. *The Corporation In American Politics.* Englewood Cliffs, N.J.: Prentice-Hall, 1969.

Foster, James C. *The Union Politics: The CIO Political Action Committee.* St. Louis: University of Missouri Press, 1975.

Goulden, Joseph C. *The Super-Lawyers: The Small and Powerful World of Great Washington Law Firms.* New York: Weybright and Talley, 1972.

Green, Mark J. *The Other Government: The Unseen Power of Washington Lawyers.* New York: W. W. Norton & Co., 1978.

Greenstone, J. David. *Labor in American Politics.* Chicago: University of Chicago Press, 1977.

Greenwald, Carol S. *Group Power: Lobbying and Public Policy.* New York: Praeger Publishers, 1977.

Grupenhoff, John T., and Murphy, James J. *Nonprofits' Handbook on Lobbying: The History and Impact of the New 1976 Lobbying Regulations on the Activities of Non-Profit Organizations.* Washington, D.C.: Taft Corporation, 1977.

Guither, Harold D. *The Food Lobbyists: Behind the Scenes of Food and Agri-Politics.* Lexington, Mass.: Lexington Books, 1980.

Hall, Donald R. *Cooperative Lobbying: The Power of Pressure.* Tucson: University of Arizona Press, 1969.

Halper, Thomas. *Power, Politics, and American Democracy.* Glenview, Ill.: Scott, Foresman & Co., 1981.

Hayes, Michael T. *Lobbyists and Legislators: A Theory of Political Markets.* New Brunswick, N.J.: Rutgers University Press, 1981.

Holsworth, Robert D. *Public Interest Liberalism and the Crisis of Affluence.* Cambridge, Mass.: Schenkman Publishing Co., 1981.

How Money Talks In Congress, a Common Cause Study of the Impact of Money on Congressional Decision-Making. Washington, D.C.: Common Cause, 1979.

Howe, Russell W., and Trott, Sarah H. *The Power Peddlers: How Lobbyists Mold America's Foreign Policy.* Garden City, N.Y.: Doubleday & Co., 1977.

Hrebenar, Ronald J., and Scott, Ruth K. *Interest Group Politics In America.* Englewood Cliffs, N.J.: Prentice-Hall, 1982.

Ippolito, Dennis S., and Walker, Thomas G. *Political Parties, Interest Groups, and Public Policy: Group Influence in American Politics.* Englewood Cliffs, N.J.: Prentice-Hall, 1980.

Isaacs, Stephen D. *Jews and American Politics.* Garden

City, N.Y.: Doubleday & Co., 1974.

Key, V. O. *Politics, Parties and Pressure Groups.* New York: Thomas Y. Crowell Co., 1964.

Kingdon, John W. *Congressmen's Voting Decisions.* New York: Harper & Row, 1973.

Koen, Ross Y. *The China Lobby in American Politics.* New York: Harper & Row, 1974.

Lipsen, Charles B., and Lesher, Stefan. *Vested Interest.* Garden City, N.Y.: Doubleday & Co., 1977.

Mahood, H. R. *Pressure Groups in American Politics.* New York: Charles Scribner's Sons, 1967.

Mahood, H. R., and Maleck, E. S. *Group Politics.* New York: Charles Scribner's Sons, 1972.

Malbin, Michael J. *Parties, Interest Groups, and Campaign Finance Laws.* Washington, D.C.: American Enterprise Institute for Public Policy Research, 1980.

Malielski, S. J., Jr. *Pressure Politics In America.* Lanham, Md.: University Press of America, 1980.

Mazmanian, Daniel A., and Nienaber, Jeanne. *Can Organizations Change? Environmental Protection, Citizen Participation and the Corps of Engineers.* Washington, D.C.: The Brookings Institution, 1979.

McCormick, Robert E., and Tollison, Robert D. *Politicians, Legislation, and the Economy: An Inquiry Into the Interest-Group Theory of Government.* Hingham, Mass.: Kluwer Boston, 1981.

McFarland, Andrew S. *Public Interest Lobbies: Decision-Making on Energy.* Washington, D.C.: American Enterprise Institute for Public Policy Research, 1976.

Milbrath, Lester W. *The Washington Lobbyists.* Chicago: Rand McNally & Co., 1963.

Moe, Terry M. *The Organization of Interests: Incentives and the Internal Dynamics of Political Interest Groups.* Chicago: University of Chicago Press, 1980.

Murphy, Thomas P. *Pressures Upon Congress: Legislation by Lobby.* Woodbury, N.Y.: Barron's Educational Series, 1973.

Oppenheimer, Bruce I. *Oil and the Congressional Process.* Lexington, Mass.: Lexington Books, 1974.

Ornstein, Norman J., and Elder, Shirley. *Interest Groups, Lobbying and Policymaking.* Washington, D.C.: CQ Press, 1978.

Platt, Alan, and Weiler, Lawrence D. *Congress and Arms Control.* Boulder, Colo.: Westview Press, 1978.

Pratt, Henry J. *The Gray Lobby.* Chicago: University of Chicago Press, 1976.

Schriftgiesser, Karl. *The Lobbyists: The Art and Business of Influencing Lawmakers.* Boston: Little, Brown & Co., 1951.

Trice, Robert H. *Interest Groups and the Foreign Policy Process: U.S. Policy in the Middle East.* Beverly Hills, Calif.: Sage Publications, 1977.

Truman, David B. *The Governmental Process.* New York: Alfred A. Knopf, 1964.

Vogel, David. *Lobbying the Corporation: Citizen Challenges to Business Authority.* New York: Basic Books, 1978.

Wilson, James Q. *Political Organizations.* New York: Basic Books, 1973.

Ziegler, L. Harmon, and Peak, Wayne G. *Interest Groups in American Politics.* 2d ed. Englewood Cliffs, N.J.: Prentice-Hall, 1972.

Articles

Becker, Bob. "Grass-Roots Lobbying by Business, Another Headache for the White House? *National Journal,* March 7, 1981, pp. 388-389.

"Business Lobbying: Threat to the Consumer Interest." *Consumer Reports,* September 1978, pp. 526-531.

Cameron, Juan. "Small Business Trips Big Labor: Grass-Roots Organizations by the Hundreds Were Organized to Stop George Meany's Favorite Bill." *Fortune,* July 31, 1978, pp. 80-82.

Campo, Terry T. "Lobbyists and How They Work." *Illinois Issues,* June 1980, pp. 11-12.

Chapman, S. "Welfare Tractors: Farmers' Subsidies and Protest in Washington, D.C." *New Republic,* March 3, 1979, pp. 16-19.

Cohen, Richard E. "New Lobbying Rules May Influence Grass-Roots Political Action." *National Journal,* May 27, 1978, pp. 832-836.

——. "The Business Lobby Discovers That In Unity There Is Strength . . . ." *National Journal,* June 28, 1980, pp. 1050-1055.

"Curbing Political Action Committees." *Commonweal,* Oct. 12, 1979, pp. 547-548.

Danilenko, V. "The Money Bag Behind the Elections." *International Affairs,* October 1980: 55-62.

Demkovich, Linda E. "It's a Whole New Budget Ball Game, But Lobbyists Are Playing by Old Rules." *National Journal,* Oct. 10, 1981, pp. 1806-1809.

Dickson, Douglas N. "CorPacs: The Business of Political Action Committees." *Across the Board,* November 1981, pp. 13-22.

Eddinger, John M., and Brightup, Craig S. "The Power of the Political Action Committee." *Nation's Business,* May 1982, pp. 32-35.

Ehrbar, A. F. "Backlash Against Business Advocacy." *Fortune,* Aug. 28, 1978, pp. 62-64.

Emerson, S. "The Petrodollar Connection." *New Republic,* Feb. 17, 1982, pp. 18-25.

Epstein, Edwin M. "An Irony of Electoral Reform: The Business PAC Phenomenon." *Regulation,* May/June 1979, pp. 35-41.

Evans, B. "Lobbying: A Question of Resources." *Sierra,* October 1978, pp. 54-55.

Fisher, John M. "The Disarmament Lobby." *American Legion Magazine,* November 1978, pp. 6-7.

"For Trade Organizations: Politics Is the New Focus." *Business Week,* April 17, 1978, pp. 107-115.

Gall, Peter, and Hoerr, John. "The Growing Schism Between Business and Labor." *Business Week,* Aug. 14, 1978, pp. 78-80.

Golden, L. L. L. "Dangerous Rush to Political Action: Corporate Political Action Committees." *Business Week,* Sept. 25, 1978, p. 14.

"Grass-Roots Lobbying: Propaganda Non Grata." *Regulation,* May/June 1981, pp. 8-11.

Guzzardi, Walter Jr. "A New Public Face for Business." *Fortune,* June 30, 1980, pp. 48-52.

——. "Business Is Learning How to Win in Washington." *Fortune,* March 27, 1978, pp. 52-58.

"How the Weapons Lobby Works in Washington." *Business Week,* Feb. 12, 1979, pp. 128, 130, 135.

Krebs, Frederick J. "Grassroots Lobbying Defined: The Scope of IRC Section 162(e) (2)(B)." *Taxes,* September 1978, pp. 16-20.

Ladd, Everett C. "How to Tame the Special Interest Groups." *Fortune,* Oct. 20, 1980, pp. 66-68.

Land, Guy P. "Federal Lobbying Disclosure Reform Legislation." *Harvard Journal of Legislation,* Spring 1980: 295-339.

Lanouette, William J. "The Influence Peddlers: Connections Still Count, But They're Not Enough." *National Journal*, Feb. 28, 1981, pp. 355-357.

____. "Off the Hill and Off the Record, Lobbyist Clubs Dine on Gourmet Tips." *National Journal*, April 10, 1982, pp. 630-634.

Levitt, Theodore. "Corporate Responsibility: Taking Care of Business." *American Spectator*, November 1977, pp. 21-25.

Lewin, Tamar. "Navigating the Loopholes: The Invisible Lobbyists." *Nation*, June 10, 1978, pp. 659-698.

Lipset, Seymour M. "Jewish Lobby and the National Interest." *New Leader*, Nov. 16, 1981, pp. 8-10.

Malbin, Michael J. "Campaign Financing and the 'Special Interest'." *Public Interest*, Summer 1979, pp. 21-42.

Margolis, Michael, and Neary, Kevin. "Pressure Politics Revisited: The Anti-Abortion Campaign." *Policy Studies Journal*, Spring 1980: 698-716.

Marshall, E. "New Feudalism: Economic Lobbies." *The New Republic*, Jan. 20, 1979, pp. 13-14.

Massie, Robert K., Jr. "How the Chamber Lobbies: Giving America the Business." *Nation*, May 8, 1982, pp. 550-551.

McDonald, Kimberly. "The Impact of Political Action Committees." *Economic Forum*, Summer 1981: 94-103.

McGovern, George. "Pluralist Structures or Interest Groups?" *Society*, January 1977: 13-15.

McQuaid, Kim. "Big Business and Public Policy In Contemporary United States." *Quarterly Review of Economics and Business*, Summer 1980: 57-68.

____. "The Roundtable: Getting Results In Washington ...." *Harvard Business Review*, May/June 1981: 114-123.

Meier, Kenneth J., and Van Lohuizen, J. R. "Bureaus, Clients, and Congress: The Impact of Interest Group Support on Budgeting." *Administration and Society*, February 1978: 447-466.

Metzer, Peter. "Government Funded Activism: Hiding Behind Public Interest." *World Oil*, June 1980, pp. 171-174; July 1980, pp. 163-164.

Montgomery, Alan L. "Lobbying by Public Charities Under the Tax Reform Act of 1976: The New Elective Provisions of Section 501(h), Safe Harbor or Trap for the Unwary?" *Taxes*, August 1978, pp. 449-461.

Nord, David P. "The FCC, Educational Broadcasting, and Political Interest Group Activity." *Journal of Broadcasting*, Summer 1978: 321-338.

North, James. "The Politics of Selfishness: The Effect, the Growth of Special Interests." *Washington Monthly*, October 1978, pp. 32-36.

Quinn, Tony. "Political Action Committees: The New Campaign Bankrollers." *California Journal*, March 1979, pp. 96-98.

Schwartz, George. "Lobbying Effectively for Business Interest." *Business Horizons*, September/October 1981, pp. 41-46.

Singer, James W. "Labor and Business Heat Up the Senate Labor Law Reform Battle." *National Journal*, June 3, 1978, pp. 884-885.

Thomas, William V. "Special Interest Politics." *Editorial Research Reports*, Sept. 26, 1980, pp. 699-716.

Wall, J. M. "SALT and Special-Interest Politics." *Christian Century*, July 4, 1979, pp. 691-692.

Walsh, J. "Lobbying Rules for Nonprofits: New Option Sets Specific Limits." *Science*, April 1, 1977, pp. 40-41.

Wertheimer, Fred. "Has Congress Made it Legal to Buy Congressmen?" *Business and Society Review*, Fall 1978: 29-32.

Wirth, Timothy E. "Congressional Policy Making and the Politics of Energy." *Journal of Energy and Development*, Autumn 1975: 93-104.

Wise, S. "Regulating Lobbies: Easier Said Than Done." *USA Today*, July 1978, pp. 10-12.

Witt, M. "Coalesce Is More: Coalitions Between Labor and Other Interest Groups." *New Republic*, April 14, 1979, pp. 12-15.

Government Documents

U.S. Congress. House. Committee on International Relations. Subcommittee on International Organizations. *Investigation of Korean-American Relations, Part 3: Hearings, Nov. 29, 30, 1977.* 95th Cong., 1st sess. Washington, D.C.: U.S. Government Printing Office, 1978.

____. *Investigation of Korean-American Relations; Report, October 31, 1978.* 95th Cong., 2d sess. Washington, D.C.: U.S. Government Printing Office, 1978.

U.S. Congress. House. Committee on Interstate and Foreign Commerce. Subcommittee on Oversight and Investigations. *Foreign Corrupt Practices Act: Hearing, June 14, 1979.* 96th Cong., 1st sess. Washington, D.C.: U.S. Government Printing Office, 1980.

U.S. Congress. House. Committee on the Judiciary. *Legal Services Corporation Reauthorization: Hearings, Sept. 21, 27, 1979.* 96th Cong., 1st sess. Washington, D.C.: U.S. Government Printing Office, 1981.

U.S. Congress. House. Committee on the Judiciary. Subcommittee on Administrative Law and Government Relations. *Public Disclosure of Lobbying Activity: Hearings, February 28 - March 28, 1979.* 96th Cong., 1st sess. Washington, D.C.: U.S. Government Printing Office, 1979.

U.S. Congress. House. Committee on Standards of Official Conduct. *In the Matter of Representative Daniel J. Flood.* 96th Cong., 2d sess. Washington, D.C.: U.S. Government Printing Office, 1980.

____. *In the Matter of Representative John W. Jenrette Jr.* 96th Cong., 2d sess. Washington, D.C.: U.S. Government Printing Office, 1980.

____. *In the Matter of Representative Michael Myers.* 96th Cong., 2d sess. Washington, D.C.: U.S. Government Printing Office, 1980.

____. *Korean Influence Investigation.* 95th Cong., 2d sess. Washington, D.C.: U.S. Government Printing Office, 1978.

U.S. Congress. Senate. Committee on Governmental Affairs. *Lobbying Reform Act of 1977: Hearings, August 2, 1977; February 6, 7, 1978.* 95th Cong., 1st sess. Washington, D.C.: U.S. Government Printing Office, 1978.

U.S. Congress. Senate. Committee on the Judiciary. Subcommittee to Investigate Individuals Representing the Interests of Foreign Governments. *Inquiry Into the Matter of Billy Carter and Libya: Hearing, September 1980.* 96th Cong., 2d sess. Washington, D.C.: U.S. Government Printing Office, 1980.

____. *Inquiry Into the Matter of Billy Carter and Libya, vol. 1: Hearings, Aug. 4, 6, 19, 20, 21, 1980.* 96th Cong., 2d sess. Washington, D.C.: U.S. Government Printing Office, 1981.

____. *Inquiry Into the Matter of Billy Carter and Libya, vol. 2: Hearings, Aug. 22, Sept. 4, 5, 9, 10, 17, Oct. 2,*

1980. 96th Cong., 2d sess. Washington, D.C.: U.S. Government Printing Office, 1981.

——. *Inquiry Into the Matter of Billy Carter and Libya, vol. 3, Appendix: Hearings, Aug. 4, 6, 19-22, Sept. 4, 5, 9, 10, 16, 17, Oct. 2, 1980.* 96th Cong., 2d sess. Washington, D.C.: U.S. Government Printing Office, 1981.

U.S. Congress. Senate. Select Committee on Ethics. *In the Matter of Senator Harrison A. Williams Jr.* 97th Cong., 1st sess. Washington, D.C.: U.S. Government Printing Office, 1981.

——. *Investigation of Senator Harrison A. Williams Jr.* 97th Cong., 1st sess. Washington, D.C.: U.S. Government Printing Office, 1981.

——. *Korean Influence Inquiry.* 95th Cong., 2d sess. Washington, D.C.: U.S. Government Printing Office, 1978.

Index

A-7 Jet fighter - 24, 32-33, 90
Abdnor, James, R-S.D. - 60
Abortion - 59, 105-108
Abzug, Bella S. - 68
ACA, *See Americans for Constitutional Action (ACA)*
ACU, *See American Conservative Union (ACU)*
Active Ballot Club (Food & Commercial Workers International Union) - 51
ADA, *See Americans for Democratic Action (ADA)*
Adams, Brock - 72, 97
Adams, Gordon - 87-88
Adams, John - 20
Adams, John Quincy - 20
Addabbo, Joseph P., D-N.Y. - 64
AFDC, *See Aid to Families with Dependent Children (AFDC)*
AFL-CIO
  Campaign support - 10, 43
  Former congressmen as lobbyists - 97
  National Budget Coalition - 138
  Public Health Service hospitals - 34
  Social programs support - 138, 140
  Solicitations - 44
AFL-CIO COPE (Committee on Political Education)
  AFL-CIO COPE Political Contributions Committee - 50-51
  American Institute for Free Labor Development (AIFLD) - 154
  Congressional ratings - 77, 80-81
  El Salvador issue - 154
  Solicitations - 10, 44
Aged, aging
  Congressional ratings - 77
  Lobby size - 5
Agee, Philip - 154
Agriculture
  Peanut allocations - 25-27
Agriculture Department
  Congressional lobbyists - 17
  Peanut allocations - 26
Aid to Families with Dependent Children (AFDC) - 138
AIFLD, *See American Institute for Free Labor Development (AIFLD)*
Air National Guard - 32-33, 90

Air Force, U.S., *See National Security*
Air Transport Association of America - 4
Akaka, Daniel K., D-Hawaii - 80
Alaska Coalition - 5, 144
Alaska lands bill - 136, 143, 145
Albert, Bernard - 44
Alexander, Bill, D-Ark. - 27
Alexander, DeAlva Stanwood - 16
Alexander, Herbert E. - 49, 54
All Savers Certificates - 127
Allen, Lew, Jr. - 32-33
Allen, Merle F., Jr. - 32
Allen, Richard V. - 4
Alliance for Education, Welfare and Other Human Services - 142
Amalgamated Clothing and Textile Workers - 154
Amax - 4
Amendments, Constitutional
  Equal Rights Amendment (ERA) - 59
  First Amendment - 1, 35, 39
  Thirteenth Amendment - 18
American Association of State Highway and Transportation Officials - 101
American Bankers Association
  American Bankers Association (BANK-PAC) - 51, 127
  Banking deregulation - 126, 128
American Baptists - 150 *(See also Religious lobbyists)*
American Bar Association - 139 (box)
American Bus Association (ABA) - 71
American Business Network ('Biznet') (box) - 116
American Civil Liberties Union (ACLU) - 9
American Clean Water Association - 145-146, 148
American Conservative Union (ACU) - 78, 105
American Dental Political Action Committee (American Dental Association) - 51-52
American Express Co. - 64, 125
American Federation of State, County and Municipal Employees - 49, 138, 139 (box)
American Federation of Teachers - 94
American Hospital Association - 96
American Institute for Free Labor Development (AIFLD) - 154

American Iron and Steel Institute - 2
American Israel Public Affairs Committee - 150
American Legion - 37-38
American Medical Association (AMA) - 40, 46
  American Medical Political Action Committee (AMA) - 50-52
  Medicaid - 140
American Natural Resources Co. - 6
American Newspaper Publishers Association - 4
American Petroleum Institute - 4
American School Food Service Association - 139 (box)
American Security Council - 105, 154
American Soybean Association - 26
American Taxpayers League - 37
American Telephone & Telegraph Co. (AT&T) - 4, 43
American Trucking Associations - 2, 46, 65, 68, 72
Americans for an Effective Presidency - 50
Americans for Change - 50, 53-54
Americans for Common Sense - 54
Americans for Constitutional Action (ACA) - 65, 67, 72, 77
Americans for Democratic Action (ADA)
  Congressinal ratings - 77, 80
  El Salvador issue - 151, 159
  Social programs - 142
Amidei, Nancy - 142
Amnesty International - 151
Amoco - 83
Amtrak Train system - 23, 29-30
Anderson, Bill - 113, 117-118
Anderson, Hibey, Nauheim and Blair - 4
Anderson, John B. - 53, 57
Anderson, Stanton D. - 4 (box)
Andrus, Cecil D. - 143
Applied Solar Technology - 95
Araujo, Richard - 154
Archer, Bill, R-Texas - 156
Arms industry. *(See also Weapons, military)*
  Investigations - 38, 40
  Lobbying - 87-92
  Political action committees (PACs) - 91

Carr, Bob
  Fund raisers - 67
  Lobbying - 97
  Political action committee contributions - 46, 91
Carter, Harlon B. - 132
Carter, Billy - 155, 159, 161
Carter, Jimmy
  B-1 bomber - 90
  Congressional relations - 12, 20
  Legislative liaison officers - 14
  Libya investigation - 155
  Nuclear energy - 24
  Partisan communications - 49
  Presidential elections (1976)(1980) - 49
  Public relations - 16
  Religious lobbyists - 110
  Small business programs - 119
  Synthetic fuels support - 6
  Veto power - 22
Carty, Jim - 117-118
Cassidy, Jay Warren - 132
Cater, Douglass - 8
Catholic Church. (See also Religious lobbyists)
  Campaign for Human Development - 138, 139
  El Salvador issue - 150, 152-153 (box)
  Food stamp program - 111, 139
Catholic Foreign Missionary Society of America - 153
Cederberg, Elford A. - 92
Center for Community Change - 138
Center for the Study and Prevention of Handgun Violence - 133, 134 (box)
Central African Empire - 159, 161
CEP, See Council on Economic Priorities
Certificates of deposit - 126
CETA, See Comprehensive Employment and Training Act (CETA)
Chafee, John H., R-R.I.
  Congressional ratings - 82
  Political action committee contributions - 60
Chamber of Commerce, U.S., See U.S. Chamber of Commerce
Champion, Harold L. - 109
Chapoton, John E. - 124
Charities. See Public charities
Charls E. Walker Associates - 4, 66
Chasey, William C., Jr. - 106-107
Cheney, Dick, R-Wyo. - 17
Chennault, Anna C. - 69
Chicago Mercantile Exchange - 4
Child Nutrition Coalition - 139 (box)
Children's Defense Fund - 30, 138, 139 (box)
Children's Foundation - 139 (box)
China External Trade Development Council - 4
Chisholm, Shirley, D-N.Y.
  Congressional ratings - 81
  Political action committee contributions - 59
Christian Voice - 105, 107 (box), 109, 110
Christian Voters' Victory Fund - 109
Chrysler Corp. - 4, 66, 89, 94
Church, Frank
  Foreign agents - 156
  Fund raisers - 67
  'Target '80' campaign - 52, 58
Churches, See Religious lobbyists
CISPES, See Committee in Solidarity with the People of El Salvador (CISPES)

Citicorp - 125
Citizens Committee for the Right to Keep and Bear Arms - 132, 134, 135 (box)
Citizens Committee on El Salvador - 149
Citizens for an Effective Presidency - 50
Citizens for the Republic - 53 (box), 54, 56-57
Citizens Forum - 56
Civil Service system
  Carter revisions - 14
  Cleveland revisions - 18
  Patronage - 16, 18
  Postal service - 16, 18
Clanton, David - 21
Clark, William L. - 92
Clausen, Don H., R-Calif. - 148
Clay, Henry - 11, 20
Clay, William, D-Mo. - 81
Clean Air Act - 3, 145
Cleveland, Grover
  Civil service reform - 18
  Veto power - 20, 22
Clifford, Clark - 12, 155-157, 159
Clinch River breeder reactor - 23-25
Clinger, William F, Jr. - 42
Clusen, Charles M. - 147
CNI, See Community Nutrition Institute (CNI)
Coalition for a New Foreign and Military Policy - 151
Coalition for Free Elections in El Salvador - 149
Coalition lobbying - 3, 5
Coalition to Ban Handguns - 135 (box), 136
Coast Guard - 34
Coast Starlight (train) - 30
Coats, Andy - 105
Coelho, Tony, D-Calif.
  Fund raisers - 68
  White House legislative liaison officer - 21
Cohen, Benjamin - 12
Cohen, William S., R-Maine
  Congressional ratings - 82
  Presidential political action committee support - 57
Colby, William E. - 155, 157
Cole, Nancy - 66-67
Colony Project - 6-7
Colton, Sterling D. - 122
Commerce Department
  Lobby regulation - 35
Committee for Full Funding of Education Programs - 139 (box)
Committee for the Future of America - 53
Committee for the Survival of a Free Congress - 46, 50, 53-54
Committee for Thorough Agricultural Political Education (Associated Milk Producers Inc.) - 50-51
Committee in Solidarity with the People of El Salvador (CISPES) - 151-152
Committee on Political Education (COPE), See AFL-CIO COPE (Committee for Political Education)
Committee to End U.S. Intervention in El Salvador - 149
Common Cause
  Fund raising - 63, 76
  Obey-Railsback bill - 55
Communications and media
  Constituent mailings - 9
  Editorial influence - 9-10

  Media campaigning - 9-10
  Presidential use of news media - 14-16
  Radio - 15, 106, 110
  Television - 15-16, 106, 110, 116
Communications Workers of America (CWA) - 46
  CWA-COPE Political Contributions Committee - 51
Community Nutrition Institute (CNI) - 139 (box)
Community Services Administration (CSA) - 140, 141 (box)
Comprehensive Employment and Training Act (CETA) - 140
Conder, Richard - 103
Congress. (See also Campaign financing)
  'Dirty Dozen' congressmen - 83, 144
  Environmental Study Conference - 147
  Former members as lobbyists - 93-98, 155-161, 157 (box)
  Lobby regulation - 35-40
  'New Deal' legislation - 15
  Presidential relations - 11-12
  Ratings - 77-84, 79 (box), 109
  Small business committees (box) - 118
  White House liaison officers - 12-14, 17
Congress and Its Members (R. Davidson and W. Oleszek) - 9, 16, 20
Congressional Club
  Contributions and expenses - 50, 52
  Fund raising - 53 (box), 54
Congressional Record - 13, 156
Congressional Research Service - 144
Conference of Mayors, U.S., See U.S. Conference of Mayors
Connally, John B.
  Citizens Forum - 56
  Political action committee contributions - 91
Conservation Foundation - 143-144, 146-148
Conservative Caucus - 9, 100, 106
Constitution (See also Amendments, Constitutional)
  Lobby protection - 1, 35
  Presidential powers - 11
  Veto power - 20
Consumer Product Safety Commission - 136
Consumer Protection Agency - 117
Conte, Silvio O., R-Mass - 152
Conyers, John, Jr., D-Mich. - 81
Cook, Marlow - 156-157
Cook, Purcell, Hansen and Henderson - 156
Cook, Richard K. - 88-90, 92
Coolidge, Calvin - 37
Cooper, Ranny - 59
Cooperatives - 49
Coopersmith, Esther - 67
Cordia, Louis J. - 145
Corporate political action committees (PACs)
  Contributions - 10, 42-44, 45 (graph), 47 (chart), 48
  Elections, congressional (1982) - 59-60
  Federal Election Campaign Act (FECA) - 41-42
  Growth - 42-43, 45 (graph), 52
  Solicitations - 10, 44
  SunPAC decision - 42
Corcoran, Thomas G. - 12
Corman, James C. - 91
COSE, See Council of Smaller Enterprises

Peck, Carey - 74
Penn Central Corp. - 96
Pennsylvania Chamber of Commerce - 44
People for the American Way - 54
Pepper, Claude, D-Fla. - 81, 84
Pepsico - 66, 122-123
Perkins, Carl D., D-Ky. - 140
Percy, Charles H., R-Ill. - 57
Perkins, Robert J. - 64
Peters, Charles - 1
Peterson, Russell - 146
Petri, Thomas E., R-Wis. - 151
Petro-Lewis Corp. - 4
Philbro Corp. - 89
Philippines - 159
Phillips, Howard - 106
Pickens, Bill - 132
Pickle, J. J., D-Texas - 156
Pierson, Ball & Down - 4
Pillsbury - 66
Pioneer (train) - 30
Pirie, Robert B., Jr. - 88-89
Pizza Hut - 121-124
Platt, Ronald - 121-122, 124
PLO, *See Palestine Liberation Organization (PLO)*
Polisario - 158
Political action committees (PACs) *(See also Corporate political action committees (PACs); Labor political action committees (PACs))*
  Contributions and expenses - 41-44, 45 (graph), 46, 47 (chart), 48-49, 50-51 (box), 52
  Conservative - 46, 52-56
  Defense industry- 91
  Environmental movement - 145
  Fund raising - 44, 46, 52-55, 53 (chart)
  Growth - 41-43, 48
  Health - 49, 52
  Liberal - 52-56
  Membership - 49, 52, 60-61
  Non-connected - 52-55
  Obey-Railsback bill - 55
  Presidential - 56-57
  Profiles - 57-61
  Regulation - 42, 55, 60-61
  Religious - 107 (box)
  Small business - 119
  'Target '80' campaign - 52, 54, 58
  Trade - 49, 52
Political Public Relations Center of Japan - 155
Pollard, James E. - 14-15
Pollution. *See Environmental movement*
Polsby, Nelson W. - 18
Ponder, Delton - 140
Poongsan Metal Corp. - 4
Portney, Paul - 147
Postmaster General. *See Post Office Department*
Post Office Department
  Conversion to Postal Service, U.S. - 18
  Patronage - 16, 18
Postal Service, U.S. - 18
Power in Washington (D. Cater) - 8
Powers, Tom - 117-119
Presbyterian Church - 150-151. *(See also Religious lobbyists)*
President and Congress (W. Binkley) - 15
Presidential lobbying. *See White House Lobbying*
Presidential political action committees - 56-57

Presidents and the Press, The (J. Pollard) - 14-15
Press
  Grass-roots lobbying - 9-10
  Presidential press conferences - 14-15
Prince, Jeffrey R. - 140
Princeton Religion Research Center - 110
Procter & Gamble Co. - 4
Productive Alliance - 154
Progressive Political Action Committee (PROPAC)
  Fund raising and spending - 53 (box), 54
  Profile - 58-59
Project on Food Assistance and Poverty - 138
Proposition 13 - 99
Proxmire, William, D-Wis.
  Congressional ratings - 77, 80-81, 84
  Fund raisers - 67
Prudential Insurance Co. - 125
Pryor, David, D-Ark. - 82
Public charities - 39
Public Citizen Congress Watch (PCCW) - 77-78, 82
Public Health Service - 33-34
Public interest groups - 99-103
Public liaison officers - 16, 21
Public Opinion Quarterly - 134
Public Utilities Holding Company Act of 1935 - 35, 38
Purcell, Graham - 156-157

Qaddafi, Muammar - 155, 159
Quayle, Dan, R-Ind.
  Amtrak Train system - 30
  Congressional ratings - 80
Quarles, John R., Jr. - 146
Quigley, Thomas E. - 152
Quillen, James H., R-Tenn. - 82

Radio
  Presidential public relations - 15
  Religious lobbying - 106, 110
Ragan and Mason - 159
Railsback, Tom, R-Ill. - 55
Ralston Purina - 66
Rayburn, Sam - 13
Raytheon Co. - 89, 91
Reagan, Ronald
  Amtrak Train system - 29-30
  AWACS sale - 14
  Budget legislation - 14
  Caribbean Basin plan - 154
  Citizens for the Republic - 56
  Congressional relations - 12, 20
  Debt ceiling - 78
  Defense cuts - 33
  Export-Import Bank - 28-29
  Federal aid to states and cities - 99, 102-103
  Gun control - 133
  Impact aid - 27
  Legislative liaison officers - 14
  Lobbying ties - 4
  Peanut allocations - 25-26
  Political action committee contributions - 133
  Presidential elections (1980) - 49, 91
  Public relations - 16, 21
  Religious lobbyists - 110
  Social programs - 30
  Synthetic fuels support - 6-7
  Tax cut - 19
  Veto power - 22

Realtors Political Action Committee (National Association of Realtors) - 50, 52
Reconciliation Bill, See Budget
Reed, Nathaniel P. - 145
Regan, Donald T. - 128
Regulation Q - 128 (box)
Reilly, William K. - 146-148
Religious lobbyists
  Congressional ratings - 109
  El Salvador issue - 149-151, 152-153
  Established church lobbying (box) - 111
  Evangelical right legislative agenda - 106, 108
  Media use - 110
  Social programs lobbying - 111, 137-138
  Techniques - 105-106, 108, 110, 112
Religious Roundtable, The - 106, 107 (box), 110
Republic Airlines - 4
Republic Steel Corp. - 83
Republican National Committee (RNC) - 48, 57
Republican Senatorial Campaign Committee - 73
Reserve Fund Inc., The - 129
Reserve Officer Association - 33
Resources for the Future - 147
Response Marketing Group - 68
Restaurant chain lobbyists
  Growth - 121-122
  Milk prices - 123
  Subminimum wage - 124
  Tax credit - 124
  Trade associations - 123
Richard King Mellon Foundation - 143
Richards, Richard - 55-56
Rinaldo, Matthew, J., R-N.J.
  Fund raisers - 67
  Presidential political action committee support - 57
Rippey, John S. - 126
RNC, *See Republican National Committee (RNC)*
Robbins, Elizabeth - 102
Robinson, J. Kenneth, R-Va. - 82
Robinson, William J. - 7
Robison, James - 107-108, 111
Rockwell International Corp. - 89-90
Rodino, Peter W., Jr., D-N.J.
  Congressional ratings - 80
  Gun control - 134
Roe, Robert A., D-N.J. - 81
Rogers, Cheryl - 141
Rogers, William P. - 157
Rohm and Haas Co. - 69, 98
Roman Catholic Church, *See Catholic Church*
Romero, Oscar - 152
Rooney, Fred B. - 97
Roosevelt, Franklin D.
  Legislative liaison officers - 12
  'New Deal' legislation - 15
  Patronage - 18
  Public relations - 15
  Utilities lobby investigation (1935) - 38
  Veto power - 20, 22
Roosevelt, Theodore - 14
Rose, Charlie, D-N.C. - 27
Rosenthal, Benjamin S., D-N.Y. - 81
Roundtable Issues and Answers (The Religious Roundtable) - 107
Roukema, Marge, R-N.J. - 59
Russo, Paul - 57